THE UNITED STATES, SOUTHEAST ASIA, AND HISTORICAL MEMORY

The United States, Southeast Asia, and Historical Memory

SECOND EDITION

Edited by Mark Pavlick
with Caroline Luft

Unfortunately, the nature of these crimes is such that both prosecution and judgment must be by victor nations over vanquished foes. The worldwide scope of the aggressions carried out by these men has left but few real neutrals. Either the victors must judge the vanquished or we must leave the defeated to judge themselves. After the First World War, we learned the futility of the latter course. The former high station of these defendants, the notoriety of their acts, and the adaptability of their conduct to provoke retaliation make it hard to distinguish between the demand for a just and measured retribution, and the unthinking cry for vengeance which arises from the anguish of war. It is our task, so far as humanly possible, to draw the line between the two. We must never forget that the record on which we judge these defendants today is the record on which history will judge us tomorrow. To pass these defendants a poisoned chalice is to put it to our own lips as well. We must summon such detachment and intellectual integrity to our task that this trial will commend itself to posterity as fulfilling humanity's aspirations to do justice.

—From the opening address for the American case under Count I of the Indictment, delivered by Justice Robert H. Jackson, Chief of Counsel for the United States, before the Nuremberg Tribunal on November 21, 1945

Published in 2019 by
Haymarket Books
P.O. Box 180165
Chicago, IL 60618
773-583-7884
www.haymarketbooks.org
info@haymarketbooks.org

ISBN: 978-1-60846-323-7

Trade distribution:
In the US, Consortium Book Sales and Distribution, www.cbsd.com
In Canada, Publishers Group Canada, www.pgcbooks.ca
In the UK, Turnaround Publisher Services, www.turnaround-uk.com
All other countries, Ingram Publisher Services International,
IPS_Intlsales@ingramcontent.com

This book was published with the generous support of Lannan Foundation
and Wallace Action Fund.

Printed in Canada by union labor.

Cover photograph by Channapha Khamvongsa.

Library of Congress Cataloging-in-Publication data is available.

10 9 8 7 6 5 4 3 2 1

CONTENTS

This book is dedicated to the countless victims of US foreign policy in Southeast Asia and around the globe

All proceeds from this book will be distributed to nongovernmental organizations doing humanitarian work in Vietnam, Laos, and Cambodia.

For details please contact Channapha Khamvongsa at channapha@legaciesofwar.org.

Introduction

Richard Falk

> *Back here it turns out newspapers*
> *and monuments are taxidermy;*
> *there is little retribution, little learning; what is lost*
> *is forgotten; sometimes it gets so bad I'm not sure*
> *I'm the one who lived . . .*
>
> —George Evans, Vietnam veteran,
"Revelation in the Mother Lode"

I am struck by two contrasting observations about the Indochina wars: that their meaning and memory remain an unresolved cultural trauma in the American political psyche, and that the dominant social forces in the United States have successfully resisted learning the right lessons from these wars, while expending perverse energy on facilitating a repetition of the tragedy by relying on the wrong lessons supposedly learned from the failures in Indochina.

The most important correct lesson, partly pragmatic and partly a matter of respect for the human dignity and legal rights of our sovereign neighbors on the planet, is for the US government to renounce aggressive war and regime-changing intervention as a means of altering the political destiny of a foreign country. Such undertakings fail miserably on the level of policy; worse, they unavoidably implicate the United States in massive human suffering and criminality that embitters any society so victimized and, in the ugly unfolding, alienates world public opinion. The criminality occurs in various forms because there is no lawful and ethical way to overcome determined national resistance that takes the form of insurgency other than by punishing the people as a whole. Additionally, the military superiority of an invader or occupier, however destructively deployed, can inflict incredible damage but given the resilience of nationalism can rarely defeat a political movement that enjoys the strong popular backing of its own people. The foreign intervener can win every battle decisively and bomb almost at will without facing retaliation in its own homeland, and yet it will still experience political defeat and lose the war. This is the important lesson of the wars in Indochina, which urgently warrant revisiting at this time of failed interventions in the Middle East, North Africa, and Central Asia.

What transpired in Iraq beginning in 2003 evokes a variety of grim memories of the long ordeal experienced by the peoples of Vietnam, Cambodia, and Laos. This failure of aggressive war, of which military intervention is a favored contemporary form, is not just a commentary on American diplomacy. It was also the fate of the Soviet Union in Afghanistan, of Iraq in Iran, of Indonesia in East Timor, of NATO in Libya, and of Saudi Arabia in Yemen. Military superiority in the postcolonial era can be used with stunning effectiveness to destroy the military capabilities of an adversary as in the Gulf War of 1991, and can sometimes achieve impressive political results if backed by the authority of the United Nations. In the case of the Gulf War in 1991, the UN-backed intervention achieved the restoration of the sovereignty of Kuwait after its conquest and annexation by Iraq. Whether war was necessary to reach these results remains a hotly contested question of great importance; some informed observers believe that Iraq could have been persuaded to withdraw from Kuwait by a combination of sanctions and diplomacy, but we will never know for sure.

One of the many strengths of this volume is to extend the scope of wrongdoing and remembrance to the whole of Indochina, rather than restricting concern to Vietnam. There is no doubt that the Vietnam War was the epicenter of the American interventionary undertaking, but both Laos and Cambodia were treated by all sides as integral parts of the war zone, enduring human suffering on a vast scale and experiencing widespread devastation. And yet due to the sort of narcissistic geopolitics that shapes mainstream media coverage around the world, which in turn exerts such control over our understanding of historical and political reality, the wartime fates of Laos and Cambodia have been deleted unforgivably from the collective political memory of America, and to some extent from that of the world as a whole. The reality is that the Indochina wars left deep scars on all three countries that together comprise Indochina, probably leaving even deeper and more persistent painful remembrances in Laos and Cambodia than in Vietnam. A central claim being made by the contributors to this volume is that an adequate grasp of American culpability during the period of 1962–1975 needs to encompass the whole of Indochina and not be limited to Vietnam. Expanding the orbit of inquiry also accords belated and respectful recognition to the peoples of Laos and Cambodia, so often revictimized by being ignored in most retrospective accounts of the American role in the overall Indochina conflict.

Seemingly more than its Indochina neighbors, Vietnam has exhibited an exceptional cultural strength in the form of postwar resilience. This is truly remarkable considering the punishment that Vietnam experienced in the course of more than twenty-five years of almost continuous warfare, first against France and then the United States. After the American departure in 1975 Vietnam was almost immediately plunged into further violent conflict with its powerful former ally, China. This new cycle of warfare tended to make Vietnam put the struggle against the American-led occupation to one side, just as earlier it had moved toward normalcy and reconciliation almost immediately after its bloody anticolonial victory over France. Vietnam has an uncanny capacity, exhibited throughout its long history of struggle to maintain its independence, to recover rapidly from the most terrible national experiences without showing its gaping wounds to the outside world. Vietnam combines a fierce pride in its national history that features its success in resisting the periodic intrusion of powerful foreign invaders, especially China, with an unusual degree of political humility, recognizing that as a small country it must quickly reconcile with former enemies even before allowing the blood-soaked battlefields to dry or grieving for lost loved ones to end.

If we are, as this volume valiantly attempts, to pay proper homage to the unfinished agenda of the Indochina wars, we need to acknowledge the wrongs done to the peoples of Laos, Cambodia, and Indonesia as well as Vietnam. We must take account of the indiscriminate, sustained bombing that permanently turned substantial portions of the Laotian countryside into an eerie moonscape, and the extensive use of deadly chemicals to achieve environmental destruction that still is the cause of grave damage to innocent Vietnamese men, women, and children generations later.

An often overlooked dimension of the Indochina combat experience is the relevance of developments in Indonesia, arguably the most important state in Southeast Asia. The insurgency and related political massacre that drove the Sukarno government from power in 1965–66 is relevant to our understanding of the Vietnam War, and the resulting change of ideological orientation in Indonesia seriously undermined the main geopolitical argument advanced to support the war.

And we should acknowledge, however belatedly, the cynical and calculated American disturbance of the delicately balanced Cambodian neutrality in the latter stages of its Vietnam defeat that helped set the table for the genocide that was to follow shortly upon American departure from the area. William Shawcross aptly entitled his account of the Cambodian tragedy *Sideshow*.

In the end, there is much for America to atone for in Indochina, and yet the process of atonement has barely begun. Let this book serve as one small, yet genuine, beginning.

CHAPTER 1

War Crimes in Indochina and Our Troubled National Soul

Fred Branfman

Corpses float on the water, dry in the field, on the city rooftops, on the winding streets. Corpses lie abandoned under the eaves of the pagoda, on the road to the city churches, on the floors of deserted houses. Oh, springtime, corpses will nourish the plowed soil. Oh, Vietnam, corpses will lend themselves to the soil of tomorrow.

—Trinh Cong Son, Vietnam's best-known musician[1]

War Crimes: Namely violation of the law or customs of war (including) murder, ill treatment . . . and the wanton destruction of towns and villages. Crimes Against Humanity: Namely, murder . . . and other inhuman acts committed against any civilian population.

—Indictment of Nazi defendants, Nuremberg Trials, 1945[2]

I committed the same kinds of atrocities as thousands of others in that I shot in free-fire zones, fired .50-caliber machine bullets, used harass-and-interdiction fire, joined in search-and-destroy missions, and burned villages. All of these acts are contrary to the laws of the Geneva Convention, and all were ordered as written, established policies from the top down, and the men who ordered this are war criminals.

—2004 US presidential candidate John Kerry, in 1971 testimony to Congress[3]

5

A Deep Wound at the Core of Our National Soul

We live in a time in which truth has become increasingly irrelevant. Reality is indistinguishable from spin, not only from politicians but also from once-trusted sports figures, church leaders, and business executives. Statements and assertions are no longer backed up by evidence. Facts are no longer treated as facts. Words have come to mean their opposite. It seems almost pointless to note the latest untruths: who has the time to research the facts amid the welter of accusations, attacks, ripostes, and counterattacks?

There are, however, certain lies so monstrous, so odious, so malignant, and so significant that they cry out to heaven for rectification. One of these is the official lie that American leaders were not guilty in Indochina of some of the worst war crimes since World War II. This lie is not merely a matter for historians. It was at the heart of the 2008 presidential race, in which one candidate ran on his Vietnam War record, just as in the 2004 presidential race. This lie has poisoned American politics and damaged America's standing in the world for the past three decades, causing America frequently to repeat the same mistakes it made in Indochina and denying America's youth the truth of their own history. Furthermore, this lie will continue to damage America until it is exposed and rectified.

International laws on war deal with two basic issues: 1) preventing "aggressive" war, that is, wars not fought in genuine self-defense; and 2) the protection of civilians once war has begun. However one feels about the first issue—America's right to have intervened in Indochina—no sane person could deny that once the United States began to wage war in Indochina it flagrantly ignored the laws of war seeking to protect noncombatants.[4]

The United States waged massive bombing and artillery campaigns that did not distinguish between innocent civilians and enemy soldiers. US leaders dropped 6,727,084 tons of bombs on a population of sixty million to seventy million people in Indochina, more than triple the tonnage it dropped in the combined European and Pacific Theaters in World War II. The United States also conducted ground artillery bombardment of Indochina on an equally massive scale. As a result, whatever their intent, US leaders killed countless noncombatants, wounded and made homeless an officially estimated 18.7 million people, and laid waste to vast areas of farmland and forest that are still unusable due to unexploded bombs and the lingering effects of toxic chemical defoliants.

OFFICIALLY ESTIMATED BOMBING AND CASUALTY STATISTICS FOR THE WARS IN INDOCHINA, 1961–75

Note: The figures below are official US estimates of bombing tonnage dropped and casualties and refugees created during the wars in Indochina from 1961 to 1975. Please note that these figures do not include the tremendous amount of ground munitions used, and seriously underestimate the total number of Indochinese who died during the war. These figures were compiled by the Indochina Resource Center from official sources, and were placed in the *Congressional Record* by Senator James Abourezk on May 11, 1975.[5] The reader is referred to these pages for a more detailed explanation of how these figures were compiled.

US BOMBING TONNAGE DROPPED ON INDOCHINA*

SOUTH VIETNAM (6/64–1/27/73)	3,223,553
NORTH VIETNAM (8/64–1/27/73)	881,302
CAMBODIA (3/69–8/15/73)	539,129
LAOS (6/64–4/73)	2,083,100
	(Northern Laos: 320,722)
	(Southern Laos: 1,762,378)

TOTAL US BOMBING TONNAGE, INDOCHINA	6,727,084
(1964–68, Johnson/McNamara/Clifford: 2,742,521)	
(1969–73, Nixon/Kissinger: 3,984,563)	

* From official Pentagon figures.

US AERIAL BOMBING SORTIES OVER INDOCHINA**

SOUTH VIETNAM (6/64–1/27/73)	946,142
NORTH VIETNAM (8/64–1/27/73)	362,542
CAMBODIA (3/69–8/15/73)	49,640
LAOS (6/64–4/73)	541,344

TOTAL US BOMBING SORTIES, INDOCHINA	1,899,668

** From official Pentagon figures.

OFFICIALLY ESTIMATED DEATHS OF INDOCHINESE***

CIVILIANS, South Vietnam	430,000
CIVILIANS, North Vietnam	185,000
ARVN (Army of South Vietnam)	221,041
PRG/DRV (Vietcong, North Vietnamese)	1,064,656
CIVILIAN AND MILITARY, Laos	hundreds of thousands

CIVILIAN AND MILITARY, Cambodia   hundreds of thousands
TOTAL INDOCHINESE KILLED   more than 2 million

*** These official figures come from the Pentagon and US Senate Subcommittee on Refugees. They show more than 2 million Indochinese killed in Indochina. No serious estimates have been made for the number of those killed and wounded in Laos and Cambodia, but most observers estimate the number in the hundreds of thousands.

OFFICIALLY ESTIMATED INDOCHINESE, WOUNDED AND MADE HOMELESS, 1961–75

WOUNDED, South Vietnam, Civilians	1,050,000
WOUNDED, South Vietnam, Military	2,205,523
WOUNDED (Cambodia, Laos, North Vietnam)	300,000
(subtotal, wounded: 3,555,523)	
REFUGEES, South Vietnam	11,683,000
REFUGEES, Cambodia	3,000,000
REFUGEES, Laos	700,000
(subtotal, refugees: 15,383,000)	

TOTAL INDOCHINESE WOUNDED/REFUGEES	18,938,523

US SOLDIERS, KILLED AND WOUNDED IN INDOCHINA, 1961–1973

US MILITARY DEATHS	56,226
	(hostile action: 45,941)
	(non-hostile action: 10,285)
US MILITARY WOUNDED	153,654
TOTAL US KILLED AND WOUNDED	209,880

We will never know how many innocent Indochinese peasants died from this massive and unprecedented US firepower, but former US secretary of defense Robert McNamara has estimated that a total of 3.4 million Indochinese died during the war.[6] Since armed guerrillas expended far fewer munitions than the United States, directed most of their fire against military targets, and were better able both to hide and to protect themselves than the civilian population, it seems clear that a sizable number of those 3.4 million dead Indochinese were unarmed peasants.

This bombing and artillery shelling resulted in the "murder, ill treatment . . . and wanton destruction of towns and villages . . . and other inhuman acts committed against any civilian population" described in the Nuremberg

Indictment, for which the United States executed Nazi leaders at Nuremberg after World War II.

Other nations have committed major violations of international law—externally, as in the cases of Germany and Japan[7] during World War II and France in Algeria,[8] and internally, as occurred in Argentina, Chile, South Africa, Rwanda, and many other countries. Although unable or unwilling to prevent these violations of international law as they were occurring, the peoples of these nations engaged in a measure of collective soul-searching and reckoning after these conflicts ended.

US leaders, however, simply ignored US war crimes when the Indochina wars ended, ensuring that the United States would continue to ignore the laws of war in the future. America has never engaged in the kind of soul-searching that might have cleansed the country's conscience, allowed for national healing, and led to national policy-making that did not repeat the mistakes of the Indochina wars. Historians a century from now may well date America's loss of moral authority—and thus its ability to be a constructive world leader—both to its violations of international law in Indochina and to the successful erasure by US leaders of these crimes from the collective American memory.

Indochina tore America apart; the wound has yet to heal. This failure to heal has contributed greatly to the internal political divisions that make reaching a genuine national consensus to take significant domestic action virtually impossible. Consequently, on an international level, America has been unable to spearhead the global consensus necessary to address the great biospheric, economic, and geopolitical challenges of our time.

In today's increasingly polarized America, extremists vilify their enemies, twist the truth, and show no interest in compromise. Conventional opinion identifies such splits as primarily political, as divisions between "liberals" and "conservatives." Were the real differences primarily political in nature, however, American politics might more closely resemble that of present-day Western Europe, where "liberals," "conservatives," and even "socialists" and "communists" remain relatively civil to one another; where there is a broad social consensus on major issues such as national health care; where leaders focus on improving the standard of living of those who elected them; and where foreign misadventures are viewed as disasters that end up weakening the nation and depriving its citizens of basic human needs.

In reality the political differences between American "liberals" and "conservatives" are only the tip of an iceberg. What gives these labels their divisive emotionality today is what lies beneath them: deep psychological divisions within the baby-boom generation and its children over Indochina that have never been addressed, let alone allowed to heal. Much of the anger and viciousness of today's left-right split has roots in the powerful, primal emotions unleashed by the wars in Indochina. Until these root causes are dealt with, they will continue to tear America apart.[9]

The Indochina wars threw America's baby-boom generation into a moral abyss because so many young people realized, consciously or unconsciously, sooner or later, that they had been betrayed by their elders. A large number of young people—the most visible segment—reacted with fury, seeking to tear down the values and institutions that they felt had colluded in mass murder of the Indochinese and that were willing to send America's young people to pointless deaths. But many others, unable to break with their elders, reacted defensively, blaming the protestors for the breakdown of America's social consensus rather than the elders who had caused it.

Tom Brokaw's book *Boom!*, which reflects on the '60s in America, is a case study in this country's ongoing amnesia about the real issues surrounding the wars in Indochina. Brokaw authored a six-hundred-page book that does not even mention the single most important issue that propelled the domestic convulsions popularly called "the sixties": the horror felt by millions of Americans at the US murder of millions of innocent Indochinese peasants. In *Boom!* Brokaw presents the Vietnam War solely as a military conflict between two armies. Like his country, Brokaw chooses to ignore entirely the mass murder of civilians that was the war's distinguishing characteristic.

At the end of the book, Brokaw issues a passionate plea for Americans to come together to heal the divisions caused by the Vietnam War. He writes, correctly, that "the failure of goodwill, and of a willingness to find common ground in a country that in election after election is so evenly divided, is a disgrace."[10] What Brokaw fails to understand is that healing the stark divisions in American political life would require far more than platitudinous calls to civic duty.

Imagine, however, that American leaders of all political persuasions united to say that, although we still disagree about our overall right to have intervened in Indochina, we can all agree that our conduct of the wars violated both international law and also what America stands for, and that we now wish to make amends. Such an effort would be a significant first step for America to begin healing internally and to regain its standing internationally. It would, above all, be a powerful statement to our young people that America really does have a moral center, that it really does try to act in accord with its stated beliefs, and that they might want to reconsider their current, justifiable cynicism about this nation's leadership and its purposes.

It is difficult to argue against those who would suggest that such a proposal is unrealistic, even unimaginable.

If it is unimaginable, however; if no major segment of American society—not religious leaders, not artists and writers, not media figures like Brokaw, not academics, not those who educate America's youth, not business leaders, and certainly not America's political leaders—is even willing to discuss whether we should teach our children what we really did in Indochina, let alone make amends to the survivors; and if the eerie national amnesia about the millions we murdered in Indochina continues, then let us at least be clear about what we are saying.

America lost its soul in Indochina.

America will not regain its soul until amends are made.

Why American War Crimes in Indochina Still Matter

One must begin with an obvious question: why raise the issue of US war crimes in Indochina now, more than four decades since the end of the wars, at a time when new war crimes are being committed by all sides in various places around the globe?

There are many possible responses to this question, but these are among the most important:

- The United States is failing to achieve its political objectives in the world largely because it has lost its moral authority due to its widespread commission of war crimes, the most flagrant postwar examples of which were in Indochina. On one hand the United States is widely hated and feared throughout the world; on the other it is unable to achieve its objectives by force. Only if it were to regain the moral authority it held after victory in World War II would the United States once again enjoy true allies and win willing political support rather than continuing its failed strategy of coercion.

- Unwillingness to observe the laws of war leads to gigantic geopolitical blunders. Had the US honored international law, for example, it would have been unable to unilaterally occupy Iraq in the first place. Doing so clearly violated international law provisions against "aggressive war," since it cannot be plausibly argued that the United States was acting in self-defense. And restrictions against murdering civilians in time of war would also have acted as a constraint, since it was obvious that any anti-insurgency campaign would necessarily involve mass murder of civilians, given that insurgents would be indistinguishable from the mass of the population.[11]

Staying out of Iraq would have benefited the United States immeasurably. It would have made the fight against those who conducted the 9/11 attacks more effective, retained the strength of the US military, spared thousands of American lives—not to mention hundreds of thousands of Iraqi lives—and saved well over a trillion dollars desperately needed to rejuvenate America's weakening economy by investing in the new technologies and industries needed to address global warming and other biospheric challenges.

- An occupying force will always ultimately be defeated. Given that the United States did invade Iraq, however, observing international law concerning the conduct of war would have helped it achieve its objectives. Even top US military leaders admit that the United States was unable to prevail in Iraq partly because it failed to pursue proper "counterinsurgency doctrine." "Counterinsurgency doctrine" is a euphemism for the US military's practice of defining as "insurgents" the many thousands of innocents it kills and tortures in Iraq, denying them even a pretense of due process. Had the United States followed the laws of war in Iraq, there would likely have been less motivation of the opposition, both within the United States and without, and America would have been safer as a result.

- Our failure to punish US leaders for their commission of war crimes in Indochina—for which they would likely have been executed if the terms of the Nuremberg Judgment had been applied to them—has encouraged US leaders to continue and even to expand the scope of their war crimes. As a result, for the first time in American history, barbaric torture has become state policy. Knowing they can kill and torture with impunity, US leaders are far more inclined to continue to do so. Had Donald Rumsfeld, for example, been punished for covering up allegations of US war crimes during his first tour as secretary of defense, as the *Toledo Blade* documented in its Pulitzer Prize-winning October 2003 series on US war crimes in Indochina,[12] it is likely that he would not have been in a position to so grievously betray the national interest in Iraq.

- America's failure even to acknowledge US war crimes, let alone to punish the guilty, has poisoned our domestic politics. In the 2004 presidential campaign, for example, the so-called "Swift Boat Veterans" campaign, which slandered candidate John Kerry, was largely built upon the lie that US war crimes did not occur as a matter of policy in Indochina.[13]

- The most pernicious result of failing to acknowledge our war crimes in Indochina is that it denies our youth their own history. After World War II, Germany acknowledged its violations of international law and paid enormous reparations to Israel, as much for the edification of German youth as for the sake of the victims of the Holocaust. When leaders behave contrary to their words they encourage cynicism and apathy among the young. Youth growing up in America after World War II believed in their leaders, a key element in America's postwar success. Today few young people genuinely respect their leaders, partly because they know that their elders are hypocrites who violate in practice the most basic principles they claim to believe in.

This nation has no greater moral failing than our ongoing refusal to take responsibility for the countless Indochinese peasants we killed in violation of the laws of war. Those who shape opinion in this country have no higher duty to history or to the nation than to research the facts of US war crimes in Indochina and to educate our people and children about them. How can we teach "personal responsibility" to our children, for example, if we refuse to take responsibility for—or even acknowledge—our illegal murder of innumerable innocent Indochinese? Doesn't true patriotism call for perfecting our democracy by admitting our crimes and ensuring they never happen again, rather than remaining silent and repeating them?

We cannot understand the true nature of our nation unless we grapple with the contradiction that we are at once the greatest democracy on earth, and yet have also committed in Indochina the most protracted and widespread violations of the rules of war of any nation since the end of World War II. Our children cannot understand who they really are unless they grasp the grotesque fact that their parents' generation not only killed innumerable innocent peasants in Indochina but has also tried to deny this reality for more than thirty years.

Bombing and Artillery Fire Against Civilians: The Clearest US Violation of the Laws of War

The clearest US violation of the rules of war was the widespread US bombing and use of artillery against villages throughout Indochina, in violation of Article 25 of the US-ratified 1907 Hague Convention (included in subsequent war crimes legislation), which states that "the attack or bombardment, by whatever means, of towns, villages, dwellings, or buildings which are undefended, is prohibited."[14] Uncounted Indochinese peasants were burned alive by our napalm, buried alive by our five-hundred-pound bombs, shredded by our antipersonnel bombs, and obliterated by our artillery shells. By simply declaring noncombatants to be either "combatants" or their "supporters," the military justified illegal bombardment of populated areas, making millions of Indochinese peasants fair game for US bombing and/or shelling.

In *The Village of Ben Suc*, a book that strongly influenced the young John Kerry, author Jonathan Schell described how US planes would fly over vast inhabited areas declared "free-fire zones" by US officials, and bomb villages and villagers alike.[15] Equally devastating bombardment occurred from the additional millions of tons of ground artillery fired from army bases and navy ships upon undefended towns, villages, dwellings, and buildings.

I personally interviewed over two thousand peasants who had escaped from US bombing in Laos. Every single one said that their villages had been leveled by American bombing; the evidence of this is still apparent to those who visit the Plain of Jars in northern Laos today. Most of this bombing was directed at undefended villages, the only visible targets, since Pathet Lao and North Vietnamese guerrillas traveled through jungles so thick that their movements could not be detected from the air.

In Cambodia, US officials claimed that they would not bomb a village unless the bombing officer at Nakhon Phanom airbase in Thailand certified that enemy soldiers were present. This was a bald-faced lie. I tape-recorded conversations between pilots and their controllers while bombing was being conducted that showed definitively that the bombing officer was not consulted before villages were bombed. The effects of indiscriminate bombing on Cambodia were reported by Sidney Schanberg in the *New York Times* in May 1973.[16] I later interviewed the bombing officer at Nakhon Phanom airbase. He said his only task was to ensure that there were no CIA teams in the area where the bombing occurred. Undefended villages throughout vast areas of Cambodia, inhabited by two million people according to the US embassy, were leveled by US bombing.[17]

John Kerry and the 2004 "Swift Boat" Campaign Against Him

Perhaps the clearest example of how US war crimes in Indochina are still relevant occurred during the 2004 campaign for US president. A politician who courageously admitted that he and his fellows had committed massive war crimes as soldiers in Indochina was defeated in part by a campaign of lies and slander that denied these crimes of war.

John Kerry displayed remarkable integrity in his 1971 testimony to Congress and in media appearances, such as the April 1971 *Meet the Press* interview in which he acknowledged his own war crimes and those of his nation. Few other soldiers contemplating a political career were willing to be so honest.

There is no serious doubt that his statement on *Meet the Press*, quoted at the outset of this chapter, is a factual description of what occurred in Indochina, and that Kerry showed transcendent moral courage in speaking it aloud—just as those political figures who have remained silent about our war crimes, such as Bob Dole, Colin Powell, John McCain, Donald Rumsfeld, and George W. Bush, have dishonored themselves and their nation. The dozens of soldiers who testified to having committed such war crimes at the Detroit "Winter Soldier" hearings of January–February 1971, which so affected Kerry just prior to his *Meet the Press* appearance, had little reason to implicate themselves other than a desire to tell the truth.[18]

The "Swift Boat Veterans" also dishonored themselves and their nation by attacking these brave young men who described their participation in war crimes at considerable emotional cost to themselves. The "Swift Boat Veterans" were also insincere in claiming that they were personally hurt because Kerry maligned their service in Vietnam. Neither Kerry nor anyone else ever claimed that all or even that most US soldiers were personally guilty of war crimes.

US War Crimes in Indochina Were a Matter of Policy

US war crimes in Indochina were so massive because they were the result of an overall policy that did not adequately distinguish between combatants and noncombatants. Thus the major responsibility for these crimes of war lies with the superiors who created and implemented these policies, not with the individual soldiers who carried them out. The responsibility of policy makers includes not only the policies created, but also the failure to change those policies even when incontrovertible evidence existed that they were resulting in the widespread murder of civilians.

For example, the *Toledo Blade* reported that in 1967 elite army paratroopers murdered hundreds of civilians in a seven-month rampage in South Vietnam with the encouragement of superiors, and that high US officials including Donald Rumsfeld were informed about the crimes but failed to bring charges against the guilty.[19]

Official CIA involvement in widespread assassination and torture in Vietnam is also a matter of public record. William Colby, chief of the CIA's Far East Division during the Vietnam War and later head of the CIA, testified to Congress that the CIA's Operation Phoenix routinely assassinated thousands of civilians. At no time has he or any other CIA official presented any evidence that those murdered civilians were in fact guilty of the crimes of which they were accused. Numerous Phoenix program operatives have testified that local assassination teams were given quotas by Colby of the number of people they were to murder weekly, and that there was little evidence that their victims were in fact Vietcong cadre. The CIA's notorious Office of Public Safety, which trained South Vietnamese police officers, funded and participated in the torture and murder of prisoners in a Kafkaesque South Vietnamese prison system far worse than Abu Ghraib.[20]

As a result of "victor's justice," no high-ranking US official has ever been punished, or even reprimanded, for the crimes of war that they committed in Indochina. On the contrary, war criminals such as Henry Kissinger, who bears a major responsibility for laying waste to vast portions of Laos and Cambodia, have instead been awarded the highest honors our society has to offer. We do not acknowledge that our nation is capable of the same kinds of violations of the rules of war as those regimes we despise, or that American officials who commit crimes of war bear any responsibility for their actions.

Remembering the Corpses

When Trinh Cong Son, the poet-troubadour of Vietnam's Calvary, wrote of the corpses of Vietnam he was not speaking metaphorically. He was describing reality: the countless men, women, and children who were killed by American leaders in blatant violation of the laws of war.

The very fact that the issue of US war crimes was at the center of a US presidential race three decades after the end of the Indochina wars is proof that we have not yet laid these corpses to rest. America will regain neither its moral standing nor its ability to improve the world until we acknowledge that these corpses were civilians killed in violation of the rules of war, and that each person had a name, a family, dreams, aspirations, and as much of a right to live as we do.

If America is to become a nation based on truth again, let the transformation begin with one of the most important truths of all: that the United States bears responsibility for the civilian deaths it caused in Indochina and needs to make amends for them. Nations that have understood this phenomenon include South Africa, whose Truth and Reconciliation Commissions provided the basis for national healing. America could learn from this example.

Taking the necessary steps toward national healing could help America unite at home and regain a leadership position abroad. To begin to mend the deep divisions in our national soul, the United States would need to take the following steps:

1. **Seek the truth.** The US government has spent enormous sums of money to search for the remains of US soldiers in Indochina and to remember the Holocaust by building the Holocaust Museum in Washington, DC. The United States now needs to invest in determining how many civilians it killed, wounded, and made homeless in Indochina.

2. **Admit responsibility, seek forgiveness, and make amends.** Any American adult alive during 1965–1975 bears a measure of responsibility for the killing of Indochinese civilians. It is possible to view the wars as justified efforts to fight communism, and yet also to acknowledge our deep shame as a people at the innocent villagers this country killed. This profound wound within our national soul can only be healed if all Americans take responsibility for it.

The US government would need to express regret that its actions in Indochina, whatever their intent, in fact harmed innumerable civilians. The United States would also need to make amends to the people of Indochina through some sort of reparations. The first step must be the removal of the millions of antipersonnel bombs that continue to kill hundreds of Indochinese yearly.

Those who actively supported the war at home would need to acknowledge their failures to oppose illegal US killing in Indochina, as would those—like Tom Brokaw—who silently opposed the killing but failed to actively work to end it.

Antiwar protestors would need to admit their mistakes, including too often making their own behavior rather than the murder of Indochinese civilians the issue, and apologize to veterans for not having acknowledged the soldiers' willingness to sacrifice on the basis of sincere beliefs.

Pro-war veterans would need to express remorse for the killing of civilians as a separate issue from their combat experience. They would also need to acknowledge the validity of the sincere moral convictions of most of those who opposed the killing, often at the expense of careers and families.

Although it is of course unlikely that such a process could occur in today's America, at least one influential person interviewed by Tom Brokaw in *Boom!* points the way. Senator John McCain says he does not "blame the protestors for the lack of support for the war. I blame the lack of support on those who failed to tell the American people exactly what was going on. That led to cynicism." He added, "Because I had my own failings, if someone was wrong or I disagreed with them, it put me in a mood to heal those differences rather than take sides. I found out I wasn't as tough, as strong, as confident as I thought I was."[21]

If all involved could find the initiative within themselves to take similar attitudes in seeking points of reconciliation, we might be able to unite America at home and restore the faith of our young people in their leadership. Instead of remaining despised and resented around the world, a new, humbler America might find itself in a position to help forge the collective global leadership necessary to face the twenty-first-century crises yet to come.

CHAPTER 2

Excerpts from
Voices from the Plain of Jars

Collected by Fred Branfman

Starting in the fall of 1969, Fred Branfman interviewed thousands of Laotian refugees from the Plain of Jars, victims of US bombing. As director of Project Air War, founded in 1971, he helped to expose the US bombing of civilians in Indochina while it was still occurring. *Voices from the Plain of Jars* was published in 1970 and reissued by University of Wisconsin Press in 2013.

The Day Does Not Exist When We Will Forget (Artist unknown)

There was one rice farmer who was forty-eight years old. He was born in the region of Xieng Khouang in the same village as I. This old man had no children, he only had a wife. And he earned his living as a rice farmer. He had a house and cows and buffalo. One day there was a plane which came and dropped bombs on his house, but he was not at home. After that he went to look for a hole in the morning and he was shot by an airplane and died. There was a villager who saw him die. He called for his wife to go look. The wife of the man went and she cried. She was most sorry about this. She thought of her husband until she finally became sick. But we took good care of the old woman.

In the year 1968, the lives of the population in Xieng Khouang, before, had goodness. And we built progress of good kind. And we helped each other to transplant and to harvest the rice in the rice fields with happiness. But then came the time of change and until it caused the people to go into the forests in the hills. We had to live in the holes and as our houses. We couldn't go out to see the daylight. We had to stay in the forest as our home. One day the planes bombed the rice field of my village. And there was a young man about nineteen years of age [who was hit].

(Artist: thirty-three-year-old man)

In the area of Xieng Khouang, the place of my birth, there was health, good earth, and fine weather. But then the airplanes came, bombing the rice fields and the forests, making us leave our land and rice fields with great sadness. One day a plane came bombing my rice field as well as the village. I had gone very early to harrow the field. I thought, "I am only a village rice farmer, the airplane will not shoot me." But that day truly it did shoot me and wounded me together with my buffalo, which was the source of a hundred thousand loves and a hundred thousand worries for me.

This chapter would not have been possible without the courageous work of previous researchers, writers, and advocates, who dared to challenge the US government and to reveal what took place in Laos—people like Fred Branfman and Walt Haney, who testified before the US Senate about the secret bombings, and Titus Peachey of the Mennonite Central Committee, who brought new attention to this humanitarian crisis and helped initiate the first bomb removal program in Laos, and countless others who, during and since the bombing, have helped to shed light on this dark episode of American history. We greatly appreciate the expertise and comments of the above people as well as Brett Dakin, Mike Boddington, and Vinya Sysamouth of the Center for Lao Studies, who reviewed this chapter. Above all, we dedicate this chapter to the people of Laos, both those who remain in this war-torn land and Laotian refugees dispersed around the world. We would like to give special thanks, or kop chai, to the dedicated volunteers, advisors, and staff of Legacies of War. The authors hope to carry on the legacy of seeking truth and reconciliation through justice and healing for those who suffer from the bombing and war.

CHAPTER 3

Legacies of War: Cluster Bombs in Laos

Channapha Khamvongsa and Elaine Russell

Introduction

Beginning more than fifty years ago, the US government inflicted a tragic injustice on the people of Laos, an injustice that has only recently been acknowledged and one that remains to be fully rectified. The US government funded an illegal, covert bombing campaign that killed tens of thousands of innocent civilians and left the small nation of Laos burdened with a deadly legacy that lives on today. Great quantities of unexploded ordnance (UXO) contaminate approximately one third of the country and have killed or maimed thousands of people, while severely hampering efforts to eliminate poverty and hunger. The story of the "secret war" in Laos has long been overshadowed by events in Vietnam and Cambodia. It is time for this story to be told so the suffering can end. It is time for the United States to do what is morally right and make Laos whole again by fully funding and completing the removal of UXO and providing victim assistance.

Between 1964 and 1973, the United States released 2.1 million tons of ordnance over Laos and on numerous occasions bombed the civilian population[1] in direct violation of the Geneva Conventions on war to protect civilians[2] and the 1954 Geneva Accords and 1962 Geneva Agreements that prohibited the presence of foreign military personnel or advisors in neutral Laos. The US military justified the bombings as necessary to counter the illegal presence of North Vietnamese troops in Laos, but the response was vastly disproportionate. At the astonishing rate of one bombing mission every eight minutes, twenty-four hours a day, for nine years, the United States dropped more bombs on Laos than it had dropped on all countries during World War

23

II. US bombing left the tiny nation the most heavily bombed country per capita in the world and resulted in mostly civilian casualties. After the war ended, up to 80 million unexploded cluster bomblets and other ordnance remained, posing a constant threat to civilian life.

During the war, in an attempt to stop the Pathet Lao communist insurgency and to interrupt Vietnamese supply lines along the Ho Chi Minh trail (which ran through southeastern Laos), the US military and CIA trained and supplied the Royal Lao Army, recruited Laotian people for covert operations on the ground, and carried out bombing strikes and reconnaissance flights under the guise of civilian contractors delivering humanitarian aid. These activities not only violated the neutrality of Laos but were also conducted without the knowledge or authorization of the US Congress. The secret war in Laos would eventually be exposed during US Senate hearings in 1971.[3] Details did not become known until State Department memorandums were declassified years after the war ended. However, the severity of the bombing was not revealed until President Bill Clinton authorized the release of US military strike data in 2000. Additional US government records released under the Freedom of Information Act, which have not been reviewed, may contain data revealing even higher levels of bombing. CIA records on the war in Laos still remain classified.

In June 2007, a speech made by US State Department official Richard Kidd substantiated the long-term civilian casualties and impacts of UXO in Laos. Calling it the "Laos exception," the US government acknowledged that no other country in the world had suffered the long-term harm from cluster bombs that was inflicted on the people of Laos.[4] However, Kidd's comments stopped short of suggesting the United States take responsibility for its role in the secret war or that it fully fund the cost of bomb removal.

In 2016, president Barack Obama made a historic trip to Laos for a meeting of the Association of Southeast Asian Nations (ASEAN). He was the first president to visit Laos since the end of the Vietnam War. While there, he signed a joint bilateral agreement between the US and the Lao People's Democatic Republic (Lao PDR). President Obama and Lao PDR president Bounnhang Vorachit confirmed comprehensive cooperation in addressing the war legacy of UXO in Laos. President Obama stated that the US had "a moral obligation to help Laos heal" and announced that the United States would contribute $90 million over three years for the completion of a national UXO survey and to increase the level of UXO clearance in Laos.[5]

While casualties have declined significantly over the last four decades, during the last five years, UXO continued to kill or injure at least 40 to 60 people each year and posed a major impediment to economic development. Laos remains one of the poorest countries in the world. The formal cleanup of cluster bombs and other explosive remnants of war began in 1994, but moves at a snail's pace. Over one and a half million pieces of UXO have been removed, but it is estimated that around 80 million cluster munitions alone remain, along with an unknown number of big bombs, motors, rockets, and land mines from the US and other parties to the conflict.[6] The lack of sustained attention to the issue has resulted in a lack of political will to expedite removal. In the past, US contributions to the effort were modest at best, due to strained relations between the governments of the US and the Lao PDR. But US funding has increased since 2008, culminating in the commitment of President Obama in 2016 for $90 million of funding over three years.

The problem of UXO in Laos had received scant media attention, until the release of three important documentaries—the highly acclaimed 2002 film *Bombies* by Jack Silberman,[7] the 2007 Australian film *Bomb Harvest* by Kim Mordaunt and Sylvia Wilczynski,[8] and Mark Eberle's 2009 film *The Most Secret Place on Earth—CIA's Covert War in Laos*.[9]

In recent years media attention on the issue has greatly increased, and the 2016 trip of President Obama resulted in stories on major networks around the world, including BBC, Al Jazeera, PBS *Newshour*, CBS, CNN, NBC, and many others. Major newspapers and magazines carried stories on the issue as well, including the *New York Times*, the *Washington Post*, the *Nation*, and the *Diplomat*.[10]

Renewed interest in the issue was also prompted by the Laotian diaspora as it became more engaged with its former homeland and recognized that cluster bombs pose a major obstacle to the safety of the population and to economic development in Laos. Additionally, the use of cluster bombs in more recent conflicts in the Middle East triggered awareness of the harm these weapons cause; this prompted an international effort to ban cluster munitions worldwide. On May 30, 2008, at a gathering in Dublin, Ireland, 107 countries, including Laos, agreed to the text of the Convention on Cluster Munitions, banning the use, sale, and stockpiling of cluster munitions and ensuring humanitarian assistance for victims and affected communities. The parties, who met throughout 2007 and 2008, gathered in Oslo, Norway on December 3–4, 2008, to sign the convention. As of 2017, 120 states have committed to the goals of the convention, of which 104 have become full states-parties and 16 are signatories.[11]

The United States is not a party to the convention.

A History of Conflict

From its early warring kingdoms to recent times, Laos has been shaped by periods of relative peace and prosperity interrupted by protracted wars that led to subjugation and exploitation by outside interests. Western countries first recognized modern-day Laos as an independent nation in 1954. Current borders evolved from the French colonial period of 1893–1954, when administrators consolidated three Lao kingdoms into a province within French Indochina.[12]

The Lao Kingdoms

The early history of Laos is closely integrated with that of its neighbors—the countries that today are Thailand, Myanmar, Cambodia, Vietnam, and China. For hundreds of years the sparsely populated region was divided into small settlements and then into larger kingdoms or vassal states. Borders continually shifted as kingdoms fought to control fertile rice lands along the river valleys, the people that farmed them, and other natural resources. It wasn't until 1353 that the kingdom of Lan Xang, "Land of a Million Elephants," was established by Chao Fa Ngum, encompassing an area twice the size of modern-day Laos.[13] The kingdom had close ties with the neighboring Tai kingdoms of Lanna and Ayutthaya. Lan Xang lost power and territory after invasions by the Vietnamese in 1449 and the Burmese in 1563. The capital was moved from Luang Prabang to Vientiane for strategic reasons in 1560 by King Setthathirath, but Luang Prabang remained the seat of the royalty. Ongoing struggles and incursions slowly depleted the Lao population and destroyed most of the wealth, palaces, and Buddhist temples.

At the start of the eighteenth century Lan Xang was divided into three kingdoms: Luang Prabang, Vientiane, and Champasak. A period of peace and prosperity followed until the Burmese raided the region once more in the 1760s. The weakened Lao kingdoms became tributaries of Siam in 1779, and in 1828 the Siamese (present-day Thai) army ransacked Vientiane and burned the city to the ground. The kingdoms remained under Siamese control until the French arrived in the late 1800s.

French Colonization

French colonization of Indochina began in Vietnam and Cambodia during the 1870s and gradually expanded into Laos. In 1893, the French forced Siam to cede power over the three Lao kingdoms for all lands east of the Mekong River.[14] Siam retained control over the more populated farmlands west of the river, although portions of the west bank were later granted to Laos. The only royal court that remained as part of the new French province resided in Luang Prabang. The French recognized this kingdom as a protectorate rather than as a colony.

Economic development in French Indochina focused on Vietnam and Cambodia, where larger populations, more accessible natural resources, and coastal ports allowed viable export markets to enrich France. Landlocked Laos remained a relative backwater, an afterthought. Infrastructure investments in Laos were concentrated on road construction, access along the Mekong River, and telegraph lines, which attempted to connect Laos with economic activity in Vietnam and Cambodia. But these projects were unsuccessful in stemming the trade that naturally flowed between Laos and Thailand.

A 1907 census reported 585,285 people living in Laos.[15] The lack of an adequate labor force presented a major constraint to French economic development. The French maintained a monopoly over the opium trade, which provided more than half the annual revenues for the provincial government; other French business ventures in mining, timber harvesting, and coffee and tobacco plantations met with only minor success.

While economic progress remained limited, French social reforms slowly introduced modernization and Western ideas to Laos. The Lao kingdoms had been highly stratified societies with diverse ethnic populations, from the lowland Lao and other Lao-Tai groups to Mon-Khmer groups, such as the Khamu, and highland ethnic minorities, including the Hmong and Mien. For centuries, lowland Lao kings and a small group of educated Lao ruled over the population of subsistence peasant farmers. In some cases, slavery and forced labor existed. Buddhist temples served as cultural centers of lowland Lao life for religious and educational purposes, as monks provided formal education to novices and village children.

Under colonial rule, a small number of French officials were posted to Laos in top administrative jobs. The French viewed Laotians as too relaxed and unreliable and brought in educated Vietnamese to fill mid-level government posts. Soon over half the population in urban areas was Vietnamese. A large number of Chinese also settled in cities and towns to run businesses and trade. The French abolished slavery but imposed *corvée*, a form of forced labor that required farmers to build roads and other public facilities. The vast majority of Lao people remained rural farmers.

The French continued support for education in the Buddhist temples, but later built French-language elementary and secondary schools in the larger towns. The schools catered to Vietnamese settlers and the privileged lowland Lao. Wealthy families sent their children to Saigon or Hanoi for higher education and, in some cases, to Paris. Toward the end of the colonial period, schools began to serve a broader population. Over time, upland and highland ethnic minorities gained limited access to education, along with greater social standing and freedoms. Exposure to the wider world and ideas of equality and independence fostered interest in a Lao identity and a free nation. Changes to the social order during the French period undermined traditional cultural and economic relationships and highlighted resentments and tensions between different segments of society, which carried over into the years of independence and civil war.

War and Independence

World War II brought changes to every corner of the world, including Laos. A vast area west of the Mekong River, known today as Isan (population now over twenty-five million) was ceded to Thailand as a result of the 1940 Matsuoka-Henry Pact, which ended the Franco-Thai war. Portions of the Xieng Khouang region were annexed by the Vietnamese, portions of the south went to Cambodia, and China claimed considerable influence along the northern border.

Once France fell to Germany in 1940 and war erupted in the Pacific in 1941, Japanese troops occupied French Indochina, primarily in Vietnam and Cambodia, but also with a minor presence in Laos. Officials from the Vichy French government remained in Laos and coexisted with the Japanese troops. On March 9, 1945, the Japanese overthrew the Vichy French colonial regime, before surrendering to the Allies in August of that year. The Lao Issara (Free Lao movement) formed a government in October and declared Laos an independent nation.[16] But this was at odds with the Luang Prabang monarchy, which worried that Thailand had ambitions to take over the country and favored a return to a French protectorate. Meanwhile, the North Vietnamese communist movement was fostering unrest among Vietnamese residents in Laos, creating tension with the Lao population. As the world divided into communist and noncommunist countries, the United States supported the return of France to Indochina in 1946, and the Lao Issara went into exile in Thailand.

Growing nationalist sentiment within the territories forced France to designate its former colonies as independent states within the French Indochinese Union. However, "independent" was a relative term. In Laos, the new constitutional monarchy was run by an elite group of Lao families with the king's support and considerable French involvement. The struggle for greater independence limped along. In 1949, the French granted Laos the status of a nominally independent Associated State within the French Indochinese Union, while retaining control of foreign policy and defense. The Lao Issara was unwilling to settle for partial autonomy from France, but was unable to agree on how to achieve full independence. By October of 1949, the Lao Issara had split into two factions. The leaders were Prince Souvanna Phouma, who returned to Vientiane to join the Royal Lao Government, and his half brother, Prince Souphanouvong (also known as the "Red Prince"), who joined the exiled Lao resistance, allied with the Vietminh communists against the French and the Royal Lao Government.

In October 1953, the Royal Lao Government was granted full autonomy and the French withdrew in 1954. The early 1950s were a time of great hope, but the fledgling Lao government faced challenges similar to those from the French colonial period. The country still had virtually no means of generating revenue, and most of the population remained subsistence farmers. The country lacked an adequate infrastructure of roads and communications to connect the rural, mountainous provinces with the capital and other towns along the Mekong River valley. At that time there were only one hundred registered vehicles in the country, and telephone service would not reach the provinces until 1967.[17]

Due to rising Lao hostility and distrust, 80 percent of the Vietnamese population in Laos fled back to Vietnam, leaving a severe shortage of trained administrators and professionals. As the French government no longer supplemented revenues, the new Lao government turned to the United States to provide desperately needed financial aid.

In North Vietnam, Ho Chi Minh's communist organization initiated the first Indochina war in order to oust France from the region. The Vietminh helped solidify a Lao communist resistance, which eventually became known as the Pathet Lao (Nation of Laos). Guerrilla attacks on French troops increased, and in 1953 the Vietminh moved into northeastern provinces of Laos. Intense fighting led to the siege of the French fort at Dien Bien Phu on the Lao-Vietnamese border, where the French surrendered in 1954.

The first Geneva Conference in 1954 met to negotiate settlements for civil wars in Korea and Indochina, all part of the growing conflict between Western democracies and the Soviet and Chinese communist governments. The 1954 Geneva Accords established Laos as a neutral, sovereign state and called for the removal of foreign troops. A new coalition government was formed in Laos with the existing government, the Pathet Lao, and neutralists. Communist Pathet Lao forces were allowed to remain in Houaphan and Phongsali provinces in northeastern Laos, while the Royal Lao Government forces held the rest of the country. Some Vietnamese troops remained in Laos at this time, while also training and equipping new Pathet Lao recruits from their base across the border.

During this period Laos, rather than Vietnam, was the focus of US attempts to stop the communist threat. The mission in Laos greatly expanded as the United States supplied arms and training for the Royal Lao Army and large sums of aid to friendly government officials. Many in the Lao elite grew wealthier from rampant corruption and cronyism, while little of the aid trickled down to the peasant population. From 1955 to 1958, the United States provided $167 million in aid to Laos, primarily to the military.[18] The disparity in aid incensed the rural population and increased their support of the communists.

Throughout the 1950s and early 1960s American, Soviet, and Chinese interests supported various government schemes as rightist, moderate, and leftist factions—including three royal princes, ministers, and military officers—vied for power. A series of coalition governments formed and fell apart, interrupted by several military coups. Before the May 1958 elections, in an attempt to influence voters the United States started Operation Booster Shot, which disbursed close to $3 million for rural projects. But the elections gave the communists a clear majority in the National Assembly and authority over the coalition government. The United States toppled this government by withholding financial aid.[19] Once US-friendly leaders were in place, aid resumed. Around this time communist forces began a guerrilla warfare campaign in northeastern Laos.

The communists were believed to hold a wide majority as the next elections, scheduled for April 1960, approached. The United States influenced the elections by increasing aid and buying votes. Exasperated, a Royal Lao Army commander, Kong Le, carried out a coup and tried to form a moderate government. The United States supported a counter-coup headed by a rightist leader, Phoumi Nosavan, and sent in US troops to fight alongside the Royal Lao Army. As a result, the neutralists joined the communists and large-scale civil war erupted.

The escalating civil war led to a second Geneva Conference in 1961 and the Geneva Agreements of 1962, which reaffirmed Laos as a neutral state and prohibited foreign bases and troops in the country. But the agreements had little effect on the illegal fighting taking place on the ground. Allegiances shifted, fighting intensified, and "neutral" Laos earned the nickname "Land of Oz,"[20] as subterfuge and lies created a surreal atmosphere.

The US role in the civil war developed on three fronts. The United States continued support for the Royal Lao Army, providing training, supplies, and air cover. The CIA also recruited and supplied Hmong and other ethnic minorities to fight a guerrilla war in the jungles behind enemy lines. The Hmong Special Forces, led by General Vang Pao (the only Hmong general in the Royal Lao Army), carried out covert operations against enemy troops and identified positions for American bombers to target. To circumvent the Geneva Agreements, the CIA hired private contractors—Air America, Continental Air Services, and others—and temporarily reclassified military pilots as civilians. The United States maintained that the planes were delivering humanitarian aid, whereas in truth they were delivering arms and supplies and carrying out bombing missions.

At the same time that the United States expanded its military role, an increasing number of Vietnamese troops fought alongside the Pathet Lao with arms and supplies from China and Russia.

By 1963, US involvement in Vietnam had deepened. Laos took a back seat as US policy was largely determined by the need to support efforts in the Vietnam War, an attitude summed up by Secretary of State Dean Rusk: "After 1963 Laos was only the wart on the hog of Vietnam."[21]

US Bombing in Laos

"The airplanes came bombing my rice field until the bomb craters made farming impossible. And the village was hit and burned. And some relatives who were working in the fields without shelter came running out to the road to return to the village, but the airplanes saw and shot them—killing the farmers in a heart-rending manner. We heard their screams, but we couldn't go to help them. When the airplane left we went to look, but they had already died."
—Laotian villager from Xieng Khouang province, living in a refugee camp near Vientiane, Laos, 1971[22]

Attempts to form another coalition government in 1964 fell apart as two Royal Lao Army generals carried out yet another coup. US Ambassador to Laos Leonard Unger insisted that the new leaders reinstate neutralist Souvanna Phouma as prime minister. In 1964, with Souvanna Phouma's approval, the United States began flying reconnaissance flights out of bases in Thailand over the Pathet Lao–held territories. After a plane was shot down, the United States bombed Pathet Lao positions and began flying armed escorts. From June 1964 to March 1970, the US government denied conducting anything but armed reconnaissance flights; in reality bomber sortie raids over northern Laos (a sortie is counted when the aircraft returns to base for refueling) reached a peak of 405 per day in 1969.

The Ho Chi Minh trail, in reality a network of dirt trails, ran through southeastern Laos, providing a supply line for communist troops fighting in South Vietnam and Cambodia. In December 1964, the United States began a second air-strike program to disrupt deliveries along the trail, yet denied the existence of this bombing campaign as well until two planes were shot down in January 1965.

However, extensive bombing raids over North Vietnam, which began in February 1965, soon overshadowed interest in the bombing of Laos. The United States set up ground-based aircraft guidance systems, manned by US troops and Hmong Special Forces, on mountaintops in Laos to direct bombing attacks over North Vietnam. When bombing missions to North Vietnam were aborted due to weather or enemy fire, pilots often dropped their bombs over Laos rather than going through the complicated procedures of landing with a full load of ordnance back at bases in Thailand.

In 1968, US president Johnson announced first a partial halt and then a full halt to bombing in North Vietnam. On October 31, 1968, he said, "The overriding consideration that governs us at this hour is the chance and the opportunity that we might have to save human lives on both sides of the conflict."[23]

The truth was very different. Planes that had been bombing North Vietnam were now diverted to campaigns over northern and southeastern Laos. One official was quoted as saying, "We couldn't just let the planes rust."[24] From 1968 through 1971, the number of sorties increased dramatically and earlier restrictions on bombing civilian targets were substantially relaxed. In 1967, a total of 52,120 sorties were flown, while in 1969 there were 148,069—equivalent to a planeload of bombs dropped every 3.7 minutes around the clock for an entire year. The town of Xieng Khouang on the Plain of Jars was completely leveled in April 1969.

From 1964 to 1973, Laos became the most heavily bombed country per capita in the world. During its secret and illegal campaign, the United States dropped 2,093,100 tons of ordnance in 580,344 bombing missions.[25] For the first time in its military history, the United States utilized a large number of cluster bombs (called "bombies" by the Lao). Depending on the design of the cluster bomb, each bomb casing opened midair to release four to seven hundred bomblets, about the size of an orange, over a wide area. The US military strike data released in 2000 was used by Handicap International in a report on cluster munitions use and casualties worldwide, issued in May 2007.[26] The newly tabulated figures indicate that at least 260 million US cluster bomblets were released over Laos during the war—eighty-six bomblets for every person living in the country (the population was approximately three million in 1970[27]). This estimate is significantly higher than an earlier report of ninety million cluster bomblets. Clearance teams have found 186 types of munitions, including nineteen different types of cluster bombs.[28]

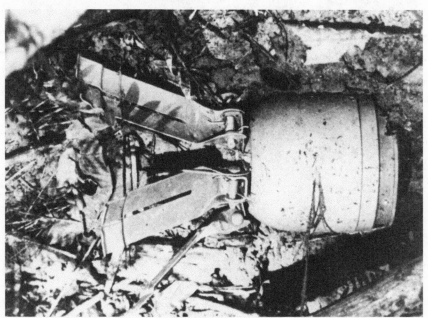

"Pineapple Bomb." Photo by Walt Haney.

The US military made a conscious decision to bomb civilian villages, crops, and livestock in addition to military targets in the Pathet Lao–held areas. The goal was to remove all means of livelihood for the communist troops. US strike data reveals that 52.8 million cluster bomblets, or 20 percent of all bombs, were dropped within one kilometer of villages. Hundreds of firsthand accounts by survivors tell of bombs dropping on civilians as they ran for cover. There are no reliable figures on the casualties of the war, but it is estimated that tens of thousands of civilians died.

"There were no soldiers in the village but the planes bombed anywhere. I lost my wife, my father, my mother, my three children, and all my belongings. All I had left were the clothes on my back."

As another villager put it, "His mother was burned up, his father was burned up, the children were burned up. Everything was burned up."
—Account of 1967 bombing by Xieng Som Di and another villager from Ban Na Sou, in a 1970 interview at a refugee camp, describing the deaths of Xieng Som Di's family. Photo by Walt Haney.

"All the villagers were living in holes then. But Tit Van Di went back to the village to get something to take to the holes. While he was in the village the jets bombed before he could flee. There were no soldiers in the village. At that time the planes came many times every day, four or five times even at night. The jets and the T-28s together. Sometimes the T-28s would drop the big bombs first and then the jets would drop the bombies."

—Account of 1968 bombing by Nang Sida from Ban Nasay, in a 1970 interview at a refugee camp, describing how her husband died.

Photo by Walt Haney.[30]

The bombings were relentless. By 1970, tens of thousands of civilians had died, while thousands more, their homes destroyed, lived in caves or holes in the ground. Another fifteen to twenty thousand were evacuated to refugee camps near Vientiane in the Royal Lao Government–controlled zone. From these refugees, the story of what had taken place began to emerge.

> By 1968, the intensity of the bombings was such that no organized life was possible in the villages. The villagers moved to the outskirts and then deeper and deeper into the forest as the bombing reached its peak in 1969, when jet planes came daily and destroyed all stationary structures; nothing was left standing. The villagers lived in trenches and holes or in caves, and they only farmed at night. All informants, without exception, had his [sic] village completely destroyed. In the last phase, bombings were aimed at the systematic destruction of the material basis of the civilian society.[31]

Throughout the war, the US military denied involvement in the illegal bombings and, once they were revealed, denied that civilians had been targeted. The truth was eventually exposed in US Senate hearings beginning in 1971. Additional details emerged with the release of State Department documents in later years. What took place in Laos sparked a temporary outcry, but it was soon lost to discord over the wider wars in Vietnam and Cambodia. The US campaign in Laos was later dubbed the "secret war" and, sadly, was relegated to a footnote in history books on the Vietnam War.

With tremendous public opposition at home to the war, the United States decided to pull out of Indochina and signed a treaty with North Vietnam in late 1972. Without American backing, the Royal Lao Government was forced to negotiate an end to war. They formed a coalition government with the Pathet Lao in 1973. Within two years, the Lao People's Revolutionary Party took power of the country and formed the Lao People's Democratic Republic (Lao PDR).

Immediately, thousands who had supported or fought on the side of the US-backed Royal Lao Government fled the country in fear of retribution, and many more followed over the years. Since 1975 at least three hundred thousand Laotians, or 10 percent of the population, have left Laos, including most of the educated and professional people. Many lived in refugee camps in Thailand and eventually resettled in the United States, Canada, France, Australia, New Zealand, or other countries.[32] Meanwhile, the people remaining in Laos attempted to resume a normal life.

Living and Dying Among the Bombs

"On March 21, 2017, a ten-year-old girl picked up a cluster bomb on her way to school and later took it home. The bomb exploded, killing one person and injuring twelve others, ages two to fifty-seven years old."

—Xieng Khouang Province, Laos[33]

Villagers who fled the fighting and bombing during the civil war returned home only to find the landscape blanketed with unexploded ordnance. Approximately 30 percent of all cluster bomblets dropped on Laos had not detonated, leaving behind close to 80 million unexploded cluster bomblets in addition to the thousands of large bombs, rockets, mortars, shells, and landmines, which contaminate close to one-third of Laos.

In 2009, the Lao PDR's National Regulatory Authority (NRA) published the *National Survey of UXO Victims and Accidents, Phase I*, which surveyed 95 percent of the villages in Laos to determine the number of victims (killed and injured).[34] The study found that from 1964 to 2008, 50,136 people were killed or injured from UXO; 20,008, or about 40 percent, of these casualties occurred after 1974 and the end of the conflict. In the 1970s about 1,500 people were killed or injured per year. Casualties declined over time to 600 per year during the 1980s and 200 to 300 per year during the 1990s. With the expansion of UXO clearance projects and better public education on the risks of UXO, casualties declined to between 40 and 300 per year in the 2000s.

Because many incidents occur in remote, rural villages without access to health care, receiving adequate treatment is very difficult, resulting in higher death rates.

Unexploded bombs remain in villages, schoolyards, rice paddies, fields, fruit orchards, bamboo stands, forests, and stream banks. The United Nations estimated the population of Laos in 2017 at 6.8 million. The majority of people are subsistence farmers who find growing adequate food supplies a constant challenge. Many farmers must choose between feeding their families and the risks of planting in bomb-laden fields. Projects to provide clean drinking water, irrigation, electricity, health care facilities, schools, and other basic needs cannot go forward until unexploded bombs have been cleared, adding substantially to the costs of development. Other casualties have occurred as desperately poor individuals try to defuse bombs in order to sell the scrap metal, even though the government has outlawed this practice.

Hundreds of children have been orphaned. Many families are left without their main breadwinners and struggle to survive. Among the UXO victims, 20,493 have lost one or more limbs and need prostheses, while many others have been blinded. Disabled fathers and mothers cannot work to support their families. The governmental and nongovernmental organizations (NGOs) in Laos providing services to disabled victims do not have enough resources to assist all those in need of artificial limbs, mental health treatment, or employment retraining.

TABLE 1: Landmine and Cluster Munition Monitor Annual Reports

Data Year	Land Cleared (km²)	UXO pieces Removed	Reported Casualties		Funding ($ million)
			killed	injured	
1996–2003	43.96	528,998	161	383	54
2004	19.50	75,371	66	128	8.1
2005	16.96	67,783	36	128	8.1
2006	47.09	102,198	16	33	13.4
2007	42.00	88,259	31	69	12.2
2008	54.09	116,158	30	69	12.7
2009	37.19	77,321	41	93	11
2010	34.98	70,518	24	93	20.8
2011	38.74	63,275	22	77	21.8
2012	41.30	80,478	15	41	80.5
2013	64.86	82,056	13	29	82
2014	67.78	93,423	16	29	93.4
2015	41.20	101,030	8	34	100.2
2016	27.40	95,581	10	49	106.6
TOTALS	577.05	1,642,449	489	1,255	624.7

Source: Landmine and Cluster Munition Monitor. Chart compiled from annual reports.

The following table, prepared by the NRA, also shows casualties from 2008–2016. Due to reporting differences, there are slightly different totals for some years. This table shows a breakdown by men, women, boys, and girls. As can be seen, 48 percent of UXO victims over the past nine years have been children, with a much higher incidence among boys. Children confuse cluster bomblets for small toys that attract their curiosity.

TABLE 2: UXO Accidents and Casualties per Year, 2008–2017

Year	Accidents	Injuries				Deaths				Total
		Males	Females	Boys	Girls	Males	Females	Boys	Girls	
2008	186	99	22	67	15	66	8	20	5	302
2009	77	50	8	25	3	25	1	6	2	120
2010	75	33	8	47	7	9	1	9	5	119
2011	64	32	9	34	4	6	0	14	0	99
2012	36	17	11	11	2	6	1	6	2	56
2013	18	9	2	12	5	5	0	7	1	41
2014	22	8	5	9	7	4	0	12	0	45
2015	27	15	1	16	1	6	1	2	0	42
2016	35	17	3	24	5	1	0	8	0	58
2017	19	12	11	8	6	3	0	0	1	41

Source: Lao National Regulatory Authority, chart provided January 20, 2017; email from Bountau Chanthavongsa, UXO Victim Assistance Officer, NRA, January 22, 2018.

For more than twenty years, the people of Laos had virtually no outside assistance in removing UXO from the land. The Lao government did not have the necessary resources and was wary of outside help. US offers of assistance were tied to the recovery of the remains of American personnel listed as missing in action (MIA). Finally in 1994, the Lao government, the British-based nongovernmental organization Mines Advisory Group (MAG), and the Mennonite Central Committee initiated a pilot program to remove UXO in Xieng Khouang province. Two years later, the government created UXO Lao, which works with the United Nations, donor countries, and humanitarian organizations on a national clearance program. In 2004, the National Regulatory Authority was designated to take over monitoring and regulatory responsibilities for the UXO program (although it did not become operational until 2006), while UXO Lao implemented removal in the field. In addition to bomb clearance efforts, the government and organizations such as MAG, World Education, and Handicap International conduct UXO awareness education in schools and villages in the hope of preventing accidents.

Based on US military strike data and a 1996 Handicap International land survey of Laos[35] it was estimated that UXO contaminates 87,200 square kilometers (33,669 square miles), or more than 37 percent of the country; of that, 12,427 square kilometers (4,798 square miles) are considered high risk, due to the presence of civilians and high concentrations of UXO. Contamination by UXO has been found in 14 of the 17 Laotian provinces and in 2,861 villages (25 percent of the villages in Laos).

However, the accuracy of this early study is unknown. In 2016 the Lao PDR committed to completing a nationwide evidence-based survey by the end of 2021, with assistance from the US and other donor countries. The survey work, which has already begun, includes nontechnical as well as technical elements to identify areas of ordnance contamination in much greater detail. As of mid-2017, the survey had already identified nearly 100,000 acres of Confirmed Hazardous Areas (CHAs) in need of clearance.[36]

UXO clearance efforts have slowly increased in scope and funding over the years. From 1996 through 2006, the United Nations Development Program (UNDP), donor countries, and a number of independent bomb clearance and humanitarian organizations provided $83.6 million for UXO clearance programs, an average of $7.6 million per year. However from 2007 to 2016 international contributions increased to a total of $541.2 million, an average of $54.1 million per year (see Table 1—Landmine and Cluster Munition Monitor Annual Reports Summary). As a result, more land has been cleared and UXO removed or destroyed. This, along with increased educational programs to alert farmers, villagers, and children to the dangers of UXO, has helped to bring down the casualty numbers.

US contributions to UXO clearance in Laos were low in the early years but began increasing in 2009. According to the 2015 US State Department report *To Walk the Earth in Safety*,[37] the United States contributed $37.5 million from 1993 through the first half of 2007, or an average of about $2.7 million per year. This represents just 3 percent of all US demining funding around the world during this period. In contrast, the United States spent $2 million *per day* (in 1960 dollars—$17 million per day in 2018 dollars) for nine years to bomb Laos during the war, and has spent close to $5 million a year on the recovery of the remains of MIA soldiers.

The level of US funding for UXO clearance has steadily increased in recent years, reaching $14 million in 2015. In keeping with President Obama's pledge for $90 million over three years, the FY 2016 original funding of $19.5 million was increased to $30 by the end of the year, and the US Congress allocated $30 million for FY 2017. Funding for FY 2018 is still uncertain. In 2018 the Trump administration budget proposed $10 million in funding. However, the US Congressional Budget, enacted in March 2018, fulfilled the pledge of $30 million.

Progress in clearing the land has been excruciatingly slow, as bomb detection and clearance work is time-consuming, dangerous, and expensive. There are two types of clearance teams. Roving teams respond to requests from villagers and farmers who have discovered UXO. The teams then detonate or defuse and remove the items. It is common for roving teams to be called back to a village numerous times as ordnance continues to be uncovered. Other teams work to clear specific tracts of land. Trained teams go over every inch of an area with metal detectors. When potential UXO is identified, the team carefully digs by hand around the site until the source is found. In many cases, the buried metal turns out to be one of the millions of exploded bomb fragments that are buried in the land alongside UXO. Unexploded cluster bomblets and other smaller UXO are usually detonated in place, while large bombs may be defused and removed. Over time, bombs rust and become even more volatile and dangerous.

New equipment is improving the efficiency of clearance work. The United States recently gave Laos fifty metal detectors designed to discriminate between metal fragments and larger live bombs. From 1996 to 2006, removal teams cleared just 144 square kilometers of land. But from 2007 to 2017 another 494 square kilometers were cleared. However, this remains a small portion of the potentially contaminated lands.

According to the annual *Land Mine and Cluster Munition Monitor* reports, 1,760,423 pieces of UXO of all types, from submunitions to big bombs, were destroyed from 1996 to 2017. In earlier years, cluster bombs represented about half of the UXO cleared, but in 2015 this went up to two-thirds and, in 2016, to three-quarters of the UXO cleared. There are an estimated 80 million unexploded cluster bomblets contaminating the land alone.

The recent expansion of UXO clearance programs must be sustained to reduce the risk to life and limb for a large portion of the Lao population.

Development—Still Struggling

Forty-five years after the end of war, the Lao government is still struggling to meet the population's basic needs for food, safe water, sanitation, health care, and education. The UN Development Program has designated Laos a "Landlocked and Least Developed Country," among the poorest nations in the world—and has identified the presence of UXO in at least 37 percent of the country as a key challenge to Laos's development.[37] The Lao PDR government adopted UN-approved Sustainable Development Goals to be achieved by 2030. The previous eight Millennium Development Challenge Goals were expanded to seventeen Sustainable Development Goals (SDG), which cover social and economic development issues. In 2016, during UN secretary general Ban Ki-Moon's visit, Lao PDR added an additional SDG goal, number 18: lives safe from UXO.

After the War

When the Lao People's Revolutionary Party (LPRP), the political wing of the Pathet Lao, took control of Laos in 1975, the economy was in ruins, and the United States stopped providing financial aid. In Xieng Khouang province and many regions around the Ho Chi Minh trail, virtually nothing remained: towns, villages, fields, and infrastructure had been obliterated. Most of the educated, professional class had already fled the country, and many of the remaining government administrators, Royal Lao military personnel, teachers, doctors, nurses, and businesspeople were sent to reeducation prison camps.

The newly formed Lao PDR immediately instituted a centrally controlled economy and collectivized agricultural land. The exodus of educated professionals resulted in a shortage of capable people to run the government and provide services. For the next ten years, Laos remained an isolated country, closely aligned with and dependent on the Soviet Union and Vietnam for military and financial assistance. After the long and bitter war, the government shunned contact with Western nations, in particular the United States. The Lao PDR suspected that the CIA was supporting ex–Royal Lao military officers and Hmong guerrillas in a continuing armed resistance within Laos and along the Thai border.

The centralized state-run economy was collapsing by the mid-1980s. The disintegration of the Soviet Union in 1990 resulted in the loss of two-thirds of the foreign aid to Laos.[38] With few remaining options, the Lao PDR government began to decentralize the economy, to allow private markets, and to seek better relations with Western countries, the UN, and humanitarian organizations. In response to international concerns, the Lao PDR closed most prison camps, adopted a constitution in 1991, and established a legal system. Today, although the people elect members to the National Assembly, there is still only one political party. Most decisions are made by the ten-member Politburo and prime minister.

In recent years, Laos has been actively engaging with regional and world economic development organizations, joining ASEAN in 1997 and applying for membership in the World Trade Organization (WTO) in 1998. Improved relations with Thailand led to more open borders and to the construction of four Lao-Thai bridges across the Mekong River, increasing access to trade and job markets for Lao citizens. Laos continues to strengthen relationships with other nations, including Australia, Japan, China, India, European Union countries, and neighboring Southeast Asian nations. It maintains membership in more than twenty-five international bodies, including the UN, the WTO, the International Monetary Fund (IMF), the World Health Organization, and the ASEAN. The United States restored full diplomatic relations with Laos in 1992, extended normal trade relations in 2004, and signed a bilateral trade agreement in 2005.

Laos Today and the Impact of UXO

The *Lao PDR 8th 5-Year Socio-Economic Development Plan 2016-2020,* [38] published in conjunction with the UN, reports that Laos has experienced sustained economic progress, with an average 7.9 percent annual growth in Gross Domestic Product (GDP) from 2010 to 2015, despite the downturn in world markets in 2008. The poverty rate fell from 27.6 percent in FY 2007–2008 to 23.2 percent in FY 2012–2013, and was expected to be approximately 20 percent in 2015. In June 2016, this plan was updated to incorporate the seventeen new Sustainable Development Goals and the Lao PDR's eighteenth goal, of reducing the impact of UXO, which is considered key to improving economic development.

Approximately one-third of economic growth in recent years has come from the development of hydroelectric power (with World Bank/IDA funding and loans) along with mining projects—copper, gold, and tin. Other growth is derived from agricultural crops, industrial forestry, food and non-food processing, and tourism. The rapid economic growth of surrounding countries has created export demand for rice, corn, sugar, coffee, rubber, and metals. Although foreign direct investment is rising, the many challenges Laos faces continue to make it difficult to attract outside private investment.

The Lao government is heavily dependent on foreign aid and loans from the UN, the World Bank/IMF, the Asian Development Bank, individual donor countries, and dozens of NGOs. The World Bank publication *Lao PDR Economic Monitor June 2018: Safeguarding Stability: An Ongoing Agenda*[39] states that the Lao fiscal deficit widened significantly in 2016–2017, to 5.3 percent of GDP, as compared to 4.3 percent in the previous year. Public debt was estimated to be around 61 percent of GDP in 2016, increasing the country's debt distress level from moderate to high.

While making progress, Laos is still struggling to lift itself out of poverty and is particularly challenged to provide adequate food supplies and health care for its citizens. Table 3 presents a comparison of conditions in Laos to those in neighboring countries and the East Asia and Pacific region in 2016. Laos has the highest rates of malnutrition and mortality for children under the age of five in the region.

TABLE 3: Data from the *World Development Indicators 2017* – World Bank[40]

	Population (millions)	Prevalence of Malnutrition Under Five	Under Five Mortality Rate Per 1,000 Births	GNI $ billion	GNI per capita $	GDP % Growth
East Asia & Pacific	2,314.4	12.2	16	23,538	10,170	4.6
Cambodia	16	33.5	30	19.7	1,230	6.8
Indonesia	264	36.4	25	934.4	3,540	5.1
Lao PDR	**6.9**	**43.8**	**64**	**15.6**	**2,270**	**6.9**
Malaysia	31.6	--	8	305.1	9,650	5.9
Myanmar	53.4	--	49	63.5	1,190	6.4
Thailand	69	16.3	10	411.7	5,960	3.9
Vietnam	95.5	23.3	21	206.9	2,170	6.8

Laos faces major challenges in addressing its economic and social problems, which are exacerbated by UXO contamination—with both direct and indirect impacts presenting significant obstacles. The UNDP found that high levels of UXO contamination correlate closely with higher levels of poverty. In a June 2007 presentation, Tim Horner, UNDP senior advisor to the UXO National Regulatory Authority in Laos, stated,

> Beyond the humanitarian impact, the presence of cluster munitions in Lao PDR is exacerbating poverty and blocking development. If we look at maps of where the reported accidents occurred, where limb disability statistics are highest, where food insecurity is at its worst and where the poorest and least developed districts are; the impact on development is undeniable.[41]

UXO contamination affects the economic and social well-being of the Lao people on many levels—directly through the contamination of the land and casualties incurred, and indirectly by contributing to the perpetuation of poverty, hunger, and a lack of services.

- *Food Production*—Because of the rugged mountains covering much of Laos, only four percent of the total land area, or 9,255 square kilometers, is arable land suitable for intensive agriculture.[42] In addition, only about 20 percent of the land in Laos is irrigated, leaving most farmers dependent on rain and, as a result, limited to a single growing season each year. Up to 50 percent of arable land is contaminated with UXO, creating a major impediment to expanding agricultural production.[43]

Continued population growth increases pressure for greater food production. The World Food Program's Lao People's Democratic Republic Country Strategic Plan (2017–2021) issued in January 2017,[44] states that 30 percent of the Lao people still live below the national poverty line (in contrast to the 23.2 percent reported in the Lao PDR 8th 5-Year Socio-Economic Development Plan 2016–2020). Laos ranks 139 out of 189 countries in the world (considered a "medium" rating) on the Human Development Index, and the 2017 Global Hunger Index ranks hunger issues in the country as "serious." A major problem is the stunting of growth in children, affecting 37.6 percent of boys and 33.6 percent of girls. Hunger problems are most prevalent among ethnic minorities in remote mountain villages.

With food often in short supply, many farmers are forced to plant fields despite the risk of UXO. The scarcity of food has also increased the hunting of animals for consumption, placing pressure on the forest environment and endangered species.

• *Infrastructure*—As the only country in Southeast Asia that does not border the ocean, Laos is highly dependent on roads and access along the Mekong River for economic trade and the provision of services. Efforts to provide basic physical infrastructure are hampered by mountainous geography and the fact that, according to the Lao PDR Population and Housing Census 2015,[45] 67.1 percent of the population lives in rural areas. Eight percent of the rural villages have no access to a road; in other villages, dirt roads may be inaccessible at times because of heavy rains.

The cost of building basic infrastructure increases substantially when the land must first be cleared of UXO. As a result, Laos does not have adequate roads, transportation systems, communication facilities, electricity, schools, or health care facilities. According to the data in the Land Mine and Cluster Munition Reports, UXO clearance teams working for commercial enterprises in Laos cleared more than 25,000 pieces of UXO.

The controversial 1,072-megawatt Nam Theun 2 Dam project is an example of how the presence of UXO affects capital costs. The World Bank's International Development Association (IDA) loaned funds to several of the partners in the project, including the Lao PDR, for this $1.45 billion undertaking. The dam was completed in 2010 with the expectation that electricity sales to Thailand would raise revenues for poverty reduction and environmental protection. The construction of roads, electric transmission lines, and dam facilities for the project involved extensive UXO removal. Mine Tech International spent three years clearing different facility sites, where they found some of the most heavily contaminated lands they have ever encountered. In addition, more than six thousand villagers had to be relocated to make way for the project, requiring additional UXO removal before new villages could be built.

Laos has experienced a construction surge of hydropower plants as the government attempts to reach a goal of one hundred dams by 2020. Since the contruction of the Nam Theun 2 Dam in 2010, the Ministry of Energy and Mines reported that twenty-five new dams had been constructed and over five dozen more are planned, as the Lao PDR government attempts to reach its goal. The large number of dams raises concerns for the quality of construction, safety in clearing contaminated lands, and the severity of environmental impacts. As of July 2018, all hydropower projects had been halted due to the devastating collapse of the Attapeu Dam in the south of Laos.

• *Health Care*—Health care facilities in rural areas are often extremely inadequate or nonexistent. Clinics have only rudimentary equipment and supplies, and electricity may only be available—if at all—for a few hours a day. Many UXO casualties occur in rural villages without access to any medical care. The injured are likely to be treated first at clinics, which are often located several hours away and are ill-equipped to handle the severity of the injuries. It may take an additional three to five hours to reach a hospital with better facilities. UXO casualties severely tax the already inadequate health care system, and because of treatment delays, many people die or suffer worse outcomes, such as the loss of a limb, than they might have otherwise. The NRA survey of UXO victims reveals that close to 40 percent of injuries result in upper-limb amputations.

The World Bank's report *Lao PDR Economic Monitor April 2017: Promoting More Inclusive Growth and Financing the Health Sector* states that government expenditure on health care per capita is among the lowest in the region, with high levels of out-of-pocket spending. Total government spending on health care was about $182 million in fiscal year

2013–2014, or about 6.3 percent of total government spending. Public spending on health care, per capita, was very low, at $16 in 2014, much lower than in neighboring Vietnam ($77) and Thailand ($177).

As a result, families of victims must find a way to pay for medical services, which often means selling off livestock and spending what little cash they may have. When family members must spend weeks or months caring for a victim during recovery, they cannot work outside the home, which further depletes the family's income.

The 2015 Lao census found that 2.8 percent of the population had moderate-to-severe disabilities. The percentage of people with disabilities varies by location—2.5 percent in urban areas; 2.9 percent in rural areas with roads; and 3.3 percent in rural areas without roads. The higher prevalence of disabilities in many rural districts corresponds with the higher incidence of UXO accidents in those areas.

Although there are a number of governmental organizations and NGOs providing disabled services and support, needs still outstrip resources. The Cooperative Orthotic & Prosthetic Enterprise (COPE), a joint venture of the Lao Ministry of Health and a number of NGOs, works with the National Rehabilitation Center and four regional centers. Fifty-three percent of the clients they fit with prosthetic legs were injured by UXO.[46]

An important development in 2017 was the funding of a $15 million, five-year USAID program (Okard) focused on victim assistance, which will provide services to promote the disability sector at large in Laos.[47]

In Lao society, the disabled have often been marginalized and have faced considerable physical and sociocultural barriers. Rehabilitation programs and vocational training for the disabled are not available in most rural areas, making it difficult for victims to work and support their families. Many disabled children are unable to attend school due to lack of mobility and biases about their capabilities.

Beyond the physical injuries resulting from UXO accidents, many victims suffer mental trauma as well. Laos has virtually no mental health treatment capacity, with only two practicing psychiatrists in the entire country. As a result, most victims receive no mental health assistance.[48]

• *The Impact of Poverty*—In most parts of Laos, the labor force suffers not only a shortage of available workers but also a lack of training and education. This discourages outside investment in new businesses and industries. Educational opportunities and jobs are more plentiful in population centers, such as major cities and towns along the Mekong River in the western part of the country. In sparsely populated rural areas, access is often limited to mandatory primary education. High levels of poverty discourage some families from sending their children on to further schooling, as they are needed to work in the fields. In many places, the mere act of walking to school through contaminated lands causes parents to worry about their children's safety.

Poverty leads to exploitation of the environment as people try to supplement incomes and augment inadequate agricultural production. Legal and illegal logging activities contribute to the degradation of the forests. In 1940, 70 percent of Laos was covered with forests, but by 2002 forests had been reduced to 41.5 percent of the land.[49] Many rural people are dependent on the forests for non-timber products (for example, wildlife or bamboo shoots for consumption or dammar resin and cardamom to sell). Newer methods of hunting, such as automatic guns and cable snares, have had considerable impact on wildlife populations. The growing illegal trade in live animals and animal parts with neighboring countries further depletes the existing populations of many endangered species.[50]

As discussed previously, poverty also prompts people to risk the illegal practice of collecting and defusing UXO to sell as scrap metal.

Reconciliation—Healing and Hope

The story of war in Laos, as with all stories of war, contains two separate but converging themes: the physical and emotional tolls of war. Long after the last bomb was dropped and the conflict declared over, the tremors of war continue. It is said that war does not decide who is right, only who is left. In Laos, war left in its path shattered lives, scattered communities, and lasting devastation. The US restored full diplomatic relations with Laos in 1992, but there has been no formal reconciliation process between the countries to heal the long-festering wounds of war. However, the 2016 bilateral agreement for comprehensive cooperation in addressing the war legacy of UXO in Laos signed by US president Barack Obama and Lao PDR president Bounnhang Vorachit marked a major step forward.

Since 1975, close to three hundred thousand Laotian refugees have resettled around the world in the United States, Australia, France, Canada, and other countries. Over the years, these refugees have made small gestures toward reconciliation and renewal with Laos. Since the opening of the Lao border in 1986, tens of thousands from among the Laotian diaspora have returned every year to Laos to visit family and hometown villages. Laotian refugees have contributed by sending money to family, sponsoring a child, or raising collective funds to build temples, schools, and other capital projects. Others have organized medical missions, book programs, or scholarship funds. The economic contributions from Laotians living abroad provide support at all levels.

In recent years, the Laotian diaspora and in particular Laotian-Americans have organized efforts to support greater economic and social opportunities for the people in Laos by engaging the government and people of their new homeland. A prime example is the influence of Laotian Americans in the US government's extension of normal trade relations to Laos in 2004. The US-Lao Normal Trade Relations National Coalition was instrumental in creating a powerful US-based constituency to advocate for trade policy changes. Since then, members of this coalition have established various business and trade councils to advocate for increased ease in trade and market access between the two countries. This represents a positive step toward reconciliation and collaboration between former wartime antagonists.

A new generation of Laotian-Americans—many of whom were too young to remember all the events of the war but remember the suffering and sacrifice of their parents and grandparents—has embraced the unfinished business of ending the devastation in Laos and bringing reconciliation and renewal. One vehicle that is providing momentum for this remarkable undertaking is the US-based organization Legacies of War.[51]

Legacies of War was founded in 2004 by Laotian-Americans to raise public awareness about the presence of cluster bombs in Laos and to advocate for additional US funding and assistance to address the problem. The group's advocacy has included collecting data on the UXO problem in Laos to inform key members of Congress and previous US administrations, such as secretaries of state Hillary Clinton and John Kerry; Congressional testimony; soliciting letters of support from former ambassadors; and convening and speaking at international conferences and public forums on the issue. The organization also supports efforts to ban the use of cluster munitions in other parts of the world through the Convention on Cluster Munitions.

Rooted in the power of history, healing, and hope, Legacies of War was founded to connect the experiences of war and peace across communities, continents, and generations. The project's unique perspective recognizes the parallel experiences of suffering, survival, and transformation of those who remain on the war-torn land and the refugees who fled. The organization integrates art, culture, education, dialogue, community organizing, and advocacy to bring people together to create healing and hope out of the wreckage of war. This and other initiatives by NGOs and foreign governmental organizations are examples of efforts to bring about reconstruction and reconciliation from the war in Laos.

Principles for Reconciliation

The following are suggested principles for implementing a formal reconciliation process between the United States and the Lao PDR. The problem of UXO in Laos and its effects on the people and country is a humanitarian issue, and requires that the two countries move beyond past political differences.

1. *Accepting Responsibility:* President Obama took a major step forward by acknowledging that the US has a "moral obligation to help Laos heal" from the devastation and suffering caused by its unprecedented bombing campaign over Laos and the long-term effects of unexploded ordnance. More than forty-five years later, it is time to focus on the consequences and how to resolve them. Residual US bombs continue to kill and maim innocent civilians; UXO contamination exacerbates the problems of poverty, inadequate health care, food production, and degradation of the environment.

2. *Joint Commitment:* The US and the Lao PDR have made considerable progress in the past ten years, working together on assistance programs that are acceptable to both governments, culminating in the 2016 joint agreement between the two countries. This efforts has required moving beyond past political differences to find a path for greater reconciliation that puts the welfare of the Laotian people first.

3. *Comprehensive Plan:* The first priority must be removal of UXO as quickly as possible from high-risk areas. While progress is slowly being made, these efforts have been hampered by the lack of detailed data on the exact location of UXO across the country. To this end, the recent commitment of the Lao PDR government, with support from the US and other donor countries, to completing a comprehensive survey of UXO is an important accomplishment. Other tasks include the prioritization of areas for clearance with enforceable timelines, expanded public education and awareness programs, and greater assistance for people

harmed by UXO, such as more medical funding for victims' injuries, physical therapy, and rehabilitation, along with mental health treatment and job retraining. Existing programs must be expanded to meet the extensive needs of UXO victims. US funding must remain sufficient over consecutive years to restore the long-term health and economic sustainability of the people and land in Laos in a reasonable time frame.

4. *Collaboration and Partnerships:* US assistance to Laos must continue and collaboration must increase with existing programs of the Lao PDR, the UN, and other governmental organizations as well as NGOs, such as World Education, COPE, Handicap International, HALO Trust, Friends Without Borders, MAG, and others. Assistance planning should involve partnering with existing programs and organizations in order to draw on the expertise of people both inside and outside Laos.

5. *Transparency:* Funding, administration, and accounting systems for providing assistance must be open and transparent. This might involve oversight from a third party or a joint agency with independent audits.

Designing an expanded program for removal of UXO in the near term will be a complex undertaking. The completion of the comprehensive survey of UXO contamination will greatly assist this effort. Also, the continuity of funding over a number of years is critical to hiring, training, and maintaining UXO clearance personnel.

The cost of clearing UXO can vary widely depending on a number of factors: 1) the quality and quantity of data on contamination; 2) the location and accessibility of the land to clearance teams and equipment; 3) topography and the type of land contaminated (for instance, valleys vs. mountains, grassland vs. forests); 4) the intensity of contamination and types of UXO found; 5) the training level of team members and equipment availability; and 6) administrative costs of program management. Existing removal programs are gaining efficiency with more experience and better equipment, while oversight of funds has become more transparent. These factors, along with the implementation of the risk assessment model developed for the Lao PDR by the Geneva International Center for Humanitarian Demining, will help reduce overall costs.

Conclusion

The second Indochina war was a dark and complicated episode in history. Forty-five years after the end of conflict, too little has been done by the US to heal the wounds inflicted on the Laotian people and their country. Unexploded bombs pose a constant threat and severely hamper the country's struggle to build a sustainable economy. The US has now acknowledged UXO clearance efforts in Laos will require sustained, long-term assistance. There is a moral and humanitarian imperative to continue adequately funding bomb clearance programs and to provide much-needed services to bomb victims. Laos has waited too long to be free from the threat of UXO.

The physical and emotional scars of war affect not only the people in Laos, but the hundreds of thousands of Laotians who fled Laos and are living abroad. Both the *Lao nai* (Lao inside) and *Lao nok* (Lao outside) share an interconnected journey grounded in loss and suffering, and leading eventually to survival and transformation. Within Laos some resent the aftermath of war that still confronts them in their daily lives, while others look forward to renewed relations with former enemies. Likewise, for some in the Laotian diaspora, there is still anger over the loss of their former lives and their country, while others return regularly (some permanently) and contribute to the development of Laos.

Now, a new generation of the Laotian diaspora is reconnecting with their homeland and bringing attention to the plight of the people affected by cluster bombs, hoping to create a future free from further harm and suffering. Additional momentum around this issue has been reinforced by the signing of the aforementioned Cluster Munitions Convention, an international treaty to ban the use of cluster bombs worldwide, which is supported by 120 countries, including Laos, and hundreds of NGOs.

It is time for the US and Lao PDR to put aside past differences in order to forge a path of reconciliation for the good of the Laotian people, who deserve to live free of fear and to have their country made whole again.

CHAPTER 4

Agent Orange in Vietnam

Tuan V. Nguyen

Among the most significant legacies of the war that Americans refer to as the "Vietnam War" are the lasting consequences of chemical defoliants used by the US military. The primary defoliant used was Agent Orange, which contained the toxic chemical dioxin.[1] Although the war ended more than four decades ago, millions of victims, including Vietnamese civilians and ex-servicemen in the American and Vietnamese militaries, are still suffering from exposure to these chemicals.

During the past forty years or so, a large number of scientific studies on the effects of Agent Orange or dioxin have been carried out around the world. These studies, which included basic and epidemiological research, have formed the basis upon which the US government makes decisions regarding compensation to members of the military who suffered exposure to these agents. This chapter will examine the scientific evidence of the relationship between Agent Orange or dioxin and human diseases.

Dioxin and Agent Orange

The term "dioxin" technically refers to a structurally similar group of 75 poly-chlorinated dibenzo-p-dioxins and 135 poly-chlorinated dibenzo-p-furans. The most toxic chemical in this group is 2,3,7,8-tetrachloro-dibenzo-p-dioxin (abbreviated as 2,3,7,8-TCDD). The numbers 2, 3, 7, and 8 indicate the positions at which chlorine atoms are located on the dioxin molecule. The compound 2,3,7,8-TCDD is often referred to simply as "dioxin" in the mainstream press, and will be identified as such in this chapter.

Dioxin was identified and synthesized by 1957,[2] and has since become one of the most widely studied chemical compounds due to concerns about its effects on humans and other living creatures. Dioxin has very low solubility in water, requiring a temperature of 295°C to begin dissolving; it breaks down into its component parts at 500°C. As a result, dioxin in the environment does not readily dilute or degrade—it tends to accumulate in soil and sediment. Dioxin is also a lipophilic compound (i.e., it adheres readily to fat). Higher levels of dioxin thus tend to be found in fatty tissue, and the levels bioaccumulate as one goes up the food chain.

A toxic by-product of combustion and manufacturing processes, dioxin can be found in trace amounts throughout the world in air, water, soil, and industrial waste; it consequently enters the food chain and occurs in meat, vegetables, and especially in seafood. Common industrial sources include the incineration of factory waste and medical equipment and the bleaching of paper and textiles. Dioxin is also produced through wood combustion, including forest fires and wood burning; a large forest fire may generate anywhere from a few grams to a few kilograms of the compound.

During the Vietnam War, the US Army used various defoliating chemicals, including mixtures of the phenoxy herbicides 2,4-dichlorophenoxyacetic acid (2,4-D) and 2,4,5-trichlorophenoxyacetic acid (2,4,5-T). The mixtures were shipped to Vietnam in fifty-five-gallon chemical drums marked with colored identifying stripes. By far the greatest quantity was of a one-to-one mixture of 2,4-D and 2,4,5-T, which was stored in drums with orange stripes. Hence, this substance was called "Agent Orange." Other mixtures, identified by their stripes as Agent Pink, Agent Green, Agent Purple, Agent White, and Agent Blue, were also used during the war. Agents Orange, Pink, Green, and Purple all were made with 2,4,5-T, and thus contained, in varying quantities, dioxin—a by-product of 2,4,5-T synthesis.[3] (Agent White consisted of 2,4-D and picloram; Agent Blue contained cacodylic acid, an arsenic compound.) For the purposes of this chapter, since Agent Orange was the chief defoliant used, "Agent Orange" will refer to all dioxin-containing mixtures.

A Brief History

At the end of the nineteenth century, when sodium chloride (table salt) and potash were the main substances used to kill weeds along roadsides, an inorganic selective herbicide was discovered by chance in France. Bordeaux vintners attempting to control downy mildew disease among their grape crops sprayed the grape leaves with a solution of copper sulfate and lime, and found that stray drops killed broadleaf weeds on the ground below. Subsequently, the copper sulfate component was identified as the weed-killing element of the so-called "Bordeaux mixture." Research experiments in France, Germany, and the United States determined that $CuSO_4$ (copper[II] sulfate) could be used as an inorganic selective herbicide for controlling weeds in wheat, barley, and oat crops. Experimentation with other copper and sulfur compounds led to the use of sulfuric acid, iron sulfate, and copper nitrate as popular herbicides over the next decade.

As the agricultural revolution brought Western farming into the modern age, the development of chemicals to control plant growth—not only to kill weeds, but also to improve crop yields—became a priority for agricultural scientists in the United States and Europe. During the 1930s and '40s, both inorganic and organic selective herbicides were used for weed control, including boron compounds, ammonium sulfate, sodium chlorate, carbon bisulfide, sodium arsenite, and dinitrophenols. In 1935, US scientists reported that phenylacetic acid (PAA) and naphthaleneacetic acid (NAA) could prevent premature fruit drop, induce rooting, accelerate fruit ripening, and produce seedless tomatoes.[4] In 1941, British scientists, while conducting potted experiments on the effects of NAA as a plant growth regulator on wheat, found by chance that NAA killed a few wild mustard plants (*Brassica kaber*) growing as weeds in the wheat pots.

Also in 1941, US scientists synthesized for the first time 2,4-dichlorophenoxyacetic acid (2,4-D) and 2,4,5-trichlorophenoxyacetic acid (2,4,5-T). The intention was to study the effects of 2,4-D and 2,4,5-T on fungal diseases in the hope of identifying new fungicides. In 1942, studies suggested that 2,4-D was an effective plant growth regulator, such that it induced the production of seedless tomatoes.[5] A real breakthrough in selective chemical weed control was achieved in 1945 with the commercial introduction of both 2,4-D and MCPA (4-chloro, 2-methylphenoxyacetic acid) in the United States and England.

Military scientists, however, had ideas for using herbicides that went far beyond weed control. During World War II, the US Army conducted biochemical warfare research through the Chemical Warfare Service, which was headquartered at Camp Detrick, Maryland. Extensive plans were drawn up for the use of defoliants against Japan.[6] The main objectives of this project were to develop a chemical that could destroy rice and other food crops in order to deplete the food reserves in Japan, and to use herbicides as defoliants for destroying broadleaf trees that concealed and protected Japanese soldiers from US forces. In 1944, substantial amounts of 2,4-D and 2,4,5-T were synthesized and experimentally sprayed from airplanes. However, after extensive discussion with US president Roosevelt and General William D. Leahy, the US military decided not to use the chemicals in the war against Japan.

At the end of the 1950s, following the English military's successful use of 2,4,5-T to destroy crops in their campaign against Malaysia,[7] the US Department of Defense (DOD) assigned the Advanced Research Project Agency (ARPA) to research and develop herbicides for military use. Large-scale testing on a mixture of 2,4-D and 2,4,5-T was successfully carried out at Drum Station, New York, in 1959; the spray system used in the tests was to be the model implemented a few years later in Vietnam.

As US involvement in Vietnam intensified, American political and military leaders argued in favor of using herbicides to destroy forest vegetation, thereby exposing the hiding places of North Vietnamese forces. American soldiers could then cut off the supply route from the North through Truong Son trail (also known as the Ho Chi Minh trail) by heavy aerial bombardment. On November 20, 1961, US president John F. Kennedy approved a plan for the US Army to carry out defoliant activities on Vietnamese forests.[8] This decision was enthusiastically supported by then-president of South Vietnam, Ngô Dinh Diem. Agent Orange was transported to South Vietnam from August to December 1961.

Operation Trail Dust was the name applied to the overarching program of spraying defoliants in Vietnam; within this program there were several separate campaigns. Operation Ranch Hand, the largest and longest campaign, comprised 95 percent of chemical spraying under Operation Trail Dust. In 1962, the US Air Force began spraying herbicides on a large scale in the southern and central regions of Vietnam. The majority (approximately 90 percent) of Agent Orange was sprayed from C-123 airplanes, and the remainder from helicopters, trucks, and other vehicles. Details of the specific areas to be sprayed and the chemicals to be used required the approval of the Oval Office. However, beginning in late 1962, President Kennedy assigned part of this responsibility to the US ambassador to South Vietnam, Henry Cabot Lodge, and to General William Westmoreland, commander of US forces in Vietnam.

Operation Trail Dust was harshly criticized and condemned worldwide. Virtually all major newspapers in the United States, Europe, and Asia opined that the operation was immoral and inhumane, and demanded that it be stopped immediately. The prominent British mathematician and philosopher Bertrand Russell accused the United States of conducting chemical warfare in Vietnam.

US senator Robert W. Kastenmeier also felt uneasy about the operation, and wrote a letter to President Kennedy questioning whether the use of chemicals in Vietnam was justified in light of the corrupt regime of Ngô Dinh Diem.[9]

In January 1966, Professor John Edsall of Harvard University and a group of twenty-nine prominent scientists in Boston published a letter in the magazine *Science* calling the use of chemicals in Vietnam inhuman and barbarous.[10] One year later, the White House received a letter with signatures of 5,000 scientists from all over the world, including 17 Nobel laureates and 129 members of the US National Academy of Sciences, asking that President Lyndon B. Johnson put an immediate stop to the ecocidal campaign in Vietnam.[11] In 1967, the American Association for the Advancement of Science, with the help of Professor E. W. Pfeiffer from the University of Montana, advised the US Department of Defense about unforeseen consequences to the Vietnamese people and the environment of Vietnam. In response, the DOD commissioned scientists from the Midwest Research Institute to study the effects of Agent Orange in Vietnam. Based on data at the time, the Institute concluded that the effects of Agent Orange were likely to be minor and short-lived; however, they also suggested further study of the effects of Agent Orange on human health.[12]

In 1969, Richard M. Nixon became US president. In an effort to reduce US involvement in Vietnam, he ordered the intensity of Operation Ranch Hand to be reduced by 30 percent. In the meantime, the US Senate was about to ratify a UN resolution prohibiting the use of chemical and biological weapons. Although President Nixon wanted to ratify the resolution, he argued that the use of Agent Orange in Vietnam did not contravene the resolution. Nevertheless, the UN General Assembly did not accept Nixon's argument and maintained that Operation Ranch Hand was illegal. In July 1971, President Nixon ordered the complete halt of Operation Ranch Hand.[13]

Magnitude of the Problem

By the time Operation Ranch Hand was halted, the US military had conducted 19,905 aerial spraying missions, with an average of eleven missions each day. The exact volume of herbicide used by the US military in Vietnam remains unknown. A 2003 study by Columbia University scientists estimated that, between 1962 and 1971, the US military sprayed 76.9 million liters of herbicide in central and southern Vietnam.[14] This figure was 9.4 million liters greater than a previous estimate. Of the total amount of herbicide sprayed, approximately 64 percent—49.3 million liters—was Agent Orange.

It is important to recognize that these are minimal estimates, because large amounts of chemicals that were shipped to Vietnam have never been accounted for. For instance, procurement records showed that the military purchased 464,164 liters of Agent Pink and 31,026 liters of Agent Green, but only 65,000 liters of that total were reported to have been sprayed.[15]

By far most of the herbicide—approximately 90 percent—was sprayed between 1966 and 1969. It is interesting to note that those mixtures with the highest levels of dioxin concentration, such as Agent Pink, were sprayed during the first few years of the operation. However, crop-destroying chemicals, such as Agent Blue, continued to be sprayed until 1971.

By using Hamlet Evaluation Survey (HES) records—monthly data on security and population information for each hamlet in Vietnam, collected from 1967 until the end of the war—Columbia University scientists have estimated that, in total, 2.6 million hectares (ha) of land were affected by various herbicides during the war. This number was 1.1 million ha higher than a previous estimate. Of the affected areas, the scientists estimated that approximately 1.68 million ha were directly affected by dioxin. Furthermore, of the affected areas, 86 percent were sprayed at least twice. About 11 percent of the areas were sprayed more than ten times! (See Table 1.)

Table 1: Areas Sprayed Between 1962 and 1971

Number of Times Sprayed	Area Affected by Chemicals (ha)	Area Affected by Dioxin (ha)
Once	368,556	343,426
2 times	369,844	332,249
3 times	361,862	275,770
4 times	341,037	236,232
5 times	272,709	153,192
6 times	216,724	119,127
7 times	153,391	75,062
8 times	138,610	51,371
9 times	115,103	32,988
10 times or more	293,461	60,316
Total	2,631,297	1,679,734

Source: J.M. Stellman, S. D. Stellman, R. Christian, T. Weber, and C. Tomasallo. The extent and patterns of usage of Agent Orange and other herbicides in Vietnam. *Nature* 2003; 422:681-687.

The number of villages or hamlets affected was estimated at 20,585. The number of individuals affected by herbicide was estimated at a minimum of 2.1 million. This number is likely an underestimate, because there were thousands of villages for which population statistics were not recorded or estimated. Therefore, the scientists suggested that the number of civilians affected could be up to 4.8 million.[16]

Figure 1. Areas (in dark orange color) affected by Agent Orange during the Vietnam War

Residual Concentration of Dioxin in Vietnam

Agent Orange and other herbicides were known to be highly toxic prior to and during the herbicide campaign in Vietnam. Indeed, as early as 1952, Monsanto Chemical Company—a major manufacturer of Agent Orange—already knew that 2,4,5-T was a toxic agent. In 1963, research conducted by the US Army revealed that 2,4,5-T was associated with an increased risk of respiratory complications and chloracne, a severe skin disease characterized by painful and disfiguring eruptions.[17]

Research conducted in 1966 indicated that 2,4,5-T caused many birth defects in mice and rats whose mothers had been exposed to 30 parts per million (ppm) of the chemical.[18] This finding was consistent with the toxicity of dioxin in animals. Dr. Arthur Galston, a noted herbicide expert whose early research led to the development of Agent Orange, stated that a dioxin concentration as low as 5 ppt (parts per trillion—an amount roughly equivalent to one drop in 4 million gallons of water) can,

> when supplied on a daily basis, induce a cancerous condition in rats. Concentrations about 1 ppb (part per billion) result in premature death from more acute causes, and concentrations above 50 ppb produce rapid signs of acute toxicity and early death. . . . [Researchers] have found that lower concentrations of TCDD produce the same effects as higher concentrations, but merely take longer to do so. . . . Even the purest 2,4,5-T currently available commercially contains about 0.05 ppm (mg/kg) of TCDD.[19]

Although the exact amount of TCDD (dioxin) sprayed during the Vietnam War is unknown, scientists estimated that the total amount was least 366 kg.[20]

During the past forty years or so, most of the research on dioxin and Agent Orange has been conducted in the United States. Only a few studies have been done in Vietnam. Therefore, the data on the herbicide contamination in Vietnam is rather limited. In one important study, a group of American and Vietnamese scientists analyzed the dioxin concentration in 3,242 residents from northern, central, and southern Vietnam.[21] According to the results, residents living in the northern provinces had the lowest levels of dioxin (an average of 2.7 ppt). However, residents of the central and southern regions had, on average, levels of dioxin five times higher (13.2 ppt and 12.9 ppt for central and southern residents, respectively), which is consistent with the geographical spraying of Agent Orange during the war. In some areas heavily sprayed during the war, the concentration was elevated to 32 ppt (Song Be), 28 ppt (Dong Nai–Bien Hoa), and 33 ppt (Tra Noc, Hau Giang). (See Table 2.)

Table 2: Average Dioxin Concentration in Vietnam 1995

Area / Local	Year of Sample-Collection	Number of Samples Collected	Average Age of Subjects	Average TCCD Concentration	TEQ (Dioxin Toxic Equivalents)
North Vietnam					
Hanoi (Hospital 103)	3/91	33	45	1.2	12.0
Highland areas (ex-servicemen)	11/91	35	48	6.1	40.3
Quang Binh, Dong Hoi	1/91	50	47	2.9	17.2
Thuan Hoa	11/91	50	55	2.9	18.0
Central Vietnam					
Thua Thien, Hue	1/91	30	57	11.0	57.0
Quang Tri, Quang Tri	1/91	50	51	9.5	34.0
Da Nang	2/91	49	59	18.0	77.0
Thua Thien, A Luoi	1/91	35	52	15.0	23.0
Khanh Hoa, Nha Trang	1/92	50	49	4.1	29.5
Phu Yen	1/92	43	51	6.2	26.4
Ninh Thuan, Phan Rang	1/92	33	56	2.9	31.7
Da Nang (18-40 yr)	8/92	100	30	14.0	96.3
Da Nang (>40 yr)	8/92	100	56	19.0	118.2
South Vietnam					
Dong Nai, Tri An (Ma Da forest)	3/91	50	47	12.0	19.0
Cuu Long, Vinh Long	8/91	51	59	4.3	16.9
Dong Nai, Bien Hoa	3/91	50	51	28.0	47.0
Ben Tre, Giong Trom	8/91	34	55	10.2	29.0
Kien Giang, Go Quao	8/91	37	58	10.9	27.5
Kien Giang, Rach Gia	8/91	48	58	4.9	17.3
Minh Hai, Ca Mau	8/91	52	59	7.2	19.9
Song Be	3/91	47	47	9.0	48.0
Song Be, Tan Uyen	3/91	48	54	32.0	55.0
Tay Ninh, Tan Bien	2/91	50	60	5.3	25.0
Tay Ninh, Tay Ninh	3/91	50	53	6.8	16.0
Cuu Long, Tra Vinh	8.91	48	57	7.2	27.7

Hau Giang, Can Tho	8/91	52	61	4.8	16.4
An Giang, Long Xuyen	8/91	49	62	2.2	10.5
An Giang, Chau Doc	8/91	46	56	3.5	16.8
Ho Chi Minh City, Cho Ray Hospital	2/91	48	54	10.8	30.0
Minh Hai, Bac Lieu	8/91	50	60	10.3	34.8
Gia Lai, Pleiku	1/91	50	57	4.2	34.2
Tay Ninh, Chau Thanh	8/92	100	54	4.6	19.4
Tra Noc, Can Tho	8/92	102	51	33.0	104.6
Song Be, Tan Uyen (18-40 yr old)	8/92	100	32	9.4	25.4
Song Be, Tan Uyen (>40 yr old)	8/92	100	51	5.7	18.9
Song Be, Ben Cat	8/92	100	53	12.0	49.8
Dong Nai (18-40 yr)	8/92	100	31	14.0	61.0
Dong Nai (>40 yr)	8/92	100	53	19.0	53.7
Tay Ninh, Hoa Thanh	8/92	100	50	1.0	38.8
Song Be, Dong Xoai	8/92	100	50	3.1	8.7
Tay Ninh, D.M. Chan	5/92	100	50	7.0	35.3
Dong Nai, Bien Hoa (18-40 yr)	5/92	100	47	7.3	22.8
Dong Nai, Bien Hoa (>40 yr)	5/92	100	N/A	12.0	49.0

Source: Schecter A, et al. Agent Orange and the Vietnamese: the persistence of elevated dioxin levels in human tissues. *Am J Publ Health* 1995; 85:516-22.

In 2003, University of Texas scientist Arnold Schecter and colleagues analyzed the dioxin concentration in a small sample of foodstuffs in Bien Hoa province, and found that two ducks had the highest levels of concentration (276 ppt and 331 ppt, respectively). However, the concentrations in fish, pork, and beef were lower (between 0.2 ppt and 15 ppt).[22]

It is known that the half-life of dioxin is between seven and ten years.[23] The above data clearly suggests that those areas where heavy aerial spraying was conducted during the war are still affected by dioxin. The data also indicates that dioxin has penetrated into the environment—soil, sediment, and foodstuff—in affected areas. The findings from Schecter, et al., are consistent with the contamination in Seveso, Italy, where high levels of dioxin concentration were still present thirty years after an industrial accident that released about 30 kg of dioxin into the environment.[24]

Effects of Dioxin and Agent Orange on Human Health

As was mentioned previously, there have been numerous studies on the associations between Agent Orange and human health, with the majority of studies conducted in United States and Europe. The studies have been highly controversial due to conflicting findings and differences in the interpretation of results, leaving the issue of the effects of Agent Orange without definite conclusion. In response to this uncertainty, under the Agent Orange Act of 1991 the US Congress asked the Institute of Medicine of the National Academy of Sciences to review all scientific and medical data regarding the health effects of exposure to Agent Orange. In 1992, the Institute of Medicine established the Committee to Review the Health Effects in Vietnam Veterans of Exposure to Herbicides, comprised of experts in epidemiology, occupational health, environmental health, toxicology, and biology, and chaired by Professor Irva Hertz-Picciotto. Results of the review were published in 1996 in the form of a report titled *Veterans and Agent Orange: Update 1996.* The committee regularly updates its findings approximately every two years. The latest findings were documented in the sixth publication, *Veterans and Agent Orange: Update 2006.*[25]

In the report, the associations between Agent Orange and/or dioxin exposure and human health are graded into four groups of evidence: "Sufficient Evidence of Association," "Limited or Suggestive Evidence of Association," "Inadequate or Insufficient Evidence to Determine Association," and "Limited or Suggestive Evidence of *No* Association." The findings are summarized in Table 3.

According to this grading, the committee considers that, after ruling out potential bias and confounding factors, there is sufficient evidence to conclude that a positive association exists between Agent Orange and/or dioxin and the following diseases: soft-tissue sarcoma, non-Hodgkin's lymphoma, chronic lymphocytic leukemia (CLL), Hodgkin's disease, and chloracne. During the past two decades, these diseases have consistently been shown to be linked to exposure to Agent Orange and/or dioxin.

The committee classifies the association between Agent Orange exposure and the following diseases as "limited or suggestive," because an association could be compromised by chance, bias, and confounding factors: laryngeal cancer; cancer of the lung, bronchus, or trachea; prostate cancer; multiple myeloma; AL amyloidosis; early-onset transient peripheral neuropathy; porphyria cutanea tarda; hypertension; type 2 diabetes mellitus; and spina bifida in the offspring of exposed people.

Nevertheless, recent studies have confirmed that Agent Orange exposure is associated with an increased risk of prostate cancer. In a study known as "the Ranch Hand study," investigators examined the incidence of prostate cancer in two groups of individuals: group 1 consisted of approximately 1,200 ex-servicemen who participated in Operation Ranch Hand during the war, and group 2 comprised 1,785 ex-servicemen who were not in any way involved in the handling of the Agent Orange. After twenty years of follow-up, investigators found that the risk of prostate cancer in ex-servicemen involved with Operation Ranch Hand (1966–1970) was between two and four times higher than in the general population. Among those who had served at least two years in Vietnam, the risk of developing prostate cancer was six to seven times higher than in the general population. Furthermore, the risk of melanoma among individuals in group 1 was twofold higher than in group 2.[26]

On July 15, 2005, the DOD released a press statement in which it recognized that exposure to Agent Orange is associated with an increased risk of developing type 2 diabetes. The latest scientific finding[27] suggests that the risk of type 2 diabetes in ex-servicemen who had been exposed to Agent Orange at the highest level is 2.6 times higher compared to unexposed individuals.

Table 3: Summary of Findings in Occupational, Environmental, and Veterans Studies Regarding the Association Between Specific Health Outcomes and Exposure to Herbicides

Level of evidence	Diseases
Sufficient Evidence of Association	Soft-tissue sarcoma (including heart); non-Hodgkin's lymphoma; chronic lymphocytic leukemia (CLL); Hodgkin's disease; chloracne
Limited or Suggestive Evidence of Association	Laryngeal cancer; cancer of the lung, bronchus, or trachea; prostate cancer; multiple myeloma; AL amyloidosis; early-onset transient peripheral neuropathy; porphyria cutanea tarda; hypertension; type 2 diabetes (mellitus); spina bifida in the offspring of exposed people

Inadequate or Insufficient Evidence to Determine Association	Cancers of the oral cavity (including lips and tongue), pharynx (including tonsils), or nasal cavity (including ears and sinuses); cancers of the pleura, mediastinum, and other unspecified sites within the respiratory system and intrathoracic organs; esophageal cancer; stomach cancer; colorectal cancer (including small intestine and anus); hepatobiliary cancers (liver, gall-bladder, and bile ducts); pancreatic cancer; bone and joint cancer; melanoma*; non-melanoma skin cancer (basal cell and squamous cell); breast cancer*; cancers of reproductive organs (cervix, uterus, ovary, testes, and penis; excluding prostate); urinary bladder cancer; renal cancer; cancers of brain and nervous system (including eye); endocrine cancers (thyroid, thymus, and other endocrine); leukemia (other than CLL); cancers at other and unspecified sites; infertility; spontaneous abortion (other than for paternal exposure to TCDD, which appears not to be associated); neonatal or infant death and stillbirth; low birth weight in offspring of exposed people; childhood cancer (including acute myologenous leukemia) in offspring of exposed people; birth defects (other than spina bifida) in offspring of exposed people; neurobehavioral disorders (cognitive and neuropsychiatric); movement disorders, including Parkinson's disease and amytrophic lateral sclerosis (ALS); chronic peripheral nervous system disorders; respiratory disorders; gastrointestinal, metabolic, and digestive disorders (changes in liver enzymes, lipid abnormalities, and ulcers); immune system disorders (immune suppression, allergy, and autoimmunity); ischemic heart disease*; circulatory disorders (other than hypertension and perhaps ischemic heart disease); endometriosis; effects on thyroid homeostasis
Limited or Suggestive Evidence of *No* Association	Spontaneous abortion and paternal exposure to TCDD

*The committee was unable to reach consensus as to whether these endpoints had Limited or Suggestive Evidence of Association or had Inadequate or Insufficient Evidence to Determine

Association, and so these were left in the lower category.

Source: Committee to Review the Health Effects in Vietnam Veterans of Exposure to Herbicides (Sixth Biennial Update). *Veterans and Agent Orange: Update 2006* (National Academies Press, 2007).

All these studies, however, suffered from a major drawback known as "survival bias." Exposure to Agent Orange is associated with an excess mortality risk. In an Italian study of residents of the aforementioned Seveso area, researchers found that individuals living in areas exposed to high levels of dioxin contamination had a 30 percent increased risk of mortality. Moreover, the risk of death from colon cancer among men with high levels of dioxin concentration increased by 2.4-fold compared to the general population.[28] Most of the studies on the effects of Agent Orange were done long after the Agent Orange campaign was over; it is possible that numerous individuals had died earlier due to exposure to the chemical. This makes delineation of the effects of Agent Orange exposure on human health very difficult, because the "ideal" candidates for study are no longer available for analysis, and those available for study are only the relatively healthy ones. Therefore, it could be argued that the strength of association from these studies actually underestimates the true effects of Agent Orange on human health.

Agent Orange and Birth Defects

The association between Agent Orange and birth defects remains one of the most contentious issues in science. While basic research using animal models has consistently indicated that exposure to 2,4,5-T may result in congenital malformation, studies in humans have produced conflicting results. As early as 1964, the US-based Bionetics Laboratory was commissioned by the National Cancer Institute of the Department of Health, Education, and Welfare to investigate the carcinogenic and teratogenic (i.e., causing birth defects) effects of various pesticides and industrial compounds on animals. The results indicated that 2,4,5-T in small doses caused birth defects in mice and rats. In 1969, the National Cancer Institute released the Bionetics report—but without mentioning the teratogenic effects. Nevertheless, the causative role of 2,4,5-T in birth defects was leaked to some scientists at Harvard University, who subsequently confirmed that 2,4,5-T, 2,4-D, and the mixture of n-butyl esters that constituted Agent Orange were all teratogenic in tiny doses. The leaking of this data sparked a furor in the American public, which contributed to the halt of Operation Ranch Hand in Vietnam.[29]

In a 1990 report to the U.S Congress, former naval commander Admiral E. R. Zumwalt Jr. also mentioned the findings that dioxin could cause birth defects:

Beginning as early as 1968, scientists, health officials, politicians, and the military itself began to express concerns about the potential toxicity of Agent Orange and its contaminant dioxin to humans. For instance, in February 1969 the Bionetics Research Council Committee ("BRC") in a report commissioned by the United States Department of Agriculture found that 2,4,5-T showed a "significant potential to increase birth defects."

By October 1969, the National Institute of Health confirmed that 2,4,5-T could cause malformations and stillbirths in mice, thereby prompting the Department of Defense to announce a partial curtailment of its Agent Orange spraying.

On the same day, the Secretaries of Agriculture, Health, Education, and Welfare, and the Interior, stirred by the publication of studies that indicated 2,4,5-T was a teratogen (i.e., caused birth defects), jointly announced the suspension of its use around lakes, ponds, ditch banks, recreation areas, and homes and crops intended for human consumption.[30]

Subsequent and recent studies have clearly suggested that dioxin can cause congenital malformation.[31, 32] In animal studies, maternal exposure to dioxin resulted in cleft palate and hydronephrosis in mice and hamsters, intestinal hemorrhage and renal abnormalities in rats, extra ribs in rabbits, and spontaneous abortions in lab animals. Moreover, dioxin was found to cause chromosomal anomalies in the bone marrow cells of some specific strains of rats and mice, and to stimulate RNA synthesis in rat liver.

When Operation Ranch Hand was at its peak in 1969, *Tin Sang*, a Saigon newspaper, reported a surge in the incidence of birth defects. In its issue of June 26, 1969, the paper ran a story entitled "Defoliants are causing a catastrophe of molar pregnancies at Tan Hoi hamlet." (A molar pregnancy results when damage to the egg prevents the placenta and fetus from developing normally.) The *Tin Sang* article reported that women of Tan Hoi hamlet were flocking to a Saigon hospital to "[have] their abnormal fetuses from molar pregnancies, or monsters [*sic*], taken out . . . .They unanimously say that after just about two months of being pregnant, their fetuses become unbearable to them; blood starts coming out through their vulvas until the fetus is taken out or the unfortunate pregnant woman must die."[33] However, at the time, no systematic studies were carried out to assess the problem. It has been estimated that up to fifty thousand deformed children were born to parents exposed either by proximity to Agent Orange spraying or through consumption of sprayed foodstuffs. This number is only a conjecture.

Concerned about the detrimental effects of Agent Orange, the American Association for the Advancement of Science set up a group called the Herbicide

Assessment Commission to examine the association between Agent Orange exposure and birth defects in Vietnam. In December 1970 the commission examined records of close to four thousand abnormal births in Saigon Children's Hospital from 1959 to 1968, and found a sudden rise in two types of defect, cleft palate and spina bifida, after the start of heavy spraying in 1966. Furthermore, the commission found that the rate of stillbirths in Tay Ninh provincial hospital was 64 per 1,000, approximately two times higher than the average rate of 31.2 per 1,000 in South Vietnam at the time. The commission's report noted,

> Although, as in other areas where Agent Orange has been used mainly for forest destruction (as opposed to crop destruction) the total number of directly exposed Vietnamese is probably low, the northern portion of Tay Ninh has been heavily defoliated and the rivers draining the areas of defoliants run through the remainder of the province and are a source of fish for some of the population.[34]

Thomas Whiteside, in his book *Defoliation*, estimated that, based on the standard dose of Agent Orange applied to wells and cisterns in South Vietnam, "If a Vietnamese woman who was exposed to Agent Orange was pregnant, she might very well be absorbing into her system a percentage of 2,4,5-T only slightly less than the percentage that deformed one out of every three fetuses of the pregnant experimental rats."[35]

However, the data from observational studies in the United States and elsewhere is inconsistent. Thus Agent Orange toxicity remains a controversial topic in medical science.[36, 37] As mentioned above, the Institute of Medicine has reviewed the published data and concluded that there was "inadequate/insufficient evidence" to determine whether an association exists between Agent Orange exposure and birth defects, with the exception of spina bifida.[38] However, the Institute's review relied primarily on published studies in its deliberation, without considering unpublished data from studies in Vietnam and the United States.

Recently, some colleagues and I conducted a meta-analysis of results from twenty-one studies, including thirteen Vietnamese studies and nine non-Vietnamese studies (seven American and two Australian studies), involving 205,398 individuals. We found that the risk of birth defects in individuals exposed to Agent Orange as compared to the non-exposed group increased 2.2-fold, and that this increase was statistically significant. Furthermore, we found that there was a higher risk of birth defects associated with Agent Orange exposure in the Vietnamese studies than in the non-Vietnamese studies (Table 4). This data collectively suggests that the observed association between Agent Orange/dioxin in humans and birth defects seems biologically plausible.

Table 4: Association Between Agent Orange Exposure and Birth Defects: a Meta-Analysis[39]

First Author and Year of Publication*	AO-Exposed Group		AO-Non-Ex-posed Group		Odds Ratio and 95% CI**	
	Number of Birth Defects	Number of No Birth Defects	Number of Birth Defects	Number of No Birth Defects	Odds Ratio	95% Confidence Interval
Erickson et al. (1984)	428	268	4,387	2,699	0.98	0.84 - 1.00
Lathrop et al. (1984)	76	757	44	638	1.46	0.99 - 1.57
Donovan et al. (1984)	127	123	202	205	1.05	0.76 - 1.10
CDC (1988)	130	1,661	112	1,463	1.02	0.79 - 1.06
Field et al. (1988)	137	695	41	685	3.29	2.29 - 3.52
Aschengrau (1988)	55	52	146	166	1.20	0.77 - 1.33
Wolfe et al. (1992)	229	816	289	1,313	1.28	1.05 - 1.30
Wolfe et al. (1995)	177	615	204	777	1.10	0.87 - 1.13
Kang et al. (2000)	95	1,570	85	1,827	1.30	0.96 - 1.36
Khoa et al. (1983)	33	1,163	6	581	2.75	1.14 - 4.06
Phuong et al. (1983)	30	39	31	144	3.57	1.93 - 4.33
Can et al. (1983a)	81	5,543	29	6,389	3.22	2.10 - 3.53
Can et al. (1983b)	189	26,501	521	100,774	1.38	1.17 - 1.40
Lang et al. (1983)	71	3,076	10	2,162	4.99	2.57 - 6.25
Tanh et al. (1987)	24	5,338	5	4,545	4.09	1.56 - 6.57
Phuong et al. (1989)	5	12	10	92	3.83	1.12 - 8.30
Phuong et al. (1994)	118	3,403	13	1,269	3.38	1.90 - 4.01
Phuong et al. (1994)	9	385	5	2,276	10.64	3.55 - 19.7
Dai B et al. (1994a)	151	6,356	14	1,275	2.16	1.85 - 2.53
Dai LC et al. (1994b)	11	1,639	2	1,718	5.77	1.28 - 18.4
10-80 study (2000)	283	4,027	33	1,390	2.96	2.05 - 3.17
Hung et al. (2000)	131	82	94	116	1.97	1.34 - 2.13
All studies	2,490	64,121	6,283	132,504	2.19	1.66 - 2.90

Notes: *A comprehensive list of studies with complete citations can be found in endnote 39. **Odds ratio (OR), in this context, is a measure of association between Agent Orange (AO) exposure and the risk of birth defects: an OR greater than 1 means that exposure to AO is associated with an increased risk of birth defects, whereas an OR less than 1 means that exposure to AO is associated with a decreased risk of birth defects. An association is considered statistically significant if its 95% confidence interval excludes 1.

In a subgroup analysis, we found that the strength of association between exposure to Agent Orange/dioxin and birth defects in the Vietnamese population was substantially more pronounced than that in the non-Vietnamese populations. This observation is consistent with previous findings that higher dioxin concentrations were found in the Vietnamese population in affected areas than in US Vietnam veterans. In addition, our findings were also consistent with the fact that in the Vietnamese civilian studies, both women and men were exposed, so effects could be both teratogenic and mutagenic; in the studies of North Vietnam and Ranch Hand veterans only mutagenesis was possible, since all the exposed individuals were men.

Most of the above studies found various birth defects in Vietnamese children; the major groups were malformations of the nervous system, such as hydrocephalus, and of the heart, genitals, and urinary tract. Other major defects included cleft palate, clubfoot, and hand and limb deformities. Some studies also reported an increased risk of spina bifida in children of parents exposed to Agent Orange.

Chemical Warfare?

The Vietnam War spanned fourteen years, from 1961 to 1975. During that period, Agent Orange and related chemicals were used as weapons for almost ten years (from 1961 to 1970). Of course, similar chemicals had previously been used during World War II and the Malayan war in the 1950s; however, in terms of scale and quantity, the chemical campaign in Vietnam was the largest ever in military history.

One of the questions the world has pondered since the beginning of Operation Ranch Hand is whether the spraying of Agent Orange and other herbicides during the Vietnam War was a violation of international law, or whether it was chemical warfare. The 1907 Hague Convention prohibited the use of poison or poisoned weapons or, more generally, the use of arms or materials calculated to cause unnecessary suffering.[40] The Geneva Protocol of 1925 reinforced the Hague Convention and further banned the use of asphyxiating, poisonous, or other gases usually referred to as chemical weapons.[41]

In 1966, resolutions were introduced at the UN charging the United States with violations of the 1925 Geneva Protocol for the Prohibition of the Use in War of Asphyxiating, Poisonous, or Other Gases, and of Bacteriological Methods of Warfare. In 1969 the UN General Assembly resolved that the Geneva Protocol of 1925, which outlawed the use of chemical or biological weapons, applied to herbicide and riot control agents.[42] However, the United States did not accept this interpretation and voted against the resolution. Nevertheless, the resolution was adopted on December 16, 1969, by a vote of 80 to 3 with 36 abstentions.

Therefore, the chemical campaign in Vietnam was considered by the international community to be a violation of international law. In 1964, the Federation of American Scientists had expressed opposition to herbicides in Vietnam on the grounds that the United States was capitalizing on the war as an opportunity to experiment with biological and chemical warfare. If the use of Agent Orange during the Vietnam War was chemical warfare, then it must stand as the largest waging of chemical war in human history. Indeed, at a 2002 conference at Yale University, after examining the evidence of the effects of Agent Orange, the world's leading environmental scientists concluded that the United States had conducted the "largest chemical warfare campaign in history."[43]

Issues of Reparation

Human rights organizations, such as the European Convention for the Protection of Human Rights and Fundamental Freedoms of 1953 and the American Convention on Human Rights of 1978, have argued for the right to compensation for victims of war.[44] The issue of reparation to victims of Agent Orange has been raised, as there is evidence suggesting that the US military knew of the toxicity of Agent Orange. Indeed, in a letter to Senator Tom Daschle dated September 9, 1988, Dr. James R. Clary, who worked at the Chemical Weapons Branch of the Air Force Armament Development Laboratory in Florida, wrote:

> When we [military scientists] initiated the herbicide program in the 1960s, we were aware of the potential for damage due to dioxin contamination in the herbicides. We were even aware that the military formulation had a higher dioxin concentration than the civilian version due to the lower cost and speed of manufacture. However, because the material was to be used on the enemy, none of us were overly concerned. We never considered a scenario in which our own personnel would become contaminated with the herbicide. And, if we had, we would have expected our own government to give assistance to veterans so contaminated.[45]

In 1984, American and Australian veterans brought a class action lawsuit against the chemical companies that produced Agent Orange for military use during the war. (It should be noted that the US government cannot be sued without its consent; therefore, all civil action has instead proceeded against

US companies). The suit resulted in an out-of-court settlement, in which the amount of $180 million was paid to veterans with death or total disability claims. Since 1991, the US government has been required by law and the Agent Orange Act to provide health care and disability compensation to American veterans exposed to Agent Orange and suffering from any of the Agent Orange-associated diseases listed by the Institute of Medicine in Table 3.[46]

However, the United States has yet to compensate victims in Vietnam. In 2004, the Vietnamese Association for the Victims of Agent Orange/Dioxin (VAVA) filed a class action suit against the companies that manufactured Agent Orange for military use during the war. These companies include some of the biggest names in the industry: Monsanto Chemical Co., Dow Chemical Co., Hercules Inc., Occidental Chemical Corp., Pharmacia Corp., Uniroyal Inc., Diamond Shamrock Agricultural Chemicals, American Home Products Corp., and others. In the suit, VAVA alleged that the companies violated international law and committed war crimes, crimes against humanity, torture, intentional infliction of emotional distress, and unjust enrichment.

In early 2005, Judge Jack B. Weinstein of the US District Court of New York dismissed all the charges against Agent Orange manufacturers. In his decision, the judge apparently sided with the companies' position; he stated that Agent Orange was a herbicide, not a poison, and that the agent was not used to intentionally inflict harm and suffering to people.[47] However, this position can be challenged. As described above, Agent Orange contained a significant amount of dioxin, considered one of the most (if not *the* most) toxic compounds known to humankind. In 1997, the International Agency for Research on Cancer classified dioxin as a carcinogenic substance. Four decades of scientific data, accumulated from numerous epidemiological, clinical, and basic studies, has clearly indicated that exposure to dioxin or Agent Orange is causally related to a number of cancers, diabetes, spina bifida, and possibly to other birth defects. Therefore, from a scientific point of view, it seems illogical and erroneous to state that Agent Orange is not a poison.

Concerning the intent of use of Agent Orange, the judge seems to have confused the chemical companies with the soldiers who actually sprayed the chemicals. The soldiers may not have known the extent to which Agent Orange was dangerous, and may not have used it intentionally to cause harm to people. Yet the manufacturers did know about the product's carcinogenic and teratogenic properties, and intentionally continued to manufacture the chemicals in high concentration. It should be noted here that, by analogy, cigarettes and asbestos (and, for that matter, many other products) were not initially designed to cause harm to people. However, as it is now known that they do, the manufacturers have been found liable for the resulting harm, since they knew about the damaging effects and did nothing to prevent them.

The use of Agent Orange in the Vietnam War, as mentioned above, fits the description of a war crime according to the Nuremberg rulings. Due to a lack of political resolve from the Vietnamese government and the lack of accessible judicial forums, the Vietnamese victims of Agent Orange still have not been recognized or compensated. In 2000, the Vietnamese government took a positive step toward compensation by introducing the Agent Orange Central Payments Programme. Under this program, adults and children who have partially or totally lost the ability to work due to Agent Orange exposure are eligible for financial assistance. However, the assistance is very modest, ranging from only $3.40 to $7.14 per month per person.[48]

Wars have long and lasting echoes. In Vietnam, the echoes of the war are children born to parents affected by Agent Orange, people who have survived the trauma of their births, brain-damaged infants who cannot express themselves, luckless children so enraged and depressed at their miserable fate that they are tied to their beds just to keep them safe from harm. They are the victims of Agent Orange in Vietnam. They, just like their counterparts in the United States, also share an innate belief in justice. Now that US-Vietnamese relations are increasingly cordial, it is time for the US government and the chemical companies involved in the Vietnam War to take responsibility for the damage caused by their actions and products, and to contribute toward the rehabilitation of the Vietnamese victims of Agent Orange. These actions would help heal the wounds of the war, which have been prolonged for more than thirty years.

Let us hope that neither Agent Orange nor any similar chemical will ever be used again in any world conflict.

Top: Vietnamese children in an orphanage, born with malformations as a result of Agent Orange exposure in the parents

Bottom: A teratoma removed from a patient exposed to Agent Orange

CHAPTER 5

Iraq, Another Vietnam? Consider Cambodia

Ben Kiernan and Taylor Owen

When US bombs hit a civilian warehouse in Afghanistan in late 2001, US secretary of defense Donald Rumsfeld responded: "We're not running out of targets, Afghanistan is." There was laughter in the press gallery. The bombing continued and then spread to a land of many more targets, with the United States determined to use "the force necessary to prevail, *plus some*," and asserting that no promises would be made to avoid "collateral damage."[1] Iraqi civilian casualties, in other words, were predictable if not inevitable. This show of strength aside, did the United States underestimate the strategic cost of collateral damage? If "shock and awe" worked against Saddam Hussein's regular Iraqi army, did it also nourish civilian support for the anti-US insurgency? Beyond the moral meaning of inflicting predictable civilian casualties, do the political repercussions of air strikes outweigh their military benefits?

The extension of the Vietnam War to Cambodia, which the US Air Force bombed from 1965 to 1973, is a troubling precedent. First, Cambodia became one of the most heavily bombarded countries in history. Then, in 1975–79, it suffered genocide at the hands of Pol Pot's Khmer Rouge communists, who were both military targets of the US bombing and its political beneficiaries.

Despite many key differences, an important similarity linked the 2003–2011 US war in Iraq to the 1965–75 Cambodian conflict: increasing reliance on airpower against a heterogeneous insurgency. As fighting continued to rage in Iraq and the US air war escalated, did al-Qaeda in Iraq and its eventual offshoot, ISIS or Islamic State, benefit politically? Did they continue to recruit among a widening anti-US Iraqi constituency even as they suffered military casualties from US aerial warfare? In Cambodia it was precisely the harshest, most extreme elements of the insurgency that survived the US bombing and then prevailed. The Khmer Rouge grew from a small force of fewer than ten thousand in 1970 to more than two hundred thousand troops and militia in 1973.[2] In their recruitment propaganda they highlighted the casualties and damage caused by US bombing. Within the broader insurgency, the radical Khmer Rouge leaders eclipsed their royalist and reformist allies as well as defeating their enemy, the pro-US Cambodian government of Lon Nol, in 1975.

The Nixon Doctrine had proposed that the United States could supply an allied Asian regime with the matériel to withstand internal or external challenge while the United States withdrew its own ground troops or remained at arm's length. "Vietnamization" built up the ground fighting capability of South Vietnamese government forces while American units slowly disengaged. In Cambodia from 1970, Washington gave military aid to General Lon Nol's new regime, tolerating its rampant corruption, while the US Air Force conducted massive aerial bombardment of its Vietnamese and Khmer Rouge communist opponents and their heterogeneous united front across rural Cambodia.

US policy in Iraq involved a similar shift from ground forces to air strikes in fighting the motley insurgency there. Seymour Hersh reported in December 2005 that a key element of any planned US drawdown of troops is their replacement with airpower. "We just want to change the mix of the forces doing the fighting—Iraqi infantry with American support and greater use of airpower,"[3] explained Patrick Clawson, the deputy director of the Washington Institute for Near East Policy. Indeed in 2007, US air strikes in Iraq more than quadrupled: from 229 in 2006 to 1,140 in the first nine months of 2007 alone. In Afghanistan, air strikes doubled from 2006 to 2007.[4]

Whether or not this strategy relieved the stretched US Army or appealed to a war-weary American public, air force commanders objected to their targets being selected by Iraqis. "Will some Iraqis be targeting on behalf of Al Qaeda, or the insurgency, or the Iranians?"[5] More generally, however, a shift to airpower ran the risk of inflicting even greater civilian casualties. Did this benefit the insurgency as it sought civilian support?

Andrew Brookes, former director of airpower studies at the Royal Air Force's advanced staff college, then at the International Institute for Strategic Studies in London, warned in 2007, "Don't believe that airpower is a solution to the problems inside Iraq at all. Replacing boots on the ground with airpower didn't work in Vietnam, did it?"[6] Moreover, in Cambodia it was counterproductive.

Of course, a continuing US ground troop presence in Iraq was also unlikely to resolve America's political problems there. In Vietnam, some of the 550,000 US troops committed atrocities against civilians that antagonized survivors and only strengthened the political influence of America's communist opponents. On a smaller scale, this dynamic recurred in Iraq, where opinion polls suggested most Iraqis supported attacks on US troops.[7] Conversely, air strikes today can be much more precise and accurate than they were in Indochina in the 1970s. Yet it would be perilous to ignore the disastrous precedent of the US air war against Cambodian insurgents.

On December 9, 1970, president Richard Nixon telephoned his national security advisor, Henry Kissinger, to discuss the ongoing bombing of Cambodia. Sporadic US tactical air strikes had begun there six years earlier, under the Johnson administration, but B-52s, long deployed over Vietnam, had been targeting Cambodia for only a year. In a "sideshow" to the war in Vietnam, 36,000 American sorties had already dropped many thousands of tons of munitions on Cambodia, a neutral kingdom until the US-backed General Lon Nol seized power from Prince Norodom Sihanouk in a March 1970 coup.[8] The 1969–70 "Menu" bombings of Cambodia's border areas, which American commanders grotesquely labeled "breakfast," "lunch," "supper," "dinner," "dessert," and "snack," respectively, aimed to destroy the mobile headquarters of the Vietcong and North Vietnamese Army (VC/NVA) in the Cambodian jungle. However, these and later bombardments both forced the Vietnamese communists further west and deeper into Cambodia, and ultimately radicalized Cambodian local people against Lon Nol's regime.

Nixon faced growing congressional opposition to his Indochina policy after the US ground invasion of Cambodia in May–June 1970, which had also failed to root out the Vietnamese communists there. The US president now wanted a secret escalation of air attacks further into Cambodia's populous areas. This was despite a September 1970 US intelligence report, which had warned Washington that "many of the sixty-six 'training camps' on which [Lon Nol's army] had requested air strikes by early September were in fact merely political indoctrination sessions held in village halls and pagodas."[9]

Telling Kissinger on December 9 of his frustration that the US Air Force was being "unimaginative," Nixon demanded more bombing, deeper into the country: "They have got to go in there and I mean really go in . . . .I want everything that can fly to go in there and crack the hell out of them. There is no limitation on mileage and there is no limitation on budget. Is that clear?"

Kissinger knew that this order ignored prior assurances to Congress that US planes would remain within thirty miles of the Vietnamese border and would not bomb within a kilometer of any village, and that military assessments stated that the air strikes were like "poking a beehive with a stick."[10] He responded hesitantly: "The problem is Mr. President, the air force is designed to fight an air battle against the Soviet Union. They are not designed for this war . . . in fact, they are not designed for any war we are likely to have to fight."

The equal US insistence today on using airpower against insurgencies raises this same dilemma: perhaps even more than the civilian casualties of ground operations, the "collateral damage" from US aerial attacks still appears to enrage and radicalize enough of the survivors for insurgencies to find the recruits and supporters they require.

Five minutes after his phone conversation with Nixon, Kissinger called General Alexander Haig to relay the new orders. "He [Nixon] wants a massive bombing campaign in Cambodia. He doesn't want to hear anything. It's an order, it's to be done. Anything that flies on anything that moves. You got that?" The response from Haig was barely audible, but it sounded like laughing.

As in Vietnam, the United States deployed massive airpower to fight an insurgency with growing local support. One result was more growth in the insurgency. The impact of the US bombing on Cambodia is now much better known. A recently declassified and apparently near-complete Pentagon spatial database, detailing no fewer than 230,488 US air war sorties over Cambodia from October 4, 1965, to August 15, 1973, reveals that much of that bombing was indiscriminate, that it was far more extensive than heretofore reported, and also that it had begun years earlier than was officially disclosed to Congress or the American people.

In the fall of 2000, the US government released to the governments of Cambodia, Laos, and Vietnam extensive classified air force data on all American bombings of those countries.[11] This data assists those nations in the search for unexploded US ordnance, still a major threat in much of the region, but the data can also be analyzed in map and time series formats, revealing an astounding wealth of historical information on the air wars there.

We now know, for instance, that from 1965 to 1969, even before the "secret" bombing of Cambodia is supposed to have started, the US Air Force had dropped bombs on, among other places in Cambodia, eighty-three sites at which the Pentagon database described the intended target as "Unknown" or "Unidentified." The detailed record shows that for these eighty-three cases, the US Air Force stated in its confidential reporting that it was unaware of what it was bombing. It nevertheless dropped a total of 1,039 tons of munitions on those sites that it could not identify, in a neutral country at peace.

This practice escalated after the ground war began. For the year 1970 alone, the number of US air strikes on targets recorded as "Unknown" or "Unidentified" increased to as many as 573 bombing sites. American planes also bombed another 5,602 Cambodian sites where the Pentagon record identifies no target, 15 percent of the 37,426 air strikes on the country that year. Interestingly, after Nixon's December 1970 order for wider bombing of Cambodia, the number of such attacks fell in 1971 to 182 bombings of "Unknown" targets and 1,390 attacks on "Unidentified" ones (among the 25,052 Cambodian sites bombed that year).

But the long-term trend favored more indiscriminate bombardment. In 1972, the US Air Force bombed 17,293 Cambodian sites, including 766 whose targets it explicitly recorded as "Unknown," plus another 767 sites with no target identified in the military database. These figures increased dramatically the next year. In the period January–August 1973 alone, the US Air Force bombed 33,945 sites in Cambodia, hitting as many as 2,632 "Unknown" targets and 465 other sites where the Pentagon record identified no target.

May 1973 saw the height of the bombing in Cambodia. During that month, US planes bombed 6,553 sites there. These sorties included hits on 641 "Unknown" and 158 "Unidentified" targets at an average rate of more than twenty-five such strikes per day for that month.

Overall, during the US bombardment of Cambodia from 1970 to 1973, American warplanes hit a total of 3,580 "Unknown" targets and bombed another 8,238 sites with no target identified. Such sites accounted for 10.4 percent of US air strikes, which hit a total of 113,716 Cambodian sites in under four years.

Also unknown is the human toll from these specific air strikes on "Unknown," "Unidentified," or nonidentified targets, or from the additional 1,023 US strikes on targets identified only as a "sampan." Casualties from the former three categories, at least, are properly considered US war crimes (not genocide), although they remain unprosecuted.

However, it is possible to cross-check other information in the Pentagon bombing database with details that Cambodian survivors provided to Ben Kiernan in interviews he conducted in 1979–81.[12] We can also begin to answer important further questions concerning the strategic efficacy and political consequences of high-altitude bombing: Can insurgencies be beaten with bombs? Or with any aerial weaponry? What are the human and also the strategic costs of "collateral damage"? In terms of a strategy in Iraq of replacing ground troops with air strikes, Cambodia demonstrates how strategic bombing, at least, can go disastrously wrong.

The new data transforms our understanding of the scale of what happened to Cambodia.[13] It is accepted that from 1969 to 1973 the US dropped at least 539,000 tons of bombs on the country, perhaps more. The Pentagon's records indicate that from 1965 to 1975 Cambodia was the target of no fewer than 230,516 bombing sorties. It is now apparent that in 1969–73 alone Cambodia suffered a significant proportion of all the US bombing of Indochina (six million tons over nine years), making it even today one of the most heavily bombed countries in history.

The United States dropped 160,000 tons of bombs on Japan during World War II. The newly released Pentagon data indicates that the bombardment of Cambodia was more than three times heavier. To put this massive figure in total perspective, during all of World War II, the United States dropped 2 million tons of bombs, including 1.6 million tons in the European Theater and 500,000 tons in the Pacific Theater. This *includes* the bombs dropped on Hiroshima and Nagasaki: 15,000 and 20,000 tons respectively.[14] In the Korean War, the total US bombardment was 454,000 tons.[15] Cambodia's total was much higher.

Not only was the total payload dropped on Cambodia very large, the bombardment also began much earlier than the US government or media have previously revealed. Although the "secret" 1969–70 "Menu" bombing campaign, when first uncovered, caused congressional uproar and provoked calls for Nixon's impeachment, we now know that US bombing actually started over four years earlier, in 1965, as Cambodian leaders had claimed at that time. These early tactical strikes may have supported secret CIA ground incursions from across the Vietnamese border. During the mid-1960s, the Studies and Operations Group—US Special Forces teams in tandem with the Khmer Serei (US-trained ethnic Cambodian rebels operating from South Vietnam)—were collecting intelligence inside Cambodia.[16] Perhaps the US tactical air strikes supported or followed up on these secret pre-1969 operations.

This revelation has several implications. First, US bombing of neutral Cambodia significantly predates the Nixon administration. Earlier individual bombardments of Cambodia were known and protested by the Cambodian government. Prince Sihanouk's foreign minister, for instance, claimed as early as January 1966 that "hundreds of our people have already died in these at-tacks."[17] The Pentagon database reveals escalating bombardments. From 1965 to 1968, the Johnson administration conducted 2,565 sorties over Cambodia and dropped 214 tons of bombs there. Most of these strikes occurred under the Vietnam War policy of then secretary of defense Robert S. McNamara, which he has since publicly regretted.

Second, these early strikes were tactical, not carpet bombings. The John-son administration made a strategic decision not to use B-52s in Cambodia, whether out of concern for Cambodian lives, or for the country's neutrality, or because of perceived strategic limits of carpet bombing. However, Nixon de-cided differently, and from late 1969 the US Air Force began to deploy B-52s over Cambodia.

Why drop over half a million tons of bombs on a small, impoverished, agrar-ian country even as it attempts to stay out of a war, and what are the conse-quences of doing so?

In the first stage of the bombing (1965–69) the US goal was to destroy the Vietnamese communists' Cambodian sanctuaries and to cut off their supply routes from North to South Vietnam, through Laos to the north and, later, the southern Cambodian port of Sihanoukville. These early US attacks failed to find, let alone hit, a mobile Vietnamese headquarters, or to stop the flow of weapons and supplies.

The second phase of the bombing (1969–72) aimed to support the pullout of US troops from Vietnam, ironically by expanding the war in the hope of winning it faster. Lon Nol's 1970 coup facilitated much more extensive US action in Cambodia, including the short ground invasion and the prolonged carpet bombing.

In 1969, Nixon first introduced B-52s into the still-secret US air war in Cambodia to buy time for the US withdrawal from Vietnam. Later, as Em-ory Swank, a US ambassador to Lon Nol's Cambodia, recalled, "time was bought for the success of the program in Vietnam . . . to this extent I think some measure of gratitude is owed to the Khmers."[18] Former US General Theodore Mataxis added that it was "a holding action. You know, one of those things like a rear guard you drop off. The troika's going down the road and the wolves are closing in, and so you throw them something off and let them chew it."[19] Thus Cambodians became a decoy to protect American lives. The irony was that in its attempt to deny Vietnam to the Vietnamese communists, the United States drove them further into Cambodia, producing the domino effect that the Indochinese intervention had been intended to prevent. Phnom Penh fell two weeks before Saigon.

The final phase of the US bombing, January–August 1973, aimed to stop the Khmer Rouge advance on the Cambodian capital. US fear of the fall of the first Southeast Asian domino translated into a massive escalation of the air war that spring and summer—an unprecedented B-52 bombardment, focused on the heavily populated areas around Phnom Penh, but also sparing few other regions of the country.[20] As well as inflaming rural rage against the pro-US Lon Nol government, the rain of bombs on noncombatants also decreased the relative risk of their joining the insurgency.

The impact of the resultant increased civilian casualties may not have been a primary strategic concern for the Nixon administration. It should have been. Civilian casualties helped drive people into the arms of an insurgency that had enjoyed relatively little support until heavy bombing of rural areas began in 1970.

Even before that, the initial US bombardments of border areas had set in motion a highly precarious series of events that led to the extension of the Vietnam War deeper into Cambodia. This contributed to the 1970 coup, which also helped fuel the rapid rise of the Khmer Rouge.

The final phase of the story is better known. In 1973 the US Congress, angered at the destruction and the deception of the Nixon administration, legislated a halt to the Cambodia bombing. The great damage was already done. Having grown under the rain of bombs from a few thousand to more than two hundred thousand regular and militia forces by 1973, the Khmer Rouge took Phnom Penh two years later. They then subjected Cambodia to a genocidal Maoist agrarian revolution. Is there a lesson here on combating insurgencies?

Apart from the large human toll, perhaps the most powerful and direct impact of the bombing was the political backlash it caused. Because Lon Nol was supporting the US air war, the bombing of Cambodian villages (and the significant civilian casualties it caused) provided ideal recruitment rhetoric for the insurgent Khmer Rouge. This direct relationship between village bombings and Khmer Rouge recruitment can be demonstrated by cross-checking testimony from the 1979–81 interviews with survivors of the bombing against an analysis of the Pentagon bombing data.[21]

The Nixon administration knew that the Khmer Rouge were explicitly recruiting peasants by highlighting the damage done by US air strikes. The CIA's Directorate of Operations, after investigations south of Phnom Penh, reported in May 1973 that the communists were "using damage caused by B-52 strikes as the main theme of their propaganda."[22] Years later, journalist Bruce Palling asked a former Khmer Rouge officer from northern Cambodia if Khmer Rouge forces there had made use of the bombing for anti-US propaganda:

> Chhit Do: Oh yes, they did. Every time after there had been bombing, they would take the people to see the craters, to see how big and deep the craters were, to see how the earth had been gouged out and scorched. . . . The ordinary people . . . sometimes literally shit in their pants when the big bombs and shells came. . . . Their minds just froze up and they would wander around mute for three or four days. Terrified and half-crazy, the people were ready to believe what they were told. . . . That was what made it so easy for the Khmer Rouge to win the people over. . . . It was because of their dissatisfaction with the bombing that they kept on cooperating with the Khmer Rouge, joining up with the Khmer Rouge, sending their children off to go with them. . . .
>
> Bruce Palling: So the American bombing was a kind of help to the Khmer Rouge?
>
> Chhit Do: Yes, that's right . . . sometimes the bombs fell and hit little children, and their fathers would be all for the Khmer Rouge. . . .[23]

The Nixon administration, aware of this consequence of its Cambodia bombing, kept the air war secret for long enough that debate over its toll and political impact came far too late. Along with support from the Vietnamese communists and from Lon Nol's deposed rival, Prince Sihanouk, the US carpet bombing of Cambodia was partly responsible for the rise of what had been a small-scale Khmer Rouge insurgency. The insurgency grew capable of overthrowing the Lon Nol government in 1975, and subsequently perpetrated genocide in the country. The parallels to current dilemmas in Iraq and Afghanistan, where a genocidal al-Qaeda faction lurked among the insurgent forces and later emerged in new guise as the more powerful Islamic State or ISIS, in Syria and Libya as well as Iraq and Afghanistan, are poignant and telling.

Today the technology of US bombing has become more sophisticated, "unknown" targets are bombed less frequently, and collateral damage is lower. Yet these days information travels faster. What are the strategic consequences of the continuing civilian death tolls that US forces inflict in Iraq and Afghanistan, and of the outrage they spawn there? Are they worth the risk, let alone the moral consequences, to say nothing of the implications under international criminal law?

An aerial strike on January 13, 2006, by a US Predator drone on a village in Pakistan, which killed women and children and inflamed local anti-US political passions, seems a pertinent example of what also continues to occur in Afghanistan and Iraq. "Collateral damage," in this case, even undermined the positive sentiments created by billions of dollars of aid to that part of Pakistan following the 2005 earthquake. Aside from the killing of innocent civilians, how many new enemies does US bombing create?

In the lead-up to the Iraq war, neither the US media nor the Bush administration seriously included the impact of civilian casualties in public discussion of the overall war strategy. Even with official assurances that civilian casualties would be limited, when it came to a decision to bomb a village containing a suspected terrorist, the benefit of killing the target trumped the toll on innocents. This misguided calculus proved quite possibly a fundamental threat to long-term American security.

If the Cambodians' tragic experience teaches us anything, it is that official disregard of the immorality and miscalculation of the consequences of inflicting predictable civilian casualties stem partly from failure to understand the social contexts of insurgencies. The reasons local people help such movements do not fit into Kissingerian rationales. Nor is their support absolute or unidimensional. Those whose lives have been ruined may not look to the geopolitical rationale of the attacks; rather, understandably and often explicitly, many will blame the attackers.

Dangerous forces can reap the windfall. The strategic and moral failure of the US-Cambodia air campaign lay not only in the toll of possibly 150,000 civilians killed there in 1969–73 by an unprecedented level of carpet, cluster, and incendiary bombing, but also indirectly, in its aftermath, when the genocidal Khmer Rouge regime rose from the bomb craters to cause the deaths of another 1.7 million Cambodians in 1975–79. These successive tragedies are not unrelated. It is only predictable that an insurgency in need of recruits may effectively exploit potential supporters' hatred for those killing their family members or neighbors. That Washington has yet to fully learn from its past crimes and mistakes is a failure of strategic as well as moral calculation. Until it does, America's hopes for the Middle East and for its own improved security seem misplaced.

CHAPTER 6

My Lai and the American Way of War Crimes

Gareth Porter

I.

On March 16, 1968, two companies of US Army troops belonging to the Americal Division entered the My Lai and My Khe hamlets of Son My village and killed between three hundred fifty and five hundred Vietnamese civilians in cold blood. In November 1969 what came to be known as the My Lai massacre became public knowledge, thanks to investigative reporter Seymour Hersh's story about the atrocities committed on that day.

The My Lai massacre could have destroyed the legitimacy of the Vietnam War, had the full implications been revealed as to how and why it occurred. Instead, however, the Nixon administration and the US military acted quickly to establish what would become the dominant national narrative of the episode—that it had been merely the result of a few "bad apples." The political damage was successfully limited and, in subsequent decades, the treatment of that shameful episode in American history in the media and historical accounts of the war effectively turned it into a cautionary tale of the dangers of a breakdown of discipline under certain conditions of war.

This interpretation of My Lai was reflected in the most widely watched television series on the Vietnam War, PBS's *Vietnam: A Television History*, a thirteen-part series broadcast in 1983. Even today, a page on My Lai on the website for the series continues to suggest that the cold-blooded murders in My Lai were the result of "widespread failures of leadership, discipline, and morale among the Army's fighting units."

The PBS account continues:

As the war progressed, many "career" soldiers had either been rotated out or retired. Many more had died. In their place were scores of draftees whose fitness for leadership in the field of battle was questionable at best. Military officials blamed inequities in the draft policy for the often slim talent pool from which they were forced to choose leaders. Many maintained that if the educated middle class ("the Harvards," as they were called) had joined in the fight, a man of Lt. William Calley's emotional and intellectual stature would never have been issuing orders.[1]

This explanation for the crimes committed at My Lai thus suggests that the problem was that the command of basic US combat units in Vietnam had fallen into the hands of the uneducated lower class. Lieutenant Calley, who is described in the program as "an unemployed college dropout," was just not smart enough to have been in charge of a military operation—so goes the PBS gloss on the most notorious atrocity in the war. If not for the unfortunate narrowing of the "talent pool," it suggests, the massacre would not have occurred. The PBS view has become the standard interpretation of war crimes in Vietnam, limiting responsibility for My Lai—and by extension, for any wanton killings of civilians in the war—to a few uneducated incompetents.

But if one traces the orders and directives from the unit that committed the crimes up the chain of command, it becomes clear that My Lai was not an aberration caused by uneducated officers. Rather, it was the result of a deliberate policy, adopted at the highest level of the Department of Defense, to treat the civilian population of hamlets and villages under the control of the Vietnamese communist movement not as noncombatants but as a part of the enemy structure—just as much as the Vietcong military personnel—and therefore fair game for the US war machine.

The truth about the responsibility for My Lai has been evaded for generations, in large part because, in the Vietnam War, the US military command and the civilian leadership of the Pentagon adopted a peculiarly American way of carrying out a war strategy in which policies involving war crimes were the core element. The US commander in Vietnam, General William Westmoreland, and his staff were certainly aware of the laws of war, and they consciously devised ways to put distance between themselves and a military strategy that called for treating all civilians in the Vietcong zone as having no rights to protection from US bombing, artillery attacks, and ground operations. They generally communicated the policy to lower echelons through careful circumlocution—by a verbal wink and a nod—rather than by clear-cut statement.

This American way of war crimes was necessary to US military strategy in South Vietnam. Without it, the United States was already defeated before its war could get under way. Not only had the South Vietnamese communist political-military organization been developing for five years by the time US troops invaded the country, but the Communist Party itself had already been deeply entrenched in the South Vietnamese countryside for nearly two decades. It had the social and political legitimacy that went with having led the fight for independence and having supported resistance against returning landowners after the war. The "Vietcong," as they had come to be called by the anticommunist regime in Saigon and its US sponsors, had traditional base areas in large parts of the Mekong Delta and in the Northern provinces from Binh Dinh all the way to the demilitarized zone separating North and South Vietnam.

The US military command knew that the population strongly supported the revolutionary movement in those base areas, and therefore that defeating it would be impossible without attacking the civilian society itself. The objective of the strategy was to make it impossible for civilians to continue to live in the Vietcong base areas. The US war planners simply redefined the civilian population out of existence by categorizing and treating them as combatants, and thus as legitimate targets of military operations.

But they could not explicitly acknowledge what they were doing. The American way of war crimes in Vietnam thus involved the concealment of the actual policy toward the civilian population in the Vietcong base areas behind a veil of hypocrisy. The treatment of noncombatants—the aged, women, and children—in those zones as the enemy was never explicitly discussed in any official document or translated explicitly into orders to kill noncombatants. Such a directive was not needed, because the entire command operated on the implicit understanding that massive killing and terrorization of civilians was necessary to succeed in the war against a deeply entrenched communist political-military movement. Unit commanders knew that the official policy distinguished sharply between operations in contested and GVN areas, on one hand, and in the Vietcong base areas, on the other. In the latter case, it was clear that command authorities would look the other way at whatever force had to be used to force the population to leave Vietcong villages and hamlets.

This American way of war crimes was aimed at protecting the command from being implicated in any activities that could be considered violations of the laws of war. The first level of defense was that commanders covered up any evidence of war crimes committed by their own troops. But for the stubborn persistence of Ron Ridenhour, who served in the aviation section of the Eleventh Brigade in South Vietnam from January to December 1968, and who heard accounts of what happened in My Lai from a fellow soldier in Vietnam, it is unlikely that the My Lai massacre would have become public knowledge until decades later. Ridenhour wrote letters to political leaders alerting them to what he had been told about My Lai in March 1969, which led to Seymour Hersh's report.[2]

The second line of defense by the US military command was, effectively, to wall itself off from the political fallout of the publicity surrounding the My Lai massacre by ordering an official army inquiry into the "cover-up" of the massacre. The Peers Commission was ostensibly given the task of finding out what actually happened in My Lai, and determining responsibility not only for the actual massacre but also for any cover-up of the massacre. The Peers Commission exposed a widespread cover-up by officers at the brigade and division levels, and has been hailed ever since as a triumph of decency and honesty in the military. But the Peers Commission Report was itself essential to the much more egregious cover-up of the US command's ultimate responsibility for what happened in My Lai.

After the Peers Commission Report, serious national inquiry into higher command responsibility for My Lai—and for war crimes in Vietnam more broadly—ended completely. Except for one young serviceman, John Kerry, who returned from Vietnam to carry out his own personal crusade against those in Washington whom he blamed for war crimes in Vietnam, no figure of public note has since raised any serious question about the legal and moral responsibility of the US command and the policymakers in Washington for the war crimes that occurred in My Lai and elsewhere in Vietnam. With the Peers Commission's absolving the US political and military leadership of responsibility for the war crimes committed in My Lai, the United States settled into a long silence on the whole issue of responsibility for such crimes.

II.

The obvious defense for low-level officers accused of a war crime is to claim that they were only following orders from their superiors, and that was exactly what Lieutenant William Calley claimed. Not only did Lieutenant Calley testify under oath at his court martial that he was ordered to act as he did, but the defense mounted by his lawyers was based explicitly on the claim that the US command in Vietnam had laid the policy and legal groundwork for the killing of civilians in the Vietcong zone. They argued that "the history of operations around Pinkville [the name the US military had given to Son My village, in which the hamlet of My Lai was located] discloses villager sympathy and support for the Viet Cong so extensive and enduring as to constitute all the villagers as belligerents themselves," and that Calley's superiors "had determined the belligerent status of the villagers before the operation of 16 March. . . . " Because of that determination, they asserted, the villagers of what had been called Pinkville "were not entitled to the protection of peaceful civilian status under the Geneva Convention. . . . "[3]

The testimony presented to the Peers Commission provided evidence that Calley did indeed get just such orders from his superiors. The company commanders who carried out the operation in My Lai conveyed the message to their squad leaders and troops that all civilians were to be killed. Captain Ernest Medina's explicit orders to the squad leaders of Company C, including Lieutenant Calley, were to consider civilians as the enemy to be destroyed. "Captain Medina told us that this village was heavily fortified," a squad leader, Sergeant Charles West, recalled. "From the intelligence that higher levels had received, he said, this village consisted only of North Vietnamese army, Vietcong, and VC families. He said the order was to destroy Mylai and everything in it."[4] Another squad leader who attended Medina's briefing also recalled that Medina had told the company that My Lai was a "suspected VC stronghold and that he had orders to kill everybody that was in that village."[5]

According to another soldier, who confirmed the order to "kill everything in the village," the men in his squad "talked about this among ourselves that night" and "all agreed that Captain Medina meant for us to kill every man, woman, and child in the village."[6] The term "VC families" to which Sergeant West referred had thus appeared in informal communications within the military command as a device to erase the distinction between combatants and noncombatants in the Vietcong zone.

It was not only Captain Medina who led the troops to believe that their mission was to kill everyone in Son My. The same message was conveyed as well by Captain Earl R. Michles, the company commander, to the squad leaders and troops of B Company. One of the infantrymen in Bravo Company testified that "there was a general conception that we were going to destroy everything." Another member of B Company testified, "We had three hamlets that we had to search and destroy. They told us they had dropped leaflets and stuff and everybody was supposed to be gone. Nobody was supposed to be there. If anybody is there, shoot them."[7]

So the platoon commanders were clearly not acting on their own in giving orders to kill anyone in the hamlet. But what about their company commanders? Were they acting independently in giving their platoon commanders orders to convey to their troops that all the people of My Lai were to be considered the enemy? The Peers Commission found clear evidence to the contrary. The evidence led them straight to the command of the parent unit, the five-hundred-man strike force called Task Force Barker, commanded by Lieutenant Colonel Frank Barker.

The Peers Commission Report stated, "There is substantial evidence that the events at Son My resulted primarily from the nature of the orders issued on 15 March to the soldiers of Task Force (TF) Barker." The Commission discovered that the commander of the task force had ordered the troops under his command to burn houses, kill livestock, and destroy foodstuffs in Son My and the surrounding area—all of which the Commission acknowledged to be "clearly illegal" under the laws of war. Barker also ordered artillery fire on parts of My Lai without any effort to warn the population, which the Commission noted was "technically permissible by the directives in effect at the time."[8] Those orders reinforced the clear message to the companies making up Task Force Barker that everyone in the villages should be considered the enemy and, by implication, should be killed.

The Commission concluded,

> While the evidence indicates that neither LTC Barker nor his subordinates specifically ordered the killing of noncombatants, they did fail, either intentionally or unintentionally, to make any clear distinctions between combatants and noncombatants in their orders and instructions. . . . [T]he orders that were issued through the TF Barker chain of command conveyed an understanding to a significant number of soldiers of C Company that only the enemy remained in the operational area and that the enemy was to be destroyed.[9]

It would have been an explicit, punishable war crime to have stated in a directive or an official briefing to the commanders of Task Force Barker that they were to consider those civilians as no different from combatants and therefore subject to wanton killing. Instead, however, the task force commander had, in the words of the Peers Commission, "conveyed an understanding . . . that only the enemy remained" in My Lai, allowing the unit commanders to draw the obvious inference about how to treat the civilian population there.

The Peers Commission failed to investigate whether Barker did so deliberately. In retrospect that failure could have been due to only one reason—to avoid pursuing the obvious question: where did Task Force Barker get the idea that civilians were to be treated as the enemy and thus devoid of any protection against death and destruction? The refusal to pursue that issue reveals the hidden objective of the Commission, which was to clear the military command of any responsibility for war crimes in My Lai.

Despite its refusal to inquire formally about the relationship between Barker's orders to his subordinates and directives to Barker, the Commission went out of its way to portray the actual policy guidance issued by General William Westmoreland and the US military command in Vietnam as requiring strict adherence to the international laws of war. Chapter 9 of the Peers Commission Report employed two distinct tactics to clear Westmoreland: first, by presenting policies and directives relating to operations in government-controlled and contested areas as though they were relevant to the issue of rules of engagement for operations in Vietcong base areas; and second, by deliberately misrepresenting the most critical directive of all regarding those rules of engagement.

The Commission presented the policy guidance that existed at the time of the My Lai operation as clearly prohibiting the actions taken by the companies in question—and condoned by the command of Task Force Barker. The Commission concluded that "existing policies and directives at every level of command expressed a clear intent regarding the proper treatment and safeguarding of noncombatants, the humane handling of prisoners of war, and minimizing the destruction of private property."[10]

The report was almost rhapsodic in its praise for MACV's directives regarding the question of humane treatment of civilians. From 1965 to the time of the Commission Report, it said, "the policy they [MACV] set forth has been consistent in adhering to the humane standard of protecting the civilians within the combat zone."[11] The commanders were directed, according to the report, to "use your firepower with care and discrimination, particularly in populated areas."[12] It cited, for example, Directive 95-4, which ordered pilots to "endeavor to minimize noncombatant casualties and civilian property damage." It quoted another directive that established policies and procedures for "control, disposition, and safeguarding of private property and food supplies. . . . " Civilian dwellings and livestock were not to be destroyed by US forces, according to the Commission's account, "except as an unavoided [sic] consequence of combat actions."[13]

There was only one problem with these descriptions of MACV rules of engagement: they were all directives and policies designed solely for populated areas in which the communist forces had either temporary control or no control at all.

The rules of engagement for such areas were irrelevant to the issue before the Commission: What were MACV's policies toward civilians living in a zone that had been under the long-term control of the communist movement? Significantly, the report did not cite a single official document that related to rules of engagement designed specifically for operations targeting villages or hamlets under long-term Vietcong control. All the references to the seemingly benign language of directives thus served to divert the attention of the public from the real issue.

The only directive that has come to light that related to rules of engagement for operations against Vietcong base areas is MACV Directive 525-3, titled "Combat Operations: Minimizing Non-combatant Casualties," which was first issued on September 7, 1965, and was reissued in a slightly revised form on October 14, 1966.[14] The Peers Commission's treatment of that directive refers only to the language bearing on contested areas, suggesting that it was the only content of the directive. The Commission presented Directive 525-3 as yet another document expressing the command's caring attitude toward potential civilian victims of war and its stress on the "exercise of restraint," describing the directive as follows:

> MAC Directive 525-3 dealt with minimizing noncombatant casualties. Non-combatants were generally described as the "hapless rice farmer and the small town inhabitant, whether at any one time [he] lives in a VC or a GVN controlled hamlet" noting that where he lives depends "to a large extent upon factors and forces beyond his control." Commanders were directed to control force and not to use "unnecessary force leading to noncombatant battle casualties in area [sic] *temporarily controlled by the VC* [emphasis added]."[15]

Thus the Commission's description of the intent of the directive to limit the use of force against noncombatants was actually related only to those areas that were "temporarily" controlled by the Vietcong. The reasoning behind that rule becomes clear from the full text of the relevant paragraph, which was reported in a news dispatch from Washington in mid-1966: "The use of unnecessary force leading to noncombatant casualties in areas temporarily controlled by the VC will embitter the population, drive them into the arms of the Viet Cong and make the long-range goal of pacification more difficult and costly."[16] That incentive for restraining the use of air strikes and artillery strikes against populated areas did not apply, of course, to areas that had been under the long-term control of the Vietcong, where the population was known to be supportive of the insurgent movement. But the Commission did not address explicitly the question of what tactics were allowed with regard to civilians in those areas.

The Peers Commission Report did refer to "specified strike zones" in the context of Directive 525-3, but only to describe them, by implication, as benign. It said one of the "significant points" in the directive was that such zones "should be configured to exclude populated areas." But it did not quote from the text of Directive 525-3 in this regard because, if it had done so, it would have been clear that this description was deliberately misleading. The text of the directive did not actually refer to "specified strikes zones" but to "free fire zones," areas in which US artillery and air strikes could be launched without prior approval by the South Vietnamese government. (It was only in the later MACV Directive 95-2 of December 20, 1965, that the term was changed from "free fire zones" to "specified strike zones."[17]) What Directive 525-3 actually said was, "Specified strike zones should be configured to exclude populated areas, *except those in accepted VC bases* [emphasis added]."[18]

The term "accepted VC bases" referred, of course, to the large parts of South Vietnam in 1965 through 1968, both in the Mekong Delta and in central Vietnam—including Quang Ngai province, where My Lai was located—that had long been revolutionary strongholds. These were areas in which the Vietminh had mobilized the population to fight the French and in which the Communist Party had built strong organizations during the struggle against the Ngô Dinh Diem regime and the subsequent American invasion. As of March 1965 secretary of defense Robert S. McNamara reported to president Lyndon B. Johnson that the Vietcong controlled about 40 percent of the total land area of South Vietnam, and that in twenty-two of the forty-three provinces they controlled 50 percent or more of the land area. Even more telling was the fact that in a number of provinces the Vietcong controlled virtually the entire province. McNamara reported that in the Mekong Delta alone, they controlled 90 percent of Kien Tuong, Long An, and Kien Hoa provinces, and 85 percent of An Xuyen.[19] More precisely, in terms of actual numbers of rural villages, the Vietcong were estimated in April 1964 to be in complete control of 866 villages, or 34 percent of a total of 2,538, while contesting for control of another 187.[20] For the most part, these villages were in long-term Vietcong base areas, and as of early 1965 had highly effective party and mass organizations. Over the next few years, the population of those base areas was reduced drastically by US bombing and shelling—in many cases by as much as 80 to 85 percent, according to data collected by US government–funded interviewers.[21]

So the Peers Commission's bland assertion that free-fire zones were "usually free of any known populace"[22] was a blatant falsehood that was necessary to carry off the cover-up of the actual rules of engagement guiding the operations of Task

Force Barker and other ground operations in long-term Vietcong base areas. Although neither he nor any of his subordinates stated that premise explicitly—and indeed they were at pains to obscure it in their public pronouncements and directives during the war—Westmoreland made that intention explicit in his own memoirs, published in 1976. He wrote that, once the free-fire zones were established, "anybody who remained had to be considered an enemy combatant," and operations in those areas "could be conducted without fear of civilian casualties."[23] Westmoreland's intent in issuing Directive 325-3 could hardly be mistaken by military officers under his command. They obviously could and did draw the conclusion that they should not be concerned about the deaths of any civilians remaining in the free-fire zones—or "specified strike zones"—established under the directive, because those noncombatants were all to be considered as "Viet cong" and therefore could be regarded as deserving of no protection.

Only two days after the My Lai massacre, a South Vietnamese government field worker reported from Son My village that 427 people had been killed in My Lai, including both civilians and guerrillas. Lieutenant Colonel William Guinn, the deputy province advisor for Quang Ngai, read a translation of the report. He later testified to the Peers Commission that he had not believed the report, but that, even if it were true, he "didn't consider it a war crime." He explained that "these people had been killed by an act of war . . . because that was a free fire zone out there. . . . "[24] That reaction reflected the general understanding of the military command that civilians in Vietcong base areas were fair game for US military assaults in those zones. It was not recorded, however, in the Peers Commission Report.

One month after the massacre, on April 24, 1968, the commander of the Eleventh Infantry Brigade, Colonel Oran K. Henderson, sent a letter to the commander of the Americal Division, Major General Samuel W. Koster, in which he dismissed the idea that a massacre could have happened in My Lai, because "this area has long been an enemy stronghold. . . . " The letter further cited the fact that the district chief "does not give the allegations any importance and . . . points out that the two hamlets where the incident is alleged to have happened are in an area controlled by the VC since 1964."[25] In dismissing the reports of the massacre on the basis of the area's status, Henderson was clearly suggesting that the fact that My Lai was in a long-time Vietcong base area was prima facie evidence that any killings in the hamlet would have been legal by definition.

Westmoreland avoided stating this equation explicitly in any official document, but in a 1967 visit to a unit of the 101st Airborne Division, called the Tiger Force, in Quang Ngai province, he conveyed the message without any ambiguity. As recounted by members of the Tiger Force who were present, Westmoreland told them, "If there are people who are out there—and not in the camps—they're pink as far as we're concerned. They're communist sympathizers. They were not supposed to be there."[26]

That message, which obviously paralleled the oral instructions from Westmoreland to Task Force Barker, gave the Tiger Force the idea that they were authorized to kill anyone who chose to remain in Vietcong base areas. In a prize-winning investigation of the operations of that unit, two *Toledo Blade* reporters found that the Tiger Force had carried out no fewer than nineteen killing sprees against civilians in "specified strike zones." The unit's commanders justified the wanton murder of civilians to army investigators by explaining that the creation of a free-fire zone gave US troops the right to "kill anything that moved."[27]

General Peers had a powerful personal incentive for covering up Westmoreland's responsibility for what happened at My Lai that was never mentioned in news media coverage of the Peers Commission. At the time he was ordered to undertake the investigation, Peers was a three-star general who was chief of the army's reserve forces. But it was Westmoreland, by then promoted to army chief of staff, who had appointed Peers, and Westmoreland remained in that position during the entire Peers Commission investigation. Thus Peers was still subject to Westmoreland in the chain of command. He could not investigate Westmoreland's responsibility for My Lai without putting his own career in jeopardy.

Jerome K. Walsh Jr., a civilian lawyer who was associate special counsel to the Peers investigation, recalled in a telephone interview with this writer in March 2008 that Peers had confided to him that he hoped to become commander of the Eighth Army in South Korea after the My Lai investigation. In order to get such a top-level command post, Peers needed the support of the army chief of staff—Westmoreland himself. Another general had already been named commander of the Eighth Army in the autumn of 1969, weeks before the decision to create the Peers Commission. Peers was, in fact, appointed deputy commander of the Eighth Army in early 1972, reflecting Westmoreland's rewarding of his role in obscuring the relationship between the MACV directives and My Lai. Peers expected to be named to the commanding general when the rotation in command came up in late 1972. But then General Creighton Abrams replaced Westmoreland as army chief of staff in June 1972, before Westmoreland could recommend Peers as commander of the Eighth Army. And Abrams was extremely hostile to the entire Peers investigation, as Peers's legal adviser Walsh told this writer in 2008. So Peers was passed over and took early retirement from the army in 1973, at the age of fifty-nine.[28]

Although the American way of war crimes depended on avoiding explicit written authorization by the command in Vietnam for such wanton killing of civilians, General Creighton Abrams (overall commander of US forces in Vietnam from 1968 to 1972) came very close to committing that policy to a formal document. In a message to commanders on November 23, 1969, Abrams reasoned that the probability of killing or injuring innocent civilians in hamlets situated in "specified strikes zones" was zero by definition.[29] That message made it clear that US forces could not be found guilty of war crimes committed against innocent civilians in any village under long-term Vietcong control.

It is worth noting that the Abrams message went out more than two months after Lieutenant William L. Calley Jr. was charged with the murder of 109 civilians in My Lai, and shortly after newspaper articles began to reveal the extent of the massacre in My Lai.[30] Thus, clear evidence of war crimes by US troops, carrying out the general directive from the US command about treatment of civilians within Vietcong base areas, had absolutely no impact whatever on the readiness of the top US commander in Vietnam to encourage his subordinates to act as though there were no civilians protected by the laws of war in those areas.

The guidance from the US command that civilians in the Vietcong zone were to be treated as no different from military combatants was implemented in part by systematic air and artillery strikes against the entire populated area under Vietcong control. An official directive made public in mid-1966 said that the civilian population was to be warned in advance of any impending air strikes "wherever possible." But in reality, as an army information officer candidly acknowledged to veteran reporter Richard Dudman of the *St. Louis Post-Dispatch*, such warnings were in fact seldom given. The officer explained the military logic of the actual policy: "We give a warning only when we're after something other than personnel, like an enemy ammunition factory, when we don't care whether the people get out or not," said the officer.[31] In other words, most attacks were to be carried out without warning, which would maximize casualties among the civilian population. That policy was in line with the objective of making the Vietcong hamlets uninhabitable.

No specific military justification was required for laying waste to Vietcong population centers. Jonathan Schell's classic account of the US military in the northernmost provinces of South Vietnam, *The Military Half*,[32] reported the policy of the Third Marine Amphibious Force in 1966 and 1967 that a village could be destroyed if the population had provided food to the Vietcong or done any labor on their behalf. The marines understood quite explicitly that they were destroying entire villages as punishment for political support for the enemy. A Vietnamese-language leaflet used by Task Force Oregon in Quang Ngai province, entitled "Marine Ultimatum to Vietnamese People," carried the following statement: "Many Vietnamese have paid with their lives and their homes have been destroyed because they helped the Vietcong in an attempt to enslave the Vietnamese people. Many hamlets have been destroyed because these villages harbored the Vietcong. The hamlets of Hai Mon, Hai Tan, Sa Binh, Tan Binh, and many others have been destroyed because of this. We will not hesitate to destroy every hamlet that helps the Vietcong. . . . "

Another leaflet dropped on villages after they had been bombed said in part, "Your village was bombed because you gave help to the Vietcong in your area." It also said, "Your village was bombed because you gave food to the Vietcong." Schell documents the fact that entire clusters of villages in certain parts of Quang Ngai province were declared to be a zone in which "[n]o one may be in this area except on the road. You may not leave the road inside this area." Failure to heed the warning would expose civilians to being "fired upon," according to the leaflet.[33]

Thus the logic of treating the civilians in free-fire zones as the enemy, which was conveyed by the US command to its units in Task Force Barker, clearly had its origins in the directive on free-fire zones issued by Westmoreland in September 1965. The free-fire zone directive, commanders were given to understand, removed any responsibility for humane treatment of noncombatants in those zones. That understanding, clearly conveyed through private conversations as well as the obvious implications of the authorization to carry out indiscriminate air and artillery attacks on Vietcong hamlets, was the central artifice underlying the American way of war crimes in South Vietnam.

III.

Was the Westmoreland strategy of treating the civilian population in effect as enemy combatants ordered or condoned by the civilian authorities to whom Westmoreland was responsible? More precisely, what did secretary of defense Robert S. McNamara know about the Westmoreland policy, when did he know it, and what did he do about it? Up to now McNamara has not been connected with the American way of war crimes used by the US command to weaken the Vietnamese revolutionary movement. No documentary evidence of involvement by McNamara in the drafting or discussion of the MACV directive creating free-fire zones has come to light.

But that does not end the matter. The scope and impacts of the US assault on the hamlets under Vietcong control was not an obscure question that escaped the notice of the Pentagon. The Department of Defense was intensely interested in the results of indiscriminate use of air and artillery strikes on Vietcong hamlets. In order to determine whether these strikes had been a "success," beginning in 1964 it ordered the RAND Corporation to carry out a "Viet Cong Motivation and Morale" project to gather detailed information on that subject. The project consisted of interviews with Vietcong prisoners of war, defectors, and refugees, designed to gather evidence that could be used to assess the strengths and vulnerabilities of the NLF.[34] Those RAND interviews provide abundant evidence that the bombing and shelling attacks on Vietcong hamlets made life virtually impossible for the civilian population and forced most of them to leave their native villages.

In a monograph on life and politics in the South Vietnamese communist zone, based entirely on the RAND interview transcripts, historian David Hunt writes that they conveyed "a vivid sense of what this bombardment meant to people." He quoted one respondent in a RAND interview as saying, "One can die there any moment, and most of the time one has to live in a shelter. Even while eating, one has to stay near a shelter because of the continued mortar-shelling. I finally could not stand such a life."[35]

Hunt goes on to describe the life reported by these villagers interviewed for the RAND study:

> Wherever they went in the village, peasants needed shelters near at hand, and as a result hours of labor time were devoted to the task of digging trenches. The villagers had to be constantly alert, since survival depended on reacting immediately after the first report of long-range guns, the sound of airplane engines, or even the hiss of falling bombs (B-52s could not be heard at ground level). At the first sound, villagers "ran into hiding, gasping for breath." They had to get used to spending a good part of their existence underground, some even sleeping in subterranean shelters. Eventually they would almost become accustomed to the perpetual crashing of bombs and shells. As one respondent summed up: "The villagers often said: 'Each morning, when we wake up, we don't know whether we are living until we open our eyes.'"[36]

In December 1965, the RAND office in Saigon wrote an analysis based on the interviews conducted during the previous six months. The analysis confirmed that the attacks "often cause more damage and losses to civilians than to the VC . . . " and that fear of the air and artillery attacks was the primary reason civilians were leaving the Vietcong zone for refugee camps. It quoted a "typical refugee" comment: "We were afraid of death. We came to the GVN side because we wanted to live." The authors concluded, "The VC are finding that the popular 'sea' in which they said they must 'swim' in order to win is receding," and that the population exodus was already beginning to weaken its economic base. They recommended that what they carefully referred to as "air and ground harassment of VC forces"—even though it was clearly intended as harassment of the civilian population—be "further intensified."[37]

A preliminary version of the report soon reached the desk of secretary of defense Robert S. McNamara. In secret testimony to the Senate Armed Services Committee in January 1966, McNamara quoted directly from the RAND study to show that the indiscriminate attacks on the Vietcong zone were causing more casualties to civilians than to Vietcong military personnel. When his testimony was sanitized for public release, however, the fact that civilian casualties were greater than the military casualties was deleted, an implicit recognition that such operations would not be regarded as legitimate by those outside the national security bureaucracy. Thus the sentence in the published version of McNamara's testimony read, "The air and artillery attacks often appear to cause [deleted] damage and casualties to the villagers [deleted]. . . ."[38] McNamara then explained clearly how attacks that caused civilian casualties could be very useful to the war effort: "The villagers are primarily concerned with their own survival, and regardless of their attitude toward the GVN they prefer to move where they will be safe from such attacks." McNamara quoted, word for word, the conclusion of the RAND report that the Vietcong were "finding that the popular 'sea' in which they said they must 'swim' in order to win is receding." He noted that the bombing and artillery attacks against Vietcong villages were causing a "noticeable reduction in the manpower available to the VC," as well as threatening "a major deterioration of their economic base." McNamara cited interviews with some Vietcong captives who reported that "their units sometimes went hungry when they were unable to buy food in abandoned villages."[39]

Thus McNamara understood that air and artillery attacks against Vietcong villagers were being carried out systematically, that they were making it impossible for civilians to live normal lives in the Vietcong zone, and were having the effect of depleting the population of that zone. His testimony in January 1966 clearly reflected his approval of the Westmoreland policy of creating free-fire zones—a violation of the laws of war—as a strategy for weakening the Vietcong, and implied that he accepted the recommendation of the

RAND Corporation study that the indiscriminate attacks against civilian centers in the Vietcong zone be "further intensified."

We do not know whether Westmoreland consulted with McNamara about the orders regarding the treatment of the civilian population that were given to the commanders of ground combat units entering Vietcong base areas. Nevertheless, the fact that McNamara was made aware of the consequences of the policy of denying the civilian population of Vietcong zones the protection from air and artillery attacks required by the international laws of war, and that he expressed his enthusiastic assent to that policy in testimony before Congress, provides sufficient evidence of his personal responsibility for the US command's strategy of treating all civilians effectively as enemy combatants.

CHAPTER 7

The Indonesian Domino

Clinton Fernandes

Could the war against Vietnam have ended in 1966? Events in Indonesia certainly made such a scenario plausible. This chapter discusses the geopolitical importance of Indonesia, Western fears of revolutionary social change there, attempts to break up the country, and the destruction of the Indonesian Communist Party, including implications for the war in Vietnam.[1]

The Geopolitical Importance of Indonesia

With its vast natural resources, a population in excess of 250 million (in 2017), and a strategic location along the main sea and air lanes between the Indian and Pacific Oceans, Indonesia is of great geopolitical significance. Military planners in neighboring Australia have long recognized that Indonesia is "of great strategic importance to Australia and constitutes a most important factor in both Australian and regional defence."[2] In the first half of the twentieth century, Indonesia was a Dutch colony known as the Netherlands East Indies. It was occupied by the Japanese during the Pacific phase of World War II.

Immediately after the Japanese surrendered, the Indonesian nationalist leader Sukarno proclaimed independence, on August 17, 1945. His proclamation inspired major uprisings throughout Java. British forces that were supposed to take over from the Japanese encountered fanatical Republican resistance during the Battle of Surabaya in October 1945. Similar defiance confronted the Dutch administration that arrived to retake its former colony. Australia supported Indonesia's independence after World War II despite Dutch objections. The US government tried to persuade the Dutch to grant independence in Indonesia but it did not coerce it; it even watered down an Australian proposal that called for Dutch troops to withdraw from Republican territory.

When the Dutch used force against the independence movement, the Australian government referred the matter to the United Nations Security Council (UNSC) as a "breach of the peace" under Article 39 of the UN Charter. So deeply did the Indonesian nationalist Republican leadership appreciate this support that it nominated Australia as its representative on the UN Good Offices Committee. Indonesia's foreign minister, Dr. Subandrio, described Australia as the "midwife" of the Indonesian Republic.[3] The Australian government's actions were based primarily on its assessment that the era of Dutch colonialism was coming to an end. In addition, key Australian policymakers sympathized with Indonesia's anticolonial nationalist cause. A further consideration was the need to prevent the Communist movement from growing stronger inside Indonesia. The secretary of Australia's External Affairs Department, Dr. John Burton, warned that if Indonesia's Republicans were unsuccessful, then "the Dutch [would] be in the position of finding a Left Wing militant movement which [would] soon gather strength throughout Indonesia." If Australia did not assist in bringing about a settlement, then Indonesia would be "lost to a potentially hostile Republican Left Wing movement. Commercially and in every other way this should be avoided at all costs."[4]

Indonesia won its independence on December 27, 1949, but the fear of a left-wing republican movement was all too real. The new republic had been devastated by years of war, military occupation, and revolution. Its plantations and industries had been damaged and food production could not keep up with population growth. It had a literacy rate of not more than 10 percent.[5] In addition, the new government was forced to "take over the Netherlands Indies debt of 4,300 million guilders, of which 1,291 million guilders . . . was external debt and thus to be repaid in foreign currency."[6] Indonesia's postwar recovery was slow, and non-Indonesian interests controlled important parts of the economy: foreign corporations like Shell, Caltex, and Stanvac dominated the oil industry; Dutch, British, and Chinese interests controlled the banking sector; and Dutch interests controlled inter-island shipping.[7] However, thanks to the Korean War, there was a boom in commodity prices and a consequent increase in Indonesia's export earnings, particularly in its main export of rubber.[8] The new government gave education a high priority. The number of entrants to primary schools rose from 1.7 million to 2.5 million. High schools and university-level institutions sprang up everywhere, especially in Java, and many achieved high standards. The adult literacy rate, which had been 7.4 percent in 1930, shot up to 46.7 percent by 1961.[9]

The problem, as Australian and US strategic planners were beginning to recognize, was that Indonesia had "a strong Communist party with considerable prospects of increasing its popular appeal."[10] The Indonesian Communist Party (PKI) defended the interests of the poor and was rapidly increasing its support among landless peasants. The PKI was allied with the left wing of the Indonesian Nationalist Party (PNI). Under this allied leadership, an organized movement of workers and peasants campaigned to make landlords comply with statutes on land reform and sharecropping. This resulted in violent responses by landlords and several physical clashes between security forces and peasants.[11] The movement supported national liberation movements around the world and called for the nationalization of foreign companies and greater economic equality inside Indonesia.[12]

According to a standard source on the subject, the PKI "had won widespread support not as a revolutionary party but as an organisation defending the interests of the poor within the existing system."[13] The USSR had almost no involvement in Indonesia. In 1958, US Secretary of State Dulles advised the National Security Council—with the "vociferous" agreement of President Eisenhower—that there was no Soviet role in Indonesia.[14] The newly opened Soviet archives have also confirmed, according to Russian Cold War historian Larissa Efimova, that "the USSR in the closing period of [World War II] and in the immediate post-war period had no plans concerning Indonesia, neither in the aspect of its Sovietisation nor imperial aggression."[15] Indonesia and the PKI "remained on the periphery of Soviet foreign policy."[16]

Indonesia's president Sukarno, like many other Third World leaders, was trying to stay out of Cold War alliances led by the US and the USSR. Sukarno called for a conference of "new emerging forces," based on states that had gained their independence after World War II. The Australian government worried that Indonesia was "a leading member of the Afro-Asian bloc. This, together with her appeal to other Asian nations, which arises from her recent struggle against Dutch 'colonialism,' would place her in a position to influence them." It feared that the PKI had "considerable prospects of increasing its popular appeal," and warned that a Communist victory in the elections "would be a considerable blow to Western prestige in South East Asia and would assist in the growth of Communist and neutralist sentiment" throughout the region.[17] The United States agreed, warning that "Indonesia would provide a powerful example for the underdeveloped world and hence a credit to communism and a setback for Western prestige."[18]

The Outer Islands Rebellion

By the mid-1950s Indonesia's nonalignment, coupled with the growing popularity of the PKI, was a matter of serious concern to Western policymakers. US president Dwight Eisenhower asked, "Why the hell did we ever urge the Dutch to get out of Indonesia?"[19] As a consequence, the US and Australia tried to break up Indonesia by encouraging rebellions on the islands of Sumatra and Sulawesi. The US/Australian plan was to exacerbate tensions between these islands and the main island of Java. Since Java was much more heavily populated than the other islands, more consumers lived in Java, even though the Outer Islands contained Indonesia's major sources of revenue, such as oil, rubber, tin, and coconut copra. In the 1950s, a number of foreign-exchange allocation systems favored consumers over producers by maintaining an overvalued rupiah exchange rate. As a consequence, barter trade and smuggling occurred in the export areas of the Outer Islands in order to keep profits there, in defiance of the central government. Key personnel in the army had close ties to regional economic interests and, having played important roles in Sumatra and Sulawesi during the independence struggle, they had a hand in local commercial ventures and operated like warlords in their domains. They also took the lead in organizing smuggling operations.

The central government, in contrast, wanted to strengthen its authority over the regions; so the army commander, General Abdul Haris Nasution, began to reorganize the Indonesian army. In defiance, Colonel Maludin Simbolon, commander of the rich North Sumatran region, announced that North Sumatra had stopped obeying the central government. Similar developments occurred on the island of Sulawesi, where military and political leaders from the north and south gathered in Makassar on March 2, 1957, to declare martial law and sign a Charter of Inclusive Struggle (Piagam Perjuangan Semesta Alam, abbreviated to Permesta). General Nasution prevailed upon President Sukarno to declare martial law on March 14, 1957, giving the military the authority to confront the rebels.

Sensing an opportunity to increase the pressure on Sukarno, the United States began to contemplate fanning the flames of rebellion. A taskforce chaired by Hugh Cumming, the State Department's intelligence chief and former ambassador to Indonesia, presented a submission to the US National

Security Council in September 1957. It argued that the US should "contribute to the establishment of a government able and willing to pursue vigorous anti-communist domestic policies and actions . . . [and consider] . . . exploiting the not inconsiderable potential political resources and economic leverage available in the outer islands, particularly in Sumatra and Sulawesi."[20]

The next month, Australia's foreign minister, Richard Casey, was in Washington for an ANZUS meeting. He met US secretary of state John Foster Dulles and his brother, Central Intelligence Agency (CIA) director Allen Dulles, both of whom shared his hostility to Sukarno. Casey said that recent elections in Java had seen a 20 percent increase in public support for the PKI, and the forthcoming national elections might have a similar effect throughout the archipelago. He therefore suggested that it might be prudent to start thinking about breaking up Indonesia. The CIA director agreed that this had to remain an option, although the first objective was to help provincial leaders defy president Sukarno's policies. By helping provincial leaders in this manner, "Java by itself would become economically non-viable"; and, because Java depended on the Outer Islands for much of its export earnings, the possibility "of pressure being exerted on it by leaders in the outlying areas" would be opened up.[21]

Casey endorsed the CIA's view. In December 1957, Secretary of State Dulles had expressed his desire to "see things to a point where we could plausibly withdraw our recognition of the Sukarno government and give it to the dissident elements on Sumatra."[22] His message was conveyed to the rebels, who understood that they could count on US recognition as soon as they broke with Jakarta. Accordingly, on February 15, 1958, Lieutenant Colonel Ahmad Husein of Sumatra announced the formation of the Revolutionary Government of the Republic of Indonesia (Pemerintah Revolusioner Republik Indonesia, or PRRI). Permesta figures from Sulawesi were enlisted in the PRRI cabinet and became the eastern wing of the rebellion.

The rebels began their military action by arresting several hundred local Communists in Sumatra. They sought to "win American support by emphasizing the communist danger," and were rewarded with a substantial airdrop of American weapons at a Sumatran airfield.[23] But they failed to make decisive progress on the ground. Colonel Maludin Simbolon requested another delivery of weapons, which he received in an airdrop near the American-run Caltex oil fields at Pekanbaru in Central Sumatra. Allen Dulles dispatched the US Navy's Seventh Fleet to Singapore, hoping to give the central government's forces "a bloody nose" if Nasution bombed the Caltex installations.[24]

He intended to justify this direct military intervention on the grounds of protecting US citizens and property.

Australia's foreign minister, Richard Casey, was an enthusiastic supporter of these actions, even if it meant the use of Australian aircraft on bombing operations to support the rebels. The Australian government also made Christmas Island available as a forward base for US submarines engaged in supplying and transporting the rebels, and the Australian Department of Defence deployed ships to stand off the Sumatran shore to provide logistical and medical support to them. Casey urged greater support for the rebellion, advising Prime Minister Menzies that "it is in the interests of the UK government and the West that the dissidents in Sumatra should at the worst be able to make a draw of it," and that "this means considerable support for the dissidents from the West."[25]

However, Nasution's forces made swift work of the rebels in a preemptive strike three days ahead of schedule, moving "with a speed and decisiveness that surprised and bewildered both the PRRI military commanders and the United States."[26] The rebellion could not be saved. Rebel troops fled the scene, leaving the Caltex installations intact. They also left behind boxes filled with US weapons that had been dropped by the CIA a few hours earlier. The boxes were captured by Nasution's forces and shown to the Indonesian public. Soon afterward the Sumatran rebels' weakness was demonstrated to the world when an improvised Indonesian invasion fleet, commanded by General Ahmad Yani, easily recaptured Padang, the center of PRRI strength in West Sumatra. CIA director Allen Dulles was forced to acknowledge that the Sumatran rebels had no stomach for a fight and denied them air cover.

The Sulawesi-based Permesta rebels fought on a little longer, receiving air cover from the so-called Revolutionary Air Force (Angkatan Udara Revolusioner, or AUREV). This air force was a CIA front, with aircraft piloted by Taiwanese, Polish, Filipino, and American personnel. It started its campaign by bombing the Makassar and Balikpapan airfields, followed by Ternate, Jailolo, Morotai (in Maluku), and central Sulawesi. Permesta forces occupied Morotai, securing an airstrip from World War II that was long enough to accommodate B-29 long-range bombers. Ambon Harbor, commercial shipping vessels, and central government installations and warships were repeatedly attacked. But the whole operation came unstuck when a rebel aircraft carrying out a bombing raid against Ambon was shot down and its American pilot, Allen Lawrence Pope, was captured alive. Pope was carrying US military identification papers and substantial evidence of his previous bombing missions, leaving no room for US denials. The US and Australia immediately wound up operations in support of the rebellion.

The Indonesian military had demonstrated its strength by crushing the Outer Islands rebellion. The US ruefully concluded that it would have to find another solution to the problem of Indonesia's president. It therefore decided to develop closer links with the Indonesian military, providing it with limited military aid in order to sustain anticommunist elements in the officer corps. So began the strong US and Australian support of the Indonesian military.

The Indonesian Communist Party

The PKI opposed the US war in Vietnam and supported national liberation movements around the world. The influence of the PKI continued to increase: its members began to hold a range of bureaucratic and political posts. From 1957, several cities on Java had communist mayors, and several provincial governors were close to the party. However, the PKI and the left wing of the Indonesian Nationalist Party did not occupy any but the most symbolic positions in cabinet. Control over the productive capacity of the economy rested in the hands of senior bureaucrats and military officers who did not support Sukarno's economic program. It was they, not the PKI, who implemented strategic economic decisions.

Between 1960 and 1965, the PKI and its allied peasant organizations began to carry out a program of land seizures in order to make landlords comply with existing laws. These actions resulted in violent responses by landlords and fights between security forces and peasants. Mass mobilizations began to increase very rapidly, with large protests in the main cities and a growing number of smaller protests in towns and villages. The party also took up the cause of plantation and industrial workers in North Sumatra, and of Javanese migrants in North and South Sumatra. It supported Hindus against East Javanese orthodox Muslims who were members of the local elite, as well as opponents of the Hindu priestly authority in Bali. All this grassroots activity contributed to a substantial increase in the membership of the PKI and the left wing of the Indonesian Nationalist Party.

By 1965, the PKI had three million members and was said to be the largest communist party in the world outside the Soviet Union and China. In addition to its vast membership, more than 15 million people had indirect connections to it through their membership in the peasant associations, labor unions, and other affiliates. According to US intelligence assessments at the time, the PKI was by far the best organized and most dynamic political entity in Indonesia. Within a few months, it would be destroyed by the Indonesian military and right-wing Islamic organizations in a cataclysmic act of terror and mass murder.

The PKI was opposed by sections of the commercial and land-owning establishment, senior figures in the bureaucratic apparatus, a number of right-wing intellectuals and students, and several smaller Islamic parties. Crucially, this conservative alliance was backed by the powerful Indonesian military. The divisions in Indonesian society found expression inside the military, and—although there were important left-wing and populist forces within the army—the right was always stronger. Indeed, the army had demonstrated its power and anticommunist credentials in 1948, when it put down an uprising supported by the PKI in the Madiun region of Central Java. In subsequent years, particularly from 1962 to 1965, there were increasingly intense internal struggles between left-wing populists and right-wing forces within the military.

Western intelligence analysts turned their attention to Sukarno, describing him as an "intuitive politician" and a "mass leader of extraordinary skill." US State Department analysts believed that Sukarno operated according to "opportunistic, play-it-by-ear policies" rather than by a long-range fixed plan. The CIA concluded that his "Marxist inclinations" were "largely emotionally based," and characterized his relationship with the communists as one of "mutual exploitation."[27] Sukarno needed the PKI because he lacked a mass political organization of his own; the PKI needed Sukarno for protection against the army. The army saw Sukarno as the best person to hold the far-flung and diverse parts of Indonesia together, while Sukarno used the army to counterbalance the PKI.

Indonesia's poor economic performance under military management was compounded by the fact that sales of rubber, its major export earner, were shrinking as a result of competition from synthetic alternatives. Indonesia was therefore deprived of an important source of foreign currency. Despite the economic problems, an influential US assessment acknowledged the country's "resilience to economic adversity" because "over half the population live outside the monetized sector of the economy as self-sufficient farmers." As for the Indonesian government, it "occupies a dominant position in basic industry, public utilities, internal transportation and communication." The US believed that, if the drift toward PKI dominance continued,

> [it] is probable that private ownership will disappear and may be succeeded
> by some form of production-profit-sharing contract arrangements to be

applied to all foreign investment. . . . The avowed Indonesian objective is "to stand on their own feet" in developing their economy, free from foreign, especially Western, influence.[28]

The US decided to reduce its visibility "so that those opposed to the communists and extremists may be free to handle a confrontation, which they believe will come, without the incubus of being attacked as defenders of the neo-colonialists and imperialists." It realized that any attempt to foment military rebellion along the lines of 1958 would fail because "the ideal of national unity is an overriding obsession with practically all Indonesians, stronger by far than any real divisive regional feeling."[29]

Tensions within a now thoroughly polarized Indonesian society continued to build until they exploded into open conflict in the early morning of October 1, 1965, when a small number of middle-ranking, left-wing army officers staged a mutiny. They may have been trying to prevent a coup by a right-wing council of generals. The mutineers killed six generals and a lieutenant but failed to arrest key generals, including Major General Suharto, who was commander of the Army's Strategic Reserve Command. Suharto had long been a personal friend and professional colleague of two of the key mutineers, Lieutenant Colonel Untung and Colonel Latief. There are good reasons to believe that Suharto had been forewarned about the mutiny. The mutiny did not appear to have been planned in much detail: no serious measures were taken to seize choke points in the capital; the worker and peasant movements had been given no forewarning, and most of them were caught unaware; the PKI did not try to mobilize its massive party membership.

According to a US clandestine source, the PKI central committee reacted only after hearing the mutineers' radio broadcast. Sir Andrew Gilchrist, the British ambassador, also suspected that the PKI had not been kept in the loop, joining in only "because they feared that if the army crushed Untung it would crush them as well." The Australian Joint Intelligence Committee noted that, while individual Communist groups clearly participated in the mutiny, "evidence of actual PKI involvement—that is, of prior planning by the Central Committee—is largely circumstantial."[30]

The Destruction of the PKI

The Indonesian military moved swiftly and decisively. It arrested PKI members and took control of the media, using Radio Indonesia and the Antara news agency to encourage anti-PKI action. A major theme in its propaganda campaign was the murder of the six Indonesian generals who, it was claimed, had been tortured and had their genitals cut off by members of the PKI-affiliated women's organization Gerwani. Members of Pemuda Rakyat, the PKI's youth organization, were alleged to have kidnapped two youths in Sumatra and tortured them for five days, removing their eyes and cutting off their hands and testicles before killing them, and to have tortured and murdered Muslims praying on the bank of a river. Other extremely successful propaganda stories alleged that PKI leader Aidit had encouraged Gerwani and Pemuda Rakyat members to take part in sexual orgies. Major General Suharto said that "it was obvious for those of us who saw [the bodies] with our own eyes what savage tortures had been inflicted by the barbarous adventurers calling themselves The September 30th Movement."[31]

The events, as noted above, actually occurred on October 1, not September 30. But the expression Gestapu (Gerakan September Tigapuluh, or G30S) was always used, in a deliberate allusion to the Gestapo of Nazi Germany. According to autopsies ordered personally by Major General Suharto, these stories were false; none of the victims' eyes had been gouged out, and their penises were intact. Sukarno and his foreign minister Subandrio tried to inform the public that the post-mortem certificates had not mentioned any abnormalities, but the army was firmly in command of the media and these messages did not get through. The propaganda continued unabated.

Full-scale massacres of PKI members across the Indonesian archipelago occurred when special forces or paratroops went into the regions. These soldiers participated in the killings, but more frequently used local militias to liquidate suspected PKI sympathizers. Local military units made it clear that they wanted to annihilate the PKI, and they provided weapons, equipment, training, and encouragement to youth organizations such as the Muslim Ansor in Central and East Java. These groups usually went from village to village, grabbing PKI members and taking them away to be murdered. In some cases, entire villages were obliterated, but more typically the killers used hit lists and local informants to identify their victims. US embassy officials compiled these lists and handed them over to the Indonesian military. While these kinds of lists were based entirely on previous reporting by the Communist press, they proved invaluable to the military, which seemed "to lack even the simplest overt information on PKI leadership at the time."[32]

When an Indonesian general secretly approached the US embassy to ask for assistance in the army's operations against the PKI, Marshall Green advised the state department that "we should do what we can as soon as we can, to meet request for medical supplies." As for the army's requests for small arms, Green said that he "would be leery about telling army we are in position to provide same, although we should act, not close our minds to this possibility. . . . We could explore availability of small arms stocks, preferable of non-US origin, which could, if necessary, provide covert assistance to army for purchase of weapons."[33]

Green also authorized the provision of 50 million rupiahs to assist the crackdown. Overall, the US provided the Indonesian army with money, medicines, communications equipment, weapons, and intelligence. It was satisfied with the return it received on this investment.

According to Helen-Louise Hunter, an analyst in the CIA's Directorate of Intelligence at the time of these events:

> The massive purge of the Indonesian Communist Party organisation, following the coup, in which thousands of people lost their lives was one of the ghastliest and most concentrated bloodlettings of current times. . . . While there may never be an exact figure of the numbers dead, the anti-PKI massacres in Indonesia rank as one of the worst mass murders of the twentieth century, along with the Soviet purges of the 1930s, the Nazi mass murders during the Second World War, and the Maoist bloodbath of the early 1950s.[34]

Once the killings were under way, Western policymakers and diplomats were keen to support the Indonesian army. The problem they faced was that President Sukarno's anti-imperialist rhetoric had resonated strongly with the Indonesian public. Any overt support would therefore serve only to expose the army as a tool of the West. Sukarno's towering reputation presented a significant obstacle. A deft touch was required. US ambassador Marshall Green understood that economic aid should not be offered, because economic difficulties hurt the reputation of the civilian administration, not the army. His military contacts told him that there was an urgent need for food and clothing in Indonesia, but it was more important to let Sukarno and Subandrio "stew in their own juice."[35] The information campaign in support of the killings was informed by similar principles. The Indonesian army secretly urged that foreign broadcasts not give the army "too much credit" or criticize Sukarno; rather, they should emphasize PKI atrocities and the party's role in the mutiny. While Sukarno could not be directly attacked, an Indonesian general offered to send background information on foreign minister Subandrio, who was regarded as more vulnerable.

Australian ambassador Keith Shann was told that Radio Australia should never suggest that the army was pro-Western or right wing. Instead, credit should be given to other organizations, such as Muslim and youth groups. Radio Australia had an important role to play because of its high signal strength and huge listening audience. Its listeners included the elite as well as Indonesian students, who liked it because it played rock music, which had been officially banned. The station was therefore told to "be on guard against giving information to the Indonesian people that would be withheld by the Army-controlled internal media." The Australian ambassador worked to ensure that it gave "prominent coverage" to "reports of PKI involvement and Communist Chinese complicity" while playing down or not broadcasting "reports of divisions within the army specifically, and armed services more generally." Another senior official recommended that Radio Australia "not do anything which would be helpful to the PKI"; rather, it "should highlight reports tending to discredit the PKI and show its involvement in the losing cause."[36]

The US, Britain, and Australia cooperated closely in the propaganda effort. US ambassador Marshall Green urged Washington to "spread the story of PKI's guilt, treachery, and brutality," adding that this was "perhaps the most needed immediate assistance we can give the army if we can find [a] way to do it without identifying it as [a] sole or largely US effort." The British Foreign Office hoped to "encourage anticommunist Indonesians to more vigorous action in the hope of crushing communism in Indonesia altogether," and sought to emphasize the PKI's brutality in murdering generals and families, its dependence on arms shipments from China, and its role in subverting Indonesia in the interests of foreign communists.[37] British ambassador Sir Andrew Gilchrist wrote: "I have never concealed . . . my belief that a little shooting in Indonesia would be an essential preliminary to effective change."[38] Throughout this period, Western radio stations continued to recycle stories from Radio Jakarta or the army newspapers and broadcast them back to Indonesia.

The New Order

On February 21, 1966, Sukarno tried to reshuffle his cabinet and sack General Nasution as defense minister, but, with the public cowed and in fear of the killings, the attempt to reassert his authority failed. There were large demonstrations backed by the army, and on March 11, 1966, armed troops mounted a show of force outside the presidential palace, pressuring Sukarno to hand over executive power to General Suharto. In retirement, Sukarno continued to defend the PKI and to campaign against the massacres and anti-Chinese racism. Without access to the media, however, his speeches failed to achieve political traction.

The best account of this episode notes that the killings saw the rise to power "of people who viewed massacres and psychological warfare operations as legitimate and normal modes of governance."[39] By March 1966, Suharto had obtained key political and military powers and become head of the armed forces. A year later, he was installed as acting president. Australia's minister for External Affairs, Paul Hasluck, secretly called for financial and political support for Suharto. The Australian prime minister shared his view, telling the River Club of New York City that "with 500,000 to 1,000,000 Communist sympathizers knocked off, I think it is safe to assume a reorientation has taken place."[40]

Known as the Orde Baru, or New Order, the Suharto regime shut down Indonesia's preeminent cultural and intellectual organizations, such as the Peoples' Cultural Institute, the National Cultural Institute, and the Indonesian Scholars' Association. It arrested many of those organizations' members and handed control of the universities, newspapers, and cultural institutions to conservative writers and intellectuals. The Armed Forces History Center rewrote Indonesian history by ensuring that textbooks and films reflected official perspectives. Ordinary men and women from all walks of life who had played a part in winning independence from the Dutch were written out of history. Instead, Indonesian military personnel were depicted as the alleged heroes of independence.

Along with the violence, certain cultural values were strongly promoted: discussion of personal, religious, and consumerist issues was encouraged, while discussion of politics was considered to be in bad taste. The conservative establishment also monopolized Indonesia's external cultural relations.

The Extinction of Political Activity at the Village Level

All trade union activity was frozen for several years. The PKI was physically annihilated, and popular organizations associated with it were suppressed. More than one and a half million Indonesians passed through a system of prisons and prison camps. The whole of Indonesian society was forcibly depoliticized. In village after village, bureaucrats backed by the army imposed a control matrix of permits, rules, and regulations. Citizens were required to obtain a "letter of clean circumstances," certifying that they and their extended families had not been associated with the left before 1965.

A new level of command, the KORAMIL (military subdistrict command), was established after 1965 in Central and Eastern Java, which were regarded as having the most number of PKI sympathizers. KORAMILs soon became an integral part of the Indonesian military's structure. The only political activity permitted at the village level was voting—only at election time and only for regime-approved parties. Accordingly, the regime combined four Muslim parties into a single United Development Party (Partai Persatuan Pembangunan, or PPP), and five non-Muslim parties into a single Indonesian Democratic Party (Partai Demokrasi Indonesia, or PDI). The regime-backed organization GOLKAR (Sekretariat Bersama Golongan Karya or Joint Secretariat of Functional Groups) comfortably won the 1971 elections, securing 236 of the 360 elected seats in the 460-member lower house of the legislature. The remaining 100 members were mainly army officers who were directly appointed by President Suharto. Membership of the 920-seat People's Consultative Assembly was even more heavily dominated by GOLKAR and the Indonesian military.

The Suharto regime adopted an antidemocratic political ideology known as Organicism, which holds that the state and society form an organic unity. There was no room in this ideology for political competition or a democratic opposition. Organicism had been influential among Indonesian legal scholars who drafted the constitution in 1945. They had been influenced by anti-Enlightenment Dutch orientalism, Japanese protofascism, and elitist Javanese political thought.[41] Under Suharto, Organicism was revived in full measure. Accompanying it was a political concept known as the "floating mass," whereby "people in the villages" were not to "spend their valuable time and energy in the political struggles of parties and groups" but rather to "be occupied wholly with development efforts." Accordingly, the people were a "floating mass" who "are not permanently tied to membership of any political party."[42]

The Implications for Vietnam

Suharto had shown that he could defeat a strong peasant movement even as American forces were being confronted with a popular peasant resistance in Vietnam. Suharto therefore earned the immediate support of the US, which was making every effort to create loyal, capitalistically prosperous, authoritarian, and anticommunist regimes—typically, but not invariably, dominated by the military. McGeorge Bundy, the US national security advisor for presidents Kennedy and Johnson, and one of the main architects of the Vietnam

War, later said that the anticommunist purges in Indonesia had achieved the broader objective of preventing independent economic nationalism in the region. While Vietnam may have seemed "vital" until 1965, he said, "at least from the time of the anticommunist revolution in Indonesia, late in 1965, that adjective was excessive, and so also was our effort."[43] In other words, the US should have terminated its war in Vietnam after the Indonesian massacres, because it was no longer necessary.

The rationale was based on the so-called domino theory. President Johnson "frequently told visitors to the White House that if we did not take our stand in Vietnam, one day we would have to make our stand in Hawaii." Leaders of the domino countries—Malaysia, Singapore, Thailand, and others—reportedly "privately told the American government that it was vital for the United States to stay the course in Vietnam so as to save them from being crushed between China and Indonesia." But "the arms of the nutcracker fell off" as a result of the Indonesian massacres. US defense secretary Clark Clifford "toured Asia and found that the domino leaders were no longer vitally concerned about Vietnam."[44]

The Truth of the Domino Theory

It is a commonplace today to scoff at this "domino theory," but it contained an important element of truth; national independence and social transformation may well have spread from one subjugated people to another. If the Vietminh were successful, then the military leadership of neighboring Thailand would fear that they had lost the West's willingness and ability to help them stave off revolutionary social change or to counter a domestic insurgency. Thailand's military leadership had collaborated with the Japanese during World War II to such an extent that they even declared war on the United States and Great Britain. It was the only country in Southeast Asia to have done so.[45] The Japanese collaborator, Phibun Songkhram, had overthrown the government of Thailand in April 1948 after his failure in the elections. The US supported him, helping him become the "first pro-Axis dictator to regain power after the war," according to Frank Darling, a CIA expert on Thailand. The Thai dictatorship established a police state and proceeded to enrich themselves. They "took over the directorships of banks, private companies, and government corporations, and they diverted large amounts of public funds to themselves." The police chief "derived most of his funds from the opium trade; while the army chief collared the profits of the national lottery."[46] But the dictatorship was willing to serve Western strategic interests, open its economy to Western economic interests, and allow its soil and military personnel to be used to suppress Southeast Asian nationalism.

Australia sent a RAAF Sabre jet fighter squadron to Ubon in Thailand as part of its Vietnam commitment. Australian troops fought alongside members of the Thai Volunteer Force in South Vietnam as well. Like Australia, Thailand was a member of the South East Asia Treaty Organization (SEATO), whose headquarters were in Bangkok, and many thousands of Royal Thai Armed Forces personnel received education and training programs coordinated by the Australian Defence Force. Australian strategic planners recognized that Thailand "provides the Allies with bases from which to operate against the Communists on the mainland of South East Asia, and has interior lines of communications and port facilities of limited capacity."[47] Australia's support for Thailand was of a piece with its objective in Southeast Asia: the establishment of Western-oriented regimes that would cooperate economically and politically with the West.

The objective was the reinforcement of local rulers who would protect freedom and stability of a particular kind—economic freedom, which means the freedom of businesses to invest and repatriate profits, and investment stability, which means a political and military order that ensures a stable climate for business operations and affords access to human and material resources. Development was acceptable only under Western terms. Australia's minister for external affairs, Percy Spender, proposed a "Colombo Plan" for foreign aid to keep anticommunist regimes in power while ensuring that South and Southeast Asia would make "a substantial contribution towards solution of the dollar problem by way either of direct dollar earnings or replacement of supplies on which the sterling area and Western Europe are dependent."[48] Developing countries must not undertake national liberation along Chinese lines, removing themselves from the global economy in order to focus on internal needs, and mobilizing material and human resources for domestic improvement. The Colombo Plan was not a humanitarian program but an instrument of anticommunist statecraft, designed to prevent revolutionary change in places like South Vietnam, the Philippines, and Thailand. The Australian Security Intelligence Organization trained the Thai police in antisubversive techniques under the Colombo Plan budget. According to a detailed study of the Colombo Plan:

> By October 1955, training was well underway and state police departments expressed a willingness to participate in a much larger program . . .

A complete record of the number who undertook these courses does not exist, but there is direct evidence of security training of Asian officials taking place in Australia. One notable trainee was Tran Van Khiem, ex–press secretary to the President of Vietnam, who completed four months of training in the period 1955–56 with ASIO and the Victorian and New South Wales police on a Colombo Plan scholarship. He was trained in security methods that he hoped would provide him with the skills to "cope with the terrorist war in Saigon."[49]

Likewise, in the next domino of Malaysia, the Australian Defence Committee's paper noted that there was "no possible land threat to the mainland of Australia" and that "the external threat to Malaya from Chinese armies operating over long and difficult lines of communications is not likely to be very great."[50] The Australian Chiefs of Staff Committee said in 1950 that for the next decade, "neither the Soviet nor the Chinese communists are likely to be able to mount a seaborne invasion of Australia."[51] And yet policymakers repeatedly expressed their fears about military threats emanating from precisely these places. There is a systematic aspect to the threats that are claimed to exist. They approximate in quite predictable fashion to the roles played by various actors in maintaining a benign international environment for Western capital to operate with relative freedom. As such, these threat constructions served as a convenient explanatory framework to justify wars with economic motives—otherwise, popular support might not be forthcoming.

It was not that Malaya or Thailand would be invaded or even heavily infiltrated by outside Communist forces but that local forces would be emboldened to overthrow local dictators' systems on which triangular trade depended. Malaya had gained independence on August 31, 1957. The first prime minister, Tunku Abdul Rahman, led the United Malays National Organisation (UMNO) with a cabinet consisting of Malay aristocrats and Chinese business leaders. The Cambridge-educated Tunku was a member of the royal family in Kedah Sultanate. A law student who had failed the English bar exams, he returned home and joined the Kedah Civil Service. He later served the Japanese Military Administration during its occupation of Malaya. As a member of the Malay aristocracy, he ensured that an independent Malaysia did not threaten Britain's economic interests in the country. Even a decade after independence, less than one-tenth of the labor force was employed in the manufacturing sector. In the mid-1970s, 67 percent of directors in Malaysia's top 100 companies were still non-Malaysian, and 30 percent were British. Economist Lim Mah Hui remarked that Malaysia's political independence came "without substantive economic independence. Politicians find themselves unable to meaningfully determine the level of employment or unemployment, to change the distribution of income, to determine the types of investment or to use societal resources the way they want to in their own society. The making of Malaysia allowed Britain to transfer political power while retaining its economic power."[52]

The Anglophile, racehorse-owning Tunku, who was willing to preserve Britain's dominance of Malaysia's economy, was no threat to this objective. Neither were the Thai generals, Indonesia's General Suharto, or Vietnam's Bao Dai and Ngô Dinh Diem. All of them were willing to accept their countries' subordinate roles in the global economy and to protect the freedom of foreign businesses to invest and repatriate profits. Global South leaders who rejected these functions were threatening. In foreign affairs, "benign" and "hostile" reflect the central importance of economic interests. Such a policy could hardly be stated quite so cynically. It was recast in terms of threat—a vast Communist movement bent on world conquest, in which indigenous forces were ultimately the forward elements of an international communist wave.

For these reasons, as this chapter has shown, the destruction of the Indonesian Communist Party terminated the prospect of revolutionary social transformation in Southeast Asia. As US defense secretary McNamara said in 1967, "To the extent that our original intervention and our existing actions in Vietnam were motivated by the perceived need to draw the line against Chinese expansionism in Asia, our objective has already been attained."[53]

CHAPTER 8

"So Many People Died": The American System of Suffering, 1965–2014

Nick Turse

Pham To looked great for seventy-eight years old. (At least, that's about how old he thought he was.) His hair was thin, gray, and receding at the temples, but his eyes were lively and his physique robust—all the more remarkable given what he had lived through. I listened intently, as I had so many times before to so many similar stories, but it was still beyond my ability to comprehend. It's probably beyond yours, too.

Pham To told me that the planes began their bombing runs in 1965 and that periodic artillery shelling started about the same time. Nobody will ever know just how many civilians were killed in the years after that. "The number is uncountable," he said one spring day a few years ago in a village in the mountains of rural central Vietnam. "So many people died."

And it only got worse. Chemical defoliants came next, ravaging the land. Helicopter machine gunners began firing on locals. By 1969, bombing and shelling were day-and-night occurrences. Many villagers fled. Some headed further into the mountains, trading the terror of imminent death for a daily struggle of hardscrabble privation; others were forced into squalid refugee resettlement areas. Those who remained in the village suffered more when the troops came through. Homes were burned as a matter of course. People were kicked and beaten. Men were shot when they ran in fear. Women were raped. One morning, a massacre by American soldiers wiped out twenty-one fellow villagers. This was the Vietnam War for Pham To, as for so many rural Vietnamese.

One, Two ... Many Vietnams?

At the beginning of the Iraq War, and for years after, reporters, pundits, veterans, politicians, and ordinary Americans asked whether the American debacle in Southeast Asia was being repeated. Would it be "another Vietnam"? Would it become a "quagmire"?[1]

The same held true for Afghanistan. Years after 9/11, as that war, too, foundered, questions about whether it was "Obama's Vietnam" appeared ever more frequently.[2] In fact, by October 2009, a majority of Americans had come to believe it was "turning into another Vietnam."[3]

In those years, "Vietnam" even proved a surprisingly two-sided analogy—after, at least, generals began reading and citing revisionist texts about that war.[4] These claimed, despite all appearances, that the US military had actually won in Vietnam (before the politicians, media, and antiwar movement gave the gains away). The same winning formula, they insisted, could be used to triumph again. And so, a failed solution from that failed war, counterinsurgency, or COIN, was trotted out as the military panacea for impending disaster.

Debated comparisons between the two ongoing wars and the one that somehow never went away came to litter newspapers, journals, magazines, and the internet—until David Petraeus, a top COINdinista general who had written his doctoral dissertation on the "lessons" of the Vietnam War, was called in to settle the matter by putting those lessons to work winning the other two.[5] In the end, of course, US troops were booted out of Iraq, while the war in Afghanistan continues to this day as a dismally devolving stalemate, now wracked by "green-on-blue" or "insider" attacks on US forces, while the general himself returned to Washington as CIA director to run covert wars in Pakistan and Yemen before retiring in disgrace following a sex scandal.[6]

Still, for all the ink about the "Vietnam analogy," virtually none of the reporters, pundits, historians, generals, politicians, or other members of the chattering classes ever so much as mentioned the Vietnam War as Pham To knew it.[7] In that way, they managed to miss the one unfailing parallel between America's wars in all three places: civilian suffering.

For all the dissimilarities, botched analogies, and tortured comparisons, there has been one connecting thread in Washington's foreign wars of the last half century that, in recent years at least, Americans have seldom found of the slightest interest: misery for local nationals. Civilian suffering is, in fact, the defining characteristic of modern war in general, even if only rarely discussed in the halls of power or the mainstream media.[8]

An Unimaginable Toll

Pham To was lucky. He and Pham Thang, another victim and a neighbor, told me that, of the two thousand people living in their village before the war, only three hundred survived it. Bombing, shelling, a massacre, disease, and starvation had come close to wiping out their entire settlement. "So many people were hungry," Pham Thang said. "With no food, many died. Others were sick, and with medications unavailable, they died, too. Then there was the bombing and shelling, which took still more lives. They all died because of the war."

Leaving aside those who perished from disease, hunger, or lack of medical care, at least 3.8 million Vietnamese died violent war deaths, according to researchers from Harvard Medical School and the University of Washington. The best estimate we have is that 2 million of them were civilians. Using a very conservative extrapolation, this suggests that 5.3 million civilians were wounded during the war, for a total of 7.3 million Vietnamese civilian casualties overall. To such figures might be added an estimated 11.7 million Vietnamese forced from their homes and turned into refugees, up to 4.8 million sprayed with toxic herbicides like Agent Orange, an estimated 800,000 to 1.3 million war orphans, and 1 million war widows.[9]

The numbers are staggering, the suffering incalculable, the misery almost incomprehensible to most Americans but not, perhaps, to an Iraqi.

No one will ever know just how many Iraqis died in the wake of the US invasion of 2003. In a country with an estimated population of about 25 million at the time, a much-debated survey—the results of which were published in the British medical journal *The Lancet*—suggested more than 601,000 violent "excess deaths" had occurred by 2006.[10] Another survey indicated that more than 1.2 million Iraqi civilians had died because of the war (and the various internal conflicts that flowed from it) as of 2007.[11] The Associated Press tallied up records of 110,600 deaths by early 2009.[12] An Iraqi family health survey fixed the number at 151,000 violent deaths by June 2006.[13] Official documents made public by Wikileaks counted 109,000 deaths, including 66,081 civilian deaths, between 2004 and 2009. Iraq Body Count has tallied as many as 121,220 documented cases of violent civilian deaths alone.[14]

Then there are those 3.2 million Iraqis who were internally displaced or fled the violence to other lands, only to find uncertainty and deprivation in places like Jordan, Iran, and now war-torn Syria.[15] By 2011, 9 percent or more of Iraq's women, as many as 1 million, were widows (a number that skyrocketed in the years after the US invasion).[16] A recent survey found that 800,000 to 1 million Iraqi children had lost one or both parents, a figure that only grows with the continuing violence that the United States unleashed but never stamped out.[17]

Today, the country, which experienced an enormous brain drain of professionals, has a total of two hundred social workers and psychiatrists to aid all those, armed and unarmed, who suffered every sort of horror and trauma.[18] (In just the last seven years, by comparison, the US Veterans Administration has hired seven thousand new mental health professionals to deal with Americans who have been psychologically scarred by war.[19])

Many Afghans, too, would surely be able to relate to what Pham To and millions of Vietnamese war victims endured. For more than thirty years, Afghanistan has, with the rarest of exceptions, been at war. It all started with the 1979 Soviet invasion and Washington's support for some of the most extreme of the Islamic militants who opposed the Russian occupation of the country.[20]

The latest iteration of war there began with an invasion by US and allied forces in 2001, and has since claimed the lives of many thousands of civilians in roadside and aerial bombings, suicide attacks and helicopter attacks, night raids, and outright massacres.[21] Untold numbers of Afghans have also died of everything from lack of access to medical care (there are just two doctors for every ten thousand Afghans) to exposure, including shocking reports of children freezing to death in refugee camps last winter and again this year.[22] They were among the hundreds of thousands of Afghans who have been internally displaced during the war. Millions more live as refugees outside the country, mostly in Iran and Pakistan.[23] Of the women who remain in the country, up to 2 million are widows.[24] In addition, there are now an estimated 2 million Afghan orphans.[25] No wonder polling by Gallup this past summer found 96 percent of Afghans claiming they were either "suffering" or "struggling," and just 4 percent "thriving."[26]

American Refugees in Mexico?

For most Americans, this type of unrelenting, war-related misery is unfathomable. Few have ever personally experienced anything like what their tax dollars have wrought in Southeast Asia, the Middle East, and Southwest Asia in the last half-century. And while surprising numbers of Americans do suffer from poverty and deprivation, few know anything about what it's like to live through a year of war—let alone ten, as Pham To did —under the constant threat of air strikes, artillery fire, and violence perpetrated by foreign ground troops.[27]

Still, as a simple thought experiment, let's consider for a moment what it might be like in American terms. Imagine that the United States had experienced an occupation by a foreign military force. Imagine millions or even tens of millions of American civilians dead or wounded as a result of an invasion and resulting civil strife. Imagine a country in which your door might be kicked down in the dead of night by heavily armed, foreign young men in strange uniforms, helmets, and imposing body armor, yelling things in a language you don't understand. Imagine them rifling through your drawers, upending your furniture, holding you at gunpoint, roughing up your husband or son or brother, and marching him off in the middle of the night.

Imagine, as well, a country in which those foreigners kill American "insurgents" and then routinely strip them naked; in which those occupying troops sometimes urinate on American bodies (and shoot videos of it); or take trophy photos of their "kills"; or mutilate them; or pose with the body parts of dead Americans; or from time to time—for reasons again beyond your comprehension—rape or murder your friends and neighbors.[28]

Imagine, for a moment, violence so extreme that you and literally millions like you have to flee your hometowns for squalid refugee camps or expanding slums ringing the nearest cities. Imagine trading your home for a new one without heat or electricity, possibly made of refuse with a corrugated metal roof that roars when it rains. Then imagine living there for months, if not years.

Imagine things getting so bad that you decide to trek across the Mexican border to live an uncertain life, forever wondering if your new violence- and poverty-wracked host nation will turn you out or if you'll ever be able to return to your home in the United States.[29] Imagine living with these realities day after day for up to a decade.

After natural disasters like Hurricane Sandy or Katrina, small numbers of Americans briefly experience something like what millions of war victims—Vietnamese, Iraqis, Afghans, and others—have often had to endure for significant parts of their lives. But for those in America's war zones, there will be no telethons, benefit concerts, or texting fund drives.[30]

Pham To and Pham Thang had to bury the bodies of their family members, friends, and neighbors after they were massacred by American troops passing through their village on patrol. They had to rebuild their homes and their lives after the war with remarkably little help. One thing was as certain for them as it has been for war-traumatized Iraqis and Afghans of our moment: no Hollywood luminaries lined up to help raise funds for them or their village. And they never will.

"We lost so many people and so much else. And this land was affected by Agent Orange, too. You've come to write about the war, but you could never know the whole story," Pham Thang told me. Then he became circumspect. "Now, our two governments, our two countries, live in peace and harmony. And we just want to restore life to what it once was here. We suffered great losses. The US government should offer assistance to help increase the local standard of living, provide better healthcare, and build infrastructure like better roads."

No doubt—despite the last decade of US nation-building debacles in its war zones—many Iraqis and Afghans would express similar sentiments.[31] Perhaps they will even be saying the same sort of thing to an American reporter decades from now.

Over these last years, I've interviewed hundreds of war victims like Pham Thang, and he's right: I'll probably never come close to knowing what life was like for those whose worlds were upended by America's foreign wars. And I'm far from alone. Most Americans never make it to a war zone, and even US military personnel arrive only for finite tours of duty, while for combat correspondents and aid workers an exit door generally remains open. Civilians like Pham To, however, are in it for the duration.

In the Vietnam years, there was at least an antiwar movement in this country that included many Vietnam veterans who made genuine efforts to highlight the civilian suffering they knew was going on at almost unimaginable levels.[32] In contrast, in the decade-plus since 9/11, with the rarest of exceptions, Americans have remained remarkably detached from their distant wars, thoroughly ignoring what can be known about the suffering that has been caused in their name.[33]

As I was wrapping up my interview, Pham Thang asked me about the purpose of the last hour and a half of questions I'd asked him. Through my interpreter, I explained that most Americans knew next to nothing about Vietnamese suffering during the war and that most books written in my country on the war years ignored it. I wanted, I told him, to offer Americans the chance to hear about the experiences of ordinary Vietnamese for the first time.

"If the American people know about these incidents, if they learn about the wartime suffering of people in Vietnam, do you think they will sympathize?" he asked me.

Soon enough, I should finally know the answer to his question.

CHAPTER 9

Bloodbaths in Indochina: Constructive, Nefarious, and Mythical (1979)

Noam Chomsky and Edward S. Herman

The sheer scope and intensity of the violence imposed on Indochina by the US war machine forced a great deal of information into the public domain and consciousness. The public was, nevertheless, spared a full picture of the war's true nature, and was kept in a state of confusion by a steady flow of allegations of enemy terror, assertions of Washington's benevolent intentions, and the pretense that the enormous destruction of the civil societies of Indochina resulted from the fact that "war inevitably hurts many innocent people." Enough got through the propaganda filter, however, to open many eyes to the ugly reality and to shatter the complacent faith of large numbers of Americans in the competence, humanity, and integrity of their leaders.

In reconstructing the faith it has been necessary to expunge from many memories the brutalities and lies of the war, and to transform the historical record so as to obfuscate its causes, minimize the toll it exacted upon its victims, and discount its meaning and historic significance. Much progress has been made along these lines by a simple process of non-discussion and suppression, allowing the war to fade, except where anticommunist points can be scored. The propagandists have proven their mettle already on the crucial issue of cause and intent; they have succeeded in wiping the record clean of the substantial documentary evidence of rational imperial planning that provided the framework for the US interventions, interpreting them more comfortably in terms of neutral categories such as "error" or "ignorance" in a framework of concern for freedom. A renewed effort has also commenced to show that the policies of search-and-destroy, harassment-and-interdiction fire, and na-palming and high-level bombing of densely populated areas were really not intended to kill civilians.[1] Rather, as Sidney Hook had already emphasized back when the United States was blowing up villages "suspected" of harboring "terrorists,"[2] the resulting casualties were not "deliberate American atrocities" but merely "the unfortunate accidental loss of life incurred by the efforts of American military forces to help the South Vietnamese repel the incursions of North Vietnam and its partisans"; or in a later version, "unintended conse-quences of military action."[3]

Here we will review very briefly some salient features of the US on-slaught, soon to be lost in the mist of obfuscation and deceit as the propa-ganda system turns to the tasks that lie ahead. We will restrict the discussion to South Vietnam[4] and will not make any effort to touch on more than a few issues and examples. We have written on the subject extensively elsewhere, as have many others.[5]

I.

Constructive Bloodbaths in Vietnam

French and Diemist Bloodbaths

Although the only pre-1965 bloodbath recognized in official doctrine is that which occurred in North Vietnam during its land reform of the mid-'50s, there were others. In 1946, without warning, the French bombarded Haiphong, killing an estimated six thousand civilians,[6] perhaps more than the number of victims of the well-publicized North Vietnamese land reform episode.[7] But as part of the French recolonization effort, and with Vietnam of little interest to the American leadership, this bloodbath was ignored and has not been mentioned by US official or non-official propagandists in their historical reconstructions of terror in Indochina.

Diem's bloodbaths also were impressive, but as they were in the service of anticommunism and the preservation of our client, they fall into the construc-tive or benign categories. Under our tutelage, Diem began his own "search-and-destroy" operations in the mid- and late 1950s, and his prison camps and the torture chambers were filled and active. In 1956 the official figure for po-litical prisoners in South Vietnam was fifteen thousand to twenty thousand.

Even Diem's friend and advisor, P. J. Honey, concluded on the basis of talks with former inmates that the majority of these were "neither Communists nor pro-Communists."[8] The maltreatment and massacre of political prisoners was a regular practice during the Diem period, although these problems became much more acute in later years.[9] The 1958 massacre of prisoners in Diem's concentration camp Phu Loi led to such an outcry that P. J. Honey was dispatched to inquire into these events; according to Lacouture, Honey could not verify more than twenty deaths at Phu Loi.[10]

"Pacification" as it developed from the earliest Diem period consisted in "killing, or arresting without either evidence or trials, large numbers of persons suspected of being Vietminh or 'rebels.'"[11] This resulted in many small bloodbaths at the local level, plus larger ones associated with military expeditions carried out by Diem against the rural population. One former Vietminh resistance fighter gave the following account of the Diemist terror and bloodbath in his village:

> My village chief was a stranger to the village. He was very cruel. He hunted all the former members of the Communist Party during the Resistance to arrest and kill them. All told, he slaughtered fourteen Party members in my village. I saw him with my own eyes order the killing of two Party members in Mau Lam hamlet. They had their hands tied behind their backs and they were buried alive by the militia. I was scared to death.[12]

Another former resistance fighter in central Vietnam claimed that

> in 1956, the local government of Quang Nam started a terrorist action against old Resistance members. About 10,000 persons of the Resistance Army were arrested, and a good many of them were slaughtered. I had to run for my life, and I stayed in the mountains until 1960. I lived with three others who came from my village. We got help from the tribal population there.[13]

The general mechanics of the larger bloodbaths were described by Joseph Buttinger, a former Diem supporter and advisor.[14]

> In June 1956 Diem organized two massive expeditions to the regions that were controlled by the Communists without the slightest use of force. His soldiers arrested tens of thousands of people. . . . Hundreds, perhaps thousands of peasants were killed. Whole villages whose populations were not friendly to the government were destroyed by artillery. These facts were kept secret from the American people.[15]

According to Jeffrey Race, a former US Army advisor in South Vietnam who had access to extensive documentation on recent Vietnamese history,

> . . . the government terrorized far more than did the revolutionary movement—for example, by liquidations of former Vietminh, by artillery and ground attacks on "communist villages," and by roundups of "communist sympathizers." Yet it was just these tactics that led to the constantly increasing strength of the revolutionary movement in Long An from 1960 to 1965.[16]

During the period 1955–60 the Vietminh mission was political, and "though it used assassinations and kidnapping," according to the *Pentagon Papers* historian it "circumspectly avoided military operations."[17] A USMAAG (US Military Assistance and Advisory Group) report of July 1957 stated: "The Viet Cong guerrillas and propagandists . . . are still waging a grim battle for survival. In addition to an accelerated propaganda campaign, the Communists have been forming 'front' organizations . . . seeking to spread the theory of 'Peace and Coexistence.'"[18] On the other hand, Diem, at least through 1957, was having "marked success with fairly sophisticated pacification programs in the countryside."[19] In a precise analogy to his sponsor's pacification efforts of 1965–72, "By the end of 1956, the civic action component of the GVN pacification program had been cut back severely."[20] The Pentagon historian refers to "Diem's nearly paranoid preoccupation with security," which led to policies that "thoroughly terrified the Vietnamese peasants, and detracted significantly from the regime's popularity."[21] According to the Pentagon historian, "No direct links have been established between Hanoi and perpetrators of rural violence."[22] The phrase "perpetrators of rural violence" is applied by the Pentagon historian only to the Vietminh, who admittedly were concentrating on political activities, and not to the Diem regime, which as he notes was conducting a policy of large-scale reprisals and violence, so extensive and undiscriminating as to be counterproductive. It is not difficult to establish "direct links" between Washington and perpetrators of the Diemist repression, incidentally. Once again it is clear that "constructive" bloodbaths can never involve "violence" for establishment propagandists and scholars; the word is reserved for those seeking social change in an illegitimate direction and under improper auspices.

Diem's extensive use of violence and reprisals against former Resistance fighters was in direct violation of the Geneva Accords (Article 14c), as was his refusal to abide by the election proviso.[23] The main reason for Diem's refusal to abide by this mode of settlement in 1955–56 was quite evident: the expatriate mandarin imported from the United States had minimal popular support and little hope of winning in a free election. (This sequence of events has not prevented the liberal establishment from claiming that our intervention in South Vietnam was to assure "self-determination.") Diem was a typical subfascist tyrant, compensating for lack of indigenous support with extra doses of terror. Violence is the natural mode of domination for those without local roots or any positive strategy for gaining support, in this instance the United States and its client regime. It is striking that irrespective of the facts, American officials and journalists throughout the succeeding struggle formulated the issues in terms of "control of the population" (how can we wrest areas from Vietcong "control"?, etc.), projecting their own inability to conceive of "support" on the hated enemy, who was not so limited in either policies or programs that might yield political successes without violence.

Diem's immediate resort to violence was in marked contrast to the behavior of those designated in the *Pentagon Papers* as "perpetrators of rural violence"; we return below to Race's detailed and well-documented study of how the Communist Party rejected the use of violence "even in self-defense, against the increasing repressiveness of the government,"[24] while winning popular support through its social programs, until driven by Diem's repression to resorting to force in order to survive. Wherever detailed studies have been carried out, the conclusions are rather similar.

As for the toll exacted among the South Vietnamese during the Diem period, there are no firm estimates. Bernard Fall reports figures, which he seems to regard as realistic, indicating a death toll of over one hundred fifty thousand "Viet Cong" from 1957 to April 1965—that is, before the first North Vietnamese battalion was allegedly detected in the South. These South Vietnamese, in his words, had been fighting "under the crushing weight of American armor, napalm, jet bombers and, finally, vomiting gases."[25] These one hundred fifty thousand (or whatever the actual numbers may be) have also never been counted among the victims of a pre-1965 "bloodbath." Rather, they were physically eliminated in a classic exercise of constructive violence, and are now being eliminated from the historical record in a no less classic exercise of a hegemonic system of ideology and propaganda.

The Overall US Assault as the Primary Bloodbath

In a very real sense the overall US effort in South Vietnam was a huge and deliberately imposed bloodbath. Military escalation was undertaken to offset the well-understood lack of any significant social and political base for the elite military faction supported by the United States. Despite occasional expressions of interest in the welfare and free choice of the South Vietnamese, the documents in the *Pentagon Papers* show that US planners consistently regarded the impact of their decisions on the Vietnamese as a peripheral issue at most, more commonly as totally inconsequential. Nonintervention and an NLF takeover were unacceptable for reasons that had nothing to do with Vietnamese interests; they were based on an assumed adverse effect on our material and strategic interests. It was assumed that an American failure would be harmful to our prestige and would reduce the confidence of our satellite governments that we would protect them from the winds of change.[26] The Thai elite, for example, might "conclude that we simply could not be counted on" to help them in suppressing local insurgencies. What is more, there was the constant threat of a "demonstration effect" of real social and economic progress in China,[27] North Korea,[28] and North Vietnam.[29]

In spite of official reiterations of the alleged threat of Chinese and North Vietnamese "expansionism," it was recognized by US policy makers that a unified communist Vietnam probably would have limited ambitions itself, and would provide a barrier to any Chinese moves further south.[30] It is not the threat of military expansion that official documents cite as the justification for the huge assault on Vietnam. Rather, it was feared that by processes never spelled out in detail, "the rot [might] spread to Thailand"[31] and perhaps beyond. The "rot" can only be the communist "ideological threat"; that is, the possibility of social and economic progress outside the framework of US control and imperial interests, which must be fought by US intervention against local communist organizing or uprisings, whether or not any communist armed attack is involved. This is the rot that might spread to Thailand and beyond, inspiring communist-led nationalist movements. But no skillful ideologists would want such implications spelled out too clearly to themselves or to others. Consequently, the central factors involved remain vague, their place taken by rhetoric about aggression, threatened bloodbaths, and our interest in self-determination.

It is important to bear in mind that these concepts—in fact, even the terminology in which they were expressed—were not invented by Vietnam planners. Rather, they merely adopted a standard mechanism of proven effectiveness in mobilizing support for US intervention. When Dean Acheson faced the problem of convincing the "leaders of Congress" (his quotes) to support the Truman Doctrine in February 1947, he outlined the threat to them as follows:

In the past eighteen months, I said, Soviet pressure on the Straits, on Iran, and on northern Greece had brought the Balkans to the point where a highly possible Soviet breakthrough might open three continents to Soviet penetration. Like apples in a barrel infected by one rotten one, the corruption of Greece would infect Iran and all to the east. It would also carry infection to Africa through Asia Minor and Egypt, and to Europe through Italy and France, already threatened by the strongest domestic Communist parties in Western Europe.[32]

As Acheson well knew, Soviet pressure on the Straits and Iran had been withdrawn already and Western control was firmly established. Further, there was no evidence of Soviet pressure on northern Greece—on the contrary, Stalin was unsympathetic to the Greek guerrillas. Still the rot might spread unless the United States undertook to rescue the terrorist regime in Athens, and a "Soviet breakthrough" was a useful propaganda device with which to mobilize domestic support. Acheson was concerned with the more remote dominoes—the Middle East and the industrial societies that were subject to the "threat" of internal democratic politics that might bring communist parties to power, thwarting US intentions. Similarly in the case of Indochina, it was the potential exit from the Free World of Indonesia with its rich resources, and ultimately industrial Japan, that obsessed US planners as they contemplated the threat of falling dominoes and rotting apples.

Gabriel Kolko comments accurately that "translated into concrete terms, the domino theory [previously invoked with regard to Greece and the Middle East, as he notes] was a counterrevolutionary doctrine which defined modern history as a movement of Third World and dependent nations—those with economic and strategic value to the United States or its capitalist associates—away from colonialism or capitalism and toward national revolution and forms of socialism."[33] In its specific application to Indochina, the falling dominoes led inexorably to Japan, the "superdomino" in the nightmare of the planners, investing their effort to prevent an unwelcome form of independence in Indochina with cosmic significance.[34] Again, mainstream scholarship is assiduously at work removing this no less unwelcome issue from the realm of discussion.

As the *Pentagon Papers* and other documentary evidence show beyond question, top-level US planners never had any doubt that in backing French colonialism and later intervening directly they were placing themselves in opposition to the main currents of Vietnamese nationalism, though a show of rage about aggression directed from Moscow or "Peiping" was always considered necessary for public relations purposes, and was always saleable to the mass media and important segments of academic scholarship. Illusions about a unified international communist movement responsible for events in Indochina were not only fostered by propagandists, but also came to be accepted doctrine among high-level planners themselves, even surviving the China-Soviet schism that was apparent by the late 1950s. A similar mixture of pretense for the population and internal delusion was standard with regard to the situation in South Vietnam, as we can see from the account of the *Pentagon Papers* historians and the government documents they provide.[35]

The US leadership knew that in Vietnam the "primary sources of Communist strength in the South remain indigenous," with a corresponding "ability to recruit locally"; and it was recognized that the NLF "enjoys some status as a nationalist movement," whereas the military government "is composed primarily of technicians" lacking in "positive support from various key segments of the populace" and determined "to remain the real power in South Vietnam" without any "interference from the civilians in the conduct of the war."[36] The experienced pacification chief, John Paul Vann, writing in 1965, puts the matter more brutally:

> A popular political base for the Government of South Vietnam does not now exist. . . . The existing government is oriented toward the exploitation of the rural and lower class urban populations. It is, in fact, a continuation of the French colonial system of government with upper class Vietnamese replacing the French. . . . The dissatisfaction of the agrarian population . . . is expressed largely through alliance with the NLF.[37]

It was thus well known to US authorities in 1965, as before, that they were fighting a nationalist mass movement in the name of a corrupt oligarchy that lacked popular backing. The Vietnam War was fought to return this nationalist mass movement to that measure of "passivity and defeatism" identified by Pool as necessary for "stability" in the Third World.[38] It must be brought under comprador-military control of the sort that the United States has imposed or supported in Brazil, the Dominican Republic, Guatemala, Bolivia, Thailand, etc. As we have noted, however, the power to rationalize self-interest is great, and some US leaders may have been able to keep their minds from being cluttered with inconvenient facts. In so doing, they preserved the belief that because we were the "good guys" our purposes must be benign and democratic and must have some positive relationship to the interests of the South Vietnamese people. Even the evidence that we were directing a large part of our military effort to assaulting and uprooting the rural population of the South, already overwhelming before 1965, was easily assimilated into the Orwellian doctrine of "defense against aggression."

The decision to employ technologically advanced conventional weaponry against the Southern countryside made a certain amount of sense on two assumptions: first, that the revolutionary forces were predominant in the rural areas, so that the war had to be a true anti-population war to force submission; and second, that the "demonstration effect" is important to US interests, so that our job was to terrorize, kill, and destroy in order to prove that revolution "doesn't pay." The first assumption was true in fact and must be assumed to have contributed to the gradual emergence of a full-fledged policy of search-and-destroy and unrestrained firepower, whatever the human consequences. The second assumption was evidently important in the thinking of high-level US planners and advisors and also contributed to the evolution of policy.[39]

The very terminology of the planners reflected these accurate perceptions, as is noted occasionally by the *Pentagon Papers* analysts. A US official commented that "essentially, we are fighting Vietnam's birth rate," in accordance with Westmoreland's concept of a "meat grinder" ("where we could kill large numbers of the enemy, but in the end do little better than hold our own," in the words of the *Pentagon Papers* historian). Some in the United States remained optimistic. Robert ("Blowtorch") Komer, who was in charge of the "other war," cheerfully reported in early 1967 that "we are grinding the enemy down by sheer weight and mass" in what he correctly perceived as a "revolutionary, largely political conflict," though he never drew the obvious conclusions that follow from these conjoined observations.[40] Komer went on to recommend, rationally enough from the point of view of a major war criminal, that the United States must "*step up refugee programs deliberately aimed at depriving the VC of a recruiting base*" (his emphasis). Thus the United States could deprive the enemy of what the Combined Campaign Plan of 1967 identifies as its "greatest asset," namely, "the people."

In January 1966, the well-known humanitarian Robert McNamara, now a passionate spokesman for the world's poor in his capacity as head of the World Bank, introduced evidence in congressional testimony on the success of air and artillery attacks, including B-52 raids ("the most devastating and frightening weapons used so far against the VC"), in forcing villagers "to move where they will be safe from such attacks . . . regardless of their attitude to the GVN." One can gain certain insight into the mentality of pro-war intellectuals from the fact that McNamara's evidence was reprinted in the pro-war journal *Vietnam Perspectives* (May 1966) to show how well things were going for our side. A month earlier, General Westmoreland had predicted "a tremendous increase in the number of refugees,"[41] an expectation that was soon fulfilled as a result of B-52 bombings and other tactics. Meanwhile other humanitarians (e.g., Leo Cherne, chairman of the International Rescue Committee) thoughtfully explained how refugees were fleeing from communism.[42]

The character of US policy was also influenced by the gradual recognition of two additional facts: first, that the South Vietnamese victims of "pacification" were essentially voiceless, unable to reach US or world opinion even as effectively as the North Vietnamese, with the result that the population being "saved" could be treated with virtually unrestrained violence. The second fact was that relevant US sensitivities (i.e., those of politically significant numbers of people) were almost exclusively related to US casualties and costs. Both of these considerations encouraged the development of an indiscriminate war of firepower, a war of shooting first and making inquiries later; this would minimize US casualties and have the spin-off benefit of more thoroughly terrorizing the population. The enhanced civilian casualties need not be reported—the enormous statistical service of the Pentagon always had difficulty dredging up anything credible on this one question—or such casualties could be reported as "enemy" or "Vietcong." Years of familiarity with this practice did not cause the news services to refrain from transmitting, as straight news, Saigon and Pentagon handouts on "enemy" casualties.

The retrospective judgment of the generals themselves on the accuracy of casualty reports makes interesting reading. General Douglas Kinnard published a study based on responses of army generals who had been commanders in Vietnam to a variety of questions, including one on the accuracy of "body counts." Only 26 percent of the respondents felt that body count figures were "within reason accurate." The query elicited such responses as these: "The immensity of the false reporting is a blot on the honor of the Army"; "They were grossly exaggerated by many units primarily because of the incredible interest shown by people like McNamara and Westmoreland"; "A fake—totally worthless"; "Gruesome—a ticket punching item"; "Often blatant lies."[43] Most generals felt that the body count was exaggerated, but that reaction must be coupled with a recognition that much of the air and artillery barrage was directed against targets where casualties would never be known or counted. Kinnard, for example, reports that when he returned to Vietnam in May 1969 as commanding general of the II Field Force Artillery he discovered that targets were being selected at random in areas where nighttime firing was authorized—quite substantial areas, as we know from other sources. Who might be killed by such random fire will never be known in the West. Reporters on the scene have made similar observations. Katsuichi Honda of *Asahi Shimbun*, perhaps the only pro-Western correspondent to have spent any time in the liberated areas of South Vietnam, described the incessant attacks on undefended villages by gunboats in the Mekong River and helicopter gunships "firing away at random at farmhouses":

> They seemed to fire whimsically and in passing even though they were not being shot at from the ground nor could they identify the people as NLF. They did it impulsively for fun, using the farmers for targets as if in a hunting mood. They are hunting Asians. . . . This whimsical firing would explain the reason why the surgical wards in every hospital in the towns of the Mekong Delta were full of wounded.[44]

In the Mekong Delta, there were virtually no North Vietnamese troops when Honda reported in the fall of 1967. The victims of these hunting trips were not listed in the "body counts" and are not included in any accounting of "bloodbaths."

Still other factors were involved in making the entire US enterprise in Vietnam a huge bloodbath; faith in technological solutions, racism reinforced by the corruption of "our" Vietnamese and the helplessness of the victimized population, and the frustrations of war. But essentially the initial high-level decision to bomb freely, to conduct search-and-destroy operations, and to fight a war against the rural population with virtually unlimited force were the source of the bloodbath. The essence of the US war in "saving" South Vietnam was well expressed by a US Marine, in a 1967 letter to Senator William Fulbright:

> I went to Vietnam, a hard charging Marine 2nd Lieutenant, sure that I had answered the plea of a victimized people in their struggle against communist aggression. That belief lasted about two weeks. Instead of fighting communist aggressors I found that 90 percent of the time our military actions were directed against the people of South Vietnam. These people had little sympathy or for that matter knowledge of the Saigon Government. . . . We are engaged in a war in South Vietnam to pound a people into submission to a government that has little or no popular support among the real people of South Vietnam. By real people I mean all those Vietnamese people who aren't war profiteers or who have [not] sold out to their government or the United States because it was the easy and/ or profitable thing to do.[45]

The immensity of the overall US-imposed bloodbath can be inferred to some degree from the sheer volume of ordnance employed, the nature of the weaponry, and the principles that governed their use. Through the end of 1971 over 3.9 million tons of bombs were dropped on South Vietnam from the air alone—about double the total bomb tonnage used by the United States in all theaters during World War II—with ground ordnance also employed in historically unprecedented volume.[46] A large fraction of the napalm used in Indochina was dropped in South Vietnam, an illustration of the abuse visited on the voiceless South Vietnamese (in protecting them from "aggression!") by the US command in collaboration with its client government in Saigon. Over 90 percent of the air strikes in South Vietnam were classified officially as "interdiction,"[47] which means bombing not carried out in support of specific ongoing military actions, but rather area bombing, frequently on a programmed basis, and attacks on "what are suspected" to be "enemy base camps," or sites from which a shot may have been fired.

One former military intelligence officer with the Americal Division in South Vietnam told a congressional subcommittee: "Every information report (IR) we wrote based on our sources' information was classified as (1) unverifiable and (2) usually reliable source. . . . The unverified and in fact unverifiable information, nevertheless, was used regularly as input to artillery strikes, harassment and interdiction fire (H&I), B-52 and other air strikes, often on populated areas."[48] In the words of Army Chief of Staff General Johnson, "We have not enough information. We act with ruthlessness, like a steamroller, bombing extensive areas and not selected targets based on detailed intelligence."[49] This is an expression of indiscriminateness as a principle—deliberate, calculated, and discriminate indiscriminateness—and it is a perfect complement to the other facets of a policy that was from the beginning semi-genocidal in purpose and method, resting in large part on the fact that the civilian population has been regarded as enemy or, at best, of no account.

The number of civilian casualties inflicted on South Vietnam is unknown, but is very likely underestimated by the Senate Subcommittee on Refugees at 400,000 dead, 900,000 wounded, and 6.4 million turned into refugees.[50] Conservative as these figures are, however, they mean "that there is hardly a family in South Vietnam that has not suffered a death, injury, or the anguish of abandoning an ancient homestead."[51]

That the overall US assault on South Vietnam involved a huge bloodbath can also be inferred from the nature of "pacification," both in general concept and in the details of implementation. We shall not here go into the general concept and the ways in which it was applied and was rapidly transformed into the wholesale killing and forced transfer of civilians.[52] We shall confine ourselves to an examination of three cases: a specific operation by US forces over a brief time period; a series of atrocities perpetrated over a six- or seven-year period by our South Korean mercenary allies, with the certain knowledge and tacit acceptance of US authorities; and the Phoenix program of extralegal "counterterror" against enemy civilians. These are by no means the only bloodbaths that typify the constructive mode, but they are offered as illustrative and deserving of greater attention.

Operation Speedy Express

The atrocities committed by Westmoreland's killing machine as it was "grinding the enemy down by sheer weight and mass" are readily discerned even in the bureaucratic prose of the *Pentagon Papers* and other government reports, but it was only after the Tet offensive of January–February 1968, when the *Pentagon Papers* record terminates, that the full force of US power was launched against the defenseless population of South Vietnam. Operation Speedy Express, conducted in the first six months of 1969, was only one of many major pacification efforts. It is unusual primarily in that it was studied in detail by Alex Shimkin and Kevin Buckley,[53] who examined the military and hospital records of the operation and interviewed South Vietnamese inhabitants and pacification officials of the Mekong Delta province of Kien Hoa, the target of Speedy Express.

For many years, the province had been "almost totally controlled" by the NLF:

> For a long time there was little or no military activity in the Delta. The 9th Division [which carried out the operation] did not even arrive until the end of 1966. Front activities went far beyond fighting. The VC ran schools, hospitals and even businesses. A pacification study revealed that an NLF sugar cane cooperative for three villages in the Mo Cay district of Kien Hoa produced revenue in 1968 which exceeded the entire Saigon government budget that year for Kien Hoa.

There appear to have been no North Vietnamese units present. As late as January 22, 1968, Defense Secretary McNamara had testified before the Senate that "no regular North Vietnamese units" were engaged in the Delta,[54] and while some entered after the massive killing of NLF guerrillas and civilians during the Tet offensive and after, there is no indication in the reports that the "enemy" in Kien Hoa included units of the North Vietnamese army.

Despite the success of the NLF, the "aggressive military effort carried out by the US Ninth Infantry Division" had succeeded in establishing some degree of government control.[55] In the six months of Speedy Express, this control was significantly extended; "a total of some 120,000 people who had been living in VC controlled areas" came under government control. This result was achieved by application of the "awesome firepower" of the Ninth Division, including air strikes using napalm, high explosives and anti-personnel bombs, B-52 bombing, and artillery shelling "around the clock" at a level that "it is impossible to reckon." Armed helicopters "scour[ed] the landscape from the air night and day," accounting for "many and perhaps most of the enemy kills." Buckley's *Newsweek* account describes the events as follows:

> All the evidence I gathered pointed to a clear conclusion: a staggering number of noncombatant civilians—perhaps as many as 5,000 according to one official—were killed by US firepower to "pacify" Kien Hoa. The death toll there made the My Lai massacre look trifling by comparison....
>
> The Ninth Division put all it had into the operation. Eight thousand infantrymen scoured the heavily populated countryside, but contact with the elusive enemy was rare. Thus, in its pursuit of pacification, the division relied heavily on its 50 artillery pieces, 50 helicopters (many armed with rockets and mini-guns) and the deadly support lent by the Air Force. There were 3,381 tactical air strikes by fighter bombers during "Speedy Express"....
>
> "Death is our business and business is good," was the slogan painted on one helicopter unit's quarters during the operation. And so it was. Cumulative statistics for "Speedy Express" show that 10,899 "enemy" were killed. In the month of March alone, "over 3,000 enemy troops were killed ... which is the largest monthly total for any American division in the Vietnam War," said the division's official magazine. When asked to account for the enormous body counts, a division senior officer explained that helicopter gun crews often caught unarmed "enemy" in open fields. But Vietnamese repeatedly told me that those "enemy" were farmers gunned down while they worked in their rice fields....
>
> There is overwhelming evidence that virtually all the Viet Cong were well armed. Simple civilians were, of course, not armed. And the enormous discrepancy between the body count [11,000] and the number of captured weapons [748] is hard to explain—except by the conclusion that many victims were unarmed innocent civilians....

The people who still live in pacified Kien Hoa all have vivid recollections of the devastation that American firepower brought to their lives in early 1969. Virtually every person to whom I spoke had suffered in some way. "There were 5,000 people in our village before 1969, but there were none in 1970," one village elder told me. "The Americans destroyed every house with artillery, air strikes, or by burning them down with cigarette lighters. About 100 people were killed by bombing, others were wounded and others became refugees. Many were children killed by concussion from the bombs which their small bodies could not withstand, even if they were hiding underground."

Other officials, including the village police chief, corroborated the man's testimony. I could not, of course, reach every village. But in each of the many places where I went, the testimony was the same: 100 killed here, 200 killed there. One old man summed up all the stories: "The Americans killed some VC but only a small number. But of civilians, there were a large number killed. . . ."

Buckley's notes add further detail. In the single month of March, the Ben Tre hospital reported 343 people wounded by "friendly" fire as compared with twenty-five by "the enemy." And as a US pacification official noted, "Many people who were wounded died on the way to the hospitals," or were treated elsewhere (at home, in VC hospitals or ARVN dispensaries). And, of course, unknown numbers were simply killed outright. Buckley's actual citation about the "perhaps as many as 5,000 deaths" is that of a senior pacification official who estimated that "at least 5,000" of those killed "were what we refer to as non-combatants"—to which we may add that the "combatants," who are considered fair game in most US reporting and historical analysis, were of course also South Vietnamese attempting to resist the overwhelming power of a foreign enemy. (Do we exculpate the Nazis for the killing of Resistance fighters in Europe?)

Interviews in the "pacified" areas add to the grim picture. One medic reported that this hospital took care of at least one thousand people in four villages in early 1969. "Without exception the people testified that most of the civilians had been killed by a relentless night and day barrage of rockets, shells, bombs and bullets from planes, artillery and helicopters." In one area of four villages, the population was reduced from sixteen thousand to sixteen hundred—which raises some questions about the official figures of casualties, largely fantasy in any event. Every masonry house there was in ruins. Coconut groves were destroyed by defoliants. Villagers were arrested by US troops, beaten by interrogators, and sent off to prison camps. The MACV location plots for B-52s show that the target center for one raid was precisely on the village of Luong Phu, near the village of Luong Hoa where the village elder cited above reported that every house was destroyed. Pounding from the air was "relentless." Helicopters chased and killed people working in fields. Survival was possible in deep trenches and bunkers, but even in bunkers children were killed by concussion, as noted in the *Newsweek* article.

An experienced US official compared My Lai to the operations of the Ninth Division:

> The actions of the 9th Division in inflicting civilian casualties were worse. The sum total of what the 9th did was overwhelming. In sum, the horror was worse than My Lai. But with the 9th, the civilian casualties came in dribbles and were pieced out over a long time. And most of them were inflicted from the air and at night. Also, they were sanctioned by the command's insistence on high body counts. . . . The result was an inevitable outcome of the unit's command policy.

That command policy can be traced directly back to Westmoreland and his civilian overseers, and derives immediately from the conditions of a war against a civilian population, already outlined.

On the matter of My Lai, misleadingly regarded in the West as somehow particularly evil (or perhaps, a shocking exception), Buckley also has relevant comments. The My Lai massacre was one of many that took place during Operation Wheeler/Wallowa. In this campaign, over ten thousand enemy were reported killed, including the victims of My Lai, who were listed in the official body count. Buckley writes:

> An examination of that whole operation would have revealed the incident at My Lai to be a particularly gruesome application of a wider policy which had the same effect in many places at many times. Of course, the blame for that could not have been dumped on a stumblebum lieutenant. Calley was an aberration, but "Wheeler Wallawa" was not.

The real issue concerning this operation, Buckley and Shimkin cabled to the US office of *Newsweek*, was not the "indiscriminate use of firepower," as is often alleged. Rather, "it is charges of quite discriminating use—as a matter of policy, in populated areas."

By the standards applied at the trials of Axis war criminals after World War II, the entire US command and the civilian leadership would have been hanged for the execution of this policy of discriminating use of firepower.

My Lai was indeed an aberration, but primarily in the matter of disclosure. Though the press concealed evidence of the massacre for over a year, the news broke through, largely because of the pressure of mass peace movement demonstrations. In the subsequent investigation by a military panel, it was discovered that a similar massacre had taken place only a few miles away at the village of My Khe. Consider the likely density of such massacres, given this accidental discovery.

Proceedings against the officer in charge at My Khe were dismissed on the grounds that he had carried out a perfectly normal operation in which a village was destroyed and its population forcibly relocated,[56] with close to a hundred people reported killed. The panel's decision to exonerate the officer tells us all we need to know about Operation Wheeler/Wallowa, and in fact reveals more about the Vietnam War than a dozen books.

Earl Martin, a Mennonite volunteer in Vietnam who is fluent in Vietnamese, was living in Quang Ngai city near My Lai at the time of the massacre, in close and regular contact with many Vietnamese. He writes that "the tragedy at My Lai never was talked about in Quang Ngai as it was in the United States . . . in the succeeding months we never once heard specific mention of My Lai from any of our friends" apart from a vague reference from a young boy. "The primary reason we heard little about My Lai," he writes, "was that the Vietnamese were afraid to tell an American—or even another Vietnamese who might have been a secret police for the Saigon government—for fear they would be accused of being *than-cong*, Communist sympathizers." He writes of the "tremendous pressure to cover up such atrocities," in the Saigon zones just as in the United States, though for different reasons, and discusses other "similar killings" that he heard about only years later from villagers near Quang Ngai, for example, a massacre at Truong Khanh where some Americans were killed when they triggered a mine and in retaliation "the troops stormed the hamlet, which was occupied mostly by old people, women and children," going from house to house, killing everyone they found, in the end, sixty-two villagers. The people of the village were broom makers. When they were dead, Martin was told by a friend, "the troops put the bodies on a pile, covered them with broom-straw and set them on fire." How many other incidents of this kind took place the West will never know, and in fact does not much care.[57]

Returning to Speedy Express, *Newsweek* reported that although John Paul Vann found that Speedy Express had alienated the population (a profound discovery), the army command considered its work well done. After all, "the 'land rush' succeeded. Government troops moved into the ravaged countryside in the wake of the bombardments, set up outposts and established Saigon's dominance of Kien Hoa"—a notable victory for "our Vietnamese."

Operation Speedy Express was regarded by the army as a "stunning success." Lauding the commanding general on the occasion of his promotion, General Creighton Abrams spoke of "the great admiration I have for the performance of the 9th Division and especially the superb leadership and brilliant operational concepts you have given the Division." "You personify the military professional at his best in devotion and service to God and country," Abrams rhapsodized, referring specifically to the "magnificent" performance of the Ninth Division, its "unparalleled and unequaled performance." During Operation Speedy Express, for example. On another occasion, when awarding him the Legion of Merit, Abrams referred to George Patton III, one of the men best noted for converting "pacification" into plain massacre, as "one of my finest young commanders."[58]

While the Ninth Division was at work in the field, others were doing their job at home. One well-known behavioral scientist who had long deplored the emotionalism of critics of the war and the inadequacy of their empirical data penned the following observations as Operation Speedy Express ground on: "The only sense in which [we have demolished the society of Vietnam] is the sense in which every modernizing country abandons reactionary traditionalism."[59]

Speedy Express, as noted, was unusual in that it was investigated and publicly reported, not in the fact that it occurred. Most of our information about comparable operations is derived by accident, when US observers happened to make an effort to find out what had happened (the same is true of My Lai, incidentally). For this reason, something is known about US operations at the same time in areas where Quaker relief groups were operating, for example, Operation Bold Mariner in January 1969. In the course of this campaign, some twelve thousand peasants (including, it seems, the remnants of My Lai) were driven from their homes in the Batangan Peninsula after having lived in caves and bunkers for months in an effort to survive constant bombardment,[60] and were then shipped to a waterless camp near Quang Ngai over which floated a banner that said, "We thank you for liberating us from communist terror." After the population was forcibly removed, the land was leveled with artillery barrages and bombing and then cleared by "Rome plows," one of the most destructive weapons in the US campaigns of ecocide in Vietnam. Since the dikes protecting rice paddies from the sea had been bombed, it was impossible to grow rice; rice purchased elsewhere was confiscated, according to inhabitants, since the population was regarded as sympathetic to the enemy and likely to give them rice. As of April 1971, the dikes—which had been purposely destroyed to deny food to the enemy—had not been repaired. Refugees who returned lived under guard in camps surrounded by ten-foot rows of bamboo, from which they might look over the flooded paddies to the hills where their huts had been, now a ruin of bomb fragments, mines, unexploded artillery shells and B-52 craters nearly twenty feet deep.[61] All of this just another episode in which this "modernizing country abandons reactionary traditionalism" under the guidance of its benevolent big brother.

In one of the postwar efforts to diminish the significance and scale of the US war in Vietnam, historian Guenter Lewy, describing the "spectacular" results of Operation Speedy Express, writes that "the assertion of Kevin P. Buckley of *Newsweek* that perhaps close to half of the more than 10,000 killed in Operation SPEEDY EXPRESS were noncombatants remains unsubstantiated. . . ."[62] The assertion was not Buckley's; he cited it from a high US pacification official. But it is true that it remains "unsubstantiated," as does the official record of 10,899 dead, which is, of course, an ugly joke, down to the last digit. The US command had no idea how many people were killed by their B-52 and helicopter gunship attacks or the artillery barrage, napalm, and antipersonnel weapons. Perhaps five thousand "noncombatants" were killed, or perhaps some other number. An honest review of the matter would at least have mentioned some of what Buckley and Shimkin discovered concerning civilian casualties in their detailed investigation, and would have considered the significance of the operation, casualties aside, under the circumstances just reviewed. Lewy, however, prefers to keep to official sources, merely expressing some skepticism as to whether what he calls "the amazing results of Operation SPEEDY EXPRESS" should "be accepted at face value," avoiding the question of what is implied by this successful operation of "pacification" in an area where South Vietnamese had successfully resisted the US invasion.

The Forty-Three-Plus My Lais of the South Korean Mercenaries

South Korean mercenary forces were contracted for and brought into South Vietnam by the Johnson administration in 1965, and they remained there into 1973.[63] News reports in 1965 and 1966 described these South Korean forces as "fierce" and "effective," but only in January 1970 was it disclosed publicly that their effectiveness rested on a policy of deliberate murder of South Vietnamese civilians. At that time it was reported that they had carried out a policy of simply shooting one of ten civilians in villages that they occupied.[64]

Not until 1972, however, did the scale of South Korean civilian murders become public knowledge (although still of little interest to the mass media—these murders fall into the "constructive" category).[65] Two Vietnamese-speaking Quakers, Diane and Michael Jones, carried out an intensive study of a portion of the area that had been occupied by the South Koreans for half a decade. To summarize their findings:

(a) The South Korean "rented soldiers," as the South Vietnamese describe them, committed a whole series of My Lai–scale massacres. Twelve separate massacres of one hundred or more civilians were uncovered in the Joneses' study. These soldiers carried out dozens of other massacres of twenty or more unarmed civilians, plus innumerable isolated killings, robberies, rapes, tortures, and devastation of land and personal property. The aggregate number of known murders by the South Koreans clearly runs into many thousands; and the Joneses examined only a part of the territory "pacified" by these "allied" forces.

(b) The bulk of the victims of these slaughters were women, children, and old people, as draft-age males had either joined the NLF, had been recruited into the Saigon army, or were in hiding.

(c) These mass murders were carried out in part, but only in part, as reprisals for attacks on the South Korean forces or as a warning against such attacks.[66] Briefly, the civilians of the entire area covered by the South Koreans served as hostages; if any casualties were taken by these mercenaries, as by an exploding mine, they often would go to the nearest village and shoot twenty, or a hundred twenty, unarmed civilians. This policy is similar to that employed by the Nazis, but South Korean hostage murders of civilians were relatively more extensive and undiscriminating than those perpetrated by the Nazis in Western Europe during World War II.

(d) These mass murders were carried out over an extended time period, and into 1972, with knowledge by US authorities.[67] There is no evidence that US officials made any effort to discourage this form of "pacification" or that any disciplinary action was ever taken in response to these frequent and sustained atrocities. In fact, there is reason to believe the South Korean policy of deliberate murder of civilians was not merely known and tolerated but was looked upon with favor by some US authorities. Frank Baldwin, of Columbia University's East Asia Institute, reports that the Korean policy was "an open secret in Korea for several years." US officials admitted to Baldwin that these accounts were true, "sometimes with regret, but usually with admiration."[68]

(e) In its request for $134 million for fiscal 1973 to support the continued presence of South Korean troops in Vietnam (raising the 1966–73 total to $1.76 billion), the DOD pointed out to Congress that South Korean troops "protect" an important section of South Vietnam. It is a fact that South Koreans "protected" and gave "security"[69] to people in South Vietnam in precisely the Orwellian official US sense in which Nixon, Westmoreland, and the pacification program in general did the same.[70]

The acceptability of this form of pacification, and the now well-established and consistent propensity of US forces and each of their "allies"—not merely South Koreans[71]—to carry out systematic acts of violence against South Vietnamese civilians, suggest that such atrocities and bloodbaths were "built in" to the US effort and mission; they constituted an integral part of the task of "pacifying" a poor, virtually defenseless, but stubbornly uncooperative, foreign population.

Phoenix: A Case Study of Indiscriminate "Selective" Terror

With unlimited resources available for killing, one option fitfully pursued by the US invaders of Vietnam—supplementing bombing, search-and-destroy, and the organization of forces of mercenaries—was selective "counterterror."[72] If the NLF had a political infrastructure that was important to its success, and if their own terror responding to that of the Saigon political machine effectively had made a shambles of the latter, why not duplicate and better their program of selective force? By doing so we would, as in providing them with the South Koreans and the US Ninth Division, help "to protect the Vietnamese people against terrorism" (to quote [then-CIA head] William Colby),[73] and thus bring "security" to the peasantry, threatened by the terror employed by their relatives among the NLF cadre.

Phoenix was a latecomer on the stage of selective counterterror. It points up the ease with which US programs were absorbed into (and added further corrupting impetus to) a system of rackets and indiscriminate torture and killings, and the willingness of the US political-military bureaucracy actively to support and rationalize the most outlandish and brutal systems of terror. The defense of this degenerate program by Komer, Colby, Sullivan, and other US officials is also noteworthy in the quality of the rationalizations offered for US-planned and financed bloodbaths.[74]

The immediate predecessor[75] of the Phoenix program was the Intelligence Coordination and Exploitation (ICEX) programs initiated in mid-1967,[76] under the direction of Westmoreland and Komer, and involving CIA, US civilian and military personnel, and the Saigon military-intelligence-police apparatus. Early internal directives describe the Phoenix program as a US effort of advice, support, and assistance to the Saigon Phung Hoang program. Later modifications delete reference to "Phoenix" and refer merely to the Saigon Phung Hoang program, in line with the approach of "keep[ing] the GVN foremost in the picture presented to its own people and the world at large."[77] On March 4, 1968, the US secretary of defense recommended that "Operation Phoenix which is targetted [sic] against the Viet Cong must be pursued more vigorously in closer liaison with the U.S." while "Vietnamese armed forces should be devoted to anti-infrastructure activities on a priority basis."[78]

After Westmoreland's and Komer's ICEX became Phoenix, the coordinated US-Saigon intelligence-military-police program succeeded in "neutralizing"[79] some eighty-four thousand "Viet Cong infrastructure," with twenty-one thousand killed, according to one set of reported official figures.[80] The Saigon government claims that under Phoenix, 40,994 suspected enemy civilians were killed, from its inception in August 1968 through the middle of 1971.[81] Just who these victims were is not entirely clear to William E. Colby, former head of Civil Operations and Rural Development [sic] Support Program (CORDS), later head of the CIA, and now a respected figure on the campus and community lecture circuit. Colby told a congressional committee that he had "never been highly satisfied with the accuracies of our intelligence efforts on the Vietcong infrastructure," conceding that "larger numbers" than the thousand suggested to him by Congressman Reid "might have been improperly identified" as Vietcong infrastructure (VCI) in the course of Phoenix operations.[82] However, he assured the committee that things are steadily "improving" (everyone's favorite word), and while we have not yet reached perfect due process or comprehensive knowledge of VC infrastructure, Phoenix has actually improved the quality of US-Saigon counterterror by its deep concern with accurate intelligence and its dedication to "stern justice."[83] Most of the Vietnamese killed, Colby (like Sullivan) assured the committee, were killed "as members of military units or while fighting off arrest."[84] Conveniently these dead enemy have usually had incriminating documents on their person to permit identification. ("What they are identified from is from documents on the body after a fire fight.")[85] Thus although things are not perfect, South Vietnam is not the "pretty wild place" it was at one period "when the government was very unstable." Though there are "unjustifiable abuses," "in collaboration with the Vietnamese authorities we have moved to stop that sort of nonsense."[86]

Colby's suggestions that intelligence concerning VC infrastructure had improved, that such intelligence had been relevant to Phoenix operations, and that deaths had occurred mainly in combat were contradicted by substantial nonofficial testimony on the subject. The program initially was motivated by the belief that US forces were developing much valuable information that was not being put to use.[87] Actually, much of this intelligence was unverified and unverifiable even in the best of circumstances. And Komer and his colleagues were aware of the fact that the "primary interest" of Saigon officials "is money"[88] with the potential, therefore, that a counterterror program using Saigon machinery would be corrupt, indiscriminate, and ineffective, except for the "spinoff" from mass terror. Potential corruption would be further heightened under a body quota system, which was quickly installed and subsequently enlarged with specific prize money of $11,000 offered for a live VCI and half that for a dead one. Corruption would be maximized by using dubious personnel to carry out the assassinations. And, in fact, assassinations were carried out regularly by former criminals or former communists recruited and paid by the CIA, by CIA-directed teams drawn from ethnic minorities, US military men, and Nationalist Chinese and Thai mercenaries. A US IVS volunteer reports picking up two hitchhikers in the Mekong Delta, former criminals, who told him that by bringing in a few bodies now and then and collecting the bounty, they could live handsomely.[89]

The quota system was applied at many levels. Michael J. Uhl, a former military intelligence (MI) officer, testified that a Phoenix MI team "measured its success . . . not only by its 'body count' and 'kill ratio' but by the number of CD's [civil detainees] it had captured. . . . All CD's, because of this command pressure . . . were listed as VCI. To my knowledge, not one of these people ever freely admitted being a cadre member. And again, contrary to Colby's statement, most of our CD's were women and children . . . "[90] Quotas were also fixed for local officials in an effort to produce "results" on a wider front; and as one US advisor noted, "They will meet every quota that's established for them."[91]

Torture, a long-standing policy of the Saigon regime, was greatly encouraged by quotas and rewards for neutralizing "Vietcong infrastructure." A sardonic saying favored by the Saigon police was: "If they are innocent beat them until they become guilty."[92] According to Uhl, "Not only was there no due process . . . but fully all detainees were brutalized and many were literally tortured."[93] A woman interviewed by Tom Fox after her release from a Saigon interrogation center in July 1972 claimed that more than 90 percent of those arrested and taken to the center were subjected to torture.[94] K. Barton Osborn, who served in a covert program of intelligence in Vietnam, not only testified to a wide variety of forms of torture used by US and Saigon personnel, but also made the startling claim that "I never knew an individual to be detained as a VC suspect who ever lived through an interrogation in a year and a half, and that included quite a number of individuals."[95]

By mid-1971, when the Saigon government had reported over forty thousand eliminated, the pacification program was being accelerated with "top priority" reportedly being given to neutralization of the VC political apparatus, at a reported cost of over $1 billion to the United States and an undisclosed amount to the Saigon government.[96] A rare statistic for April 1971 reveals that in that month, of two thousand "neutralized" more than 40 percent were assassinated.[97] According to British journalist Richard West, a US intelligence officer assigned to the Phoenix program stated that when he arrived in his district, he was given a list of two hundred names of people who were to be killed; when he left six months later, two hundred sixty had been killed, but none of those on his list.[98]

In some respects the Phoenix system was biased in favor of the NLF and its cadres and against the ordinary citizen. The former were more elusive and better able to defend themselves and sometimes established a modus vivendi with local officials. But Phoenix was "widely used to arrest and detail [sic] non-Communist dissidents," according to Theodore Jacqueney, a former AID and CORDS employee in Vietnam.[99] The Phoenix program also reportedly served for personal vendettas or for obtaining cash rewards for producing bodies. Meeting quotas was always possible in Free Vietnam by simply committing violence against the defenseless.

A system of terror-run-amok was facilitated by the incompetence and chronic irrelevance of the "intelligence" system that Colby claimed to be "improving" and which gave him hopes of "stern justice." According to Michael Uhl, Colby's claim of increasingly adequate intelligence as a basis for the huge number of Phoenix victims simply reflects Colby's "general lack of understanding of what is actually going on in the field."[100] According to Uhl, the MI groups in South Vietnam never had the capacity to do such a major intelligence job. "A mammoth task such as this would greatly tax even our resourceful FBI, where we have none of the vast cross-cultural problems to contend with." In the reality of practice:

We had no way of determining the background of these sources, nor their motivation for providing American units with information. No American in the team spoke or understood Vietnamese well enough to independently debrief any "contact". . . . Our paid sources could easily have been either provocateurs or opportunists with a score to settle. Every information report (IR) we wrote based on our sources' information was classified as (1) unverifiable and (2) usually reliable source. As to the first, it speaks for itself; the second, in most cases, was pure rationale for the existence of the program.

The unverified and in fact unverifiable information, nevertheless, was used regularly as input to artillery strikes, harassment and interdiction fire (H&I), B-52 and other air strikes, often on populated areas.[101]

Osborn testified that the Phoenix bureaucracy unofficially encouraged killing on the spot rather than going through the required administrative procedure:

After all, it was a big problem that had to be dealt with expediently. This was the mentality. This carries a semiofficial or semi-illegal program to the logical conclusion that I described here. It became a sterile depersonalized murder program. . . . There was no cross-check; there was no investigation; there were no second options. And certainly not whatever official modus operandi had been described as a triple reporting system for verification. There was no verification and there was no discrimination.[102]

The indiscriminateness of the Phoenix murders was so blatant that in 1970 one senior AID advisor of the Danang City Advisory Group told Jacqueney that he refused ever to set foot in the Provincial Interrogation Center again, because "war crimes are going on there."[103] A UPI report of November 1971 cites another US advisor, who claims that local officials in the Delta decided simply to kill outright 80 percent of their "suspects," but US advisors were able to convince them that the proportion should be reduced to 50 percent.[104] This is the "selective counterterror" by which the United States and its clients brought "security" to the peasants.[105]

For all its lack of discrimination in selection of victims, the Phoenix program and other techniques of "pacification" were not without impact on the Southern resistance movement. In fact, they may have been so successful as to guarantee North Vietnamese dominance over the wreckage left by the US war.

The Last Years of the Thieu Regime

As the war ground to a bloody end, the Saigon system of counterrevolutionary "stabilization" continued to function with new atrocities. The end product of "Vietnamization" was a centralized, corrupt, and exceptionally brutal police state. It became the ultimate satellite—the pure negative, built on anticommunism, violence, and external sustenance. The base of the Thieu regime was a huge foreign-organized and financed military and police apparatus; the population under its control was increasingly brutalized and "pacified" as enemy.

With US "know-how" placed in the hands of the most fanatic and vicious elements of the dying order in South Vietnam, the modes and scope of torture and systematic police violence in the Thieu state reached new heights.[106] Electrical and water torture, the ripping out of fingernails, enforced drinking of solutions of powdered lime, the driving of nails into prisoners' bones (kneecaps or ankles), beatings ending in death, became *standard operating procedure* in the Thieu prisons.[107] In Quang Ngai, for example, Dr. Marjorie Nelson saw "dozens of patients who had coughed up, vomited, or urinated blood after being beaten about the chest, back and stomach."[108] In another AFSC report: "A 17 year old boy, near death, had been unable to urinate for four days and was in extreme pain. After treatment by a Quaker doctor, we were informed that the prisoner had been tortured by electrical charges to his genital organs. A young girl had seizures, stared into space and exhibited symptoms of loss of memory. She said she had been forced to drink a lime solution many times while being interrogated."[109]

Following the release of ten students from Thieu's jails, these students put themselves on display in a college laboratory. One of them was in a state of semi-shock and was still being fed dextrose intravenously. His fingernails were blackened as a result of pins and slivers of wood being inserted under them. His hearing had been impaired by soapy water having been poured into his ears. Luu Hoang Thao, deputy chairman of the Van Hanh Student Association, described what happened to him after his arrest, as follows:

> For the first three days, the police beat me continuously. They didn't ask me any questions or to sign anything. They just beat my kneecaps and neck with their billy clubs. Then they beat me with chair legs. When a chair leg broke, they took another one. I was beaten until I was unconscious. When I regained consciousness, they beat me again. Finally, after three days, they asked me to sign a paper they had already written. They read the paper but would not let me see it. I wouldn't sign it, so they beat me some more.
>
> They put pins under my fingernails. They attached electrodes to my ears, my tongue and my penis. They forced soapy water into my mouth,

tramping on my stomach when it became bloated with water. They then hung me from the ceiling and extinguished lighted cigarettes in my nipples and penis.[110]

In a 1972 study of the treatment of prisoners in South Vietnam, the Quaker team from Quang Ngai reported that there had been a further increase in torture in that stricken province.[111] Ngô Cong Duc (former Catholic deputy and president of the Saigon publishers association and now returned to Vietnam as publisher of the journal *Tin Sang*) claimed that the typical prisoner in South Vietnam "undergoes three torture sessions at the arresting agency," with the most brutal designed to force the divulgence of names.[112] The evidence that was streaming in from all over the Thieu state indicated that it was probably the torture capital of the world.

Under Vietnamization the previously tenuous rule of law was terminated completely; the other side of the coin was the rise and triumph of essentially unrestrained police powers to seize, imprison, and molest. We have already quoted former military intelligence officer Michael Uhl, who pointed out that large numbers of detainees, the majority women and children, were "captured" in repeated dragnet operations, "and whatever looked good in the catch, regardless of evidence, was classified as VCI. . . . Not only was there no due process" applied to these prisoners, "fully all detainees were brutalized and many were literally tortured."[113] In 1972 arrests were proceeding at an estimated rate of fourteen thousand to fifteen thousand persons per month.[114] The victims of this process had no protection in the US-Thieu state, especially if they were ordinary citizens seized in countryside villages.

The breakdown of anything resembling a "legal system" was paralleled by a huge increase in the numbers of police. The National Police Force, which was only one of a dozen agencies legally authorized to make arrests, was enlarged from sixteen thousand in 1963 to eighty-eight thousand in 1969; under Vietnamization the numbers rose to 122,000 in 1972. Concurrently, a pervasive police-intelligence network spread throughout South Vietnam.

A police state is a prison state, and the Thieu state may have led all others (even Indonesia) in the number of political prisoners. Over two hundred national prisons and hundreds of local jails in South Vietnam housed a prisoner population that many estimated at over two hundred thousand.[115] A great many of these prisoners were middle-of-the-road students, clergy, intellectuals, and labor leaders who showed some interest in political affairs and therefore constituted a threat to the leaders of the police state. One should add that the prisoners were drawn from that sector of the population that was more favorably treated by the US-Saigon system; those beyond its reach were subjected to the full rigors of mechanized war. Under Vietnamization the Thieu government engaged in a determined effort to destroy any noncommunist opposition to its rule, largely by means of intimidation and violence. The vast repressive machinery of the Thieu regime was employed to a great extent against these center elements, which it properly regarded as threatening to its rule. The degeneration of this state was so extreme that a great many subjects of police terror were essentially "random" victims—brutalized as a matter of course once they fell into police hands (as in the dragnet seizures described by Uhl, above).

Many of the maltreated were victims of attempts at shakedowns. Staff of the American Friends Service Committee reported speaking with a young woman who had been imprisoned and tortured for rejecting the advances of an ARVN officer who had friends in the police.[116] And many arrests had payoffs in bribes from the families of the imprisoned, solicited or offered with knowledge that these might be useful in reducing the severity of tortures to be applied.[117]

As the threat of a political settlement became manifest in 1972–73, the repression intensified. The reason was simple. The Saigon diplomatic representative in Phnom Penh in 1959 told a reporter: "You must understand that we in Saigon are desperate men. We are a government of desperadoes."[118] True enough, though Diem was an authentic nationalist and relatively benign in comparison with the collaborationist regimes that followed as the US intervention grew to full-scale war against rural South Vietnam where the vast majority of the population had lived. The desperation stemmed in part from the fact that, as each successive US client found, terror does not build popular support, but on the contrary generates more "communists," or at best leaves demoralization and apathy. More violence was always required to give the people "security." Thus, after many years of US-sponsored protective terror, Thieu acknowledged to Saigon officials in January 1973 his continued inability to compete with the communists *on a purely political basis*: "If we let things go the population may vote for the Communists, who know how to make propaganda."[119] The occasion was the signing of the peace agreements that were to establish parallel and equivalent authorities in South Vietnam (Thieu and the PRG), which were to reach a peaceful political settlement. But Thieu did not have to fear that the United States would help expedite any such arrangement. Recognizing no less than Thieu the hopelessness of political competition,[120] the US government unilaterally rescinded these provisions.

But even the *possibility* of political competition sent shivers through the Thieu government. In June 1972 several thousand persons were arrested and shipped to Con Son island, many of them "merely relatives of political suspects" and many of them women and children.[121] George Hunter reported that

> special Branch Police swooped down on houses all over South Vietnam and arrested anyone under the remotest suspicion of being "left wing". . . .The government has a blacklist of suspects, but I understand that wives, mothers and fathers—anyone with the slimmest association with those on it are being caught in the net.[122]

Another roundup took place during the period of the threat of a Peace Agreement in October and November of 1972. On November 9, Hoang Duc Nha (Thieu's closest advisor) announced to a group of Vietnamese journalists the seizure of over forty thousand "communists" over the previous two-week period, thanks to a vast network of police.[123] The mammoth scale of arrests to which Free Vietnam had been accustomed was sharply intensified, at just the time that Thieu and Nixon were theoretically readying themselves to sign an agreement committing them to a policy of national reconciliation.

After the agreements were signed, measures were taken that laid the basis for imprisonments with the potential of simple extermination—whether realized or not, it is hard to determine. In an official telegram sent by the commander in chief of Thieu's police and the Saigon head of Phoenix on April 5, 1973, police and other arresting agents were advised as follows on the proper classification of detainees: "Do not use the expression 'condemned communist or communist agent.' Write only: 'Disturbs the peace.'"[124]

Disturbers of the peace might be regarded as common criminals; a communist agent would be a political prisoner covered by the January 27th Agreement. This practice was supplemented by the reclassification of current prisoners to common-law status. For example, Madame Ngô Ba Thanh, president of the Saigon-based Women's Committee Struggling for the Right to Live, with a law degree from Columbia University, was among those transferred to a prison for common-law criminals in Bien Hoa province. Documents from inside the prisons alleged that prison authorities incited common-law prisoners to provoke and even to kill reclassified political prisoners.[125]

Another technique used by the Thieu government was the alleged release of political prisoners, not to the PRG and DRV as stipulated in the January Agreements, but at large within South Vietnam. In early February, Thieu announced the release of forty thousand prisoners, with no specifics as to names and places of release.[126] The media failed to perceive the most significant aspect of this action, portrayed as a magnanimous act although in technical violation of the Agreements. The crucial point missed was that, by this device, prisoners who were murdered could be alleged to have been "released" and thus no longer a Thieu responsibility.[127] Previously, families of prisoners held at Phu Quoc whose terms had expired were informed of the prisoners' release, yet these individuals had disappeared.[128]

Accelerated mistreatment of political prisoners was also reported as the threat of peace mounted, including further sharp reductions in the rice ration (which had already been reduced severely in January 1972), the practice of mingling healthy prisoners with others in advanced stages of contagious diseases such as tuberculosis—another happy innovation in pacification—and direct physical violence.[129] Jean-Pierre Debris, who had recently been released from Chi Hoa prison, wrote that "the aim of the Thieu regime is to break the prisoners physically so that they will never be able to take any part in national life again. . . . The conditions under which thousands are held is critical and becoming more dramatic at the present time."[130]

Finally, reports of the direct killing of prisoners began filtering through with increased frequency. The two French prisoners released in December reported that just prior to their departure "there were massive deportations to the Paulo Condor [Con Son] camp," the scene of numerous reported atrocities in the past. They speculated that their sudden release might have been motivated by concern that they might witness what they expected would then take place, "a liquidation operation which might begin in the prisons."[131] Amnesty International cited "evidence that selective elimination of opposition members had begun" in the prisons, and a report that three hundred prisoners being moved from Con Son to the mainland were killed.[132] On Sunday, March 25, *NBC Monitor News* transmitted a report from the Swedish office of Amnesty International that observers had sighted thousands of bodies in prison uniforms floating in the area off South Vietnam. The PRG and DRV reported a steady stream of killings and disappearances, impossible to verify but frequently specific as to place, and hardly to be ruled out in light of the processes then at work in the Thieu state.

Although it was sometimes said that the Thieu government was "a coalition of the extreme Right" (a description by the pro-Thieu *Saigon Daily News*), this characterization was rejected by informed Vietnamese, who preferred the term "Mafia" to describe the Thieu coalition; they pointed to the huge thievery, the common involvement in the heroin trade, and the long and parasitic dependence of this tiny faction on a foreign power for survival. The repressive character of the Thieu state epitomized the long-term incapacity of the Diem regime and its increasingly militarized successors to respond to grievances except by violence. With Thieu the blend of egotism, fanatical anticommunism, and a life of professional military service under foreign sponsorship brought repression and police state violence to a new level of refinement.

The US role in the police repression apparatus of the Thieu state was straightforward. In the broadest sense, the long US intervention was the only reason that a Thieu-type regime could exist in the first place; more specifically, the United States financed, advised, provided technological improvements, and afforded a public relations cover for the direct instruments of terror. From the time of Diem the United States placed great weight on the police and intelligence; the funding and advising of the prison-police-intelligence ensemble of South Vietnam began at once, as the United States entered the scene directly after the Geneva Accords of 1954. A spokesperson for AID told Congress: "AID and its predecessor agencies have supported public safety programs [essentially police] in Vietnam since 1955. . . . AID's task has been to assist the National Police in recruiting, training and organizing a force for the maintenance of law and order."[133]

AID provided police specialists to train Saigon's police and advise them at all levels, and to work in Thieu's "public safety" programs. Over $100 million was spent on public safety in Vietnam from 1968 through 1971.[134] The Provincial Interrogation Centers, which were reported by Americans on the scene to have uniformly employed torture, were funded directly by the United States.[135] The pacification programs in general, including Phoenix, were paid for by the United States, at a cost estimated conservatively at about $5 billion for the period 1968–71.[136] AID put more money into South Vietnamese prisons than schools, and even after the discovery and notoriety of "tiger cages," it funded the construction of additional tiger cages for Con Son prison, even smaller than those already located on the island.[137]

Advice was also continuous, extending both to general strategy and specific tactics. William Colby indicated: "The function of US advice and support was to *initiate* and support a Vietnamese effort which can be taken up and maintained by the Vietnamese alone . . . [and] a considerable degree of advice and support of the GVN pacification program has come from the US side over the years."[138] In later years, in addition to Phoenix, US advice and funds went toward provision of commodity and advisory support for a police force of 108,000 men by the end of Fiscal 1971; . . . assisting the National Identity Regis- tration Program (N.I.R.P.) to register more than 12,000,000 persons 15 years of age and over by the end of 1971; continuing to provide basic and specialized training for approximately 40,000 police annually; providing technical assistance to the police detention system, including planning and supervision of the construction of facilities for an additional 8,000 in- mates during 1970; and helping to achieve a major increase in the number of police presently working at the village level.[139]

Advice included the introduction of Western technology to improve Third World "security." Some examples are mentioned in the AID statement quoted above. Another illustration was provided by a former prisoner in the Con Son tiger cages, who reported on the ingenuity of US advisors in improv- ing the technique of torture.[140]

It is not in question that the United States played the decisive role in the evolution of South Vietnamese political life from 1955 to 1975. US authorities did not merely accommodate to events thrust upon them from the outside; as advisor, controller of the purse strings, and occupying power, the United States had critical leverage, which it exercised time and again to make spe- cific choices. The character of the Thieu regime reflected a series of consistent decisions made in Washington, and expressed a preference and choice as to the nature of a client state that is not confined to South Vietnam. The Saigon authorities, in general, went along with US advice, partly because of their proclivities, partly because they were dependents, but also because each new policy innovation meant an additional inflow of cash, which the Saigon lead- ership knew could be absorbed readily into the existing system of corruption.

In addition to funding, advising, and providing the equipment and know- how, the United States provided a moral cover for the Thieu state. This re- sulted in part from the fact that the United States is a democracy; its officials pretend that democracy and an open society are among its serious objectives in intervening. Thus moderate scholars and others determined to think well of the United States have found it possible to employ the argument from long- run benefit. This mystification was furthered by the constant reference of US officials to "encouraging developments" in their client police states, and to the fact of "our working with the Vietnamese government," which is making "very substantial strides" toward eliminating the unjustifiable abuses that we all recognize and are doing our level best to eradicate.[141]

The apologetics include more or less continuous lying, especially at the higher levels of officialdom, as when Colby and Sullivan suggested that many of the twenty-one thousand or forty-one thousand killings under Phoenix might be combat deaths. Or in Colby's constant reference to pacification as a program for the "defense of the people" against somebody else's terror. Or the statement of Randolph Berkeley, chief of the Corrections and Detention Division of AID: "Generally speaking we have found the Vietnamese very light in their punishment."[142] Or the statement of Frank E. Walton, Director of the AID Public Safety Program, that Con Son prison is "like a Boy Scout Recreational Camp."[143] The same Frank Walton who denied any knowledge of the tiger cages in 1970 signed a report dated October 1, 1963, which stated that:

> In Con Son II, some of the hardcore communists keep preaching the 'party' line, so these 'Reds' are sent to the Tiger Cages in Con Son I where they are isolated from all others for months at a time. This confinement may also include rice without salt and water—the United States prisons' equivalent of bread and water. It may include immobilization—the prisoner is bolted to the floor, handcuffed to a bar or rod, or leg irons with the chain through an eyebolt, or around a bar or rod.[144]

The Paris Agreements of January 1973 brought no reprieve to the suffering people of South Vietnam. As already noted, the United States announced at once that it would disregard the central provisos of the Agreements it had signed in Paris and proceeded to do so, a fact effectively concealed by the press.[145] The Thieu regime, as always a creature of the United States, persisted in the sole program that it was equipped to conduct: violence and terror. The evidence is voluminous. We will give only one illustrative example as the appendix to this chapter, a discussion of the activities of the US-Thieu regime after the January 1973 ceasefire, presented by two US relief workers in Quang Ngai province. Here we only emphasize the obvious: the many years of US savagery in South Vietnam devastated the land, tore the society to tatters, decimated both the popular resistance and the noncommunist opposition, and left a legacy of horror that may never be overcome and will certainly have bitter consequences for many years, long after the true story of the US war has been excised from history and safely forgotten in the West. But those elements in United States society and political life that could impose such suffering on South Vietnam and the rest of Indochina will not hesitate to organize another constructive bloodbath if needed to save people elsewhere from any foolish attempt to exit from the Free World.

II.

Nefarious and Mythical Bloodbaths

Revolutionary Terror in Theory and Practice

The Vietnamese revolutionaries shed considerable blood over the years in individual acts of terror, some deliberate and calculated, others reflecting sporadic breakdowns in the discipline of cadres under enormous pressure, along with occasional sheer vengeance killing. There are very few authenticated cases, however, in which the insurgents killed significant numbers of unarmed civilians in deliberate acts of mass murder.[146] This appears to have been a result of a longstanding revolutionary philosophy and strategy, their relationship to the underlying population, and superior discipline.

Despite the widely held belief to the contrary, a product of decades of officially inspired propaganda, the Vietnamese revolutionary movement always gave force and violence a lower rating in the spectrum of *means* than did the Diem government and its successors or their US sponsors. This was in close accord with classical Maoist principles of revolutionary organization, strategy, and behavior. The NLF view in early 1960 was:

> Armed activities only fulfill a supporting role for the political struggle movement. It is impossible to substitute armed forces and armed struggle for political forces and political struggle. Formerly we erred in slighting the role of armed activity. Today we must push armed activity to the right degree, but at the same time we must not abuse or rely excessively on armed activity.[147]

Douglas Pike, the official US government authority on the NLF, confirmed the great weight given by it to the political struggle as opposed to "violence."

> It maintained that its contest with the GVN and the United States should be fought out at the political level and that the use of massed military might was itself illegitimate. Thus one of the NLF's unspoken, and largely unsuccessful, purposes was to use the struggle movement before the onlooking world to force the GVN and the United States to play the game according to its rules: The battle was to be organizational or quasi-political, the battleground was to be the minds and loyalties of the rural Vietnamese, the weapons were to be ideas; . . . and all force was automatically condemned as terror or repression.[148]

The United States and the Diem regime would not play by the rules of any such game, and as Pike states, in the end "armed combat was a GVN-imposed requirement; the NLF was obliged to use counterforce to survive."[149]

According to Jeffrey Race, before 1960 the South Vietnamese revolutionaries carried out an official policy of "non-violence," which led to a serious decimation of their ranks, as violence was monopolized almost entirely by the US-sponsored Diem regime. Race contends:

> By adopting an almost entirely defensive role during this period and by allowing the government to be the first to employ violence, the Party—at great cost—allowed the government to pursue the conflict in increasingly violent terms, through its relentless reprisal against any opposition, its use of torture, and particularly after May 1959, through the psychological impact in the rural areas of the proclamation of Law 10/59.[150]

The idea that the success of the Vietnam revolutionaries was based on "terrorizing" the population is shown by Race to be a serious misperception; in fact, it was the Saigon government, sponsored and advised by the United States, that in the end helped destroy itself by its inability to respond to problems and threats except by terror. Race's discussion is worth quoting at length:

> The lessons of Long An are that violence can destroy, but cannot build; violence may explain the cooperation of a few individuals, but it cannot explain the cooperation of a whole social class, for this would involve us in the contradiction of "Who is to coerce the coercers?" Such logic leads inevitably to the absurd picture of the revolutionary leader in his jungle base, "coercing" millions of terrorized individuals throughout the country[151] . . . . The history of events in Long An also indicates that violence will work against the user, unless he has already preempted a large part of the population and then limits his acts of violence to a sharply defined minority. In fact, this is exactly what happened in the case of the government: far from being bound by any commitments to legality or humane principles, the government terrorized far more than did the revolutionary movement . . . [and] *it was just these tactics that led to the constantly increasing strength of the revolutionary movement in Long An from 1960 to 1965.*[152]

Race indicates that official communist executions "actually were the consequence of extensive investigation and approval by higher authority." Furthermore, many careless executions during the resistance prior to 1954 had had adverse effects on the party, so that after it became stronger it "exercised much tighter control over the procedures for approving executions . . ."[153] This concern for the secondary effects of unjust executions sharply contrasted with the policies of the Saigon regimes under US sponsorship, and even more with the policies of the United States itself from 1965 to 1975.

Race's study shows how the Communist Party's refusal to authorize violence "except in limited circumstances . . . even in self-defense, against the increasing repressiveness of the government," while at the same time it was gaining support through its constructive programs, gave rise to an "anomaly"; "the revolutionary organization [was] being ground down while the revolutionary potential was increasing."[154] In response to angry demands from Southern party members who were being decimated by US-Diem terror, a May 1959 decision in Hanoi authorized the use of violence to support the political struggle.[155] From this point on the threat of terror was "equalized" and violence was no longer a government monopoly. In the province near Saigon that Race studied intensively (Long An), the result was that the revolutionary forces quickly became dominant while the government apparatus and its armed forces dissolved without violent conflict, undermined by party propaganda and disappearing from the scene.[156] The revolutionary potential had become a reality. By late 1964 parts of the province were declared a free-strike zone and by early 1965, when the full-scale US invasion took place, "revolutionary forces had gained victory in nearly all the rural areas of Long An."[157] As for the "North Vietnamese aggressors," their first units entered the province at the time of the 1968 Tet offensive.[158]

Revolutionary success in Vietnam both in theory and practice was based primarily on understanding and trying to meet the needs of the masses. Race noted that government officials were aware of the fact that "communist cadres are close to the people, while ours are not."[159] Yet they appeared to be unaware of the reasons, which he believes were traceable to a recruitment pattern for government office that systematically "denied advancement to those from majority elements of the rural population." The reasons also were related to a total failure on the part of the government to meet the real needs of the rural masses, in contrast with the revolutionary forces who "offered concrete and practical solutions to the daily problems of substantial segments of the rural population. . . ."[160] A movement geared to winning support from the rural masses is not likely to resort to bloodbaths among the rural population. A government recruiting wholly from an elite minority centered in the cities and admittedly "out of touch" with its own people, dependent on a foreign power for its existence and sustenance, generously supplied with weapons of mass destruction by its foreign sponsor—this type of government could well be expected to try to "pacify" its own people and to rely on its foreign protector to do so more effectively, while both speak of their objective as "protecting" the rural masses from "revolutionary terror."

Numerous cases of atrocities have been attributed to the NLF or DRV,[161] and several were nurtured by US government propaganda as cornerstones of the justification for US intervention. We focus briefly on the two most important mythical bloodbaths[162]: that associated with the North Vietnamese land reform of the mid-1950s, and the Hue massacres of 1968.

Land Reform in the Mid-'50s

In an address on November 3, 1969, President Nixon spoke of the DRV communists having murdered more than fifty thousand people following their takeover in the North in the 1950s. Six months later, in a speech given on April 30, 1970, he raised the ante to "hundreds of thousands" who had been exposed in 1954 to the "slaughter and savagery" of the DRV leadership. Then, one week later, on May 8, 1970, apparently in some panic at the public's response to his invasion of Cambodia, Mr. Nixon invoked the image of "millions" of civilians who would be massacred if the North Vietnamese were ever to descend into South Vietnam. Subsequently, in the calm of a press interview on April 16, 1971, President Nixon reported that "a half a million, by conservative estimates . . . were murdered or otherwise exterminated by the North Vietnamese."

It is obvious that a credibility problem exists with periodic variations in numbers of alleged victims, but there are three elements in this particular bloodbath myth worthy of discussion. First, whatever the numbers involved in the DRV land reform abuses, they had little or nothing to do with retaliatory action for collaboration with the French. Even in the sources relied on by official propagandists, the intended victims were identified primarily as landlords being punished for alleged past offenses against their dependent tenants, rather than wartime collaborators. Thus the attempts to use this episode as proof of a probable bloodbath in retaliation for collaboration with the United States or noncooperation during the continuing fighting were somewhat strained.

Second, the North Vietnamese leadership was upset by the abuses in the land reform, publicly acknowledged its errors, punished many officials who had carried out or permitted injustices, and implemented administrative reforms to prevent recurrences. In brief, the DRV leadership showed a capacity to respond to abuses and keep in touch with rural interests and needs.[163] It was a "bitter truth" for Professor Samuel Huntington that the "relative political stability" of North Vietnam, in contrast with the South, rested on the fact that "the organization of the Communist party reaches out into the rural areas and provides a channel for communication of rural grievances to the center and for control of the countryside by the government."[164] What Huntington missed is that the DRV and NLF leadership were not prevented by class interest, as were the successive regimes in Saigon, from responding constructively to rural grievances. In the South, as Jeffrey Race points out, even when the reactionary elites came into possession of captured documents that stressed rural grievances that the insurgents felt they could capitalize on (and for which *they* offered programs) "the government did not develop appropriate policies to head off the exploitation of the issues enumerated in the document."[165]

Third, and perhaps most important for present purposes, the basic sources for the larger estimates of killings in the North Vietnamese land reform were persons affiliated with the CIA or the Saigon Propaganda Ministry. According to a Vietnamese Catholic now living in France, Colonel Nguyen Van Chau, head of the Central Psychological War Service for the Saigon army from 1956 to 1962, the "bloodbath" figures for the land reform were "100% fabricated" by the intelligence services of Saigon. According to Colonel Chau, a systematic campaign of vilification by the use of forged documents was carried out during the mid-1950s to justify Diem's refusal to negotiate with Hanoi in preparation for the unheld unifying elections originally scheduled for 1956. According to Chau the forging of documents was assisted by US and British intelligence agencies, who helped gather authentic documents that permitted a plausible foundation to be laid for the forgeries, which "were distributed to various political groups and to groups of writers and artists, who used the false documents to carry out the propaganda campaign."[166]

The primary source of information on the land reform for many years was the work of Hoang Van Chi, formerly a substantial landholder in North Vietnam, and employed and subsidized by the Saigon Ministry of Information, CIA, and other official US sources for many years.[167] D. Gareth Porter undertook the first close analysis of his work and demonstrated that Chi's conclusions were based on a series of falsehoods, nonexistent documents, and slanted and deceptive translations of real documents. For example, Chi stated that the DRV authorities fixed a minimum quota of three landlords to be *executed* in each village, when in fact they placed an *upper* limit of three who could be *denounced and tried*, not executed.[168] In another passage Chi quotes Giap as saying, "Worse still, torture came to be regarded as normal practice during Party reorganization," when in fact Giap actually said: "Even coercion was used in carrying out party reorganization." Other passages cited by Chi as evidence of a plan for a "deliberate excess of terror" were shown by Porter to be "simply cases of slanted translation for a propaganda purpose."[169]

His estimate of seven hundred thousand, or 5 percent of the population of North Vietnam, as victims of the land reform, Chi eventually conceded to be merely a "guess," based largely on experience in his own village where ten of two hundred persons died, although only one was literally executed.[170] This admission came after Porter had made Chi's falsifications public. Given Chi's proven willingness to lie, his figure of ten deaths attributable to the land reform can hardly be taken at face value, but his extrapolation of this sample to the entirety of North Vietnam, which even Chi explicitly recognized as nonhomogeneous, is not even worth discussing.[171] Although scientifically worthless, and surely fabricated for propaganda purposes, Chi's "guess" served well for many years in providing authoritative and "conservative" estimates, not only for political leaders and their media conduits, but even for serious students of the war. Bernard Fall was taken in by Chi, and Frances FitzGerald in her influential *Fire in the Lake* followed Fall in giving a "conservative estimate" that "some fifty thousand people of all economic stations were killed" in the course of the land reform.[172] Because of their reputations as opponents of the war, Fall and FitzGerald played an especially important role in the perpetration of a myth that still flourishes in its third decade of life.[173]

On the basis of an analysis of official figures and credible documents, plus an estimate made by the Diem government itself in 1959, Porter concluded that a realistic range of executions taking place during the land reform would be between 800 and 2,500.[174]

The North Vietnamese land reform has been subjected to a more recent and exhaustive study by Edwin E. Moise.[175] To Porter's "negative" argument, based largely on his demonstration that "the documentary evidence for the bloodbath theory seems to have been a fabrication almost in its entirety," Moise adds "some positive evidence": namely, he points out that Saigon propaganda contained little about land reform until Saigon had learned from international press agency dispatches in 1956 of the North Vietnamese discussions of errors and failures. Even Hoang Van Chi, in 1955 interviews, did not make any accusations about atrocities; "It was only in later years that his memories began to alter," that is, after the United States and the Saigon regime learned about the land reform problems from the discussion in the Hanoi press, which, Moise writes, was "extremely informative" and "sometimes extraordinarily candid in discussing errors and failures." After a detailed discussion of sources, Moise concludes that "allowing for these uncertainties, it seems reasonable to estimate that the total number of people executed during the land reform was probably in the vicinity of 5,000, and almost certainly between 3,000 and 15,000, and that the slaughter of tens of thousands of innocent victims, often described in anti-Communist propaganda, never took place." These victims, Moise concludes, were not killed in the course of a government program of retribution and murder but rather were victims of "paranoid distrust of the exploiting classes," lack of experience on the part of poorly trained cadres, and the problems inherent in attempting to engage poor peasants and agricultural workers directly in a leadership role. "One of the most extraordinary things about the land reform," he writes, "was the fact that its errors were not covered up, or blamed on a few scapegoats, after it was over," but were publicly admitted by the government and party, which "corrected them to the extent possible." "Economically, the land reform had succeeded"; land was given to peasants who lacked it and agricultural production rose rapidly, overcoming the severe food shortages and famine of earlier years, and thus saving many lives. Subsequent steps toward cooperatives proceeded "without any significant amount of violence," largely on the basis of persuasion.

However one may choose to evaluate these efforts at social reform in the countryside under harsh conditions and in the aftermath of a bitter war, the picture is radically different from what has filtered through journalism and scholarship to the Western reader and continues to be repeated today as proof of communist barbarism. We might point out, finally, that the indiscriminate massacre in the single operation Speedy Express claimed as many victims as the land reform that has served US propaganda for so many years, and that the perpetrators of this massacre, which was quite clearly a direct expression of high-level policy aimed at systematic destruction and murder, were not punished or condemned but rather were honored for their crimes.

The Hue Massacre of 1968

The essential claim of the myth of the Hue massacre (see note 166) is that during their month-long occupation of Hue at the time of the Tet offensive of 1968, NLF and North Vietnamese forces deliberately, according to an advance plan and "blacklist," rounded up and murdered thousands of civilians, either because they worked for the government or represented "class enemies." The basic documentation supporting the myth consists of a report issued by the Saigon government in April 1968, a captured document made public by the US Mission in November 1969, and a long analysis published in 1970 by US Investigations Services (USIS) employee Douglas Pike. Both the Saigon and Pike reports should have aroused suspicions on the basis of their source, their tone, and their role in an extended propaganda campaign, timed in the latter case to reduce the impact of the My Lai massacre. But, even more important, the substance of these documents does not withstand scrutiny.[176]

As in the case of the land reform bloodbath myth just discussed, official estimates of alleged NLF-DRV killings of civilians at Hue escalated sharply in response to domestic political contingencies, in this case, in the fall of 1969, coincident with the Nixon administration's attempt to offset the effects of the October and November surge of organized peace activity and to counteract the exposure of the My Lai massacre in November 1969. Shortly after the Tet offensive itself, Police Chief Doan Cong Lap of Hue estimated the number of NLF-DRV killings at about two hundred,[177] and the mass grave of local officials and prominent citizens allegedly found by the mayor of Hue contained three hundred bodies. (The authenticity of these numbers and responsibility for these bodies is debatable, as is discussed below.) In a report issued in late April 1968 by the propaganda arm of the Saigon government, it was claimed that about one thousand executions had been carried out by the communists in and around Hue, and that nearly half of the victims had been buried alive. Since the story was ignored, the US embassy put out the same report the following week, and this time it was headlined in US papers. The story was not questioned, despite the fact that no Western journalist had ever been taken to see the grave sites when the bodies were uncovered. On the contrary, French photographer Marc Riboud was repeatedly denied permission to see one of the sites where the province chief claimed three hundred civilian government workers had been executed by the communists. When he was finally taken by helicopter to the alleged site, the pilot refused to land, claiming the area was "insecure."[178]

AFSC staff people in Hue were also unable to confirm the reports of mass graves, though they reported many civilians shot and killed during the reconquest of the city.[179]

Len Ackland, an IVS worker in Hue in 1967 who returned in April 1968 to investigate, was informed by US and Vietnamese officials that about seven hundred Vietnamese were killed by the Vietcong, an estimate generally supported by his detailed investigations, which also indicate that the killings were primarily by local NLF forces during the last stages of the bloody month-long battle as they were retreating.[180] Richard West, who was in Hue shortly after the battle, estimated "several hundred Vietnamese and a handful of foreigners" killed by communists and speculated that victims of My Lai-style massacres by the US–ARVN forces might have been among those buried in the mass graves.[181]

In the fall of 1969, a "captured document" was discovered that had been mysteriously sitting unnoticed in the official files for nineteen months, in which the enemy allegedly "admitted" having killed 2,748 persons during the Hue campaign. This document is the main foundation on which the myth of the Hue massacre was constructed. At the time it was released to the press, in November 1969, Douglas Pike was in Saigon to push the Hue massacre story, at the request of Ambassador Ellsworth Bunker. Pike, an expert media manipulator, recognized that American reporters love "documents," so he produced documents. He also knew that virtually none of these journalists understood Vietnamese, so that documents could be translated and reconstructed to conform with the requirements of a massacre. He also knew that few journalists would challenge his veracity and independently assess and develop evidence, despite the long record of official duplicity on Vietnam and the coincidence of this new document with official public relations needs of the moment[182]—the My Lai story had broken, and organized peace activity in the fall of 1969 was intense. Pike was correct on this point also, and the few indications of skepticism by foreign reporters were not allowed to interfere with the institutionalization of the official version.

The newly captured document and its interpretation by a well-known official propagandist were thus promptly accepted without question by many reporters (e.g., Don Oberdorfer, in his book *Tet*). Frances FitzGerald swallowed completely the official tale that "the Front and the North Vietnamese forces murdered some three thousand civilians" in their month of terror at Hue in 1968, and she took at face value all Saigon allegations of grave findings as well as the "piecing [of] various bits of evidence together" by Douglas Pike.[183] In the hysterical propaganda effusions of Robert Thompson, the number of people executed by the communists was escalated to 5,700, and we learn that "in captured documents they gloated over these figures and only complained that they had not killed enough."[184] No documents were identified, nor was any explanation advanced for such odd behavior. Senator William Saxbe insisted on no less than seven thousand murdered by "North Vietnamese," considerably more than the total number reported killed from all causes during this period in Hue.[185]

Thus, in the fall of 1969 the press in general once again headlined the refurbished story, quoting from the captured document: "We eliminated 1,892

administrative personnel, 39 policemen, 790 tyrants, 6 captains, 2 first lieu-
tenants, 20 second lieutenants and many noncommissioned officers." This sentence and document were accepted as confirmation of the US-Saigon version
of what had taken place, despite the fact that nowhere in the document is it
claimed or even suggested that any civilians had been *executed*. Furthermore,
the quoted sentence was taken out of the context of the document as a whole,
which had nothing to do with the punishment of individuals, but was rather
a low-level report, describing the military victory of the NLF in a particular
district of Hue. But the press was too interested in reaffirming the cruelty of
the Vietcong to pay attention to such fine distinctions.

In manipulating this document for propaganda purposes, the Vietnamese word "diet" was translated as "eliminate," which implies killing, although
the word was used by the NLF in the military sense of putting out of action
(killing, wounding, capturing, or inducing to surrender or defect). If the NLF
had intended to describe plain killing or deliberate executions, they would
have used any number of Vietnamese terms, but not "diet." The government
propaganda version also disregarded the fact that the 2,748 figure clearly included estimated numbers of enemy troops killed and wounded in combat.
This deception was facilitated by mistranslating the word "te" as "administrative personnel" in the version circulated to journalists when, in fact, according
to a standard North Vietnamese dictionary it has the broader meaning of
"puppet personnel," which would include both civilian administrators and the
military. The propaganda operation also produced a list of fifteen categories
of "enemies of the people" allegedly targeted for liquidation, when the documents in question never used the quoted phrase and suggested only that those
categories of people should be carefully "watched." Those targeted for repression, let alone liquidation, were in completely different categories.[186] Finally, it
was claimed that the NLF had blacklists for execution that included "selected
non-official and natural leaders of the community, chiefly educators and reli-
gionists," when in fact the testimony of Hue's chief of secret police contradicts
this. According to the latter, the only names on the list of those to be executed
immediately were the officers of the secret police of Hue. Other lists were of
those who were to be "reeducated."[187] Porter states that no captured document
has yet been produced that suggests that the NLF and DRV had any intention
of executing any civilians. Porter claims further that the general strategy of
the NLF conveyed in the documents, and misrepresented by Douglas Pike
and his associates, was to try to mobilize and gain support from the masses,
organized religious groups, and even ordinary policemen.[188]

The documents uniformly attest to an NLF policy of attempting to rally large numbers with minimum reprisals. Furthermore, the killings that did take place occurred after the NLF realized that it would have to evacuate the city, then under a massive US attack, and during that evacuation. In Porter's words:

> The real lesson of Hue, therefore, is that in circumstances of peace and full political control, the basic Communist policy toward those associated with the Saigon regime would be one of no reprisals, with the exception of key personnel in Saigon's repressive apparatus (and even in these cases, officials can redeem themselves at the last moment by abandoning resistance to the revolutionary forces).[189]

This lesson, the opposite of that which the US-Saigon propaganda machines succeeded in conveying, gains plausibility in view of the events of postwar Vietnam.[190] There is no credible evidence that the behavior of the victors resembles that of the gloating butchers who "only complained that they had not killed enough." In fact, the long-predicted bloodbath in Vietnam did not materialize.

Apart from the "captured documents," the most persuasive support for the alleged massacre came from the finding of mass graves—but this evidence is as unconvincing as the managed documents. A fundamental difficulty arises from the fact that large numbers of civilians were killed in the US-Saigon recapture of Hue by the massive and indiscriminate use of firepower. David Douglas Duncan, the famous combat photographer, said of the recapture that it was a "total effort to root out and kill every enemy soldier. The mind reels at the carnage, cost and ruthlessness of it all."[191] Another distinguished photographer, Philip Jones Griffiths, wrote that most of the victims "were killed by the most hysterical use of American firepower ever seen" and were then designated "as the victims of a Communist massacre."[192] Robert Shaplen wrote at the time: "Nothing I saw during the Korean War, or in the Vietnam War so far has been as terrible, in terms of destruction and despair, as what I saw in Hue."[193] Of Hue's 17,134 houses, 9,776 were completely destroyed and 3,169 more were officially classified as "seriously damaged." The initial official South Vietnamese estimate of the number of civilians killed in the fighting during the bloody reconquest was 3,776.[194] Townsend Hoopes, undersecretary of the air force at the time, stated that in the recapture effort 80 percent of the buildings were reduced to rubble, and that "in the smashed ruins lay 2,000 dead civilians. . . . "[195] The Hoopes and Saigon numbers exceed the highest estimates of NLF-DRV killings, including official ones, that are not demonstrable propaganda fabrications. According to Oberdorfer, the US Marines put "Communist losses" at more than five thousand, while Hoopes states that the city was captured by a communist force of one thousand, many of whom escaped—suggesting again that most of those killed were civilian victims of US firepower.

Some of the civilian casualties of this US assault were buried in mass graves by NLF personnel alongside their own casualties (according to NLF-DRV sources), and a large number of civilians were bulldozed into mass graves by the "allies."[196] The NLF claims to have buried two thousand victims of the bombardment in mass graves.[197] Oberdorfer says that 2,800 "victims of the occupation" were discovered in mass graves, but he gives no reason for believing that these were victims of the NLF-DRV "political slaughter" rather than people killed in the US bombardment. He seems to have relied entirely on the assertions of the Ministries of Propaganda. Fox Butterfield, in the *New York Times* of April 11, 1975, even places all three thousand bodies in a single grave! Samuel A. Adams, a former analyst with the CIA, wrote in the *Wall Street Journal* of March 26, 1975, that "South Vietnamese and Communist estimates of the dead coincide almost exactly. Saigon says it dug up some 2,800 bodies; a Viet Cong police report puts the number at about 3,000." There are no known "police reports" that say any such thing; and it apparently never occurred to Adams that the 2,800 figure might have been adjusted to the needs of the mistranslated document.

An interesting feature of the mass graves, as noted earlier, is that independent journalists were never allowed to be present at their opening, and that they had difficulty locating their precise whereabouts despite repeated requests.[198] One of the authors spoke with a US Marine present at the first publicized grand opening, who claims that the reporters present were carefully hand-picked reliables, that the bodies were not available for inspection, and that he observed tracks and scour marks indicative of the use of bulldozers (which the DRV and NLF did not possess).[199] Perhaps the only Western physician to have examined the graves, the Canadian Dr. Alje Vennema, found that the number of victims in the grave sites he examined were inflated in the US-Saigon count by over sevenfold, totaling only 68 instead of the officially claimed 477; that most of them had wounds and appeared to be victims of the fighting, and that most of the bodies he saw were clothed in military uniforms.[200]

Little attention has been paid to the possibility that massacre victims at Hue may have been killed neither by the NLF-DRV nor US firepower, but rather by the returning Saigon military and political police. Many NLF sympathizers "surfaced" during the Tet offensive, cooperated in the provisional government formed by the revolutionaries in Hue, or otherwise revealed their support for the NLF. With the retreat of the NLF and DRV forces from Hue in 1968 many cadres and supporters were left in a vulnerable position as potential victims of Saigon retribution. Evidence has come to light that large-scale retaliatory killing may have taken place in Hue by the Saigon forces *after* its recapture. In a graphic description, Italian journalist Oriana Fallaci, citing a French priest from Hue, concluded that "Altogether, there have been 1,100 killed [after 'liberation' by Saigon forces]. Mostly students, university teachers, priests. Intellectuals and religious people at Hue have never hidden their sympathy for the NLF."[201]

One of the US reporters who entered Hue immediately after the US Marines had recaptured part of it was John Lengel of AP. He filed a report on February 10 concerned primarily with the extensive war damage, and then added the following intriguing comment:

> But few seasoned observers see the devastation of Hue backfiring on the communists. They see as the greatest hope a massive and instant program of restoration underlined by a careful psychological warfare program pinning the blame on the communists.
>
> It is hard, however, to imagine expertise on such a broad scale in this land.[202]

It seems quite possible that the "seasoned observers" whom Lengel cites gave the matter some further thought, and that contrary to his speculation, there was sufficient psywar expertise to manage the media—never very difficult for the government—and to "pin the blame on the communists." That seems, at least, a very reasonable speculation given the information now available, and one that gains credibility from the early reaction of "seasoned observers" to the havoc wrought by the US forces reconquering the city.

In any case, given the very confused state of events and evidence plus the total unreliability of US-Saigon "proofs," at a minimum it can be said that the NLF-DRV "bloodbath" at Hue was constructed on flimsy evidence indeed. It seems quite likely that US firepower "saving" the Vietnamese killed many more civilians than did the NLF and DRV. It is also not unlikely that political killings by the Saigon authorities exceeded any massacres by the NLF and DRV at Hue. Porter's analysis of the NLF documents used by US-Saigon propagandists suggests that mass political killings were neither contemplated nor consistent with revolutionary strategy at Hue. The evidence indicates that "the vast majority of policemen, civil servants, and soldiers were initially on 'reeducation' rather than on liquidation lists, but the number of killings mounted as the military pressure on the NLF and North Vietnamese mounted."[203] It is also of interest here, as in the land reform case, that the retreating Front forces "were severely criticized by their superiors for excesses which 'hurt the revolution.'"[204] We have not yet heard of any such self-criticism coming from US and Saigon superiors for their more extensive killings at Hue.

As noted earlier, the apparent absence of retributory killings in postwar Vietnam is suggestive of where the truth may lie on the question of the Hue massacre. The Pike-Thompson version led to forecasts that have been refuted by history. Nonetheless the force of the US propaganda machine and US influence are such that the Hue massacre (by the communists!) is still an institutionalized truth, not only in the United States but overseas as well. For example, Michel Tatu of Le Monde has taken the Pike version as established truth. And in his letter proposing Sakharov for the 1973 Nobel Peace Prize, Aleksandr Solzhenitsyn also refers to "the bestial mass killing in Hue" as "reliably proved"—and we can be sure he is not referring to the nearly four thousand civilians mentioned by the Saigon authorities themselves, most of whom were buried in the rubble created by US firepower.

We have discussed several of the more blatant exercises of the US-Saigon propaganda machines, but it must be emphasized that even their day-to-day reports, which constituted the great mass of information about Indochina, should have been treated with comparable skepticism. On the rare occasions when competent reporters made serious investigations, the information presented by US and Saigon sources turned out to be no less tainted. The Japanese reporter Katsuichi Honda once undertook to investigate the weekly report of the General Information Bureau of the US Army in Saigon entitled "Terrorist Activities by Viet Cong." Pursuing "one isolated case" that interested him, he discovered

> that not only was amazingly brutal and persistent terrorism occurring regularly, it was actually being shielded from public scrutiny by Saigon's "information control." It soon appeared that the murders were not done by the National Liberation Front at all. There were, it seemed, innumerable "terrible facts" which had been secretly hushed up behind the scenes of the intensifying Vietnam War.[205]

In the case in question, he discovered that the assassination of five Buddhist student volunteers, officially victims of Vietcong terror, had apparently been carried out by government forces. In another case, "drunken soldiers of the Government army quarreling among themselves threw grenades, and some civilian bystanders were killed," the case again being reported "as another instance of 'Viet Cong terrorism.'"

In other cases, the facts have emerged only by accident. To mention one particularly grotesque example, the camp where the remnants of the My Lai massacre had been relocated was largely destroyed by ARVN air and artillery bombardment in the spring of 1972. The destruction was attributed routinely to Vietcong terror. The truth was revealed by Quaker service workers in the area.[206]

These examples point up the fact that in the instances in question the official reports were lies and deceptions, and in some cases were converted into official myths; the more important conclusion is that official sources in general have extremely limited credibility. They raise questions, but provide no reliable answers.

CHAPTER 10

From Mad Jack to Mad Henry: The United States in Vietnam (1975)

Noam Chomsky

At 8 a.m. on April 30, 1975, the last US Marine helicopter took off from the roof of the American embassy in Saigon. Less than five hours later, General Minh made the following announcement over Saigon radio:

> I, General Duong Van Minh, President of the Saigon Government, appeal to the armed forces of the Republic of Vietnam to lay down their arms and surrender to the forces of the NLF unconditionally. I declare that the Saigon Government, from central to local level, has been completely dissolved.[1]

For the United States, these events signaled the end of a quarter-century effort to maintain Western domination over all or part of Indochina. For the Vietnamese, it meant that the foreign invaders had finally been repelled and their colonial structures demolished, after more than a century of struggle.

Mad Jack Attacks

With fitting symmetry, history had come full circle. "The first act of armed intervention by a Western Power in Vietnam," according to the Vietnamese historian Truong Buu Lam, "is generally held to have been perpetrated in 1845 by a ship of the US Navy, the *Constitution*," in an effort to force the release of a French bishop.[2] The skipper of "Old Ironsides" was Commander John Percival, known as "Mad Jack." Sailors under his command "disembarked at Danang and proceeded to terrorize the local population . . . United States sailors fired on an unresisting crowd and several dozens were killed . . . " before Mad Jack withdrew in failure.[3] A few years later the French navy returned and took Danang, and in the years that followed, established their imperial rule over all of Indochina, bringing misery and disaster. The agronomist Nghiem Xuan Yen wrote in 1945 that under French colonization "our people have always been hungry . . . so hungry that the whole population had not a moment of free time to think of anything besides the problem of survival."[4] In the northern parts of the country, two million people are reported to have died of starvation in a few months in 1945.[5]

Throughout this period, resistance never ceased. Early French eyewitnesses reported that

> We have had enormous difficulties in imposing our authority in our new colony. Rebel bands disturb the country everywhere.[6] The fact was that the centre of resistance was everywhere, subdivided to infinity, almost as many times as there were Annamese. It would be more exact to consider each farmer busy tying up a sheaf of rice as a centre of resistance.[7]

Meanwhile, the French complained, the only collaborators were

> Intriguers, disreputable or ignorant, whom we had rigged out with sometimes high ranks, which became tools in their hands for plundering the country without scruple. . . . Despised, they possessed neither the spiritual culture nor the moral fibre that would have allowed them to understand and carry out their task.[8]

A century later, the imperial overlords had changed, but their complaints never varied. The resistance, however, did significantly change its character over the years:

> At that, the partisans fought to recover the independence of their country, to avenge their king, and to safeguard their traditional pattern of life. By the 1900s, as the occupation developed into a systematic exploitation of the colony's economic resources, creating in its wake large-scale social disruptions, slogans of explicit social and political values were added to the original calls for independence from the French. The spontaneous reaction against foreigners, the armed struggle to oust them, had grown into a demand for revolutionary—political and later social—changes.[9]

The August revolution of 1945, led by the Vietminh, was the culmination of a struggle of revolutionary nationalism. On September 2, President Ho Chi Minh proclaimed the independence of Vietnam:

Our people have broken the chains which for a century have fettered us, and have won independence for the Fatherland. Viet Nam has the right to be free and independent and in fact it is so already. The entire Vietnamese people are determined to mobilize all their physical and internal strength, to sacrifice their lives and property, in order to safeguard their freedom and independence.[10]

It was to be another thirty years, however, before the promise was realized. The French Foreign Legion returned,[11] its path cleared by British bayonets. Chiang Kai-Shek's troops invaded from the North. In March 1946, France signed an agreement with Ho Chi Minh in which France "recognize[d] the Republic of Vietnam as A Free State with its Government, its Parliament, its Treasury, its Army, within the framework of the Indochinese Federation and of the French Union," thus establishing the Ho Chi Minh government as *"the only legal government of Vietnam."*[12] But the French military authorities proceeded to dismantle this agreement. War was inevitable after the naval bombardment of Haiphong on November 23, 1946, in which thousands were killed in order to "teach the Vietnamese a good lesson" according to French commander in chief Valluy.[13] The United States backed France from the start, ignoring repeated appeals from Ho Chi Minh (eight messages from Ho between October 1945 and February 1946 received no reply). By April 1946 the United States acknowledged French control of Indochina, and "thereafter, the problems of US policy toward Vietnam were dealt with in the context of the US relationship with France."[14] Thus, as French historian Philippe Devillers correctly states:

> The United States approved a policy which was not basically different from those followed by the Third Reich in Norway (with Quisling), or by Japan in occupied China (with the Nanking government of Wang Ching-Wei). It was the policy of imposing a regime and policy on a country through Quisling or puppet governments.[15]

With Eyes Open

It is important to bear in mind that the US government was never in any doubt as to the basic facts of the situation in Vietnam. Intelligence reports describe the "intense desire on the part of the Annamese for independence and thorough hatred by them of the French and any other white people who happen to be in any way supporting or sympathizing with the French."[16] The headquarters of the Office of Special Services (OSS), China Theater, reported to the chief of the Intelligence Division on September 19, 1945, that Emperor Bao Dai, in an interview, "stated that he had voluntarily abdicated, and was not coerced by the Provisional Government," because he approved "the nationalistic action of the Viet Minh" and preferred to "live as a private citizen with a free people than rule a nation of slaves." On the same date, the same source reported an interview with Ho Chi Minh, "the President of the Provincial Government of Viet Nam," in which Ho assured him that "his people are prepared for a long struggle of ten or twenty years, and are willing to fight for the freedom, not of their own, but of future generations." He reported the personal opinion that "Mr. Ho Chi Minh is a brilliant and capable man, completely sincere in his opinions," and that "when he speaks, he speaks for his people, for I have traveled throughout Tonkin province, and found that in that area people of all classes are imbued with the same spirit and determination as their leader." The new government, he reported, "is an outgrowth of the controlling forces in the military resistance"; "Viet Nam looks to America for moral support in their struggle, almost expects it." A "personal observation" of October 17 certifies "to the fact that the great mass of the population supports Ho Chi Minh and his party, and to the anti-Japanese action in which they have engaged. . . . In traveling through Tonkin, every village flew the Viet Minh flag. . . . The women and children were also organized, and all were enthusiastic in their support." The report continues that American observers "saw how well the majority of the people follow the orders of Ho Chi Minh and the Provisional Government," apart from "some of the wealthy merchants and former high Annamese officials."

As for those at the receiving end of these communications, the State Department's assessment of Ho Chi Minh and the Provisional Government of Vietnam was summed up this way from Abbot Low Moffat, the chief of the Division of Southeast Asian Affairs:

> I have never met an American, be he military, OSS, diplomat, or journalist, who had met Ho Chi Minh who did not reach the same belief: that Ho Chi Minh was first and foremost a Vietnamese nationalist. He was also a Communist and believed that Communism offered the best hope for the Vietnamese people. But his loyalty was to his people. When I was in Indochina it was striking how the top echelon of competent French officials held almost unanimously the same view. Actually, there was no alternative to an agreement with Ho Chi Minh or to a crushing of the nationalist groundswell which my own observations convinced me could not be done. Any other government recognized by the French would of

necessity be puppets of the French and incapable of holding the loyalty of the Vietnamese people.[17]

An Irrelevant Question

Thus, the United States committed itself with its eyes open and with full knowledge of what it was doing to crushing the nationalist forces of Indochina. "Question whether Ho as much nationalist as Commie is irrelevant," Secretary of State Dean Acheson explained. Quite to the contrary, he urged in May 1949 that "no effort should be spared" to assure the success of the French Quisling government, since there seemed to be "no other alternative to estab[lishment] Commie pattern Vietnam." And on the eve of the Korean War, in March 1950, Acheson observed that French military success "depends, in the end, on overcoming opposition of indigenous population"; we must help the French "to protect IC from further Commie encroachments."[18]

Two years earlier, a State Department Policy Statement of September 1948 had spelled out the fundamental "dilemma" that the United States faced in Indochina. It was a "dilemma" that would never cease to haunt American policy makers. The "dilemma" was this. The communists under Ho Chi Minh had "captur[ed] control of the nationalist movement," thus impeding the "long-term objective" of the United States, namely "to eliminate so far as possible Communist influence in Indochina." The State Department analysis added that "our inability to suggest any practicable solution of the Indochina problem" was caused by "the unpleasant fact that Communist Ho Chi Minh is the strongest and perhaps the ablest figure in Indochina, and that any suggested solution that excludes him is an expedient of uncertain outcome." But to the very end, the United States continued to back former agents of French colonialism, who easily transferred their allegiance to the successor imperial power, against the nationalist movement "captured" (by implication, illegitimately) by the Vietminh and its successors.

The Central Dilemma

This "dilemma" is absolutely central to the understanding of the evolution of American policy in Indochina. The *Pentagon Papers* historian, considering the situation after the Tet offensive of 1968, asks whether the United States can "overcome" the apparent fact that the Vietcong have "captured" the Vietnamese nationalist movement while the GVN has become the refuge of Vietnamese who were allied with the French in the battle against the independence of their nation. It does not occur to him to ask whether the United States *should* attempt to "overcome" this fact. Rather, the problem is a tactical one: how can the fact be overcome? In this analysis, the historian reflects quite accurately the tacit assumptions that were unquestioned in the extensive documentary record.

Protecting Indochina from Aggression

For propaganda purposes, the issue was reformulated. It was our noble task to protect Indochina from "aggression." Thus the *Pentagon Papers* historian, in the musings just cited, continues by observing that the question he raises is "complicated, of course, by the difficult issue of Viet Cong allegiance to and control by Communist China." Again, the historian accurately reflects the mentality revealed in the documents. He does not try to *demonstrate* that the Vietcong owed allegiance to communist China, or were controlled by Peking. Rather, he adopts the premise as an a priori truth, untroubled by the fact that no evidence was ever brought forth to substantiate it.

Not that intelligence didn't try. Elaborate attempts were made to demonstrate that the Vietminh and its successors were merely the agents of some foreign master. It was, in fact, a point of rigid doctrine that this must be true, and no evidence to the contrary served to challenge the doctrine. Depending on date and mood, the foreign master might be the Kremlin or "Peiping,"[19] but the principle itself could not be questioned.

The function of the principle is transparent: It served to justify the commitment "to defend the territorial integrity of IC and prevent the incorporation of the ASSOC[iated] States within the COMMIE-dominated bloc of slave states" (Acheson, October 1950), or to safeguard Vietnam from "aggressive designs Commie Chi [*sic*]"(Acheson, May 1949) by support for the French puppet regime. One of the most startling revelations in the *Pentagon Papers* is that in the twenty-year period under review, the analysts were able to discover only one staff paper (an intelligence estimate of 1961) "which treats communist reactions primarily in terms of the separate national interests of Hanoi, Moscow, and Peiping, rather than primarily in terms of an overall communist strategy for which Hanoi is acting as an agent."

Intelligence labored manfully to provide the evidence required by the doctrine. But their failure was total. It was impossible to establish what had to be true, that Ho Chi Minh was a puppet of the Kremlin or "Peiping." Faced with this problem, American officials in Saigon reached the following casu-istic conclusion: "It may be assumed that Moscow feels that Ho and his lieu-tenants have had sufficient training and experience and are sufficiently loyal to be trusted to determine their day-to-day policy without supervision." In short, the absence of evidence that Ho was a puppet was held up as conclusive proof that he "really" was an agent of international communism after all, an agent so loyal and trustworthy that no directives were even necessary.

The whole amazing story gives a remarkable indication of how effective are the controls over thought and analysis in American society. It is a gross error to describe the *Pentagon Papers*, as is commonly done, as a record of gov-ernment lies. On the contrary, the record reveals that the top policy planners and, for the most part, the intelligence agencies were prisoners of our highly ideological society. No less than "independent intellectuals" in the press and the universities, they believed precisely those doctrines that had to be believed in order to absolve the United States of the charge of aggression in Indochina. Evidence was—and remains—beside the point.

"Internal Aggression"

Not only were the Vietminh necessarily agents of a foreign power, they were also literally "aggressors." The National Security Council, in February 1950, held that France and the native armies it had assembled "is now in armed conflict with the forces of communist aggression." A presidential commission of early 1954 added that France was fighting "to defend the cause of liberty and freedom from Communism in Indochina" while the cause of the Viet-minh is "the cause of colonization and subservience to Kremlin rule as was the case in China, in North Korea, and in the European satellites." Later internal documents refer generally to the VC aggression in the South, and refer to the Pathet Lao in Laos as "aggressors." Indeed, the joint chiefs of staff went so far as to characterize "political warfare, or subversion" as a form of aggression. And Adlai Stevenson informed the UN Security Council that "the United States cannot stand by while Southeast Asia is overrun by armed aggressors," adding that "the point is the same in Vietnam today as it was in Greece in 1946," where the United States was also defending a free people from "inter-nal aggression," a marvelous new Orwellian construction.

By and large, the New Frontiersmen were quite at home with this rhetoric. With "aggression checked in Vietnam," writes Arthur Schlesinger, "1962 had not been a bad year."[20] In fact, 1962 was the first year in which US military forces were directly engaged in combat and combat support, the bombing of villages, the gunning down of peasants from helicopters, defoliation, etc. Only three years later, in April 1965, did US intelligence report the presence of the first North Vietnamese battalion in the South (see note 45).

It is important to recognize that these ridiculous rationalizations for American aggression in Indochina were accepted in their essentials within the American "intellectual community." Left-liberal opinion, regarding itself as "opposing the war," called for a peace settlement between South and North Vietnam with American troops in place in the South—in short, a victory for American imperialism.[21] The war is described in retrospect as a "tragic error," where worthy impulse was "transmuted into bad policy," a case of "blundering efforts to do good." Such assessments are offered even by people who became committed opponents of the war in its later phases. The plain and obvious fact that the United States was guilty of aggression in Indochina is rejected with horror and contempt, or, to be more accurate, it is simply dismissed as beyond the bounds of polite discourse by liberal commentators. These facts give an important insight into the nature of the liberal opposition to the war, which later developed largely on "pragmatic" grounds, when it became obvious that the costs of the war to us (or, to the more sensitive, to the Vietnamese as well) were too great for us to bear.[22]

Enlisting the Intellectuals

The fundamental dilemma, perceived from the start, permitted only two outcomes to the American involvement in Indochina. The United States might on the one hand choose to come to terms with the Vietnamese nationalist movement, or it might bend its efforts to the destruction of the Vietminh and its successors. The first course was never seriously contemplated. Therefore, the United States committed itself to the destruction of the revolutionary nationalist forces of Indochina. Given the astonishing strength and resiliency of the resistance, the American intervention in Vietnam became a war of annihilation. In every part of Indochina, the pattern was repeated. As in the days of the early French conquest, "each farmer busy tying up a sheaf of rice" might be "a centre of resistance." Inevitably, the United States undertook to destroy the rural society.

"Urbanization and Modernization"

American intellectuals dutifully supplied the rationale. We were engaged in a process of "urbanization and modernization," they explained, as we drove the peasants out of their villages by bombs, artillery, and search-and-destroy missions, simultaneously destroying the countryside to ensure that return would be impossible. Or, the United States was helping to control "village thugs" in violent peasant societies where "terrorists can operate largely unmolested whether or not the population supports them" (Ithiel de Sola Pool). More generally:

> In the Congo, in Vietnam, in the Dominican Republic, it is clear that order depends on somehow compelling newly mobilized strata to return to a measure of passivity and defeatism from which they have recently been aroused by the process of modernization. At least temporarily, the maintenance of order requires a lowering of newly acquired aspirations and levels of political activity . . .

—as "we have learned in the past thirty years of intensive empirical study of contemporary societies."[23] By the end, even the more cynical and sadistic were driven to silence as the horrendous record of the achievements they had sought to justify for many years was slowly exposed to public view.

The terminology of the behavioral sciences was continually invoked in an effort to delude the public and the colonial administrators themselves. "Counterinsurgency theorists" explained in sober terms that "all the dilemmas are practical and as neutral in an ethical sense as the laws of physics."[24] It is simply a matter of discussing the appropriate mix of aversive conditioning (B-52 raids, burning of villages, assassination, etc.) and positive reinforcement (the detritus of the American presence) so as to overcome the unfair advantage of the revolutionaries—revolutionaries who in fact had won popular support by virtue of their constructive programs,[25] much to the dismay of the social scientists who persisted to the end with claims to the contrary based on "empirical studies," which they never produced.

"Social Engineering"

In a report to President Kennedy after a 1962 study mission in Southeast Asia, Senator Mike Mansfield discussed the "widespread support of the peasants for the Vietcong," and remarked that any "reorientation" of peasant attitudes "involves an immense job of social engineering." He anticipated the unpleasant need of "going to war fully ourselves against the guerrillas—and the establishment of some form of neocolonial rule in South Vietnam," which he "emphatically" did not recommend. Others, however, took up the task of social engineering with zeal and enthusiasm. The Australian social psychologist

Alex Carey, who has studied the matter in some detail, concludes that the American pacification program was "neither more nor less than a nationalized sociological experiment in bringing about changes, desired by American policy, in the attitudes and values of a physically captive population."[26] The more sophisticated analysts went further still. They derided the concern for popular attitudes—such mysticism has no place in a scientific civilization such as ours—and urged instead that we concern ourselves solely with more objective matters, that is, with controlling behavior. This advance to the higher stages of applied science was necessitated by the miserable failure of the colonial agents in the efforts to mimic native revolutionaries.[27]

I cannot survey here the techniques that were attempted. Perhaps the mentality of the "scientists" is sufficiently indicated in one minor experiment in operant conditioning reported in congressional hearings.[28] An American psychiatrist working in a mental hospital in Vietnam subjected one group of patients to "unmodified electroconvulsive shock," which "produces systemic convulsions similar to a grand mal epileptic seizure and in many patients is very terrifying." Others were offered work, "including tending crops for American Special Forces—Green Berets—in Viet Cong territory 'under the stress of potential or actual VC attack or ambush.'" Asked about the "research value" of this amusing study, Dr. Veatch, who was testifying, replied that "the entire field of behavior conditioning is of great interest in the treatment of mental patients as well as prisoners. . . . " This example, insignificant in context, reveals very clearly who was insane, the patients or the "scientists," just as academic studies on "control of village violence" leave no doubt as to who are the violent individuals who must somehow be controlled in a civilized society.

Commenting on the "experiment" just cited, Alex Carey observes that "to be mentally ill and Asian deprives a man of most of his humanity; to be a communist and Asian deprives him of all of it." He goes on to show how this experiment exhibits in microcosm the major features of the program of social engineering devised by the American descendants of Himmler's SS and the Nazi physicians as they sought to design a more appropriate culture for the benighted Vietnamese once control had been gained over the population by violence and terror.

An Interview with Vann

While studying the American pacification program, Carey interviewed John Paul Vann, field operations coordinator of the US Operations Mission, who was generally regarded as the most important American official in Vietnam after the ambassador and the chief military commander.[29] Vann provided him with a remarkable 1965 memorandum, since privately circulated, "in response to a request for material on the concepts and theory that had guided the pacification programme."[30] In this memorandum, Vann noted that a social revolution was in process in South Vietnam, "primarily identified with the National Liberation Front," and that "a popular political base for the government of South Vietnam does not exist." But it is "naive" to expect that "an unsophisticated, relatively illiterate, rural population [will] recognize and oppose the evils of Communism." Therefore, the United States must institute "effective political indoctrination of the population," under an American-maintained "autocratic government."

Vann was not a brutal murderer in the style of those who designed the military operations. He objected strongly to the ongoing destruction of the civilian society by American terror. His view was that of the benevolent imperialist, the bearer of the white man's burden, who urged that "we should make it clear [to the Vietnamese villagers] that we continue to represent that permanent revolution of mankind which the American revolution advanced; and that only the principles of that revolution can ultimately produce the results for which mankind longs." We must overcome "the pseudo-science of communism" by the techniques of the behavioral sciences, "psywar," firm in our conviction that "our system . . . is more in keeping with the fundamentals of human nature," as John F. Kennedy once explained.[31] If the Vietnamese are too stupid to comprehend these well-known facts, then we must drill them in by force—with the most benevolent of intentions. Indeed, it would be immoral to do otherwise, just as we do not permit children or the mentally disabled to injure themselves in their innocence.

Two Tasks for the US Government

1. Destroy the Countryside

The US government and its agents in the field had to carry out two essential tasks. The first and most crucial was to destroy the society in which the resistance was rooted—the society "controlled by the Viet Cong," in the terminology of the propagandists. In South Vietnam, the primary victim of American aggression, a vast expeditionary force was let loose to accomplish this task. But by the late 1960s Washington came to understand why earlier imperial aggressors—the French in Indochina, for example—had relied primarily on

hired killers or native forces organized under colonial management to conduct a war against a resisting civilian population. To its credit the invading
American army had begun to disintegrate, necessitating its withdrawal.[32] The
disintegration was in part due to revulsion against its tasks, and in part to the
indirect influence of the peace movement at home, which—as apologists for
state violence lamented—was "demoralizing public opinion."[33] Washington's
response was to assign the job of destruction to more impersonal agencies—
helicopter gunships, bombers, and artillery. American technology devised
fiendish devices to maximize the damage done to "enemy personnel." These
were particularly effective in northern Laos, where the peasant population
was totally defenseless. Here, "experiments in population control" involving
the highest level of technology could be conducted without the unwelcome
intrusion of irrelevant variables. In North Vietnam, Laos, and Cambodia the
war remained "capital intensive" in this sense. Especially in the case of Laos
and Cambodia, the US government was abetted by the press, which kept the
war "secret" by self-censorship for many years, and only occasionally revealed
its true horrors.

2. Rebuild Vietnam's Society

The task of destruction was accomplished with partial success. In South Vietnam, the society was virtually demolished, though the resistance was never
crushed. But the aggressors faced a second and more difficult job: to construct
a viable Quisling regime out of the wreckage, and to rebuild the society in
accordance with the imperial vision. This effort was a dismal failure. Like the
French before them, the American conquerors were able to assemble "a crew
of sycophants, money-grubbers, and psychopaths,"[34] but rarely more. Efforts
were made to integrate the ruined societies into "the free world economy" by
encouraging American and Japanese investment. Academic studies explained
how foreign investment "must be liberated from the uncertainties and obstacles that beset it" so that it might take advantage of the cheap labor offered
by a society of rootless, atomized individuals driven from their villages by
American urbanization, a virtually ideal labor market.[35] It was hoped that
with the vast flow of arms and the expansion of the police, the merry crew
of torturers and extortionists placed into power by the United States would
somehow manage to control the population.

To the very end, the American government was committed to victory, at
least in South Vietnam. To fend off liberal criticism, Kissinger and his press
entourage spoke vaguely of a "decent interval," but there is no evidence that

they looked forward to anything short of total victory for the American client regime. Nonetheless, success was beyond their grasp. When Washington was no longer able to call forth the B-52s, the whole rotten structure collapsed from within, virtually without combat.

The "Fall of Danang"

Symbolic of the American failure in its second task—reconstruction of the society it had demolished—was the "fall of Danang," where the foreign aggression began more than a century before. Three intact ARVN divisions with more than one hundred thousand men and enough ammunition for a six-month siege were stationed in Danang as of March 26. "Thirty-six hours later, without a single shot having been fired, the ARVN ceased to exist as a fighting unit." What happened is described by a French teacher who remained:

> The officers fled by air taking with them the ground crews so that the pilots that had stayed could not get their planes started. Left without leaders the army fell apart. On March 28 widespread looting started. The rice stocks were sacked and in the hospitals the army and the local staff stole all the drugs in order to sell them on the black market. Then the army started shooting civilians at random, often to steal their motorcycles. By then half of the army was in civilian clothes. For 36 hours, with the Vietcong nowhere in sight but the rumors of their arrival constantly spreading, the city became a nightmare. By that time the population had but one hope: that the Vietcong would arrive as quickly as possible to restore order, any order.

Many civilians fled, "because the Americans told us the Communists would kill us," as they explained to reporters. America "left behind in Danang . . . an empty shell and a good deal of hatred, which will probably endure."[36]

The fact of the matter is that there never was any hope for the population of Indochina apart from a victory for the forces of revolutionary nationalism. That this was the case was even recognized by some members of the ruling elites. I once had a lengthy discussion with a high official of the Laotian government in the offices of the ministry that he directed. He described in detail the poisonous effects of the colonial (now American) presence—the corruption, the venality, the social decay. Pointing to the foreign-owned shops in the street below, he predicted that Laos would virtually cease to exist under the rule of the American-backed regime. As a wealthy aristocrat and intellectual, he did not personally look forward to a Pathet Lao victory. But, he added, they would find some use for a person with his skills, though his privileges would be lost. The only hope for Laos, he concluded, was a Pathet Lao victory. How many more people there were like him, I cannot say. But no one with even a pretense of rationality can fail to comprehend that throughout Indochina, the communist-led revolutionary forces received significant and even passionate support from much of the rural population, the overwhelming mass of the people of these countries, before the American policies of "urbanization" were undertaken. It was, of course, precisely because of this fact that the policy of "inducing substantial migration of people from the countryside to the cities"[37] was undertaken in the first place.

Consequences of US Policy

The Nazi-like brutality of the American assault on Indochina is the most searing memory of these terrible years. Even though the ideologists and propagandists will labor to erase it, I cannot believe they will succeed. Nevertheless, it must be understood that the savage programs put into place by the government and justified or ignored by much of the intelligentsia did not merely result from some sadistic streak in the American character. To be sure, the element of racism cannot be dismissed. One may doubt whether such maniacal "experiments in population control" would have been conducted—at least, with such self-satisfaction and lack of guilt—on a white population. But in a deeper sense, the savagery of the American attack was a necessary and unavoidable consequence of the general policy that was adopted in the late 1940s—the policy of crushing a revolutionary nationalist movement that was deeply rooted in the population, a movement that gained its support because of the appeal of its commitment to independence and social reconstruction.

This policy remained in force until the final collapse of the Saigon regime. During the 1950s, the United States hoped to regain control over all of Indochina. The National Security Council in 1956 directed all US agencies in Vietnam to "work toward the weakening of the Communists in North and South Vietnam" in order to bring about "the eventual peaceful reunification of a free and independent Vietnam under anti-Communist leadership." Policy for Laos was stated in similar terms: "In order to prevent Lao neutrality from veering toward pro-Communism, encourage individuals and groups in Laos who oppose dealing with the Communist [bloc]—support the expansion and reorganization of police, propaganda, and army intelligence services, provided anti-Communist elements maintain effective control of these services—terminate economic and military aid if the Lao Government ceases to demonstrate a will to resist internal Communist subversion and to carry out a policy of maintaining its independence."[38] In Cambodia as well, the United States made significant efforts (in part through the medium of its Thai, South Vietnamese, and Philippine subordinates) to reverse the commitment to neutralism.[39] A few years later, it was recognized that Vietminh control over North Vietnam was irreversible, and the imperial managers lowered their sights. The goal was now a "non-Communist South Vietnam" instituted and guaranteed by American military force (since there was no other way), and a Western-oriented Laos and Cambodia.

A Gang of Murderers

Given this continuity of policy, it is hardly surprising that many Vietnamese saw the Americans as the inheritors of French colonialism. The *Pentagon Papers* cite studies of peasant attitudes demonstrating that "for many, the struggle which began in 1945 against colonialism continued uninterrupted throughout Diem's regime: in 1954, the foes of nationalists were transformed from France and Bao Dai to Diem and the U.S. . . . but the issues at stake never changed." By early 1964, even the US-backed generals were warning of the "colonial flavor to the whole pacification effort," noting that the French in their worst and clumsiest days never tried to control the local society as the Americans were planning to do. But the American leadership saw no alternative, and rejected the objections of their clients as "an unacceptable rearward step." A systems analysis study concluded that unless the Vietcong infrastructure ("the VC officials and organizers") "was destroyed, US-GVN military and pacification forces soon degenerated into nothing more than an occupation army." They did not add that if this "infrastructure" were destroyed, the US-GVN forces would be nothing but a gang of murderers. Both conclusions are, in fact, correct, and reflect the natural consequences of the implementation of the Indochina policy first mapped out in the late 1940s.

It was only after the Tet offensive that American terror was unleashed against South Vietnam in its full fury. What was to come was indicated by the tactics employed to reconquer the urban areas that quickly fell into the hands of Vietnamese resistance forces in January–February 1968. The events in Hue were typical. Here, thousands of people "were killed by the most hysterical use of American firepower ever seen," and then designated "as the victims of a Communist massacre."[40] The "accelerated pacification program" that followed was a desperate effort to reconstruct the shattered American position. It had some success. Describing the "massive" increase that had been achieved by August 1970, John Paul Vann estimated that "we control two million more people than we controlled two years ago," although he added that "occupation is only the first step in pacification." As for that second step—the "willing cooperation of the people with the Government and the overt rejection of the enemy"—contrary to the pretense of ignorant social scientists, that step had not been and never would be achieved.[41]

It is impossible in these pages even to sample the catalog of horrors, whether in Vietnam or in Laos and Cambodia, where the American murder machine was let loose to similar effect though the victims who survived were spared the viciousness and hypocrisy of the "pacifiers" and the "peace researchers" who followed in the wake of the military elsewhere. If anything, the destruction of these countries by American terror is even more appalling than Vietnam. Thus, in northern Laos, hundreds of miles from any zone of combat, the American military unleashed its air armadas (with particular intensity, when planes were released by cessation of the bombing of North Vietnam) for the sole purpose of demolishing a peaceful civilian society that was undergoing a mild social revolution under Pathet Lao leadership. Cambodia was subjected to a similar murderous attack on the pretext that the Vietnamese resistance forces were violating its neutrality, after massive American military operations had driven much of the Vietnamese population across the border in 1967. The story has been told elsewhere and need not be repeated here.[42]

Calculated Enterprise

Again, it is important to bear in mind that the character of the American war cannot be attributed solely to a sadistic military leadership or to incompetent or deranged civilian advisors. It was a calculated and rational enterprise undertaken to realize goals that could be achieved in no other way: namely, the goal, clearly stated in the 1940s, of preventing communist domination in a region where, it was always understood, the communists had "captured" the national movement. Furthermore, the tactics employed were by no means novel. To cite only the most obvious analogy, recall the air war in Korea, and significantly, the manner it which it was later analyzed. Since the rhetoric is itself revealing, I quote from an air force study of "an object lesson in air power to all the Communist world and especially to the Communists in North Korea," a lesson delivered a month before the armistice:

On 13 May 1953 twenty USAF F-84 fighter-bombers swooped down in three successive waves over Toksan irrigation dam in North Korea. From an altitude of 300 feet they skip-bombed their loads of high explosives into the hard-packed earthen walls of the dam. The subsequent flash flood scooped clean 27 miles of valley below, and the plunging flood waters wiped out large segments of a main north-south communication and supply route to the front lines. The Toksan strike and similar attacks on the Chasan, Kuwonga, Kusong, and Toksang dams accounted for five of the more than twenty irrigation dams targeted for possible attack—dams up-stream from all the important enemy supply routes and furnishing 75 percent of the controlled water supply for North Korea's rice production. These strikes, largely passed over by the press, the military observers, and the news commentators in favor of attention-arresting but less meaningful operations events, constituted one of the most significant air operations of the Korean war. They sent the Communist military leaders and political commissars scurrying to their press and radio centers to blare to the world the most severe, hate-filled harangues to come from the Communist propaganda mill in the three years of warfare.

In striking one target system, the USAF had hit hard at two sensitive links in the enemy's armor—his capability to supply his front-line troops and his capability to produce food for his armies. To the U.N. Command the breaking of the irrigation dams meant disruption of the enemy's lines of communication and supply. But to the Communists the smashing of the dams meant primarily the destruction of their chief sustenance—rice. The Westerner can little conceive the awesome meaning which the loss of this staple food commodity has for the Asian—starvation and slow death. "Rice famine," for centuries the chronic scourge of the Orient, is more feared than the deadliest plague. Hence the show of rage, the flare of violent tempers, and the avowed threats of reprisals when bombs fell on five irrigation dams.[43]

This report, no less typical of Nazi archives than some of those cited earlier, should have left little doubt in the minds of any rational observer as to how the United States would respond to a challenge to its imperial power in Indochina a few years later.

The same fundamental "dilemma" that made inevitable the savagery of the war always compelled the United States to evade any serious moves toward a negotiated settlement, and to reject the "peaceful means" that are required by "the supreme law of the land." In the second Mansfield Report (December 1965), it is explained that

... negotiations at this time, as a practical matter, would leave the Viet Cong in control of the countryside (much of which, by the way, they have controlled for many years and some of it since the time of the Japanese occupation). The Nationalists (and only with our continued massive support) would remain in control of Saigon, provincial capitals and the coastal base-cities. The status of the district seats would be in doubt.[44]

This conclusion was based on the reasonable assumption that "negotiations merely confirm the situation that exists on the ground."

Thus, despite the massacre of some two hundred thousand people in the preceding decade, despite the direct engagement of American military forces for four years, and despite the massive invasion and aerial bombardment of 1965, a political settlement was unthinkable, because the National Liberation Front controlled the countryside.[45]

Refusing to Negotiate

Similar reasoning had impelled the United States to undertake overt aggression earlier in the year. Throughout 1964, the NLF made repeated efforts to arrange a negotiated settlement based on the Laos model, with a neutralist coalition government. But the United States rejected any such "premature negotiations" as incompatible with its goal of maintaining a noncommunist South Vietnam under American control. The reason was quite simple. As American officials constantly reiterated, the NLF was the only significant political force and the US-imposed regime had virtually no popular base. Only the politically organized Buddhists could even conceive of entering into a coalition with the NLF, and the Buddhists, as General Westmoreland sagely observed, were not acting "in the best interests of the Nation." Ambassador Lodge later regarded them as "equivalent to card-carrying Communists," according to the *Pentagon Papers* historian. This, the US government position, was that only General Westmoreland and Ambassador Lodge understood "the interests of the Nation," all political groupings in South Vietnam being automatically excluded from any possible political settlement. To be sure, as William Bundy explained, we might be willing to consider the peaceful means required by law "after, *but only after*, we have established a clear pattern of pressure" (i.e., military force; his emphasis). As noted earlier, pacification specialist Vann took the same view, as did all other knowledgeable observers.

The United States therefore supported General Khanh and the Armed Forces Council. But by January 1965, even that last hope went up in smoke.

As Ambassador Taylor explained in his memoirs,[46] the US government "had lost confidence in Khanh" by late 1965. He lacked "character and integrity," added Taylor sadly. The clearest evidence of Khanh's lack of character was that by late January he was moving toward "a dangerous Khanh-Buddhist alliance which might eventually lead to an unfriendly government with which we could not work." Moreover, as we now know from other sources, he was also close to political agreement with the NLF.[47] Consequently, Khanh was removed. And in late January, according to the *Pentagon Papers*, Westmoreland "obtained his first authority to use US forces for combat within South Vietnam." The systematic and intensive bombing of South Vietnam (accompanied by a more publicized but less severe bombing of the North) began a few weeks later, to be followed by the open American invasion.

At every other period, much the same was true. The 1954 Geneva Accords were regarded as a "disaster" by the United States. The National Security Council met at once and adopted a general program of subversion throughout the region to ensure that the political settlement envisioned in the Accords would not be achieved.[48] In October 1972, just prior to the US presidential election, the DRV offered a peace proposal that virtually recapitulated the Geneva Accords and also incorporated the central positions in the founding documents of the NLF. Nixon and Kissinger could not openly reject this offer just prior to the elections, but they indicated clearly that the proposal was unacceptable while claiming deceitfully that "peace was at hand." Abetted by the subservient press, they were able to carry off this charade successfully, but their later efforts to modify the proposals, including the Christmas bombings, failed utterly. They were compelled to accept the very same offer, with trivial changes in wording, in January 1973.

As in the case of Geneva 1954, this agreement was purely formal. Even before the Paris Agreements of January 1973 were signed, Kissinger explained to the press that the United States would reject every essential principle in the Agreements. And in fact, the United States at once committed itself to subverting these agreements by intensifying the political repression in South Vietnam and by launching military actions against PRG territory through the medium of its client regime, massively supplied with arms. Again, the treachery of the mass media served to delude the public with regard to these events, helping to perpetuate the slaughter.[49]

By mid-1974, US government officials were reporting enthusiastically that their tactics were succeeding. They claimed that the Thieu regime had conquered about 15 percent of the territory of the PRG, exploiting its vast advantage in firepower, and that the prospects for further successes were great. As in the 1950s, the whole structure collapsed from within as soon as the communists were so ungracious as to respond.

No Political Solutions

The point of this brief resume has been to illustrate the complete refusal of the United States to consider any political settlement. The reason was always the same. It was always understood that there was no political base for US aggression, so that a peaceful political settlement would constitute a political defeat. This was precisely the dilemma of 1948, and it was never resolved.

Something similar happened with Laos. In 1958, the Pathet Lao won an important election. The American subversion system was therefore put into operation to prevent the political settlement from taking effect. At one point (December 1960), the United States was backing a military rebellion against the government that it regarded as the "duly constituted government" of Laos. By 1961, Kennedy approved "an immediate increase of 2,000 in the number of Meos being supported to bring the total to a level of 11,000," with an increase in US "mobile training teams in Laos to include advisors down to the level of the company." This "clandestine army" was conducting operations in territories controlled by the Pathet Lao and the neutralists under command control "exercised by the chief CIA Vientiane with the advice of chief MAAG Laos." Throughout this period, while the CIA was buying elections, subverting governments, supporting rebellions, and commanding its clandestine armies, American officials and independent newsmen conceded that—as in South Vietnam—there was no organized force that could challenge the communists in the political arena. Here too this was the main reason why American military forces were subsequently used to systematically demolish the rural society of Laos.[50]

Two Reasons for Murder

As I noted earlier, it was after the Tet offensive of early 1968 that the American murder machine really went into high gear in South Vietnam. The reasons were essentially two. It was feared that a political settlement of some sort would be inescapable, given the mounting pressures within the United States and the international arena to limit or terminate the American war. And with the American military forces disintegrating in the field, it was evident that they would soon have to be withdrawn and replaced by native mercenaries. Given all this, it was decided to carry out the maximum amount of destruction possible in South Vietnam in the time remaining. The hope was that a US-imposed regime might maintain control over a sufficiently demoralized and shattered society. As noted, American officials like Vann felt that the post-Tet accelerated pacification campaigns had been partially successful in bringing the population under American "occupation," though "pacification" would, of course, still require substantial efforts.

"Thrust for American Policy"

Imperialist ideologues in the academic community generally shared this analysis. Henry Kissinger, in his last contribution to scholarship before ascending to high office, outlined "the thrust for American policy in the next phase" as follows: "the United States should concentrate on the subject of the mutual withdrawal of external forces and avoid negotiating about the internal structure of South Vietnam for as long as possible."[51] Putting aside his irrelevant rationalizations, the meaning of this prescription is obvious. If American terrorism could succeed in at last demolishing the Southern resistance, an American client regime might be able to maintain itself. This would, however, only be possible if the North Vietnamese could be compelled to withdraw (the war planners had always expected that the bombing of the North and the direct American invasion of the South would draw the DRV into the conflict). Then, with North Vietnam out of the way, the United States could bring to bear the socioeconomic programs mentioned earlier to maintain the stable, noncommunist South Vietnam it had always sought. Of course, Kissinger's prescription required that the Southern resistance be smashed before the withdrawal of American troops. This is why, under his regime, such operations as Speedy Express were launched against the South Vietnamese, while the air war was stepped up in Laos and Cambodia.

It is not surprising that Kissinger was, for a time, the great hope of American liberals. As I have already noted, left-liberal "opponents" of the war had themselves urged that the solution was a peaceful settlement between South and North Vietnam with American military forces remaining in the South. Indeed, to this day they feel that their proposals to this effect might have occasionally been questionable in "nuance," but nothing more.[52] Thus it was perfectly natural that Kissinger should have been able to pacify much of the liberal opposition with his analysis of how an American military victory over the South Vietnamese might yet be attained.

To be sure, Kissinger was fully aware of the fundamental dilemma that had always plagued American policy makers. His way of phrasing the problem was as follows:

> The North Vietnamese and Viet Cong, fighting in their own country, needed merely to keep on being forces sufficiently strong to dominate the population after the United States tired of the war. We fought a military war; our opponents fought a political one . . . our military operations [had] little relationship to our declared political objectives. Progress in establishing a political base was excruciatingly slow. . . . In Vietnam—as in most developing countries—the overwhelming problem is not to buttress but to develop a political framework. . . . One ironic aspect of the war in Vietnam is that while we profess an idealistic philosophy, our failures have been due to an excessive reliance on material factors. The Communists, by contrast, holding to a materialistic interpretation, owe many of their successes to their ability to supply an answer to the question of the nature and foundation of political authority.[53]

Translating to simple prose: our problem is that the Vietnamese live there and we do not. This has made it difficult for us to develop a viable Vietnamese regime, whereas the Vietminh and their successors had long ago created a functioning and successful social order in which they gained their support. There is no "irony" here. Rather the problem is one that all imperial aggressors confront when faced with stubborn resistance, magnified in this case by the appeal of the social revolution.

Why Was the War Necessary?

Given the fundamental commitment to destroy the national movement, the United States was compelled to conduct a war of annihilation in South Vietnam and the surrounding region, and to reject any political settlement of the conflict. The question, however, remains: why was it always regarded as necessary to pursue this course? As noted earlier, the fundamental "dilemma" was clearly perceived in 1948, when State Department analysts explained that the "long-term objective" of the United States was "to eliminate so far as possible Communist influence in Indochina." The rationalization offered was that we must "prevent undue Chinese penetration and subsequent influence in Indochina" because of our deep concern "that the peoples of Indochina will not be hampered in their natural developments by the pressure of an alien people and alien interests." Therefore, the United States attempted to restore French rule, in accordance with another "long-term objective": "to see installed a self-governing nationalist state which will be friendly to the US and which . . . will be patterned upon our conception of a democratic state," and will be associated "with the western powers, particularly with France with whose customs, language, and laws the peoples of Indochina are familiar, to the end that those peoples will prefer freely to cooperate with the western powers culturally, economically and politically" and "will work productively and thus contribute to a better balanced world economy," while enjoying a rising standard of income.

The subsequent history in Indochina (and elsewhere) reveals just how deep was the American commitment to self-government, to democracy, and to a rising standard of living for the mass of the population. We may dismiss this as the usual imperialist tommyrot.

A Real Concern

But the concern that Indochina "contribute to a better balanced world economy" was real enough. There is compelling documentary evidence from the *Pentagon Papers* and other sources, that this and related concerns dominated all others and impelled the United States on its course in Indochina. As the record clearly demonstrates, American planners feared that the success of revolutionary nationalism would cause "the rot to spread" to the rest of mainland Southeast Asia and beyond to Indonesia and perhaps South Asia, ultimately impelling Japan, the workshop of the Pacific, to seek an accommodation with the communist powers. Should all this happen, the United States would in effect have lost the Pacific phase of World War II, a phase that was fought in part to prevent Japan from constructing a "new order" closed to American penetration.

The mechanisms by which the rot would spread were never clearly spelled out. But there is ample evidence that the planners understood that it would not be by military conquest. Rather, the danger was seen to lie in what they sometimes called "ideological successes," the demonstration effect of a successful revolution in Indochina (as in China). To counter this danger, pressure was put on Japan to reject "accommodation" with China. Access to Southeast Asia was promised as a reward for good behavior. And access was granted. By 1975 "Japanese commercial interests in Southeast Asia account for one-third of its US $100,000 million annual trade, more than 90% of the total $4,000 million 'yen credits' and a substantial share of the $10,000 million overseas investment balance,"[54] transactions that "have tended to enrich only a privileged few in Southeast Asia and their business and political counterparts in Japan."

It is no surprise, then, "that Japan was the only major country which had fully supported the American war policy in Indochina, including all-out bombing of North Vietnam in [1972]."[55]

Unacceptable to Ideologists

In spite of the fact that there is now substantial documentary evidence to support this analysis of American intentions,[56] it cannot be accepted by ideologists.[57] Instead they emphasize other peripheral factors—the need to gain French support for American programs in Europe, concern for some mystic "image," etc. To be sure, these factors were real enough. Thus restoration of European capitalism was the primary objective of American postwar policy, and it was achieved in a manner that, not coincidentally, supported an immense expansion of overseas investments by American corporations. And there is no doubt that the United States was concerned to reinforce the image of a grim destroyer that would tolerate no challenge to its global order. But the primary reason why the long-term objective of destroying the communist-led nationalist movement could not be abandoned is precisely the one that is repeatedly and clearly stressed in the documentary record: the United States could not tolerate the spreading of the rot of independence and self-reliance over Southeast Asia, with its possible impact upon Japan, the major industrial power of the Pacific region.

The precise weight of the motives that led US leaders to commit themselves to the destruction of the Vietnamese nationalist movement may be debated; however, the extensive documentary record now available, and briefly surveyed here, leaves no doubt that the commitment was undertaken in full awareness of what was at stake. This fact is difficult for many American intellectuals to accept, even those who opposed the war. To cite one striking and not untypical example, Professor John K. Fairbank of Harvard argues that a "factor of ignorance" lies at the source of what he called "our Vietnam tragedy." Lacking "an historical understanding of the modern Vietnamese revolution," we did not "realize that it was a revolution inspired by the sentiment of nationalism while clothed in the ideology of communism as applied to Vietnam's needs. . . . The result was that in the name of being anti-communist, vague though that term had become by 1965, we embarked on an anti-nationalist effort." We misconceived "our role in defending the South after 1965," conceiving it as aimed at blocking aggression from North Vietnam and "forestalling a southward expansion of Chinese Communism."[58] As we have seen, this analysis is refuted at every point by the historical record. The top planners knew from the start that the revolution was inspired by nationalism while clothed in the ideology of communism, and consciously embarked on an effort to destroy the nationalist movement. They always understood that intervention from the North was a response to American aggression (which they, like Fairbank, called "defending the South"). "Chinese expansion" was fabricated to provide a propaganda cover for American aggression in Indochina. At the very moment when they were planning the 1965 escalation, William Bundy and John McNaughton noted that unless the United States expanded the war, there would probably be "a Vietnamese-negotiated deal under which an eventually unified Communist Vietnam would assert its traditional hostility to Communist China . . . "[59]

As to why scholars choose to ignore the factual record, one may only speculate. We may note that it is convenient to blame the American "failure" on ignorance—a socially neutral concept—thus deflecting analysis of the systematic and institutional factors that brought about the American war.

A study group sponsored by the Woodrow Wilson Foundation and the National Planning Association once defined the primary threat of "communism" as the economic transformation of the communist powers "in ways which reduce their willingness and ability to complement the industrial economies of the West";[60] American hegemony in "the West" was naturally assumed. The comment is accurate and astute. The United States, as the dominant power in the global capitalist system (the "free world"), will use what means it can muster to counter any move toward independence that will tend to "reduce" this "willingness and ability."

Three-quarters of a century ago, Brooks Adams proclaimed that "our geographical position, our wealth, and our energy pre-eminently fit us to enter upon the development of Eastern Asia and to reduce it to part of our own economic system."[61] As Oliver Wendell Holmes admiringly commented, Adams thought that the Philippine War "is the first gun in the battle for the ownership of the world."[62] American victory in the Pacific war of 1941–45 appeared to lay the basis for success in achieving this "long-term objective." The US government was not prepared to see its vision—which, in the familiar manner, was presented as utterly selfless and benign—threatened by a nationalist movement in a small and unimportant country where the peasants were too naive to understand what was in their best interests. The policy planners and intellectuals who stood by while hundreds of thousands were slaughtered in Indonesia as the "Communist menace" was crushed and the country's riches again flowed toward the industrial powers, or who watched with occasional clucking of tongues as countries of the Western hemisphere fell under the rule of American-backed fascist torturers, could hardly have been expected to react differently in the case of Indochina, nor did they, until the domestic costs of the war mounted beyond tolerable levels, and a spontaneous movement of protest and resistance threatened to shatter domestic tranquility and authority.

Epilogue

On May 12, 1975, the US merchant ship *Mayaguez* was intercepted by Cambodian patrol boats within three miles of a Cambodian island, according to Cambodia; within seven miles, according to the ship's captain. Shortly after midnight US time on May 14, US planes sank three Cambodian gunboats. That afternoon, the secretary-general of the UN requested the parties to refrain from acts of force. At 7:07 p.m. the Cambodian radio announced that the ship would be released. A few minutes later, US Marines attacked Tang Island and boarded the deserted ship nearby. At 10:45 p.m., a boat approached the US destroyer *Wilson* with the crew of the *Mayaguez* aboard. Shortly after, US planes attacked the mainland. A second strike against civilian targets took place forty-three minutes after the captain of the *Wilson* reported to the White House that the crew of the *Mayaguez* was safe. US Marines were withdrawn after heavy fighting. The Pentagon announced that its largest bomb, fifteen thousand pounds, had been used. The operation cost the lives of forty-one Americans, according to the Pentagon, along with an unknown number of Cambodians.

A few days later, in an incident barely noted in the press, the US Coast Guard boarded the Polish trawler *Kalmar* and forced it to shore in San Francisco. The ship was allegedly fishing within the twelve-mile limit established by the United States. The crew was confined to the ship under armed guard as a court decided the penalty, which might include sale of the ship and its cargo. There have been many similar incidents. In one week of January 1975, Ecuador reportedly seized seven American tuna boats, some up to one hundred miles at sea, imposing heavy fines.

President Ford stated in a May 19 interview that the United States was aware that Cambodian gunboats had intercepted a Panamanian and a South Korean ship a few days before the *Mayaguez* incident, then released the ships and crews unharmed. Kissinger alleged that the United States had informed companies that Cambodia was defending its coastal waters, but the President of the American Institute of Marine Underwriters was unable to verify any such "forewarning."

Evidently, the *Kalmar* and *Mayaguez* incidents are not comparable. Cambodia had just emerged from a brutal war, for which the United States bears direct responsibility. For twenty years, Cambodia has been the victim of US subversion, harassment, devastating air attacks, and direct invasion. Cambodia has announced that hostile US actions continue, including espionage flights and "subversive sabotage and destructive activities" and penetration of coastal waters by US spy ships "engaged in espionage activities there almost daily." Thai and Cambodian nationals have been landed, Cambodia alleges, to contact espionage agents, and have confessed that they are in the employ of the CIA. There can be no doubt that Cambodia has ample reason, based on history and perhaps current actions, to be wary of US subversion and intervention. In contrast, Poland poses no threat to the security or territorial integrity of the United States.

According to Kissinger, the United States decided to use military force to avoid "a humiliating discussion"—failing to add that the "supreme law of the land" obliges the United States to limit itself to "humiliating discussion" and other peaceful means if it perceives a threat to peace and security. Aware of its legal obligations, the United States informed the UN Security Council that it was exercising the inherent right of self-defense against armed attack, though evidently it is ludicrous to describe the Cambodian action as an "armed attack" against the United States in the sense of the UN Charter.

Despite official denials, the American military actions were clearly punitive in intent. The *Washington Post* reports that US sources privately conceded "that they were gratified to see the Khmer Rouge government hit hard" (May 17, 1975). Cambodia had to be punished for its insolence in withstanding the armed might of the United States. The domestic response indicates that the illegal resort to violence will continue to enjoy liberal support, if only it can succeed. Senator Kennedy stated that "the President's firm and successful action gave an undeniable and needed lift to the nation's spirits, and he deserves our genuine support."[63] That everyone's spirits were lifted by still another blow at Cambodia, after years of US terror and savagery, may be doubted. Still, this reaction, from the senator most closely concerned with the human impact of the American war, is important and revealing. Senator Mansfield explained that Ford's political triumph weakens antimilitarist forces in Congress. Supporting his conclusion, on May 20 the House voted overwhelmingly against reducing American troop commitments overseas. House Majority Leader Thomas P. O'Neill reversed his earlier support for troop reductions.

There have been a few honorable voices of protest. Anthony Lewis observed that "for all the bluster and righteous talk of principle, it is impossible to imagine the United States behaving that way toward anyone other than a weak, ruined country of little yellow people who have frustrated us."[64] We need only add that the world was put on notice—as if notice were needed—that the United States will tolerate no reproach for its sadistic war against Cambodia or the rest of Indochina. And more generally, that the world's most violent power intends to persist in the illegal use of force for global management, confident that success will bring support within the political mainstream.

On the liberal wing of the mainstream, John Osborne chided Lewis in the *New Republic* for his failure to see "some good and gain" in the *Mayaguez* incident. Osborne himself felt that the president acted "properly, legally, courageously, and as necessity required." There were, to be sure, some "flaws." One of these flaws, "disturbing, avoidable, and to be deplored," was the tentative plan to use B-52s. But our honor was saved, according to Osborne, when the plan was rejected for the following reasons: "partly because of predictable domestic and world reaction and partly because heavy bombing would almost certainly have worsened rather than bettered the lot of the *Mayaguez* crewmen."[65]

Another possible consideration comes to mind: bombing of defenseless Cambodia with B-52s, once again, would have constituted another major massacre of the Cambodian people. But no such thoughts trouble the mind or conscience of this austere tribune of the people, who sternly admonished those "journalistic thumbsuckers" who raised questions in the wrong "manner and tone" in "a disgrace to journalism."

Here we see again the Nazi-style mentality—I use the term advisedly—that has characterized much of the reaction to the American war in Indochina among the liberal intelligentsia. They understand nothing; they have learned nothing.

Top administration officials have informed the press that it was Henry Kissinger who "advocated bombing the Cambodian mainland with B-52's during the recent crisis over the captured ship *Mayaguez*."[66] Thankfully, he was overruled by others who felt that carrier-based bombers would be punishment enough.

From "Mad Jack" in 1845 to "Mad Henry" in 1975; that is the story of the United States in Indochina.

CHAPTER 11

After "Mad Henry": US Policy Toward Indochina Since 1975

Ngô Vĩnh Long

After the 1968 Tet offensive, I founded the Vietnam Resource Center in Cambridge, Massachusetts, with the aim of providing the American public as well as interested individuals or organizations anywhere in the world with information and analyses on the war in Vietnam that were not otherwise available in English. One of the publications of the Center was the monthly English-language newsletter *Thoi Bao Ga*. The first issue came out in March 1969; for the next six years *Thoi Bao Ga* documented the conduct of the war and its many social, economic, and political consequences for Vietnam, especially for South Vietnamese society. With the end of the war I thought the newsletter had served its purpose, so I terminated it in May 1975. In its place I wanted to start a new magazine, *Vietnam Quarterly*, to serve as a vehicle for people with differing expertise from around the world to address the many issues concerning Vietnam's rebuilding and development, as well as to facilitate reconciliation and ties between Indochina and the United States.

I asked my friend of many years, Professor Noam Chomsky, to serve as an editor of the *Vietnam Quarterly* and to write an article summarizing the history of relations between the United States and Indochina, with implications for the future. Noam sent the manuscript for "From Mad Jack to Mad Henry" very quickly, and the entire editorial board—which included several American Nobel laureates in various fields—was proud to publish this piece in the first issue, which came out in January 1976. Subsequently the article was reprinted in the journal *Bridge: An Asian-American Perspective*, when the

Vietnam Resource Center and the Asian American Association in New York collaborated to publish two special issues of *Bridge* devoted to Indochina.

"From Mad Jack to Mad Henry" ends with an epilogue of several pages on the *Mayaguez* incident and Henry Kissinger's involvement. Yet the piece does not mention another of Kissinger's decisions during the same time period, which was to have much more disastrous consequences for both Cambodia and Vietnam in years ahead: On May 14, 1975, although preoccupied with the *Mayaguez* incident and many other urgent tasks, Henry Kissinger somehow found time to recommend to the secretary of commerce that the strictest trade sanctions be imposed on Cambodia and South Vietnam.[1] Without consulting Congress, as of May 16 the Treasury Department began to carry out a series of measures that prevented American citizens from sending any humanitarian aid to people in those countries. Americans were repeatedly denied licenses to send items such as pencils, chalk, machinery to make prosthetic devices, fishing nets, and farming equipment. Even letters and telegrams between refugees and their families in Cambodia and Vietnam were prohibited.[2] Only two other countries, Cuba and North Korea, were relegated by the United States to this most-restrictive embargo category, known as Category Z.[3]

The brutality of these sanctions clearly demonstrated the Ford administration's hostile attitude toward postwar Vietnam, but the justifications offered for extending the sanctions to South Vietnam were even more revealing. At a congressional hearing in June 1975 State Department officials explained that the language used to place a full embargo on North Vietnam in 1958 stated only "Communist-controlled areas of Vietnam" and not "the Democratic Republic of Vietnam" or "North Vietnam." And since all of Vietnam now was "communist-controlled," not extending the sanctions to the South would be tantamount to lifting the trade embargo. This, they argued, would in effect be rewarding the Vietnamese communists for defeating the United States and its South Vietnamese allies. When asked why it was a matter of national security to impose a trade embargo on Vietnam, deputy assistant secretary of state Robert Miller explained that the controls would permit the US government "to monitor the evolving attitudes of these new regimes toward the United States and toward its citizens."[4] In other words, this policy was meant not just to punish the Vietnamese people for their success in having liberated themselves from the American occupation of their country, but also to preempt any objectionable future attitudes and actions of the nascent governments.

This preemptive policy seemed even more blatantly hostile to the Vietnamese given the repeated statements by Vietnamese leaders that they desired diplomatic cooperation and good relations with the United States. A few days after the liberation of South Vietnam, for example, Premier Pham Van Dong of the Democratic Republic of Vietnam sent a message to Washington through Sweden in which he stated that a chapter had been closed, and that Hanoi was looking forward to enjoying "good relations with the United States." In this letter Premier Dong never broached the subject of an American "contribution to healing the wounds of war" as stipulated in the Paris agreement.[5] On May 14, 1975, the very day that Kissinger ordered the trade embargo, the *Washington Star* reported that Hanoi wanted good relations with the United States and would welcome without any precondition an American diplomatic mission in Saigon under a new South Vietnamese government.[6]

Before the collapse of the Saigon government in 1975, both the government in Hanoi and the Provisional Revolutionary Government (PRG) in the South had often stated that they envisioned the reunification of Vietnam proceeding step by step over a period of twelve to fourteen years. After liberation the Vietnamese sent two official observer delegations to the United Nations, one representing North Vietnam and the other representing the South. In mid-July North Vietnam and South Vietnam submitted applications for membership to the UN as two independent states. The United States strongly opposed these applications. Daniel Patrick Moynihan, then US ambassador to the UN, explained in his memoirs that, at the time, the admission of the two states of Vietnam would have symbolized and confirmed that the United States had been "utterly humiliated" in Vietnam. However, Moynihan was also concerned about the consequences of an outright veto. In a cable to the White House he stated, "For us to veto the admission of the Vietnams would be a calamity. . . . *We would be seen to act out of bitterness, blindness, weakness and fear. . . . The overwhelming response would be contempt.*"[7] Instead, Moynihan proposed that the United States should link the Vietnamese applications to the upcoming South Korean application. In a telegram to Kissinger, Moynihan suggested that since "there is not now a sufficient number of votes available even to get the South Korean application inscribed on the Council agenda," the United States should use the rejection of the South Korean application as a pretext to veto the Vietnamese admissions. Moynihan explained that otherwise a US veto would be seen as no less than a direct continuation of the war against Vietnam on the diplomatic level.

On July 30, 1975, the UN Security Council voted twelve to one to put the Vietnamese membership applications on the UN agenda, but opposed even allowing a discussion of the South Korean case. Moynihan immediately made an announcement before the UN National Security Council that the United States would veto the Vietnamese admissions, citing Washington's desire for "universality" of admissions. The United States, Moynihan stated, could not tolerate the rejection of South Korea alongside the admission of the two Vietnamese states.[8] A few days before the vote on August 11, in the hope of softening Washington's position, Hanoi offered to return the bodies of three American pilots shot down during the war.[9]

The uncompromising stance of the United States had the effect of strengthening the hands of hard-liners in North Vietnam who favored early reunification with the South. Only two months after the US veto of the two independent Vietnamese applications to the UN, the Central Committee of the Communist Party declared at its Twenty-Fourth Plenum in September 1975 that Vietnam had entered a "new revolutionary phase." The tasks at hand were as follows: "To complete the reunification of the country and take it rapidly, vigorously and steadily to socialism. To speed up socialist construction and perfect socialist relations of production in the North, and to carry out at the same time socialist transformation and construction in the South . . . in every field: political, economic, technical, cultural and ideological." The Resolution of the Twenty-Fourth Plenary Session of the Party Central Committee stressed that in order to carry out socialist transformation and construction in the South the "comprador class" and the "vestiges of the colonial and feudal land systems" would have to be eradicated.[10]

In order to understand some of the reasons for these transformational policies and their subsequent impact on Vietnam, it is necessary to begin with a summary of the incredible human toll, the physical destruction, and the social and economic dislocations created by the war. Figures regarding human casualties are admittedly incomplete. After years of study the Vietnamese Ministry of Labor, Wounded War Veterans, and Social Problems announced in October 1993 that approximately two million civilians had been killed, two million wounded, and two million contaminated by various chemical agents sprayed by the US Armed Forces. The majority of these casualties occurred in South Vietnam. As for combat casualties, the ministry gave only the total figures for North Vietnamese soldiers and NLF guerrillas without any breakdown. These totaled 1.1 million killed, 600,000 wounded, and 300,000 missing in action.[11] US estimates of Vietnamese civilian deaths during the US phase of the war include some 300,000 Vietnamese killed by both sides and 65,000 North Vietnamese killed by US bombs. Between 1959 and 1975 the Republic of Vietnam Armed Forces—those based in Saigon—suffered some

224,000 killed and more than 1 million wounded, excluding losses in the final phase of the war, for which figures are unavailable.[12]

Official estimates for the consequences of the war in Vietnam have consistently understated the magnitude of the problems. This was true, for example, in the case of Agent Orange and other herbicides sprayed in Vietnam. In 1974, the US National Academy of Sciences published estimates of the extent and distribution of herbicides sprayed. Since it had been thought that these estimates were inaccurate, Congress passed the Agent Orange Act (AOA) of 1991, which requested that the Institute of Medicine (IOM) assess the evidence of an association between exposure to military herbicides and disease in order to determine the need for further epidemiological studies. This recommendation resulted in a report published in the April 17, 2003 issue of *Nature*. The article states, "Here we present revised estimates, developed using more complete data. The spray inventory is expanded by more than seven million litres, in particular with heavily dioxin contaminated herbicides. Estimates for the amount of dioxin sprayed are almost doubled. Hamlet census data reveal that millions of Vietnamese were likely to have been sprayed upon directly."[13] The *Nature* study used the Hamlet Evaluation Survey (HES), which during the war amassed monthly data on almost every hamlet, to come to the conclusion that

> among the hamlets with some population data, 3,881 were sprayed directly and at least 2.1 million but perhaps as many as 4.8 million people would have been present during the spraying. Another 1,450 hamlets were also sprayed, but we cannot estimate the population involved. In all, at least 3,851 out of 5,958 known fixed-wing missions had flight paths directly over the hamlet coordinates given in the HES and gazetteer data and about 35% of the total herbicides sprayed was flown by these missions, although, in general, the flight paths extended beyond hamlet borders.[14]

Herbicides were first sprayed in Vietnam with the intent of destroying crops and thus cutting off food supply to the NLF; later they were used to drive the civilian population out of areas supposedly under NLF control. (Ed. note: For more information on the lasting consequences of Agent Orange on Vietnam and the Vietnamese people, see chapter 3 of this book.) In a 1968 article entitled "Our Chemical War," Seymour M. Hersh wrote:

> But by early 1967, Presidential advisers had a different reason for using herbicides, one that wasn't directly linked to cutting off Viet Cong food supplies. The rationale was presented to a group of scientists who met in

February with Donald Hornig, President Johnson's chief scientific adviser, to protest the use of anticrop chemicals. According to one scientist who attended the session, Hornig explained that the anticrop program was aimed chiefly at moving the people.[15]

According to US estimates, the total population of South Vietnam in 1964 was around 15.7 million, with about 4.2 million urban and 11.5 million rural. The population in 1970 was 18.3 million total, with about 6.7 million urban and 11.6 million rural. In 1964 the total population of the Mekong Delta was estimated at about 6.3 million with 400,000 urban and 5.9 million rural. By 1970 the total Mekong Delta population had increased slightly to 6.8 million, but its urban population had jumped to 1.2 million while the rural population had decreased to 5.6 million.[16]

Perhaps even more significant were residential and occupational shifts within the rural population itself. According to a US Senate investigation, by 1972 South Vietnam had more than 10 million refugees.[17] Official Saigon sources claimed that actually only about 3.9 million refugees—out of a total population of about 18.7 million—were living in and around urban areas and in refugee camps.[18] Although Saigon provided no figure for the total rural population, its economic ministry disclosed that there were one million peasant families and another million households that engaged principally in the marketing and processing of agricultural products.[19] This meant that about half the rural population had been shifted to non-agricultural occupations. As a result, staple production had stagnated. According to US figures, rice production in the Mekong Delta was 2.6 million metric tons (MT) in 1964 and 2.7 million MT in 1970; for all of South Vietnam, rice production was about 3.5 million MT in 1964 and 3.3 million MT in 1970. Throughout this period rice consumption in the Mekong Delta remained steady at around 2 million MT a year, so South Vietnam had to import huge amounts of staples in order to feed its growing population. In 1970, for example, imports included some 560,000 MT of rice, 250,000 MT of wheat, and 17,000 MT of other food grains.[20]

The food and economic situations in South Vietnam became much worse after the signing of the Paris Peace Accords in January 1973. This was partly because the United States supplied the Thieu government with so much armament that it was encouraged to undertake "military operations to saturate the national territory" (*hanh quan tran ngap lanh tho*) through ground assaults on and indiscriminate bombing and shelling of the areas under the control of the PRG.[21] The February 16, 1974 issue of the *Washington Post* quoted Pentagon officials as saying that the Thieu armed forces were "firing blindly into free zones [i.e., PRG-controlled areas] because they knew full well they would get all the replacement supplies they needed from the United States."

Worse still, because of the increase in economic aid to the Thieu regime in 1973 and 1974, the Thieu government felt confident enough to carry out an "economic blockade" designed to inflict hunger and starvation on the PRG areas.[22] Thieu was frequently quoted as exhorting his armed forces to do their utmost to implement the "economic blockade" in order to defeat the "Communists" by starving them out.[23] This blockade, known as the "rice war" in the American press at the time, included prohibitions on the transport of rice from one village to another, the milling of rice by anyone except the government, storage of rice in homes, and the sale of rice outside the village to anyone other than government-authorized buyers.

Widespread hunger and starvation resulted. According to reports by Saigon deputies and Catholic priests, up to 60 percent of the population of the central provinces was reduced to eating bark, cacti, banana roots, and the bulbs of wild grass. Children and the aged were the first victims. In some central Vietnamese villages, deaths from starvation claimed 1 to 2 percent of the total population each month.[24] Even in the wealthiest section of Saigon itself, Tan Dinh district, a poll conducted by Catholic students in late summer 1974 disclosed that only 22 percent of the families had enough to eat. Half the families could afford only a meal of steamed rice and a meal of gruel per day; the rest went hungry.[25] And in the once rice-rich Mekong Delta, acute rice shortages became commonplace in many provinces.[26] In addition to hunger and starvation, Thieu's policies precipitated a major depression. On February 25, 1974, *Hoa Binh* ("Peace," a conservative Catholic daily newspaper in Saigon) quoted Deputy Premier Phan Quang Dan as complaining that there were three million to four million unemployed persons in the Saigon-controlled areas alone.

With the end of the war in 1975 the Southern half of Vietnam found itself in an even worse socioeconomic situation. To the unemployed and hungry mentioned above, one must factor in the several million Saigon soldiers and police forces as well as the three hundred thousand to five hundred thousand prostitutes who suddenly found themselves out of work. There were also several hundred thousand disabled war veterans and eight hundred thousand orphans. The priority of the policy makers in Hanoi, as expressed repeatedly in official party journals, was to feed and provide jobs for the eight million unemployed people in the urban areas in the South—more than one-third of the total population.[27] The dire situation was exacerbated in May 1975 by the strict trade embargo imposed by the United States and supported by most of its allies, which left the Vietnamese government with few options. These developments played an important role in the decision spelled out in the Party Central Committee's Twenty-Fourth Plenum resolution of September 1975 to combine the "eradication of the comprador class" with the "elimination of the vestiges of colonialist and feudalist land system" in the South.

The party perceived that the commercialization of the South's rural economy, particularly production by the middle peasants, was tightly linked to the comprador capitalists in the urban areas. The middle peasants produced the most food surplus in the South. If the government allowed them to maintain close ties with the capitalists in the urban areas, it would be difficult for the government to procure enough staples and other agricultural products to supply the urban population and the huge numbers of people in its administration and its military.[28] Therefore, transformation of the rural economy had to be tightly coordinated with transformation of the private commercial and industrial sectors.

On the morning of September 11, 1975, the so-called "X-1 campaign" was launched when army units, public security agents, local militia, and self-defense units raided the houses of comprador capitalists in the Saigon-Cholon area and seventeen other provincial cities. This campaign lasted until December 1976. *Vietnam Courir*, a magazine of the foreign ministry, stated in its November 1975 issue that this was "the logical continuation of the military and political campaign against the puppet regime rigged up by US imperialism."[29]

There were relatively few targets for the X-1 campaign in the countryside since most of the landlords had already fled to the cities. The land they left behind had either been confiscated and distributed among the poor peasants by the NLF, or it had been sold to the peasants on an installment basis by the Thieu regime through the so-called "Land to the Tiller" program, which had paid the landlords several billion dollars in US aid money.[30] The official party daily *Nhan Dan* ("People") concluded on December 1, 1975, that there was no need to carry out land reform in the southern part of Vietnam. According to the party, only a slight adjustment of the landholding patterns—allotting "surplus lands" belonging to rural capitalists and rich peasants to landless peasants—was called for.[31]

During the X-1 campaign 670 heads of household in the Saigon-Cholon area and in seventeen other provincial cities were considered compradors. About 70 percent of those who were categorized as compradors were Vietnamese citizens of ethnic Chinese background (*Hoa*), prompting China to accuse Vietnam of discriminating against the ethnic Chinese and thereby increasing tensions between the two countries. Moreover, although the government had explained clearly when the X-1 program started that the sole targets were the compradors and not the "national capitalists," the dividing line between the two groups had blurred as the campaign widened. In the zeal to emulate the large cities, many smaller urban centers tried to produce a couple of compradors although in reality there were none.[32] This situation created some panic among the wealthy, even those who had not collaborated with the Americans and the Saigon regime. To pacify public fears, the central government reexamined the situation and admitted that many people had been wrongly targeted. As a result, the original number of 670 heads of household was decreased to 159, of whom 117 were ethnic Chinese.

Contrary to the swift action taken in urban areas during the X-1 campaign, and in spite of the tough language in the Twenty-Fourth Plenum resolution and subsequent directives, the party and government were much more deliberate and cautious in dealing with the problems in the countryside. In 1975 the rural population was directed to establish so-called "production teams," aimed at encouraging the peasants to exchange labor, to help each other in production, and to produce according to the plans of the central government. Official sources reported that in 1975, 12,246 such production teams were formed in South Vietnam. However, because the teams had been assembled hastily under pressure and coercion by local party members and officials, four thousand of them disintegrated quickly when confronted with the severe natural disasters of 1976, while six thousand other teams continued to do poorly.[33]

It was not until the end of October 1976 that the Secretariat and the Standing Committee of the Government Council organized a special conference in Ho Chi Minh City (formerly Saigon) to formulate programs to carry out the wishes of the party on the land reform issue. This resulted in the redistribution of land belonging to former landlords in areas that had been under Saigon control, land belonging to Catholic and Buddhist churches that had been rented out to tenant farmers, and land donated by rich farmers to peasants with no land or inadequate land. By 1978 some 426,000 hectares (ha) had been redistributed and the peasants who worked these lands were regarded as "primary cultivators." The Politburo stated in its Directive 57 of November 15, 1978, that "the vestiges of exploitation by feudal landlords have been eradicated and the majority of the land [in South Vietnam] now belongs to the peasant laborers."[34]

Due to this land redistribution and due in greater part to the movement of approximately one million people from the North and urban areas of the South to reclaim close to one million ha of land, food production in South Vietnam increased significantly in 1976 and 1977. In 1976 total staple production reached 7.1 million MT, an increase of about 22 percent over the average annual production of 5.2 million MT during the 1961–1965 period. In 1977, despite many disastrous floods, food production in the South still reached 6.8 million MT, an increase of about 17 percent over the best pre-war years. Staple production was calculated in terms of rice and rice equivalents: one kilogram of corn, three kilograms of sweet potatoes, or five kilograms of manioc, for example, were equivalent to one kilogram of paddy rice. During the pre-escalation period of 1961–1965 the total production of corn, sweet potatoes, and manioc had been 39,000 MT, 277,000 MT, and 196,000 MT respectively. By 1977 the total production of these staples had increased to 159,000 MT, 775,000 MT, and 1,400,000 MT respectively.[35]

The increased production in South Vietnam did not, however, lead to an increase in government food procurement, which included taxes and government purchase. In 1976 and 1977 government procurement amounted to 950,000 MT and 790,000 MT respectively. Under the agricultural tax system at the time, peasants did not have to pay taxes on produce kept for family consumption, but a graduated tax was imposed on all marketed surplus. For example, a tax of 8 percent had to be paid on a surplus of 200 to 250 kilograms of rice. According to official surveys, most of the poor peasants did not have to pay any taxes or have any surplus to sell. The largest surplus came from the middle peasants in the Mekong Delta. However, procurement through taxes was inadequate because production had not increased sufficiently in other areas of the country. The government paid for much of this surplus at market prices in order to provide all registered inhabitants of urban areas, as well as all government employees, subsidized rates of one-sixth to one-tenth of the going market prices.[36]

In 1977 food production and procurement also suffered due to the escalating conflict with Cambodia and increasing tension with China. Beginning in January 1977 Khmer Rouge forces attacked civilian settlements across the border in six out of seven of Vietnam's border provinces. Similar attacks occurred again in April. The Vietnamese government decided not to retaliate and instead sent a conciliatory letter to Phnom Penh proposing negotiations to resolve the border problem. The Khmer Rouge rejected this offer and continued with the attacks. In September and December the Vietnamese counterattacked strongly, pulling back each time with an offer for negotiation. Each time Phnom Penh spurned the offer for talks and continued to attack Vietnamese territory until late 1978. During these two years of attacks Khmer Rouge troops brutally murdered about thirty thousand Vietnamese civilians, impelling tens of thousands of Vietnamese to flee the border provinces. Many people in the no-escape zones abandoned their farmland and flooded into Ho Chi Minh City and other urban areas. Several hundred thousand Cambodian refugees also fled to Vietnam during those years.[37]

Cambodia's aggressiveness and intransigence were certainly made possible, if not encouraged, by China's aid and support. According to historian D. R. SarDesai,

> Between 1975 and 1978, China supplied Cambodia with 130-mm mortars, 107-mm bazookas, automatic rifles, transport vehicles, gasoline, and various small weapons, enough to equip thirty to forty regiments totaling about 200,000 troops. There is no way of knowing how much economic assistance was additionally provided by China beyond the initial gift of $1 billion made at the time of Sihanouk's return to Phnom Penh in 1975. An estimated 10,000 Chinese military and technical personnel were sent to Cambodia to improve its military preparedness.[38]

The aim was to pressure Vietnam to join China in condemning Soviet hegemony. China also threatened to cut off all loans and grants to Vietnam if Vietnam refused to do so. In the words of SarDesai, "China did not make an exception even on humanitarian grounds. Thus when Vietnam was hit by severe food shortages during 1976–1977 because of adverse weather conditions, China did not send any food grain across its southern borders. In contrast, the Soviet Union supplied 450,000 of the 1.6 million tons of food rushed to Vietnam by external agencies."[39]

While Vietnam's domestic situation and its relations with Cambodia and China worsened, in the United States the Democratic candidate for president won the 1976 election. President Jimmy Carter wanted to improve relations with Vietnam for a number of reasons, one of which was to stabilize the political situation in Southeast Asia. Three rounds of talks lasted from May to December 1977. The US position was to establish full relations with Vietnam as soon as possible without any precondition. Vietnam's position was that the United States should lift the trade embargo and grant Vietnam the 3.2 billion dollars in aid that Nixon had promised. In return, Vietnam would do everything possible to help the United States solve the issue of MIA (missing in action) soldiers. It is not known whether Vietnam was desperate or whether there were outside pressures, but Vietnam still pressed the aid issue at the third negotiating session, held December 19–20, 1977. Consequently the negotiations broke down. Meanwhile, China increased its military pressures along Vietnam's northern borders and supported Cambodia's widespread attacks along the southwestern borders.

Confronted by economic and security crises, in March 1978 the Vietnamese government launched the X-2 campaign to "eradicate commercial capitalists" (*xoa bo tu san thuong nghiep*). As stated in many government documents at the time, the primary reason for the move against commercial capitalists was to strengthen the distribution capability of the government. By the beginning of 1978, however, 1,500 enterprises in the South had already been nationalized and transformed into 650 state-run concerns with a total of 130,000 workers, 70 percent of the total work force in this sector. Almost all large rice mills, warehouses, and transport facilities had also been placed under government control.[40] This meant that the capitalists were not hoarding and speculating in bulk commodities such as rice, but in items that could be easily concealed, such as gold, diamonds, dollars, and precision machines and their spare parts, which were extremely difficult to flush out.

The X-2 campaign was accompanied by a money-exchange scheme to replace the two different currencies used at the time in the North and South with one standardized national currency, the *dong*. In the words of one author,

> However, by this time the rich had either dispersed their wealth or transferred it into precious commodities such as gold and diamonds that could be easily hidden, so neither the X-2 campaign nor the currency replacement scheme netted the government much goods and cash. In fact, the whole program further eroded public trust in the currency in use and pushed people to speculate in gold, thereby artificially increasing the price of gold to the extent that during the 1978–1979 period an ounce of gold could support a family comfortably for the whole year. [41]

In addition, the X-2 campaign created a whole array of new problems for the Vietnamese government. First, the fact that many of the commercial capitalists targeted by the X-2 campaign were ethnic Chinese gave China the excuse to terminate all aid and all trade by mid-1978. Trade with China had accounted for 70 percent of Vietnam's foreign trade. Much of China's aid had been consumer items, such as hot water flasks, bicycles, electric fans, canned milk, and fabrics; without these items the government had little to offer the peasants for their produce as incentives to increase production. However, long before the government undertook the X-2 campaign in March 1978, the commercial capitalists had already dispersed their goods and funds among relatives and the tens of thousands of small traders belonging to their networks. Meanwhile, the commercial capitalists continued to compete with the government for the peasants' produce and to create obstacles to the government's efforts at rural transformation.

In the face of these complicated urban and rural developments, on April 14, 1978, the Politburo issued Directive 43-CT/TW, which called for the vigorous "transformation of agriculture" in South Vietnam.[42] The transformation of agriculture meant rural collectivization, in effect the imposition of the Northern model on the South. However, the collectivization in the North from 1965 to 1975 had produced many social and economic problems. This policy of centralizing production through cooperativization had as its goal the extraction of much-needed resources from the countryside to support the war effort. Land and labor utilization and income distribution in the cooperatives were made on an egalitarian—hence "socialist"—basis so as to ensure social stability and to provide psychological security for those families who sent their sons and daughters to fight in the war. The cooperative system also allowed the government to procure a certain amount of foodstuffs that it could redistribute to families of soldiers, disabled veterans, and war dead for free or at subsidized prices. During this decade the rural area in the North supplied two million able-bodied men and women for the battlefront and contributed tens of millions of workdays for national defense purposes. However, the system proved extremely inefficient. Staple production decreased from an average of 305 kilograms per capita during the 1961–1965 period to only 252 kilograms per capita for the 1966–1975 period. Production costs increased by an average of 75 percent during the 1971–1975 period while the average income of cooperative members increased by only 23 percent. Husbandry incurred an average loss of 10 percent a year. The socioeconomic consequences would have been very severe had it not been for the government's ability to give financial aid and other subsidies to the rural population, thanks to foreign aid.[43]

Hanoi knew full well the problems it faced in the rural areas in both North and South. Collectivization had proceeded cautiously in the South, especially in the Mekong Delta, until the beginning of 1978. But now the party leadership was willing to gamble that by getting the peasants into a collective framework, the government would be able to procure food more effectively in the effort to feed the burgeoning urban population and the armed forces.

In response to the conflicts with Cambodia and China, some three hundred thousand to four hundred thousand men and women had been added to the various armed forces, while hundreds of thousands of refugees had flooded into the cities. The total number of people in the armed forces and in urban areas was now estimated at 11.5 million out of a total population of around 50 million in 1980.[44] Another primary goal of collectivization was to try to increase governmental penetration into and control of rural areas, as expressed in the Twenty-Fourth Plenum resolution of September 1975. Subsequently, almost every report on the achievements of any village, district, or province assessed success or failure in the most basic terms of political control.[45]

The collectivization program met with fierce resistance, principally from the rich and middle peasants, who had been the main supporters of the revolution but whose interests and welfare were now under attack by the regime. By the end of 1980 official figures showed that in all of South Vietnam only 3,732 production teams and 173 medium-size cooperatives remained. Many peasants simply abandoned farming altogether. In 1980 the area of cultivated land had decreased by about 100,000 ha from 1978 figures, and staple production had dropped by more than 400,000 MT.[46]

Food procurement in 1978 and 1979 also decreased drastically: 457,000 MT in 1978 and only 398,000 MT in 1979. In 1978 and 1979 the government implemented the *nghia vu luong thuc* ("food obligations") policy, through which the peasants were required to sell a certain amount of paddy rice to the government at the "two-way contract" rate of 0.50 dong per kilogram. The government then provided all registered inhabitants of the urban areas with a minimum rice ration of thirteen kilograms per adult at the subsidized rate of 0.40 dong per kilogram—only one-tenth of the going market price. In return, the state sold the peasants an equivalent value of goods such as oil, gasoline, fertilizers, and fabrics at subsidized rates. But the exchange was unsatisfactory. The government goods were slow in coming due to shortages, pilferage by officials in charge, and distribution and transportation problems; moreover, many of the items pushed by the government were not necessarily what the peasants wanted. As a result, in 1979 food procurement decreased fourfold in many Southern provinces. The overall food procurement situation would have been much worse if the government had not purchased additional volumes of rice at market prices. To remedy this situation, in 1980 the government modified its pricing policies and was able to procure 1 million MT of rice. Successful food procurement, therefore, was more contingent on market and pricing mechanisms than on collectivization and its various control mechanisms.[47]

Although Vietnam had made the decision to push collectivization in the South in March 1978, in part to extract enough resources from the rural areas in order to defend against attacks by Cambodia and China, it was still hoping to improve relations with the United States. Both publicly and through the offices of countries such as France, Sweden, and the Soviet Union, Vietnam offered to drop the precondition for economic aid and promised to help the United States wholeheartedly in resolving the MIA issues. In July 1978 Vietnam repeated these proposals many times.[48] On July 31, 1978, Premier Pham Van Dong told an American delegation to Hanoi, led by Senator Edward Kennedy, that Vietnam had not only dropped the precondition for US economic aid in order to normalize relations with the United States, but that Vietnam also truly wanted to be a good friend to the United States.[49] Upon his return to the United States, Senator Kennedy called upon the US government to establish diplomatic relations with Vietnam, to lift the trade embargo, and to give Vietnam aid "according to the humanitarian traditions of our country."[50] This was followed by meetings between Assistant Secretary of State Richard Holbrooke and the Vietnamese foreign minister at the UN headquarters in New York on September 22 and 27, 1978, to discuss normalization of relations between the two countries. The two agreed on normalization without any precondition.

According to Zbigniew Brzezinski in his memoirs, on September 28, 1978, Secretary of State Cyrus Vance sent President Carter a report on the details of the agreement to normalize relations with Vietnam and recommended that normalization should proceed immediately after congressional elections in early November. Brzezinski, then national security advisor, strongly opposed this recommendation. According to Brzezinski, as of October 11, 1978, he had been successful in getting President Carter to drop the decision to normalize relations with Vietnam.[51] Instead, at the end of October 1978, "Vietnam was presented with a set of preconditions it could not possibly meet in the current situation. Recognition would not occur until three problems had been resolved to the satisfaction of the United States: the near war between Vietnam and Cambodia, the close ties between Vietnam and the Soviet Union, and the continued flood of refugees from Vietnam."[52]

Fearing that the tough stance by the United States would encourage both Cambodia and China to stage a pincer attack on Vietnam, in early November 1978 Vietnam signed a treaty of friendship and mutual assistance with the Soviet Union. On December 15 the United States announced normalization of relations with China. On December 25 Vietnam invaded Cambodia in order to preempt a pincer attack, stating, however, that it went into Cambodia to save the Cambodian people from the genocidal Pol Pot regime. In late January 1979 China's leader, Deng Xiaoping, visited the United States. He announced that China intended to "teach Vietnam a lesson" and asked President Carter for "moral support" for China's forthcoming punitive war against Vietnam. In his memoirs Brzezinski disclosed his concern that President Carter would be persuaded by Cyrus Vance's advice, and would ask Deng Xiaoping not to use force against Vietnam. Thus Brzezinski did everything in his power to ensure that President Carter would support China.[53] The result is summarized by Marilyn Young as follows:

> In February 1979, with the blessing of the United States, China launched its invasion of Vietnam, laying waste an area of the countryside that had been untouched by the United States during the war for fear of provoking Chinese intervention. . . .
>
> Brzezinski was well satisfied: the conflict had imposed "major costs on [the Vietnamese], produced a great deal of devastation, and above all, showed the limits of their reliance on the Soviets". . . .
>
> Brzezinski's policy toward Vietnam forced the country into the embrace of the Soviet Union, thus justifying America's ongoing economic war against Vietnam and drawing harsh lessons for other nationalist aspirants. American support for Chinese policy in Cambodia salvaged the defeated remnants of Pol Pot's forces and put them back into the field against the Vietnamese army of occupation so as to "bleed Vietnam." "It is wise for China to force the Vietnamese to stay in Kampuchea," Deng Xiaoping reflected, "because that way they will suffer more and more. . . ." American policymakers agreed, adding a double-bind of their own: until Vietnam withdrew from Cambodia, it would remain an international outlaw, unfit for recognition, trade, or aid.[54]

For the next ten years China and the United States exerted maximum economic and diplomatic pressures on Vietnam. To deal with the situation the Vietnamese government carried out a series of reforms in the hope of shoring up the deteriorating situation in rural areas. From 1984 to 1986 production of staples in Vietnam stagnated, hovering around 18 million MT a year. In 1987 total production declined to 17.5 million MT. Meanwhile, the total population grew about 2.3 percent annually. The result was a severe food shortage beginning in March 1988, affecting an estimated 9.3 million persons in the Northern provinces alone.[55]

The delay in carrying out more fundamental reforms resulted in part from the fact that Vietnam was suspended in a state of neither war nor peace. The cooperative system was still considered useful for extracting human and material resources from rural areas to support the armed forces and the urban population. In 1988, however, Vietnam decided that it should sue for peace and began the negotiating process with China and the United States to withdraw its troops from Cambodia. On April 5, 1988, the Politburo issued Resolution Ten, entitled "Renovation in Agricultural Economic Management," which contained two important provisions.[56] One guaranteed (*bao dam*) peasants in the collective sector greater control over their lives and the fruits of their labor. The other reaffirmed the existence of various economic sectors, including the household sector. The stated aim of Resolution Ten was to create a more productive agrarian market economy. Since the Southern provinces, especially those in the Mekong Delta, had resisted collectivization for years and had been operating largely on the basis of the household and the market, it was obvious that Resolution Ten was directed mainly at the Northern and central provinces where most cooperatives were located. What was most important to the Southern population was that this resolution officially recognized the status quo, especially the legalization of wealth and restoration of land to the peasants.

The policy changes of Resolution Ten helped to increase staple production and brought about significant developments in other sectors. In 1987 Vietnam produced a total of 17.5 million MT of rice equivalents; in 1988 and 1989 the totals increased to 19.6 million MT and 20.5 million MT respectively. Six Mekong Delta provinces produced more than 1 million MT each. Thus in 1989 Vietnam was able not only to supply food adequately to its entire population, but also to export 1.5 million MT of milled rice. More importantly, peasant households began to diversify, planting crops other than rice and raising fish, shrimp, deer, and other livestock for market. An integrated rural-urban market economy began to take shape. This finally put Vietnam on the road to recovery and development.[57]

Realizing that economic, social, and political stability—as well as access to international markets and foreign aid—required solutions to the Cambodian situation and the conflict with China, in early July 1988 Vietnam pulled its entire military command and half of its troops out of Cambodia. It placed the rest of its troops under Phnom Penh's command, stating that it would bring all troops home by the end of 1989, earlier if there were a political settlement. After it became evident that there would be no political settlement, and all efforts to solicit the support of the United States and China failed, in September 1989 Vietnam pulled its troops out of Cambodia. Over the next two years the United States insisted that Vietnam make the Hun Sen government in Cambodia accept a "comprehensive" political settlement with the other Cambodian parties. This demand was equivalent to China's position, which forced the Khmer Rouge–dominated coalition on that hapless country.

The Soviet Union also pressured Vietnam vigorously in 1988 to agree to the inclusion of the Khmer Rouge in any peace settlement with Cambodia. In 1985 the Chinese had set three conditions for normalization of relations with the Soviet Union: the withdrawal of Soviet forces from Afghanistan, the reduction of Soviet troops on the Sino-Soviet border, and the withdrawal of Vietnamese troops from Cambodia. The Soviets were eager to accommodate China and to settle the Cambodian situation quickly. This would enable them to improve diplomatic relations and open trade with the Association of Southeast Asian Nations (ASEAN), whose booming economies were of special interest to Moscow.[58] In May 1989 Mikhail Gorbachev went to Beijing to officially normalize relations with China. In late 1991 Vietnam signed the UN-sponsored settlement for Cambodia, which represented the Chinese and US positions stated above. In 1992 China and Vietnam established full diplomatic relations. However, the United States did not lift its trade embargo on Vietnam until January 1994. The sticking point was US insistence that Vietnam should account satisfactorily for the 1,677 American servicemen still listed as MIA in Indochina. Because Vietnam showed its goodwill and tried to accommodate the United States in every way possible, in 1995 the United States finally normalized relations with Vietnam.

Relations between Vietnam and the United States since then were summarized by Raymond Burghardt, US ambassador to Vietnam from 2001 to 2004 and current director of East-West Seminars at the East-West Center in Honolulu. In the November 22, 2005 issue of *Yale Global Online*, Burghardt wrote:

> In the early years after normalization in 1995, American policy toward Vietnam was focused on dealing with historical issues left over from the war: accounting for the missing in action (MIA's); reuniting the families of refugees; and humanitarian programs aimed at developing trust between the two peoples. As ties strengthened, trade grew rapidly, especially after the Bilateral Trade Agreement (BTA) was signed in December 2001.
>
> For most of the ten years since normalization, US policy toward Vietnam was not driven by geo-strategic objectives. But the administration increasingly recognized Vietnam's potential for continued rapid economic growth, its potential to play an increasingly important role in Southeast Asian regional organizations and therefore its "strategic potential."
>
> In a policy of hedging relations with China, Vietnam, with its long history of troubled relations with its huge neighbor, is an obvious partner. . . .

Bilateral military ties can be expected to continue growing, but progress will be slow. Vietnam will value America's role as strategic balance but will resist being seen as part of a containment policy against China. American policymakers understand and accept this line, as the US has no containment policy against China. Hedging is not containment.

While Vietnam will keep looking over its shoulder to ensure that big brother China has not been unduly provoked, Vietnam-US ties should progress. Our two countries have no strategic conflicts and some important areas of strategic convergence.[59]

Has history come full circle? In "From Mad Jack to Mad Henry," Noam Chomsky writes:

At the very moment when they were planning the 1965 escalation, William Bundy and John McNaughton noted that unless the United States expanded the war, there would probably be "a Vietnamese-negotiated deal under which an eventually unified Communist Vietnam would assert its traditional hostility to Communist China . . . "

Why is "strategic convergence" not seen now in the same way as it was in 1965? Is it because the United States has realized that it has successfully eliminated the primary threat of "communism" as defined back in the early 1960s and as quoted by Chomsky?

CHAPTER 12

My Experiences with Laos and the Indochina Wars

Interview with Fred Branfman

Introduction

In early September 1969, when I was twenty-seven, a moral abyss opened suddenly before me. I was shocked and horrified to the core of my being as I found myself interviewing Laotian peasants, among the most decent, humane, and kind people on earth, who described living underground for years on end while they saw countless fellow villagers and family members burned alive by napalm, suffocated by five-hundred-pound bombs, and shredded by antipersonnel bombs dropped by my country, the United States. Even more shocking was the realization that the bombing was continuing apace, and that a few hundred miles away innocent Lao rice farmers alive one day would be dead the next.

I soon learned that a tiny handful of American leaders—a US executive branch led by Lyndon Johnson, later by Richard Nixon and Henry Kissinger—had taken it upon themselves to massively bomb Laos without informing, let alone consulting, the US Congress or public. They murdered tens of thousands of subsistence-level, innocent Lao civilians who did not even know where America was and certainly never committed any offense against it. The populations bombed by the United States consisted almost entirely of innocent peasants, mainly old people and children who could not survive by hiding in the forest, as others did. The official targets of the bombing, Pathet Lao and North Vietnamese soldiers, were able to move through the heavily forested regions in Laos and were mostly untouched by the attacks.

As a Jew profoundly touched by the Holocaust, including my having known Holocaust survivors during the fourteen months I spent on an Israeli kibbutz in the early 1960s, I strongly identified with the Laotian victims and found it impossible to turn away from their plight. And I knew that postwar US leaders had specifically created the Nuremberg Principles protecting civilian populations in wartime as a precedent that applied to all nations, in the hope of deterring future leaders from committing war crimes.

It was a profound shock to realize that if the Nuremberg Principles were applied to my own leaders they would be executed for crimes against humanity. I also recognized that the judgment at Nuremberg did not leave me the moral option of claiming these murders were not my affair. I felt deeply that the continued bombing of Laos proved beyond any doubt that there was no justice in the world, that innocents could be murdered daily with the world neither knowing nor caring, let alone intervening to stop it.

The situation was stark: it was as if I had discovered Auschwitz while the killing was still going on, knowing that day after day countless more innocent civilian victims would be pitilessly murdered without the slightest moral, legal, or political justification. My immediate response was visceral and political. I sought to expose the bombing to the world and to bring it to a halt. Until the bombing finally ceased, however, tens of thousands more innocent people throughout Indochina would die.

On a deeper level, this shocking discovery was to launch me on a lifelong search to understand the roots of human evil that could produce a Johnson, a Nixon, a Kissinger—and that could allow the latter not just to go unpunished but, instead, be lauded. What kind of society could largely ignore the murder of millions occurring in its name? I felt I could not understand humanity without understanding how the richest and most powerful of the species could drop, on the poorest of the species, more than triple the bomb tonnage it had dropped during World War II on all of Europe and the entire Pacific Theater combined.

My search to understand that evil took me from the refugee camps in Laos to US air bases in South Vietnam and Thailand, including the top-secret headquarters of the Seventh Air Force; to Washington, DC to study war-making by Congress, the Pentagon, and the executive branch itself; to grassroots politics in California and then to the Governor's Office in Sacramento to understand the domestic politics that produced such leaders; back to DC to participate in and gain deeper understanding of national-level politics and policy; and, for the past fifteen years, to a period of spiritual and psychological inquiry into the deeper human drives that have produced our present politics and policies.

I was asked by Mark Pavlick, editor of this book, to describe my experiences in Laos. The questions and my responses follow.

Mark Pavlick: Please describe your early life and education.

Fred Branfman: I grew up in Great Neck, New York, an upper-middle-class and predominantly Jewish suburb of New York City. My father was a textile executive, my mother a housewife. I began college at the University of Chicago in September 1960, graduating with a BA in political science, and a few years later I received a master of education from Harvard. I was a pretty typical liberal college student in those days. My first Washington, DC demonstration was with the Student Peace Union, picketing John F. Kennedy all night in front of the White House for his hawkish nuclear policies. I attended the first major anti–Vietnam War demonstration, organized by the Students for a Democratic Society (SDS),[1] at the Washington Monument in May 1965.

As I look back on those pre-Laos years, several issues seem particularly relevant to what happened later in Laos:

1.   My mother had a particularly strong political and social conscience. A vivid memory from my early years was her weeping convulsively when Eisenhower beat Stevenson in 1952. The TV was frequently tuned to the news, my mother discussed politics all the time in a very personal way, our house was stacked with the *New Republic*, the *Nation*, etc. My mother cared about the poor and supported civil rights. My household upbringing was reinforced by my college years: I grew up with an identity that said our primary obligation as human beings was to help those most in need, and that our focus should be on acting politically to change the nation.

2.   My mother had been sexually abused when she was young. As an adult, understandably, she harbored a great deal of unconscious anger toward men, and was verbally and emotionally abusive while I was growing up. This manifested in my adult life in two key ways. First, I tended to identify with the underdog—particularly when I felt those being punished were innocent of wrongdoing. This has been a consistent theme in my life, from defending the kid in first grade that everyone else picked on, up to and including my actions in Laos. Second, while living

at home, I learned to repress my anger, which made it all the more volatile. Later, that anger would become a major source of energy for what I was to do in Laos. I do not mean to imply that my early experiences were the sole impetus behind my actions as an adult. Yet my childhood clearly played a major role in shaping my adult life, as, I have come to learn, it does with all human beings.

3. My father represented Southern textile mills that were run by racists, and begged me not to join the civil rights movement when I was in college on the grounds that the people he represented would fire him and our family would be destitute. I acceded to his wishes by not joining the civil rights movement, the major political issue at the time. (The peace movement really began after I graduated college in September 1964.) Instead I found myself looking for adventure abroad: living in an Israeli kibbutz in the Negev desert from June 1962 to September 1963, and volunteering as a teacher in a small village on the shores of Lake Victoria in Tanzania from September 1965 to February 1967. Had my father not worked for Southern textile mills, I would likely have become a Freedom Rider, gone south for Mississippi Summer, forged friendships and contacts in the struggle, found a way to get out of the draft by having an arrest record or finding a friendly doctor (as did two of my brothers), and, overall, taken a course of action more typical of "New Leftists" of that era.

4. I had a particularly strong sense of generational betrayal. The very idea that I could be drafted to go fight a war in which I did not believe shaped my every waking hour. I was not philosophically opposed to violence, however. As a Jew with strong feelings about and interest in the Holocaust, I wanted to believe that I would have fought in World War II. Thus I could not honestly file as a conscientious objector, which required opposing all violence.

In addition to opposing the US government politically—on issues of discrimination, nuclear disarmament, support for Third World dictatorships, etc.—I felt betrayed on a very *personal* level. My government was willing to see *me* die, by forcing *me* to fight in a war that was clearly both immoral and not in my nation's interest.

Part of this feeling came from my being prime draft age. There was no lottery, and the draft was very real indeed. It was no joke. The reality was that I would be forced to kill and possibly die in an unjust and insane war. My feeling was "these bastards really are out to get me."

On a deeper level, I had grown up with a strong belief in American values, due to my mother's deeply held convictions and also because my father,
who had escaped Russia at age ten, was extremely anticommunist, patriotic,
and pro-American. Believing so deeply in America, I felt particularly betrayed
when I realized beyond any serious doubt that my leaders—and much of the
generation that spawned them—were selfish hypocrites and murderers.

I experienced the undeniable fact that my government was prepared to
send me to fight and possibly die for a clearly unjust war as the deepest possible *personal* betrayal. This had a profound impact on my psyche. I came to
feel that I had no real elders or mentors, no one I could really trust from the
older generation. It was only later, when I read Erich Maria Remarque's *All
Quiet on the Western Front*,[2] that I understood more fully this phenomenon of
generational betrayal.

Though I identified with people my age in the "New Left," I didn't know
too many actual "New Leftists" since I was spending so much time out of
the country. I felt I was on my own. This had a good side: I became relatively
self-reliant, self-motivated, and thought for myself. But it also left me feeling
isolated, alone, and angry at the betrayal.

I think this strong feeling of being abandoned and betrayed by our elders
is the key to understanding the sixties and much of what has occurred since.
I believe that my generation, which grew up believing deeply in American
values, was thrown into a psychological and moral abyss from which we still
have not emerged. I believe that much of my generation's fury, which led
to so much that was positive and also to so much that was negative, can be
explained by the particular madness and fear experienced by those who are
abandoned by the parents and elders upon whom they relied for nurturance
and protection. I think this sense of betrayal has had disastrous effects upon
American politics, culture, and civilization.

I remember Morton Kaplan, a political science professor with whom I
studied at the University of Chicago. His main reason for opposing the Vietnam War, which he opposed as early as 1964, was his fear that it would divide
our nation generationally. He argued that the cost to our society of alienating
large numbers of the younger generation would far outweigh any good that
could come of fighting in Vietnam. I strongly believe today that he was right.[3]
Not only do I see evidence of this proposition everywhere, but it is also the
story of much of my own life.

What series of events led you to be committed to going to Southeast Asia?

Initially I had no interest whatsoever in going to Southeast Asia. I was living in a small village near Lake Victoria in Tanzania, a thousand miles inland, the only non-African within a fifty-mile radius. There I discovered one of Africa's central problems: rural children received just seven years of education, too much to want to remain farmers the rest of their lives, too little to find productive jobs in the city. I wrote a series of articles entitled "Utilizing the Potential of Primary School Leavers," which were published in the journal of Kivukoni College, one of Tanzania's major universities. President Julius Nyerere read them and asked me to stay on in Tanzania as an advisor to the Ministry of Education in the then-capital Dar Es Salaam, in order to try to implement my ideas. I was excited at the prospect and made plans to move to the capital.

This was January 1967, at the height of the Vietnam War. I was twenty-four. During 1966 I had, of course, realized I was prime draft age. My mother, who was in touch with my draft board, informed me that they were going after twenty-four- and twenty-five-year-olds in particular, since they wouldn't draft you if you managed to stay out of the military until age twenty-six. She urged me to plan out my next move carefully. I had received a "2-A" deferment, known as "service in the national interest," which allowed me to stay in Tanzania. It had been renewed for six months in mid-1966. During the last half of 1966 I had written a long letter to my draft board explaining why I hoped they would extend my deferment so I could remain in Tanzania.

Just in case they would not, however, I had applied to and been accepted by the Peace Corps to serve in Malaysia, by Service Civil International to work in Sri Lanka, and by International Voluntary Services (IVS) to work in Laos. I had heard about the last group by accident, and learned that they were funded by the US Agency for International Development (USAID), a government agency. I'd decided to apply, figuring that the combination of their being in Laos, part of Indochina, and being funded by USAID would give me the best shot at keeping my 2-A deferment if my draft board would not let me remain in Tanzania.

When President Nyerere asked me to work as an educational advisor in Tanzania, the US ambassador to Tanzania wrote a letter to my draft board stipulating that my remaining in Tanzania was in the national interest. I assumed the board would comply. It was thus with considerable shock that I received a telegram from my mother in early February 1967 saying that my draft board had denied my request and had made me "1-A"—"available for unrestricted military service"—and therefore likely to be drafted. I could appeal the decision if I returned home immediately. I decided to do so.

Since IVS had accepted me, and their training program was to begin back in the States in a few days, I decided both to return home and to appeal to my draft board to let me go to Laos as an educational advisor. If they would not, I decided that I would go to either Canada or prison. This twenty-four-hour period was one of the strangest of my life. I had spent the earlier part of the day running through the streets of Dar Es Salaam in shorts and a T-shirt, one of a handful of Caucasians amidst a crowd of tens of thousands of Tanzanians, stoned out of my mind, waving a green branch above my head and screaming revolutionary slogans with the crowd, celebrating the "Arusha Declaration" that was to launch Tanzania on a new path of humanitarian socialism.[4] I don't remember feeling so alive and happy in that way—a combination of hopeful, youthful idealism and the collective joy of the tens of thousands of people in whose midst we ran—before or since.

That night I received my mother's telegram. I flew to JFK the next day and got off the plane, inadequately dressed for the freezing weather, dreading the need to face a draft board that could ruin my life. Something inside me froze, and I passed the next weeks in a kind of daze. I don't remember feeling more miserable at any time in my life.

After completing the one-week preparatory training for Laos, I had a dramatic meeting with my draft board. I entered the room and the draft board chief asked me in a nasty tone of voice, "What do you want this time?" Shocked, I explained that I had wanted to remain in Tanzania as an advisor, but since I could not, I hoped as an alternative to serve as an educational advisor in Laos. "Laos?" he answered with a sneer. "How did you come up with that one?" It was clear that neither he nor his two compatriots had bothered to read the materials I had sent them from Tanzania, including the letter from the US ambassador that described my work in Tanzania as being in the national interest, and my long, heartfelt explanation as to why I wanted to go to Laos if I could not remain in Tanzania.

The draft board chief asked me whether I was willing to serve my country by fighting in Vietnam. I answered that I felt I could better serve by being an educational advisor. He then screamed at me, "Don't give me any of that college-boy bullshit! I send boys like you every day to die in Vietnam. I want a simple yes or no answer. Are you willing to serve your country in Vietnam!" I said, "I can't answer that question with a simple yes or no, sir," and my life passed in front of my eyes when he responded, "That's all right, you've answered it. Next!"

At that moment, however, one of the other two members of the board—neither of whom had yet said a word—asked me musingly, "Tasmania. I've always been interested in Tasmania. What's it like?" I responded, "Well actually, sir, it's Tanzania, you know, I was there as a teacher . . . " and began talking for my life, explaining my motivation, how I had tried to help the villagers, my interest in teaching the kids agriculture, etc. At one point he asked, "What did you make over there?" "A hundred and fifty dollars a month," I responded. "What, a Harvard graduate from Great Neck, and that's all you made?" he said, genuinely shocked. I learned later that I had received permission to keep my 2-A and go to Laos by a 2 to 1 vote. I will always wonder if I would have been drafted—and consequently wound up in Canada—had that man not been interested in "Tasmania."

A week or two later, my head still spinning, my heart still back in Tanzania, I found myself on a long plane flight to Laos.

Please describe your experiences with IVS in Laos.

My primary goal upon arriving in Laos was to live with Laotians. I studied Laotian assiduously, creating my own dictionary; hired a guy who spoke French and Laotian to serve as an interpreter; and moved to a small village, Ban Xa Phang Meuk, which, although only twelve kilometers outside the capital of Vientiane, had no running water, electricity, or even pit toilets. I lived in the village the whole time I served with IVS, from March 1967 until June 1969. During that period the people I was closest with were Laotians and Vietnamese. Most of my time was spent learning about Laotian culture, hanging out with villagers, or spending time with a Vietnamese family that I befriended downtown.

The letter I had received accepting me for work in Laos had said I would be an "educational advisor" rather than a teacher—in effect, a promotion. I was happy about this; I did not want to teach English, because I found doing so tedious and also because I opposed it philosophically. I thought it was more important that the kids learn agriculture and community development. The reality was that only a small percentage of students mastered English; they could then work for the US government or English-speaking businesses. The other 90 percent of kids learned little in school that was useful for their lives. I had no idea why I had received this promotion, but assumed it was because I had a master of education from Harvard and prior experience teaching in Tanzania.

Upon starting my job, I discovered that my services had been requested by the head of USAID Secondary Education in Laos, who wanted me to find derogatory information about his rival, the head of USAID Primary Education in Laos, with whom he was competing to become overall head of USAID Education. I ignored his desire to have me spy on his rival, but I did write a long report making several dozen suggestions about how to improve USAID's education programs in Laos. These suggestions focused on improving the education for the vast majority who would never go to college rather than the tiny minority who would.

My congressman, Lester Wolff, came to Laos and requested a meeting with me due to my mother's having visited him back in Long Island. After our meeting he introduced me to the head of USAID for Laos, Joseph Mendenhall. In response to Mendenhall's questions as to what I was doing, I mentioned my report. He said he'd like to see it, so I gave him a copy.

A few weeks later my immediate USAID superior, the one in charge of Secondary Education, called me into his office. He handed me a letter he had written to Mendenhall, dated the previous day, detailing why every one of my suggestions was wrong, calling me young and naive, and stating that I agreed my report was useless and that I had asked for it to be withdrawn from circulation. As I looked at him in shock, he explained that I was a troublemaker, that I would be teaching English from here on out, and that if I gave him any trouble he would fire me from IVS and contact my draft board to make sure they not only drafted me, but sent me to fight in Vietnam. He told me that he had done so with another IVS volunteer who had given him a hard time, and he had just heard the fellow had died in Vietnam.

I went to my IVS superior, who worked closely with my USAID superior, and suggested a deal. I had no intention of teaching English, and just wanted to live quietly in my village until I finished my tour with IVS. If USAID would leave me alone and let me do what I wanted—which was to write a textbook in Laotian to teach agriculture to primary school kids, start a school garden at a high school, and help Lao students study community development in Thailand—I would not cause him any trouble by going to Congressman Wolff or to the USAID official Mendenhall. The IVS supervisor said it was a deal. I spent the next two years living in my village, avoiding USAID Education except to write the textbook. I also visited community development training sites in Thailand and obtained funding to send some Laotian teachers to study there.

My defining experience with IVS occurred in late 1968. Upon arriving in Laos the previous year, I had quickly found myself out of sync with the IVS leadership and most of the volunteers. They seemed either nonpolitical or supportive of the war, did not speak Laotian, were uninterested in Laotians and their culture, and spent most of their free time with each other or with other Westerners. I thus tended to avoid IVS and IVSers. In late 1968, however, one of the few volunteers with whom I was friendly, Chandler Edwards, an ebullient, sweet, friendly fellow, was killed by the Pathet Lao. This happened a few months before the upcoming annual IVS conference. I launched a campaign to have IVS invite the head of the Pathet Lao delegation in Vientiane to the conference on the grounds that otherwise they would persist in seeing us as part of the US war effort, and consequently the lives of our volunteers would continue to be in danger.

At a highly dramatic meeting I led the fight to have the volunteers vote on the invitation. We won by one vote. I was ecstatic, believing this would both save the lives of my fellow volunteers and also give IVS an identity separate from the war effort.

But shortly after that meeting, the overall head of IVS, Arthur Gardiner, flew in from DC and summoned me to a meeting of IVS supervisors. (I learned many years later that Gardiner had been the US ambassador to Cuba during Batista's final days.) He informed me in no uncertain terms that, despite the vote, there was no way that IVS was going to invite the Pathet Lao to our conference. After an increasingly heated argument, I pausing dramatically and said to Gardiner, "Mr. Gardiner, I want you to look around this room. I want you to look deeply into the eyes of each person in this room. Because there is a very good chance that, due to your lack of concern for the lives of your own volunteers, one or more of these people will be killed in the next year. And if that happens, Mr. Gardiner—and I fervently pray that it does not—if it happens you will have their blood on your hands!" Then I stalked out of the room.

Within months Arthur Stillman, an IVS supervisor who had been in that room, an extremely decent fellow sincerely devoted to helping Laotians, was killed by the Pathet Lao in an ambush. As far as I am concerned, Mr. Gardiner has Stillman's blood on his hands.

When did you begin to question the US mission in Laos? Did you meet persons working with the official "enemy"–the Pathet Lao? What was your impression of these people and their work?

Although I was strongly opposed to the US war in Vietnam, which was going full-bore by the time I arrived in Laos in March 1967, I had an emotional stake in believing that Laos was different. I did not want to see myself as part of a US war effort devoted to murdering Laotian civilians. I was aided in this illusion by the fact that throughout my IVS years and beyond, the United States officially claimed that it was not bombing or fighting in Laos, and that its efforts were limited to supplying the Meo (now called Hmong) armies fighting a guerrilla war against the communist Pathet Lao and North Vietnamese. Between March 1967 and June 1969 there were almost no stories describing US war-making in Laos, and I received few first-person accounts of the war. This campaign of concealment led to its later description as "the US secret war" in Laos.

My doubts about the US effort in Laos were initially focused on my area of interest, education, and on the aid program in general. I felt strongly that USAID was helping only a small minority, who would master English, go on to college, and eventually join the pro-American Royal Lao Government (RLG), at the expense of the vast majority, who were not learning about agriculture or community development. The majority of students would wind up—as I'd seen happen in Africa—being part of an urban lumpenproletariat, working as prostitutes and low-wage urban workers rather than as productive farmers. I also decried how the Americans lived in their own American suburban compound called "K-6" (or "Kilometer 6"), which I passed on my way to my village. The Americans did not speak Laotian or learn Laotian culture, looked down on Laotians, and were not there to help the Lao people but rather to advance their own careers.

The longer I lived in Laos, spoke Laotian, and got to know the country from the inside, the more appalled I became. The United States was supporting a small, corrupt elite—including generals who supplied the opium that wound up addicting tens of thousands of US soldiers in Vietnam—at the expense of the majority of Laotians.[5]

This issue became personal to me when I discovered that the very village I was living in, Ban Xa Phang Meuk, meant "village of the deep pond," and had originally been built near a pond necessary for watering animals and growing crops.[6] Some years before I arrived, a rich outsider had paid off corrupt officials in Vientiane and sealed off the pond for his own use, refusing to allow my fellow villagers to use it. It was a huge issue for the villagers—they had appealed to the authorities, but nothing had happened.

As I made my rounds around Laos, including a six-week stay in an Edenic village in southern Laos called Lahanam, I had occasion many times to meet the poor, miserable youngsters who had been drafted into the Royal Lao Army. I never met one who believed in what he was doing; the conversation tended to focus either on sex and women or on the disgraceful behavior of their officers, e.g., how their leaders would send them into combat while themselves remaining in the rear, stealing money and forcing young peasant girls to have sex with them.

Contrary to the 1962 Geneva Accords on Laos, which declared Laos officially neutral, there was a Pathet Lao delegation in the middle of Vientiane. They would show movies on Friday night, which I began to attend after a year or so. I was immediately struck by the difference between the young soldiers at the compound and the RLG soldiers I had met. The Pathet Lao soldiers were also charming and friendly, but the conversation always revolved around politics: what I thought was happening in the Middle East, the latest developments in the war in Indochina, etc. At one point I learned that USAID had captured some Pathet Lao textbooks. It turned out that they were the very sort that I had been advocating for USAID Laos: written in Laotian and focused on agriculture and community development.

By June 1969, when I finished with IVS, I strongly opposed US involvement in Laos. I knew from experience that it was primarily helping a corrupt elite that had no interest in their own people, and that it was neglecting the interests of the vast majority of the two million people living under RLG rule. And I was favorably impressed with the Pathet Lao, whom I saw as relatively non-corrupt, and sincerely dedicated not only to freeing their country of the Americans and RLG, but also to helping their own people. I didn't know the Pathet Lao very well, however, and the focus of my attention was the wrongdoing of the Americans and RLG.

My immediate emotional focus, however, was on the villagers in Ban Xa Phang Meuk, including the "Old Father" with whom I ate every day and all the other Laotians I got to know during those years.[7]

It is hard even now, almost forty years later, to try to describe what I felt for these villagers. My life in America had been deeply disappointing to me. Though there had been people I loved, I could not relate to Americans in general, who did not seem to share my values. To pick the most dramatic example, at the time most Americans still supported the war. Seared into my memory was the train trip I'd taken from DC back to New York to face my draft board. I sat there on the train, brooding about the war, the killing, the insane situation I was about to face, and after a time went into the dining car where a party was occurring. I still remember the red, drunken, self-satisfied faces of the dozens of passengers, many badly overweight, shouting and laughing, symbolizing to me how most Americans were spending their time as tens of thousands of innocent Indochinese died and American and Vietnamese soldiers waged a senseless war.

I'd also felt estranged in all the other places I'd been, including Israel and Tanzania. But in Laos it was different. The people had a hard time pronouncing my name, and I was a foot taller than most of them. So they called me "Phouvieng," or "mountain of Vientiane," and somehow I became more me as "Phouvieng" than I had ever been as "Fred."

Laos was different from any place I had ever been. It was hard not to like Laotians in general, as well as specific individuals. And this was not only my experience, but that of most other visitors as well. Everyone loved "the Lao," even though most Westerners treated them with the kind of condescension one used with a cute terrier or naughty child.

Perhaps the best comparison of the villagers I knew in Laos would be to the hobbits in the *Lord of the Rings*: lively, funny, good-natured, devoted to the simple, human things in life.[8] They liked to have a good time. Upon the death of someone of note, like a monk, hundreds of people would come from miles around and party for three days at the foot of the casket. The Lao villagers tended to be sincere, not cynical. They were honest. They were trustworthy. And if you had a difficult task you needed to accomplish, with someone you could trust, there was no one else you would more naturally turn to.

I don't want to romanticize the Laotians I knew. They were human beings, with all the usual faults and more. I knew lying, hypocritical, and nasty Laotians. But, in general, most of the time, if you liked human beings at all, there was no one more likable and trustworthy than most of the Laotians I came across.

I not only liked but also admired these people. The Old Father, who owned the shed I rented next to his home on stilts, and with whom I ate every day, appeared from the outside little more than an illiterate peasant farmer, dressed in a sarong, puttering around his house. But as I got to know him I saw him as more of a Renaissance man than anyone I had ever met. He could build houses, make bedding, grow crops, raise animals. He had raised several children and was now raising his grandkids. He had farmed and had driven a samlaw downtown. One of his sons had traveled to the United States to learn how to make artificial limbs, and another son had become a member of the Lao Secret Police. The Old Father was also a natural doctor, making medicines from plants, roots, and branches, and helping people when they were sick. And, most striking to me, he was a devout Buddhist. He was the lay head of the village's Buddhist temple, which we lived next to. He would spend months every dry season copying the Tales of the Buddha onto dry strips of bamboo, using a piece of wood with a needle protruding from its end. It was a devotional task, and he was so absorbed in it that I once got to within six inches of his face before he was able to hear me calling to him.

Most importantly, he was a beautiful human being: funny, cheerful, generous, curious, kind, competent, loving, sincere, and earnest, a man who liked nothing better than to sit around and joke and talk with people late into the evening. His house was usually filled with visitors, and it was many a night that I fell asleep to the sound of laughter and good cheer from the house next door.

One day, the old monk in the village took sick. The villagers took him to the hospital and he returned a few days later in a coffin, dead. Rather than being a somber event, the monk's death was an occasion for a three-day feast, held a few yards away from where I lived. Hundreds of people came from miles around, laughing, drinking, and gambling all night in front of the open coffin.

The next day I approached the Old Father's house. To my amazement, I saw his wife, whom I called the Old Mother, lying prone on the ground. A villager was walking up and down on her back. This back-walking was a traditional way of treating pain, and the Old Mother was moaning and seemed quite sick. I concluded immediately that she needed to go to the hospital. I told this to the Old Father, but he replied that she wouldn't go. She overheard me and began screaming, "No! To go to the hospital is to die in the hospital!" since that is what had just happened to the monk. The Old Father shrugged. Exasperated, I began arguing with both of them when their son, the one who had studied making artificial limbs in the States, pulled up in his jeep. I told him we had to take his mother to the hospital. He told her, she refused again, and he gave up, also turning to me with a shrug.

I lost control. "Listen! Stop this nonsense! Now you just go over there and pick her up and put her in your jeep, we're taking her to the hospital!" I shouted. He complied, and we got her to Operation Brotherhood, the US-funded hospital run by Filipinos. They rushed her into the emergency room and saved her, telling us that she had been within five minutes of dying.

A few days later I had one of the most terrifying experiences in Laos; there were many more than I'd like to remember. I was awakened by loud noises in the middle of the night. I got up, saw large explosions lighting up the night sky, walked over to the home of some neighbors, and to my great surprise saw their heads sticking out of the ground. I'd had no idea that next to every home in the village was a trench, in which the villagers were now hiding. What is going on, I asked. The Pathet Lao are attacking Vientiane, they answered. What should I do, I asked them, suddenly scared for my life. Go ask the *naibahn* (village chief), they said.

I went to the village chief's house. He had always been very friendly to me, but tonight was quite cold. What should I do, I asked, still not fully awake. He answered through the door, not opening it, "Get out of here!" But, I protested, if I just get on my motorcycle and start riding around I'm more scared of being shot by the Royal Lao Government troops than the Pathet Lao. He just shrugged his shoulders.

Feeling totally isolated and afraid, I suddenly thought of the Old Father, and rushed back to his house. As I approached I saw his wife's and grandkids' heads poking up from their trench, but found the Old Father sitting out in front of it with a big smile on his face. As soon as he saw me he called out, "Hey, Phouvieng, great to see you! Come over here and sit down next to me and let's watch the movie together!" slapping the ground next to him. I did, and felt my terror evaporate in the face of his friendship and joviality.

We talked for a while, and finally I asked him what I should do, telling him the naibahn had said I should quit the village, but that I was scared of the RLG soldiers. "You're not going anywhere!" he laughed, "you just sit here with your father and watch the movie." "But Old Father," I asked, "what will you do if the Pathet Lao soldiers come and see you here with an American?" "I'll just hide you under my mattress," he laughed—a joke, since his mattress was on the floor of his bedroom. "But what will you do if they see me?" I asked. "I'll just tell them I'm your father and you're my son," he laughed again. "Don't worry about it."

Needless to say, experiences of this kind with the Old Father and his family, and many others too numerous to mention here, gave me the deepest possible appreciation for Laotians as human beings. It wasn't just that the people I was closest to were sincere, nice, decent, gentle, honest, and a lot of fun. It was that they were real, courageous, and could be counted on when it mattered.

During all my years in the village the Old Father never discussed politics. While I would rant about the US bombing or the latest example of RLG corruption or disgusting American behavior, he would just listen. I thought of him as a nonpolitical peasant, wishing only that the two sides would stop fighting—the grass in that old saying, "When the elephants fight the grass gets trampled."

It was only after the war ended and I returned for a visit in 1993 that I learned the Old Father had been the local representative of the Pathet Lao in that village throughout the years I'd lived there. To the long list of virtues that I so admired in this Renaissance man, I now added courage, idealism, and commitment.

In a sense the key steps I took in Laos were learning Laotian, living with the villagers, and growing to love them. Given that connection, it was inevitable that I would react as I did when I realized that people just like them were being pitilessly murdered by my government just one hundred miles away.

How did you discover the bombing? What did you do after discovering it?

After I finished with IVS in June 1969, I thought about returning home but decided to remain on in Southeast Asia. For one thing, I thought I was deeply in love with Kim Lien, a Vietnamese woman. She had gone to Japan for the summer and was to return in September. Another factor was that for more than two years I had spent most of my time in personal matters, socializing with Laotians, and working with the aid program. I knew very little about the war at that point, and I wanted to know more before returning to the United States. I had this idea that I would be embarrassed if people asked me about the situation in Laos and I knew nothing.

On a deeper level, looking back on it, I can see now that I really had nothing to return to. I'd missed the prime part of the sixties, having spent almost all of the period since September 1965 out of the country, had few contacts or personal ties, and on some level felt at that point more "at home" and also very much more alive in Laos. I can remember during this period looking at a map of the United States and trying to remember what it had felt like to live there.

In June 1969, as I finished my IVS tour, I came across a series of articles on the Laos bombing by Jacques Decornoy of *Le Monde*, who had been the first Westerner to visit Pathet Lao zones in the city of Sam Neua in far-northern Laos.[9] Decornoy's articles had received no notice in the United States; I was shocked to read them. I decided to go to Paris to try to convince the Pathet Lao delegation to let me visit their zones and see the bombing firsthand, on the grounds that it would take an American to be heard in America. It proved a fool's mission, since they weren't about to trust a French- and Lao-speaking American who wore black, Vietcong-like clothing and had been an IVS volunteer.

On that trip I happened to watch the moon landing in a Paris café with Kong Le, the former, "neutralist" ruler of Laos. He had informed me earlier that he had the power to make himself invisible. As we watched Neil Armstrong step onto the moon and cheered, he excitedly informed me that now the people at NASA would finally believe him! Believe what, I asked. He explained that he had told them that there was life on other planets when he visited them as head of state, but he could tell that no one believed him. Now they would, he explained, with a broad smile of self-satisfaction. I left my encounters with Kong Le shaking my head. This man who believed in magic had been the US-recognized leader of Laos? It was only one example—Hmong leader Vang Pao and Lon Nol in Cambodia being much more serious cases—of the folly of the US government supporting warlords, a policy that many advocate for Afghanistan today.

I returned to Laos and, in early September 1969, was staying a few days downtown with the journalist T. D. (Tim) Allman, who was then writing for the *Bangkok Post* and stringing for the *New York Times* and *Time*.[10] At that time Laos, unlike Vietnam, was divided into clearly demarcated communist and Royal Lao Government zones. He said he wanted to interview the first refugees from communist zones—specifically, from the Plain of Jars in northern Laos—who had been brought into US-controlled zones. Allman asked me if I would interpret for him; I said sure. We hopped on my motorcycle and drove to the That Luang Buddhist pagoda in the center of Vientiane, to a moment in time that would change my life forever.

The villagers had just been brought down from northern Laos, and there were hundreds of them sitting around the pagoda. Each family had little more than a burlap bag or two into which had been thrown a few pieces of clothing, a stove, pots, pans, utensils, and a few other necessities.

Tim and I went up to one family at random and started chatting; then, remembering the Jacques Decornoy articles, I asked them whether they'd seen any bombing. Their eyes grew wide and they began talking about how they had been bombed for the previous *five* years, but in particular during the last year. I remember clearly and often, for it is etched in my brain, how the first villager I talked with squatted down and drew an "L" in the dirt. He explained that he had lived in a cave for most of the previous year, venturing out only at night to try to salvage some food or water for his family and those animals of his that hadn't yet been killed.

Every single villager that day, and every one of the more than two thousand refugees I was to interview over the next fifteen months, told essentially the same story. The bombing began in mid-1964 and escalated gradually until, by late 1968, the planes were coming every day, raining down death and destruction, destroying entire villages, and, eventually, the whole society that had existed for the previous seven hundred years on the Plain of Jars. The refugees made clear that most of the bombing was from American jets. They knew the difference between the small, propeller-driven aircraft of the Royal Lao Air Force (many of which, I discovered later, were piloted by US-trained Thais), which were relatively few in number, and the enormous numbers of American jets that dropped huge bombs upon them day after day, month after month, year after year.

I cannot, even now, describe the shock, outrage, and horror that I experienced upon hearing these reports from the refugees. I could not, and even today cannot, fathom how humanity had reached the point that the richest and most sophisticated of the species could carry out a policy of what was in fact systematic murder of the poorest and weakest of the species—innocent, subsistence-level farmers who had not only not committed any offense against their murderers, but *didn't even know who they were.*

The first level of shock came in realizing that the executive branch leaders of my country, the United States, were conducting these massive bombing raids *secretly.* They had been lying to the media, lying to the world, and no one outside Laos even knew that this mass murder had been going on. I would learn later that they had even committed perjury in testimony to Congress, denying the bombing to members of Congress in closed sessions. At that time, September 1969, the official US position was that US planes had never dropped a single bomb in Laos. It wasn't until March 1970 that Richard Nixon finally admitted that the United States had been bombing in Laos for the previous six years. But he and the US government continued to maintain the most monstrous lie of all, which persists to this day: that the United States bombed only "military" targets and avoided hitting civilians. I knew from what had happened in South Vietnam that my leaders were lying and murdering their way into history. But realizing it in this personal way, in a Laotian refugee camp with the victims two feet away, transformed this intellectual knowledge into a deeply felt emotional experience.

The second level of shock came in trying to absorb the horror of what I was seeing and hearing. Here were these kind, beautiful, decent Laotian farmers, no different than the villagers I knew so well and loved so much from

Ban Xa Phang Meuk, who described seeing a beloved grandmother burnt alive by napalm before their eyes, a child buried alive or a wife blown to bits by five-hundred-pound bombs, a husband shredded by antipersonnel bombs. There in front of my eyes was a young boy missing a leg, a beautiful six-year-old girl with napalm wounds on her chest, stomach, and genitals. I took photos of her smiling face. When I happily came back after a few days to give one of the photos to her mother, the woman appeared tired and miserable. I handed her the photo. She informed me her daughter had died painfully just days earlier. I was also given a photo of a beautiful, sincere-looking, happy young girl named Sao Doumma, posing on her wedding day. She had later been killed by US bombing.

The horror was magnified by the slow realization that the vast majority of the people that Richard Nixon and Henry Kissinger had murdered were civilians, particularly children, mothers, and old people. Northern Laos was deeply forested and the only "targets" visible from the air were villages. The Pathet Lao and North Vietnamese soldiers moved easily through the forests. The main groups forced to remain in and near the villages were mothers with children, old people, and the children themselves. These groups comprised the vast majority of the bombing victims.

But the greatest horror was my realization that the bombing was continuing, that at the very moment I was talking with these refugees, bombs were dropping on other innocent villagers just a few hundred kilometers away. To realize that each and every day Laotians who awakened alive would be dead by the evening—burned and buried and suffocated and shredded—was almost more than I could bear.

Most people, I suppose, cannot point to a particular spot, day, or moment when their lives changed forever. But I can. I drove up to that pagoda a kind of hedonistic, well-meaning, adventurer/do-gooder. I left it a committed political activist. By the end of my first hour interviewing those refugees from the Plain of Jars, my life had changed forever. I did not decide this consciously, but someplace within me the decision was made that I would devote my every waking hour from then on, to the best of my ability, to stop this horror.

As it happened, there were other journalists besides Allman at the pagoda. One of them, Craig Spence of ABC-TV, hired me the next day to be his interpreter. He also interviewed me about the USAID program. This became a pattern: I spent much of the next fifteen months working for US journalists visiting Laos, usually for a week at a time, as an interpreter and guide. I worked with Welles Hangen of NBC, Ted Koppel of ABC, Bernie Kalb and

Ed Rabel of CBS, Henry Kamm, Flora Lewis, and Sidney Schanberg of the *New York Times*, David Greenway of *Time*, Les Whitten of Jack Anderson's column, and many others. They paid me thirty dollars a day to arrange interviews and take them out to the refugee camps to investigate a variety of stories. From my perspective, I was getting the story of the bombing onto national television and was able to support myself; I could live on three or four days of work, a hundred dollars a month, if I had to.

As I took the journalists out to the refugee camps, I also documented our interviews with photos and audio recordings, which I compiled and sent to the US Senate Subcommittee on Refugees, headed by Senator Edward Kennedy, and to the Senate Foreign Relations Committee, chaired by Senator William Fulbright. I also spent time with visiting antiwar activists such as Howard Zinn, Dan Berrigan, Dave Dellinger, and Noam Chomsky, filling them in on what was occurring. In those days, antiwar activists en route to Hanoi often stopped in Vientiane for a day or two before taking an International Control Commission (ICC) flight to Hanoi.

One of the most meaningful weeks of my life was putting around Vientiane on my motorcycle with Noam Chomsky on the back seat. During that week Noam gathered material for the Laos chapter of his book *At War with Asia*.[11] I was very impressed by Chomsky's mind. I would give him a book and several articles to read at eleven o'clock at night, and by breakfast the next morning he would have them memorized, able to cite footnoted references in discussions with US embassy officials. But I was even more impressed with Chomsky's heart. I took dozens and dozens of Westerners out to the refugee camps during that period. Chomsky and Flora Lewis were the only ones who wept at what they heard.

At the same time as my powerful emotional reaction to the murder of these innocent peasants, I had an equally powerful intellectual reaction: What was going on? How had it occurred? I have always been an inquisitive person, and this stimulated my curiosity to its maximum. I developed an almost visceral need to understand the air war, to understand the minds and beings of those who could perpetrate this horror, and to understand what it meant for the human species as a whole.

I remember well how, when I first heard these stories from the peasants, I was flabbergasted as well as horrified. So many questions came to mind. Who had ordered the bombing? Why? Who was doing the bombing? Where were the planes based? How did the bombing work? Why were there so many kinds of bombs—napalm, five-hundred-pounders, antipersonnel bombs? How did they decide which ones to drop where? Why did they bomb so much? Did they know what they were doing? What on earth was going on? I knew nothing. Literally nothing.

Thus I spent much of the next fifteen months trying to understand the bombing by talking with airmen at US air bases in Thailand and South Vietnam. My quest eventually led to my meeting Jerry Brown (not the Jerry Brown who became governor of California, with whom I later worked). This Jerry Brown had been an air force sergeant in Vientiane, disguised as a civilian, in charge of selecting bombing targets. At the time we met he was working in advertising in Bangkok. Jerry told me the whole story of the air war, providing a unique perspective that no one outside the military could have had. Later I discussed Jerry and his exploits with Seymour Hersh, who proceeded to write about Jerry in one of the longest articles ever to appear in the Sunday *New York Times Magazine*.[12]

Between September 1969 and February 1971, when I was expelled from Laos, I interviewed more than two thousand refugees, visited Udorn Air Base in Thailand and Danang Air Base in South Vietnam, and talked with CIA pilots, bombardiers, military pilots, and many others with firsthand knowledge of the bombing. I learned about the air war from both the bottom up and the top down.

How and why did you leave Laos? Were you alone in making such decisions, or were you in the company of others?

I was working for Ed Rabel of CBS News when three Laotian secret police came to arrest me one morning in early February 1971 at the Hotel Lane Xang. They were acquaintances of mine, who knew me from my friendship with the Old Father's son, one of their colleagues. They apologized profusely, saying they had been forced to arrest me by "the Americans." They explained that a bunch of Americans were meeting at the USAID Office of Public Safety—a CIA front that worked with secret police around the world—to decide how to deal with me, and that they had been ordered to take me in. They took me to the National Police headquarters. As we trudged up to the cells on the top floor, one of the officers smiled and gestured meaningfully as we walked past the door labeled "USAID Public Safety" on one of the lower floors.

I had a bunch of papers with me—the Laotian secret police had kindly let me stop off at my apartment to retrieve my papers on the way to the cell—and the deputy head of the Lao National Police came into my cell to demand that I hand them over. Although there was nothing incriminating in my huge pile of papers, I refused to surrender them. He tried to threaten me, announcing that I would be locked up indefinitely if I didn't surrender my papers. I said to him, "I don't mind if you hold me here. Every day CBS, with whom I'm working, will photograph the top of your police headquarters and tell the world that you are holding an American whose only crime is to try and stop the horrible bombing of your own people."

"Phouvieng, please don't talk that way!" the deputy police chief pleaded. "The Americans said I had to get your papers, what should I do?" I had an idea. "Look," I said. "You're a Laotian and I'm an American, right?" "Yes!" he said eagerly, hoping for a way out. "Okay," I said. "We'll go through my papers and you can have anything in Laotian; I'll keep everything in English, okay?" "Yes!" he said, even more eagerly. I then flipped through my papers rapidly, giving him a few sheets of advertisements in Laotian. He took them happily, implored me not to tell anyone of our agreement, and left the jail cell. I was released an hour later.

After that I was on my own in Laos, with the exception of two key friends: François, a French-Vietnamese teacher, and Ngeun, a refugee from the Plain of Jars and former Pathet Lao cadre and soldier, who had become my closest friend. I was even more isolated from the Americans, only one of whom besides myself—Walt Haney—had shown any visible concern for the plight of the refugees or about the ongoing bombing. François was a wonderful friend: brilliant, kind, informative, comforting. He applied a kind of Buddhist perspective to things, which comforted me more and more as I became increasingly anxious and worried about the possible consequences of what I was doing.

Ngeun played a particularly important role in my life. He was a strong, ebullient, funny-yet-serious guy, with a spontaneous, wild side, and just my age. I learned a great deal from him about the Pathet Lao from the bottom up. He buoyed my spirits at crucial times: for instance, when I felt near-total anguish as Nixon prepared to invade Cambodia, to do to that country what he had done to Laos. Ngeun also collected the drawings and stories that eventually became the book *Voices from the Plain of Jars*,[13] the only book to emerge from the Indochina wars written by the peasants themselves, who made up 95 percent of the population. The villagers would not have trusted me, a Westerner, to collect those stories and drawings. Ngeun gathered them at some risk to himself. My most moving memory from the many, many hours we spent talking was one night, when we were rooming together. After we had talked for hours, I asked him at 3 a.m. in the darkness, "Ngeun, what do you want out of all of this? What would be your highest dream for yourself?" His voice came back, disembodied: "You know, Phouvieng, I'm only twenty-five, and I've been almost killed more times than I can remember. I don't expect to live much longer. My only hope is that some time after I'm dead, some of the villagers might be sitting around and talking, and my name might come up, and somebody might say, "'Oh, yes, Ngeun. I remember him. He loved the people.'"

This wasn't propaganda or cant. The hour was too late for that, our friendship too close. This was Ngeun.

The months before my expulsion were among the most stressful in my life. A CIA operative at the US embassy, Matt Manchevsky, had taken on the mission of trying to destroy my credibility with the American press. Shortly before I was expelled from Laos, I met François's father, who told me that Manchevsky had arrested François and said he would hold him in prison indefinitely unless François publicly accused me of being a communist. François refused to do so. Manchevsky also visited Ngeun and threatened to have him inducted into the Meo army, a death sentence, unless he accused me of being a communist. I learned this just before I was expelled from Laos, and I spent much of the next twenty-two years worrying about what had happened to Ngeun and François. It was only decades later, when I found François in Paris and Ngeun in Vientiane, that I learned that both had survived their associations with me. A journalist and close friend of mine said he'd been told by a CIA operative that there had been a debate over whether or not to kill or imprison me, but that such action had been decided against because of my close ties to the press. I do not know if this story is true.

Please describe the work you did on returning to the United States with Project Air War and the Indochina Resource Center. With whom did you work on these projects? How important and effective were these organizations?

The timing of my expulsion from Laos in February 1971 was interesting. It occurred at the one point during the entire Indochina war that Laos was the focus of world attention. The Americans had sent the South Vietnamese army into Laos in an ultimately disastrous attempt to try to close off the Ho Chi Minh trail, and for a moment in time the world turned its focus to Laos. The (erroneous) view of the peace movement was "First Nixon continued the war in Vietnam, then he invaded Cambodia, now he's invading Laos."

Thus, there was particular interest in what I had to say. Upon my return to the United States at the end of February 1971, I went directly to the Dispatch

News Service[14] office in Washington, DC, and threw myself into twenty-four-hour workdays, taking naps on the couch. I was almost immediately invited to speak to peace groups, who found the message that "Nixon is bringing home US ground troops but vastly increasing the air war" vital to their ongoing efforts. I also suddenly found myself giving private briefings to congressmen. On one occasion I was briefing Phil Burton, Speaker of the House, and began to take some of the Laotian peasants' drawings out of my briefcase. "Stop right there!" he thundered. "Don't try to pull that shit on me!" Bewildered, I kept going, took the drawings out, and showed them to him and the other members in the room. It turned out that someone had recently shown Burton photos of dead Vietnamese, and he thought I was about to do the same thing. I published an op-ed article in the *New York Times* about the bombing of the Plain of Jars.[15] I publicly confronted the former US ambassador to Laos, William Sullivan, at a hearing of the US Senate Subcommittee on Refugees, when he falsely claimed that the United States had never bombed villages in Laos—an event that was carried on national television.[16]

This visibility and activity led to offers from progressive donors like Cora and Peter Weiss and Carol Bernstein to donate funds if I were to establish a nonprofit organization. The result was Project Air War. For the next four years, from the spring of 1971 until April 30, 1975, I directed first Project Air War and then the Indochina Resource Center. During this period we testified to Congress and helped write legislation, held press conferences, briefed the media and members of Congress, spoke on hundreds of occasions to peace groups, continued to research the air war, and published dozens of articles as well as the book *Voices from the Plain of Jars*. Highlights included authoring legislation that increased the funding of Food for Peace by $500 million in 1975, speaking at a rally of a million people in New York City, a full-page review of *Voices* in *Time* magazine,[17] publication of drawings by the peasants on an entire page of the *New York Times* op-ed section, and a long interview on the *CBS Evening News with Walter Cronkite*.[18]

I married a saintly Vietnamese woman during this period, Thoa Nguyen, who played a key role in inspiring and organizing our work, and who influenced my life tremendously.

After the signing of the Paris Peace Accords, I spent January–August 1973 in Indochina to research and expose the bombing of civilian targets, and also to gain understanding of the situation of political prisoners in South Vietnam. In Phnom Penh, Cambodia, I borrowed a radio from a CIA pilot friend of mine and tape-recorded pilots' conversations while they were in the act of bombing villages. These recordings, which I then transcribed, allowed me to accomplish the difficult task of proving to Sydney Schanberg of the *New York Times*, whose own credibility was on the line, that US pilots were not checking with the Seventh Air Force bombing officer to ensure that there were no civilians in the villages they were bombing, as the air force falsely claimed. This led to a front-page story in the *New York Times* indicating that pilots were bombing civilian targets, which ran on the day of a key vote to end the bombing of Cambodia.[19, 20] The legislation passed by one vote, and I've always hoped that Schanberg's story might have been a deciding factor.

Then I left Cambodia and entered South Vietnam illegally by boat—I had previously been detained while trying to enter through the airport—and remained underground for six weeks. My goal was to get to know my Vietnamese in-laws and their family, most of whom I had never met, and to investigate the situation of political prisoners in South Vietnam. I spent a good deal of time with former political prisoners. I'll never forget my first meeting, for which I arrived prior to those I was interviewing. The door opened, I looked up, and to my amazement only saw the tops of three or four heads moving into the room. It turned out that they had been crippled by being chained up for years in South Vietnam's infamous "tiger cages," and were now forced to roll themselves around on simple boards to which little wheels were attached; of course they could not afford wheelchairs. I also interviewed human rights activists and Third Force political leaders. Additionally I discovered that US Navy personnel were smoking hashish on nuclear submarines, leading to exposés by Flora Lewis and Jack Anderson.

I spent several months at US air bases in Thailand, eventually visiting the top-secret Project Blue Chip at the Seventh Air Force headquarters in Nakhon Phanom, Thailand. There I spoke with the bombing officer, who stated that no one ever checked with him about bombing villages, other than to ensure that there were no CIA teams in the area.

My nonprofit colleagues and I worked closely with a wide variety of organizations and individuals throughout the 1971–75 period, including members of Congress opposed to the war, media interested in our information, and the peace movement, for whom we served as a kind of information clearinghouse. From 1973 to 1975 we worked particularly closely with the Indochina Peace Campaign to cut aid to the Thieu regime in South Vietnam, and to bring attention to the plight of political prisoners there.[21]

I firmly believe that the peace movement as a whole was a restraining influence on the Johnson and Nixon administrations; we know this from the tape-recorded conversations of Johnson and Nixon themselves. There is also no question that the peace movement played a key role in the two key US decisions of the 1971–75 period, when I was active: the close vote to end US bombing of Cambodia in the summer of 1973 and the decision to reduce aid to Thieu from $1.2 billion to $700 million in the winter of 1975.

As for my own organizations, Project Air War and the Indochina Resource Center, it's difficult for me to know what our actual impact was. It was interesting that the US ambassador to South Vietnam, Graham Martin, came back and testified to Congress that the Indochina Resource Center and Indochina Mobile Education Project bore the major responsibility for convincing Congress to cut aid to Thieu, which he saw as the critical step toward the Thieu regime's falling apart. He described the Indochina Resource Center as "the most effective propaganda and pressure organization the world has ever seen."[22] I would like to feel that we had that kind of impact; clearly, though, the key factor determining the war's outcome was the balance of forces on the battlefield.

In your opinion, what is the continuing value of the US-Indochina antiwar movement? What might have been done differently and perhaps better?

I think the movement for peace in Indochina has had a major and beneficial impact on American foreign policy continuing to this day. As horrible and unconscionable as has been much of recent US bombing in Iraq, for example, there is far more concern for the negative public-relations impact of killing civilians wholesale than was the case during much of the Vietnam era. I think the peace movement also had a major impact on the elimination of the draft. Another major development, for which the peace movement is at least partly responsible, is that US leaders are much more reluctant to get involved in conflicts in which there could be a high number of American casualties. Even in Iraq today, US casualties are a fraction of what they were in Indochina.

The clearest example of the peace movement's influence was in halting the bombing of Cambodia on August 15, 1973. On August 14 the bombing was going full blast, as it had been for the previous five years. On August 15 it stopped, the result of extremely close votes in the House and Senate three months earlier. The peace movement deserves the lion's share of credit for that victory.

From a philosophical perspective nothing could have been done differently, given where young people's heads and feelings were at. I believe, for example, that the peace movement could theoretically have been far more successful if peace activists had been operating more out of compassion and sadness than out of anger and frustration. For example, one of the people who had the biggest early impact on my views was my upstairs neighbor in Cambridge, whom I ran into one day in late 1964. He was about to drive several hours to give a talk opposing the war to a church group. I was not against the war at that time, taking the view that the US government and North Vietnamese communists were equally wrong. He heard me out patiently and then, in a very friendly and compassionate way, told me his point of view. I can still remember his face and manner more than forty years later, and I can tell you that he started me thinking. The folks who attacked or belittled me for being too "right wing" during that period tended to reinforce my views rather than getting me to think about them.

Of course, it is appropriate to criticize the peace movement for eventually making itself, rather than the war, the issue. This was after early, more peaceful protests had been entirely ignored. But what are you going to do? Young people *were* angry, and the antiwar movement would have been much weaker and would have declined even more rapidly had it been limited only to those willing to be "Clean for Gene." The specter of hundreds of thousands of angry youth and others did inhibit Johnson and Nixon, by their own testimony. The peace movement was what it was, and it seems to me mainly idle speculation to suggest how in theory it might have been more effective.

If I were to apply the lessons of the Vietnam peace movement to today, my own view is that those of us who oppose the Iraq War will be far more effective if we focus on how the war is endangering American lives by spreading terrorism. But I understand that this way of thinking does not motivate many of the people presently working against the war, and I am happier they are doing so for their own reasons rather than remaining quiet.

What work are you doing now? What are your hopes for the future?

I was deeply disillusioned by the aftermath of the Indochina wars. I had really believed that the guerrillas of Indochina would usher in a far better society than the one they were replacing, one that would not be corrupt and that would be motivated above all by a desire to help the peasants. Although I still believe that the guerrillas behaved relatively admirably during the war, I have been sickened by the transformation that occurred after the war, particularly the widespread corruption and lack of concern for peasants and working people. Wide-scale corruption in a poor, developing country is more than mere thievery or wrongdoing. It is literally murder: money stolen by the rich is money that could otherwise go to food, health care, and agricultural aid needed to keep whole families alive. Such corruption speaks to a sickness at the very heart of a social system.

I was flabbergasted when the victors in Vietnam and Laos so quickly created corrupt societies that showed a cruel indifference to the needs of the majority. I could not, and on some level still cannot, believe that people who fought a war in which they were required to face every kind of hardship, in which they lived so purely and showed so much more concern for the majority than did their opposition, would betray their own ideology, values, and ideals so completely and so quickly.

I had been too busy during the war to try to develop my own deeper understanding of life. I more or less agreed with those who saw humanity's problems as fundamentally a question of economic and social systems, and who believed that if socialism triumphed in the Third World, or economic democracy in the First, that humanity would be launched on a path toward social justice, decency, and happiness. What the experience of Indochina dramatically suggested, and my own post-Indochina observations confirmed, is that solving human problems involves far more than social, economic, or political issues. The real questions involved are psychological and spiritual.

After working in American politics for fifteen years—serving as research director for Tom Hayden for Senate; writing the state of California's SolarCal campaign; serving as Governor Jerry Brown's director of research, a cabinet-level position, and creating his 1981 and 1982 State of the State initiatives; working as research director of Senator Gary Hart's think tank; and directing Rebuild America, which included a wide variety of future Clinton cabinet officials and other worthies—I found myself increasingly drawn to psychological and spiritual issues. What I learned from working in politics at that level was that the kind of fundamental change needed to save the global biosphere, promote peace and genuine social justice, or create a politics that served the majority, would have to come from outside the system. This kind of change would need to involve deep psychological and spiritual transformations in human consciousness.

As I was reaching these conclusions intellectually, I had a deep, life-changing experience in August 1990 in which I faced my mortality on an emotional rather than an intellectual level. I immediately left politics and embarked on a spiritual journey that included six months in India and a return to Laos, intensive meditation culminating in a silent three-month meditation retreat, marrying the second great love of my life—the Hungarian writer and activist Zsuzsa Beres—and studying extensively with Hungarian spiritual teacher Laszlo Honti. I have spent the past five years in Santa Barbara, working and studying psychology with Dr. Robert Firestone and a group of his friends.

I've remained somewhat politically active, marching against and writing about the war in Iraq and a wide variety of other issues for Salon.com, and creating a project called "For Generations to Come," which focuses on saving the biosphere.

My main focus at the moment, however, is on encouraging people to face their own mortality while still in the prime of life. I think that facing one's mortality—developing a "life-affirming death awareness"—is a necessary precondition to an individual's being fully alive. I also believe that only if large numbers of people do so will humanity be able to generate the consciousness required to save the biosphere and avoid the vast number of other calamities awaiting it in the twenty-first century. I am currently facilitating workshops and writing a book on this topic.

You ask about my "hopes for the future." Well, I have to say that my mind doesn't seem to generate too many these days. I am particularly concerned with the effect on the biosphere of the interactions among global warming, biodiversity loss, aquifer depletion, chemical contamination, and a wide variety of other new threats to the biospheric systems upon which human life depends. These are new problems for humans; our slow response to them serves only to accelerate our long-term species-suicide. When I think about these issues, combined with the fact that terrorism will most likely continue to increase in technological sophistication—possibly turning Western societies into police states—and factor in the threats facing the developing world, I find it hard to have much "hope" that the species will better itself in coming decades.

But I also reached a point in my self-inquiries where I came to dislike the whole notion of "hope." If I need to have "hope" to motivate me, what will I do when I see no rational reason for hope? If I can be "hopeful," then I can also be "hopeless," and I do not like feeling hopeless. I came to see "hope" as just one more of the many games that we humans devise to keep ourselves occupied.

When I looked more deeply at my own life, I noticed that my life was not, nor had it ever been, built around "hope." Laos was an example. I went there, I learned to love the peasants, the bombing shocked my psyche and soul to the core, and I responded—not because I was hopeful or hopeless, but because I was alive.

Although I would rather be in my current state, having a much fuller experience of life, I can honestly say that I have never felt so intensely alive and energized as I did during my Laos years, both before and after I discovered the US bombing. And I lived that way because I was alive, not because I was hopeful or hopeless. I was not hopeful that the war in Indochina would end. On the contrary—I assumed that it would continue, and that I would be opposing it, for the rest of my life.

I feel that I am at my best these days when I can allow the life-force to move through me, and move with it, as opposed to creating all sorts of intellectual constructs in my head, such as being motivated by hope, meaning, or other ideas toward which I used to gravitate.

On a good day, I have no hopes for the future; neither am I hopeless about it. I just wake up, work on opening to the forces of life, love, and energy, and do the best I can to experience life as deeply and fully as possible. That will always include doing my best to help others.

— November 2008

CHAPTER 13

Interview with Noam Chomsky

What was the existing framework of international law pertaining to war crimes and crimes against humanity at the time of US intervention in Indochina?

Same as it had been since 1945, and still is. For war crimes, basically, the UN Charter, spelled out a bit further in the Nuremberg Tribunal. The "supreme international crime differing from other war crimes in that it contains within itself the accumulated evil of the whole" (including all subsequent crimes against humanity) is the crime of aggression (the Nuremberg wording),[1] that is, the use of force that does not fall within the exceptions of the Charter: under Security Council authorization, or in "self-defense against armed attack" until the Security Council acts, a very narrow notion, adopting the Webster-Ashburton Treaty wording in the *Caroline* case about immediate necessity leaving no time for deliberation.[2] Western legal and political analysts and Western governments have sought to weaken those constraints to allow them (but not others) more latitude in the use of force, but the original wording and intent have repeatedly been upheld, recently by a high level UN panel (including prominent Western figures) in December 2004,[3] and by the UN World Summit in September 2005.[4] Crimes against humanity are defined by The Hague, Geneva, and subsequent conventions.[5]

Obviously, the United States committed the supreme international crime in Indochina, at least since 1962 when JFK launched a direct attack. Various pretexts were offered (SEATO treaty, collective self-defense, etc.).[6] They're about as credible as those offered by the Nazis hanged at Nuremberg, and nowhere near as credible as the pretexts offered by the Japanese for Pearl Harbor.

There's substantial literature on all of this from the 1960s. Of course, within the international law profession one can find plenty of justifications for the use of force by one's own state or its allies and clients. That's to be expected.

If you were going to write the chapter on "Bloodbaths in Indochina" in *The Political Economy of Human Rights*[7] today, what might you see differently?

Not much. There is more information on the early planning of the war—the kind of documentary evidence I reviewed in *Rethinking Camelot*,[8] which reveals more clearly than before the nature of the war in its early stages and Kennedy's insistence, until the assassination, that there can be no withdrawal before victory is assured.

But that's more about crimes against peace than about crimes against humanity. On the latter, Hatfield Consultants[9] and others have brought forth a lot more evidence about the chemical warfare. There's a horrifying book about it by the great British photojournalist Philip Jones Griffiths, scarcely mentioned in the United States, to my knowledge, though it merited prominent attention.[10] The powerful typically pay little attention to their crimes. Few eyebrows were raised when President Carter declared that we owe Vietnam no debt because "the destruction was mutual."[11] Or when the less forgiving George Bush I declared that we can never forget their crimes against us, but "we can begin writing the last chapter of the Vietnam War" if the Vietnamese dedicate themselves with sufficient zeal to finding the remains of Americans shot down while innocently bombing North Vietnam. "It was a bitter conflict, but Hanoi knows today that we seek only answers without the threat of retribution for the past," Bush added magnanimously.[12]

We now know more about the planning of the 1973 Cambodia bombing, including Kissinger's orders reported in the *New York Times* in May 2004: "A massive bombing campaign in Cambodia. Anything that flies on anything that moves."[13] These comments of Kissinger's did not elicit even a ripple of comment, though they are probably unique in the archival records of any state: a comment so shocking that words fail.

The record of such pronouncements is rich and unchallenged. It recalls an observation of Francis Jennings, one of those who unearthed the true story of the destruction of the indigenous population of the United States from the depths to which it had long been consigned: "In history, the man in the ruffled shirt and gold-laced waistcoat somehow levitates above the blood he has ordered to be spilled by dirty-handed underlings."[14] One of the enduring principles of intellectual history.

There has been one quite remarkable new revelation: the study by Taylor Owen and Ben Kiernan (see chapter 5), based on documents released during the late Clinton years that record what happened after Kissinger loyally transmitted the boss's orders. It turns out that the bombing of rural Cambodia was at five times the horrendous level already reported, more than total Allied bombing in all theaters in World War II. As Owen and Kiernan observe, this savage attack was also a major factor in creating the Khmer Rouge: the casualties from the intense bombing, sharply accelerated by the Nixon-Kissinger call for virtual genocide, drove an "enraged populace into the arms of an insurgency that had enjoyed relatively little support until the bombing began," setting the stage for what followed. The more that is learned, the more we discover about the criminality of the war that Kennedy launched, after years of subversion and violence. And about the validity of Jennings's acid observation.

Please discuss the movement, particularly among US intellectuals, to rewrite and revise the history of US involvement in Indochina. What are your thoughts about references to the history of the United States and Indochina in current US political discourse?

The last chapter of *Rethinking Camelot* goes into the rewriting and revision of history after the war became unpopular among elites in the late 1960s, notably the radical revision of earlier accounts by the JFK memoirists and others, part of the effort to burnish the Camelot image—an effort that still continues, with quite surprising misreading of the documentary record and fanciful accounts of Machiavellian plotting by the hero JFK that were so secret they have left no trace, matters I've discussed elsewhere. The earlier version, which conforms to the rich documentary record, is reinforced by Arthur Schlesinger's recently published journals.[15] These do not even mention Vietnam until the Johnson years, when concerns about the costs and likelihood of success were beginning to mount.

While many intellectuals tried to reconstruct themselves as "long-time opponents of the war" (in secret), many did not have to revise the record very much because their opposition to the war was so qualified: for example, the editors of *Dissent*, who wrote in the summer of 1964[16] that withdrawal of the US invading forces would be "quite as inhumane" as the ongoing policies of "hopeless attrition of the Vietnamese people," which had already reached levels that are hardly captured by the euphemistic phrase "hopeless attrition" (and if they had been "hopeful"?). Their reason was that withdrawal would "almost certainly" be followed by "a slaughter in the South of all of those who have fought against the Communists"—so therefore we must proceed to slaughter the South Vietnamese and destroy the country, the perfectly predictable consequence of continuing the aggression, and the actual consequence. As the war ended in 1975, the *Dissent* editors repeated their 1964 prediction with pride, adding that possibly "nuances" were questionable.[17] A standard argument is that those predictions were in fact fulfilled, referring to Cambodia, which is not at all what anyone predicted. That aside, the argument is an intriguing exercise in cynicism in the light of the actual course of events from the early invasion of South Vietnam to the extension of the war to Cambodia with its hideous aftermath.

During the 2004 presidential campaign it was regularly claimed that the Vietnam War was constantly invoked, perhaps too much. In reality, there is almost no serious reference to the US wars in Indochina in current political discourse. For example, in the "Swift Boat" controversy, has there been even a question about what Kerry was doing deep in the southern part of South Vietnam, in areas that had been virtually devastated by seven years of vicious US attack, and at a time when the atrocities were peaking with the post-Tet accelerated pacification campaigns? Inconceivable. Or take the reaction to McNamara's apologia,[18] which (putting aside the ludicrous falsehoods) was comparable to Goering apologizing to Germans after Stalingrad because he hadn't told them soon enough that the war would be costly to them. The hawks condemned McNamara as a traitor: the doves hailed him for vindicating their stand. One of the sicker moments of modern intellectual history. I have written about that too, in some detail.[19, 20]

The principle is simple: if we committed a crime, it didn't happen. Or at worst, it was a mistake, perhaps involving some half-crazed uneducated GI in the field, not nice folk like us.

If you were writing *After the Cataclysm*[21] today, would you change anything? What are your thoughts on the reactions—or the lack of them—to what you and Edward Herman wrote in the book?

The book you mention is Volume II of *The Political Economy of Human Rights* (*PEHR*).[22] It covered many topics. All have been completely ignored, to my knowledge, apart from the chapter on Cambodia under Pol Pot, which elicited a torrent of hysterical denunciations. Volume I—*The Washington Connection and Third World Fascism*—was also virtually ignored, in particular the chapter on East Timor, which was paired with the chapter on Cambodia in *After the Cataclysm*. The reaction to the comparison is quite telling.

As was quite explicit in *PEHR*, the two paired chapters on East Timor and Cambodia under Pol Pot illustrate dramatically a central theme of the two volumes: the reaction to atrocities is very sharply skewed by agency. When the crimes can be attributed to someone else, particularly official enemies, there is enormous outrage, bitter condemnation, laments about the depths to which evil can descend, cries of "Never again," and the rest of the familiar performance. When comparable or worse crimes are attributable to us, they are ignored, denied, or dismissed as mistakes, strange departures from our nobility, easily forgotten. A corollary is that it is considered highly meritorious to condemn ourselves for failure to respond appropriately to terrible crimes—as long as we keep to the crimes of others.

East Timor and Cambodia under the Khmer Rouge provide as close to a test case of the thesis as we can expect to find in history. The atrocities were monstrous in both cases. They took place in the same part of the world and in the same years (though in East Timor, they continued for twenty years after the Khmer Rouge were expelled from Cambodia).[23]

They also differed in crucial respects. In the case of the Khmer Rouge, responsibility could be blamed on others—if we ignore, as is conventionally done, the role of the horrendous US bombings in laying the groundwork for Khmer Rouge crimes. Furthermore, no one had any proposal as to how to end the atrocities. Finally, Pol Pot's atrocities were highly valuable for apologists for state violence. For the more cynical apologists, the crimes could be—and were—exploited as a retrospective justification for the destruction of Indochina and the acquiescence or tepid opposition of those who allowed it to happen. And the Khmer Rouge crimes could be—and were—exploited instantly to justify further US atrocities to "save people from the Pol Pot left": to support Reagan's terrorist wars in Central America, for example, which took a hideous toll—forgotten, ignored, or denied, because they are our crimes.[24-32]

I use the word "exploited" advisedly. It was exploitation because nothing was done, or even contemplated, to protect the victims of the Khmer Rouge, and when the Vietnamese finally did drive out the Khmer Rouge just as their atrocities were peaking, Vietnam was bitterly condemned, Washington supported a Chinese invasion to punish Vietnam for the crime of ending Pol Pot's atrocities, and the United States and UK turned to direct diplomatic and military support for the Khmer Rouge. All of this passed without notable comment. Further evidence for the lack of concern for the fate of Cambodians except at the hands of some enemy is the (null) reaction to the recent exposure of the extraordinary scale and character of the US attack on Cambodia, and its role in creating the Khmer Rouge. The Kissinger orders, reported in the *New York Times*, scarcely elicited a yawn. The Owen-Kiernan study, to my knowledge, did not appear in the United States apart from my posting of their paper on ZNet[33];I haven't found a mention of it elsewhere. Evidently, both the Kissinger orders and the Owen-Kiernan article would be headlined on page one if there were any genuine concern for the fate of Cambodians. These examples, and many more, reveal that the show of concern for Cambodians suffering under Pol Pot was for the most part sheer hypocrisy. The cynicism was as extraordinary as the lies, and doubtless related.

Turning to East Timor, the contrast is dramatic. The United States had decisive responsibility for the aggression and atrocities from the start, joined by Britain, France, Australia, and other Western powers as the atrocities approached genocidal levels, and there was profit to be made by supporting the Indonesian aggressors. Furthermore, there was a very simple way to terminate the huge slaughter: stop participating in it. That was obvious all along, and for those who could not figure it out for themselves, it was clearly demonstrated in September 1999 when, under great domestic and international pressure, Clinton finally told the Indonesian generals that the game was over: they instantly withdrew, allowing an Australian-led peacekeeping force to enter. I've reviewed the grotesque details elsewhere,[34] including the aftermath, so will not proceed here.

The reactions to the two comparable cases kept to the thesis just outlined, virtually to the level of caricature. In both cases there was massive lying, but in opposite directions. As we demonstrated, fabrication about Pol Pot's atrocities would have impressed Stalin, and was often repeated after it was conceded that it was fabrication. In contrast, the marginal attention to East Timor was largely restricted to lies denying the crimes and the crucial US complicity, or sometimes the cowardly evasion that the United States was too occupied with other matters and "looked away": Washington looked *right there*, and acted decisively to escalate the atrocities right through 1999. True, the educated classes chose to "look away," a standard reaction when the blood is on our hands.[35]

The relative attention to our paired chapters illustrates the same pattern.

Needless to say, the East Timor example was far more significant, precisely because we could so easily do something about it, unlike Cambodia.

That trivially obvious fact allows us to draw the obvious lessons even more sharply. The fact that it is not done, even contemplated—even intelligible— tells us quite a lot about the reigning moral and intellectual culture.

Turning to your question, which I presume is restricted to the chapter on Cambodia, Herman and I did return to the topic ten years later, in our book *Manufacturing Consent*.[36] We reviewed what had happened since, but were able to find nothing that required any change at all in what we had written in *PEHR*. In the chapter on Cambodia we had reviewed extraordinary lying about an earlier article of ours, and the reactions to this chapter were much the same. To my knowledge, not even a misplaced comma has been found, despite the massive effort to discredit our exposure of the cynicism and deceit of the media and the intellectuals. That is not too surprising. The chapter had passed through extensive review at the hands of leading specialists on Cambodia, among them David Chandler, Steven Heder, Ben Kiernan, Laura Summers, and Michael Vickery. Furthermore, the chapter had quite modest aims, so error would have been unlikely. For the most part it simply reviewed uncontroversial documentation, comparing the evidence available with what appeared as it was refracted through the ideological prisms. As we wrote in conclusion, "When the facts are in, it may turn out that the more extreme condemnations were in fact correct. But even if that turns out to be the case, it will in no way alter the conclusions we have reached on the central question addressed here: how the available facts were selected, modified, or sometimes invented to create a certain image offered to the general population. The answer to this question seems clear, and it is unaffected by whatever may yet be discovered about Cambodia in the future."

Our own tentative conclusions were those of State Department intelligence, the most knowledgeable source, which we quoted—which was rare; as can easily be determined, their conclusions were generally ignored. The reason, presumably, is that they did not conform to the imagery required by service to state power and violence.

What lessons might today's movements for social justice learn from the US domestic movement against the US wars in Indochina?

The mainstream movement against the US wars in Indochina kept pretty much to the positions expressed by prominent intellectuals at the dovish extreme: "We all pray" that the hawks are right and that more force will bring victory for the United States, and "We may all be saluting the wisdom and statesmanship of the American government" if escalation succeeds, while leaving "a land of ruin and wreck"—but it probably won't succeed (Arthur Schlesinger[37, 38]); the war began with "blundering efforts to do good" but by 1969 (a year after the business world had turned against the war) it was clear that it was a "disastrous mistake" and the United States "could not impose a solution except at a price too costly to itself" (Anthony Lewis[39]). And many others. The rhetoric can be carried over virtually unchanged to mainstream criticism of the Iraq War.

The fact that some dedicated Nazis turned against Hitler's war after Stalingrad merely increases contempt for their values. If the Russians succeed in pacifying Chechnya, as now seems likely, we do not "salute the wisdom and statesmanship" of the Kremlin. Those concerned with social justice should be able, without difficulty, to apply the conclusions to our own actions and responsibilities. A principled stand is not an easy or popular one, but anything short of it opens the way to more atrocities and crimes—always in the name of peace and justice, a primary lesson to be learned from the Indochina wars, and much else.

Another lesson that the movements for social justice should learn from these wars and much else is that among educated elites, faith in the fundamental benevolence of US policy is profound, and largely immune to fact and logic. It is simply a presupposition of discourse that is considered "responsible." Hence principled opposition to aggression is likely to be fiercely opposed in these sectors, though fortunately, the general public is less deeply indoctrinated and can be reached.

Popular opposition to the Vietnam War did develop, though slowly. There was almost no opposition when JFK launched outright aggression against South Vietnam in 1962. Popular opposition did develop on a substantial scale by 1967, but it is well to remember that by then the destruction had reached such a level that the respected military historian and Vietnam scholar Bernard Fall had warned that "Vietnam as a cultural and historic entity . . . is threatened with extinction" under the "blows of the largest military machine ever unleashed on an area of this size."[40] He was referring particularly to South Vietnam, always the main target of the US assault. But like mainstream opposition to the war, the popular movements generally focused on the bombing of the North more than on the far more extreme attack on the South. The former raised serious threats of international complications that could be harmful to US interests; the latter could be conducted with impunity. There are lessons here too, not pretty ones.

There are more hopeful lessons too. Popular opposition to the war did not keep to the paradigm of a mistake based on good intentions. By 1979 over two-thirds of the population described the war as "not a mistake" but rather "fundamentally wrong and immoral."[41] Those figures remain pretty constant up to the most recent polls in which the relevant questions were asked, a few years ago. Exactly what people meant by saying this, we do not know with confidence because the right follow-up questions were not asked. But the results are nevertheless rather striking, particularly because people who express these views are unlikely to have seen or heard them in the mainstream.

Opposition to aggression is only one of the legacies of the activism of the '60s and its aftermath. It's common to hear concerns these days about the lack of protest against the Iraq War as compared with the Vietnam protests. The comparisons, however, are misleading. At a period of the Vietnam War comparable to Iraq today, there was virtually no protest. Or take the question of withdrawal. In the case of Iraq it's a lively topic. The first call for withdrawal from Vietnam that I can recall in the mainstream was in the fall of 1969, in a *Boston Globe* editorial.[42] Simply compare the scale of the Indochina wars at that time and Iraq today.

One important lesson of the activism of the '60s is that activism can make a difference, a lasting one, and can lead to changes of consciousness to be carried forward in the future. In many respects the country has become a more civilized place, thanks to the activism of the '60s and its expansion in many directions in the years that followed.

—September 2008

Glossary of Selected Terms

(Ed. note: This glossary is not intended to be comprehensive or analytical, but rather to define abbreviations and acronyms used in the text and to provide brief, contextual descriptions of some frequently mentioned terms, individuals, and events.)

Abrams, General Creighton: Commander of Vietnam War military operations 1968–1972 and US Army chief of staff 1972–1974

AFSC: American Friends Service Committee; Quaker organization founded in 1917 with the mission of affording conscientious objectors of all faiths the opportunity to help civilian victims during times of war

ARVN: Army, Republic of Vietnam (military of South Vietnam); counterinsurgent forces allied with the United States against the PAVN and NLF

AID: See USAID

Bloodbath: Term used to argue against premature withdrawal of US forces from Vietnam; the Nixon administration predicted that bloodbaths (systematic murder of unarmed functionaries) would be enacted against noncommunist South Vietnamese by the communist forces of the North.

***Caroline* case/affair**: Term invoked to support the principle of preemptive strike or anticipatory self-defense. The *SS Caroline* was an American steamboat that supplied Canadian rebels with arms, money, and provisions during an 1837 secessionist attempt; Canadian loyalists burned the *Caroline* and sent her over Niagara Falls, inciting tensions between the United States and Britain.

Diem, Ngô Dinh: Prime minister of South Vietnam 1953–1963, installed with the backing of the Eisenhower administration. Diem was overthrown in a CIA-backed coup and executed by ARVN officers in November 1963.

DMZ: Demilitarized zone; east-west swath dividing North and South Vietnam roughly along the 17th parallel

DRV: Democratic Republic of Vietnam (North Vietnam)

Geneva Accords of 1954: Declaration granting Indochina independence from France and dividing Vietnam (provisionally, under the Geneva agreement, with unifying elections to be held in 1956) into North and South at the 17th parallel. The United States did not sign the accords but agreed to abide by them.

Giap, Vo Nguyen: Commander in chief of the People's Army of Vietnam (PAVN) during the Vietnam War; military commander of the Vietminh during the first Indochina war (1946–54). Giap subsequently served as defense minister and deputy prime minister of the Socialist Republic of Vietnam.

GVN: Government of the Republic of Vietnam (South Vietnam)

Ho Chi Minh trail: Complicated system of roads, trails, footpaths, and river routes running from North Vietnam through Laos and Cambodia to South Vietnam; logistical supply route for the PAVN and NLF

Hue: Site of a month-long battle of the Tet offensive and infamous massacre; location of First Division ARVN headquarters and former capital of Vietnam

Indochina: Strictly speaking, Vietnam, Laos, and Cambodia (former "French Indochina"); the term also refers collectively to the aforementioned countries as well as Thailand, Myanmar, Malaysia, and Singapore (mainland Southeast Asia).

IVS: International Voluntary Service; the US branch of Service Civil International (SCI), a worldwide voluntary service organization devoted to promoting peace through community development; originally founded as an alternative to military service

Khmer Rouge: Cambodian military communist movement in power 1975–1979 under the leadership of Pol Pot, whose genocidal regime killed millions. The Khmer Rouge was overthrown by the Vietnamese in 1979 but continued as a guerrilla movement until the late '90s.

Lao PDR: Lao People's Democratic Republic

LPRP: Lao People's Revolutionary Party; Communist Party of Laos, in power since 1975 (named changed in 1972 from Lao People's Party)

MACV: Military Assistance Command, Vietnam; unified command structure of all US military forces in Vietnam

McNamara, Robert: US secretary of defense 1961–1968

My Lai: Massacre on March 16, 1968, of hundreds of Vietnamese civilians by US Army troops; killing took place in My Lai and My Khe, hamlets in the village of Son My

NLF: National Liberation Front (or National Front for the Liberation of South Vietnam); also known as Vietcong

NVA: North Vietnamese Army

Office of Public Safety: US government agency founded in 1957 to train foreign police forces in paramilitary techniques. Technically part of USAID but directed and funded by the CIA, the Office of Public Safety (OPS) trained brutal forces in Latin and South America as well as South Vietnam, including Operation Phoenix assassination squads. OPS was dissolved with the passage of the Foreign Assistance Act of 1974.

Operation Phoenix: Also known as the Phoenix program, the CIA's Operation Phoenix was designed to "neutralize" VCI (Vietcong infrastructure) through assassination, capture, or "conversion." Directed by William Colby (later director of the CIA) and implemented jointly by the CIA, USMACV, and RVN (South Vietnamese) police forces, Phoenix was launched in June 1967 and ran through 1972, although similar programs were in place before and after.

Paris Peace Accords of 1973: Declared an end to US military involvement in Vietnam and provided a temporary halt to North-South fighting. US National Security Advisor Henry Kissinger was awarded the Nobel Peace Prize for his part in negotiating the agreement, signed on January 27, 1973.

Pathet Lao: Literally "Land of Laos"; Lao nationalist movement opposed to French occupation, allied with Vietminh and North Vietnamese

PAVN: People's Army of (North) Vietnam

Pentagon Papers: Documents procured (and leaked to the *New York Times*) by journalist and US Marine veteran Daniel Ellsberg in 1971. The *Pentagon Papers* comprised more than 7,000 pages of classified and top-secret government and military plans for the invasion of and subsequent war in Vietnam, spanning the Kennedy, Johnson, and Nixon administrations. The *Pentagon Papers* have subsequently been published in various editions.

Plain of Jars: Area in northeast Laos, part of Xieng Khouang province. Scattered across and buried on this plateau are thousands of huge, prehistoric stone jars (hence the name). A major archaeological site, the Plain of Jars was devastated by US bombing during the secret war in Laos.

PRG: Provisional Revolutionary Goverment (of South Vietnam); established in 1969 in opposition to the Thieu government of the RVN. Allied with the NLF, the PRG was incorporated into the ruling government after the surrender of Saigon in 1975.

Psywar: psychological warfare; the use of psychological methods (propaganda, terror, torture) to influence the mind of the opposition

Quisling: a puppet government that acts in the interests of an occupying power. The term, synonymous with "traitor," refers to Vidkun Quisling, the Norwegian politician who assisted Hitler in conquering Norway in 1940.

RAND Corporation: A not-for-profit, international research organization with the aim of improving policy and decision making. RAND (a contraction of "research and development") was originally formed by the US Armed Forces in 1946 but has been independent since 1948. RAND has conducted pioneering studies in many areas of public policy, health insurance in particular; much of the organization's work in the areas of intelligence and defense has been classified.

Rome plow: Armored US military bulldozer (manufactured in Rome, Georgia) with a massive, two-ton, angled blade on the front. Rome plows were used to clear densely forested areas in South Vietnam by shearing vegetation and chopping down trees, with the aim of exposing NLF hiding places.

RLG: Royal Lao Government

RVN: Republic of (South) Vietnam

Search-and-destroy: Also known as "S&D," search-and-destroy missions entailed sending US platoons into rural areas of South Vietnam to seek out and destroy Vietcong and NVA forces in the countryside.

SEATO: Southeast Asia Treaty Organization

Strategic Hamlet Program: Joint plan of the United States government and the Diem regime, intended to separate the rural peasants of South Vietnam from NLF influence. The Strategic Hamlet Program involved resettling peasants into "fortified villages" of about a thousand inhabitants each. Although by July 1963 an estimated 8.5 million people had been resettled, the fortification for most of these communities never materialized. The program was dissolved upon the November 1963 assassination of Diem.

Swift Boat: Refers to a smear campaign against Senator John Kerry in his 2004 presidential campaign; "Swift Boat Vets" claimed Kerry lied about his Vietnam War record. A swift boat is a US Navy vessel.

Tet offensive: Military campaign conducted by the Vietcong and North Vietnamese January–September 1968. On January 30 strikes were launched against more than two dozen cities in South Vietnam, taking US and ARVN forces by surprise (a truce had been declared for *Tet*, the lunar new year holiday.) The Tet offensive revealed the scope of the war to be larger than the US had anticipated and is often regarded to have turned US public opinion against the war.

Thieu, Nguyen Van: President of South Vietnam 1965–1975

Third Force: Buddhist peace movement in Vietnam

Tiger cages: Tiny stone compartments about five feet wide, nine feet long, and six feet high, which imprisoned political detainees at Con Son prison off the coast of South Vietnam. Prisoners were shackled to the floor, unable to stand, beaten, mutilated, and starved. Many of those who survived were permanently disabled as a result. The tiger cages were exposed to the US public in 1970 after a visit by a US congressional delegation, accompanied by former IVS head Don Luce and then-congressional aide Tom Harkin. Harkin's photos of the horrors of the tiger cages were printed in *Life* magazine July 17, 1970, and helped to sway US public opinion against the war.

UNDP: United Nations Development Program/me; a global branch of the United Nations that works to help developing countries to reduce poverty, attract international aid, increase local development, and protect human rights, among other goals. The UNDP is funded by donations from member countries.

USAID: US Agency for International Development; created in 1961 by President Kennedy. An independent federal agency under the oversight of the secretary of state, USAID's primary function is to provide non-military foreign aid and social development assistance to developing countries. USAID has come under periodic criticism for supporting US political and military partners rather than aiding humanitarian causes.

USMAAG: US Military Assistance Advisory Group, also known as Special Forces; created by the Truman administration to support and advise the French army against the Vietminh. During the Vietnam War MAAG came under the direction of USMACV and served to advise and train the ARVN and other RVN forces.

Vietcong (VC): Short for *cong san Viet Nam* ("Vietnam communist"); also known as the National Liberation Front (NLF). Founded by former Vietminh in the 1950s, the Vietcong was an army (guerrillas, cadres, and official army units) based in South Vietnam, allied with the North Vietnamese, that fought against US and South Vietnamese forces.

Vietminh: Vietnamese national liberation movement formed in 1941 in opposition to French occupation; later granted control over the civil administration of North Vietnam under Ho Chi Minh in 1954

Westmoreland, General William: Commander of Vietnam War military operations 1964–68 and US Army chief of staff 1968–72

Winter Soldier Investigation: Event held January 31–February 2, 1971, by Vietnam Veterans Against the War. One hundred nine veterans (including future senator John Kerry) and nine civilians testified about atrocities and war crimes they had committed or witnessed in Vietnam. Testimony was entered into the *Congressional Record.*

Further Action

This section is intended to help direct the interested reader toward the web-sites of human rights activist organizations and NGOs working in Indochina.

Activist Organizations

Alternative Radio
http://www.alternativeradio.org

Amnesty International
http://www.amnesty.org

Center for Constitutional Rights
http://ccrjustice.org

Human Rights First
http://www.humanrightsfirst.org

Institute for Policy Studies
http://www.ips-dc.org

National Lawyers Guild
http://www.nlg.org

Physicians for Social Responsibility
http://www.psr.org

Radio Free Maine
http://www.radiofreemaine.com

RESIST
http://www.resistinc.org

Vietnam Veterans Against the War
http://www.vvaw.org

Witness Against Torture
http://www.witnesstorture.org

ZNet, especially "Activism" and "Events" sections
http://www.zcommunications.org/znet

NGOs Working in Southeast Asia

Multicountry

CARE International
http://www.care.org

Catholic Relief Services
http://www.crs.org

Handicap International
http://www.handicap-international.us

Mêdecins Sans Frontières
http://www.msf.org

Mennonite Central Committee
http://mcc.org

Mine Advisory Group
http://www.maginternational.org

Norwegian People's Aid
http://www.npaid.org

Red Cross
http://www.redcross.org

Save the Children
http://www.savethechildren.org

UNICEF
http://www.unicef.org

UNDP
http://www.undp.org

War Legacies Project
http://www.warlegacies.org

World Concern
http://www.worldconcern.org

World Vision International
http://www.wvi.org/wvi/wviweb.nsf

Cambodia

American Friends Service Committee
http://www.afsc.org

Cambodia Trust
http://www.cambodiatrust.org.uk

Cambodian Disabled People's Organization
http://pwds.wordpress.com/2008/01/16/cambodian-disabled-peoples-orga-
nization-cdpo-got-fund

Cambodian Documentation Center
http://www.dccam.org

Cambodian School of Prosthetics
http://www.cspo.org.kh

Halo Trust
http://www.halotrust.org

Jesuit Service Cambodia
http://www.jrscambodia.org

Kien Khleang National Rehabilitation Center for the Disabled
http://www.rosecharities.net/rose-cambodia.htm

National Center of Disabled Persons
http://www.ncdpcam.org

Veterans International
http://www.apcdproject.org/trainings/2006/sts/kh-01.html

Laos

Cooperative Orthotic & Prosthetic Enterprise (COPE)
http://www.copelaos.org

Give Children a Choice
http://www.givechildrenachoice.org

Lao Disabled People's Association
http://www.ldpalaos.org

Lao Disabled Women's Development Center
http://www.apcdproject.org/trainings/web-based/pant_homepages/vieng-phet/A1.HTML

Participatory Development Training Center (PADETC)
http://www.padetc.laopdr.org

SNV Netherlands Development
http://www.snvworld.org

World Education/Consortium Lao PDR
http://www.worlded.org

Vietnam

Children of Vietnam
http://www.childrenofvietnam.org

Clear Path International
http://www.cpi.org

East Meets West
http://www.eastmeetswest.org

Landmine Survivors Network
http://www.survivorcorps.org/NetCommunity/Page.aspx?pid=313

Office of Genetic Counseling and Disabled Children
http://www.ogcdc.org

Oxfam Hong Kong
http://www.oxfamamerica.org/partners/OHK-GLO_partner

Peace Trees Vietnam
http://www.peacetreesvietnam.org

Veterans Vietnam Restoration Project
http://www.vvrp.org

Vets with a Mission
http://www.vwam.com

Vietnam Assistance for the Handicapped
http://www.vnah-hev.org

Vietnam Red Cross
http://www.redcross.org.vn/defaultEng.aspx

Vietnam Veterans Memorial Fund
http://www.vvmf.org

Vietnam Veterans of America Foundation
http://www.vva.org

Volunteers for Peace
http://www.vfp.org

Recommended Reading

Following are reading lists suggested by contributors, including references on international law as it relates to US intervention in Indochina. For additional references, please see individual notes for each chapter in the Notes section.

References on International Law and US Intervention in Indochina

Special thanks to Marjorie Cohn (http://www.marjoriecohn.com) and Richard Falk for their suggestions.

Primary Documents

Charter of the International Military Tribunal, August 8, 1945, 82 U.N.T.S. 279; 59 Stat. 1544; 3 Bevans 1238; 39 AJILs 258 (1945), available at http://avalon .law.yale.edu/imt/imtconst.asp

United Nations, Principles of International Law Recognized in the Charter of the Nuremberg Tribunal and in the Judgment of the Tribunal, August 2, 1950, U.N. Doc. A/1316 (1950); 1950 ILC Yb 374, vol. II; 44 AJIL 126 (1950), available at http://untreaty.un.org/ilc/texts/instruments/english/commentaries /7_1_1950.pdf.

General Treaty for Renunciation of War as an Instrument of National Policy, July 24, 1929, U.K.T.S. 29, available at http://avalon.law.yale.edu/subject_menus /kbmenu.asp.

Convention (IV) Respecting the Laws and Customs of War on Land, with Annex of Regulations, October 18, 1907, 1910 U.K.T.S. 9, 187 CTS 227; 1 Bevans 631, available at http://avalon.law.yale.edu/20th_century/hague04.asp.

Protocol for the Prohibition of the Use in War of Asphyxiating, Poisonous or Other Gases, and of Bacteriological Methods of Warfare, June 17, 1925, 26 U.S.T.S. 571, L.N.T.S. 65, available at http://www.state.gov/t/ac/trt/4784.htm.

Geneva Conventions (I–IV), August 12, 1949, 6 U.S.T. 3314–17, available at http://www.icrc.org/Web/Eng/siteeng0.nsf/htmlall/genevaconventions

Protocol Additional to the Geneva Conventions of 12 August 1949, and Relating to the Protection of Victims of Non-International Armed Conflicts (Protocol II), June 8, 1977, 1125 U.S.T.S. 609, available at http://www.icrc.org/Web/Eng/siteeng0.nsf/htmlall/genevaconventions.

UN General Assembly, "Resolution on the Definition of Aggression," U.N. Doc. A/9631, December 14, 1974, available at http://documents.un.org/mother.asp.

Convention on the Prohibition of Military or Any Other Hostile Use of Environmental Modification Techniques, 1108 U.N.T.S. 151, December 10, 1976, available at http://www1.umn.edu/humanrts/peace/docs/conenvironmodification.html.

The International Military Tribunal for the Far East, at Tokyo, July 26, 1946, available at http://www.cnd.org/mirror/nanjing/NMNJ.html.

Commentaries

Bass, Gary Jonathan. *Stay the Hand of Vengeance: the Politics of War Crimes Tribunals.* Princeton: Princeton University Press, 2000.

Dellums, Ronald V. and Citizens' Commission of Inquiry on US War Crimes in Vietnam. *The Dellums Committee Hearings on War Crimes in Vietnam; an Inquiry into Command Responsibility in Southeast Asia.* New York: Vintage Books, 1972.

Duffett, John and Bertrand Russell Peace Foundation. *Against the Crime of Silence; Proceedings of the Russell International War Crimes Tribunal, Stockholm, Copenhagen.* New York: Bertrand Russell Peace Foundation, 1968.

Falk, Richard A. *The Costs of War: International Law, the UN, and World Order after Iraq.* New York: Routledge, 2007.

Falk, Richard A. *Achieving Human Rights.* New York: Routledge, 2009.

Falk, Richard A. and American Society of International Law. *The Vietnam War and International Law.* Princeton: Princeton University Press, 1968.

Falk, Richard A., Gabriel Kolko, and Robert Jay Lifton, eds. *Crimes of War: a Legal, Political-Documentary, and Psychological Inquiry into the Responsibility of Leaders, Citizens, and Soldiers for Criminal Acts in Wars.* New York: Random House, 1971.

Fried, John H. E. and Lawyers Committee on American Policy Towards Vietnam. *Vietnam and International Law: an Analysis of International Law and the Use of Force, and the Precedent of Vietnam for Subsequent Interventions.* Northampton, MA: Aletheia Press, 1990.

Hersh, Seymour. *My Lai 4; a Report on the Massacre and Its Aftermath.* New York: Random House, 1970.

Jackson, Robert H. *The Case Against the Nazi War Criminals*. New York: A. A. Knopf, 1946.

Jokic, Aleksandar, ed. *War Crimes and Collective Wrongdoing: a Reader*. Malden, MA: Blackwell Publishers, 2001.

Littauer, Raphael and Norman Uphoff, eds. *The Air War in Indochina*, rev. ed. Boston: Beacon Press, 1972.

Melman, Seymour, ed. *In the Name of America: the Conduct of the War in Vietnam by the Armed Forces of the United States as Shown by Published Reports, Compared with the Laws of War Binding on the United States Government and on Its Citizens*. New York: Clergy and Laymen Concerned about Vietnam, 1968.

Minear, Richard H. *Victors' Justice: the Tokyo War Crimes Trial*. Princeton: Princeton University Press, 1971.

Minow, Martha. *Between Vengeance and Forgiveness: Facing History after Genocide and Mass Violence*. Boston: Beacon Press, 1998.

Morris, Errol. *The Fog of War: Eleven Lessons from the Life of Robert S. McNamara* [film]. Sony Pictures, 2004.

Ratner, Steven and J. S. Abrams. *Accountability for Human Rights Atrocities in International Law: Beyond the Nuremberg Legacy*. New York; London: Clarendon Press; Oxford University Press, 1997.

Russell, Bertrand. *War Crimes in Vietnam*. London: Allen & Unwin, 1967.

Taylor, Telford. *Nuremberg and Vietnam: an American Tragedy*. Chicago: Quadrangle Books, 1970.

Vietnam Veterans Against the War. *The Winter Soldier Investigation: An Inquiry into American War Crimes*. Boston: Beacon Press, 1972.

Further Readings Suggested by Mark Pavlick

The following are some important works on the United States and Indochina that might be overlooked by standard bibliographies. This list is somewhat personal; I apologize in advance for inevitable omissions.

The works of Marvin Gettleman encouraged millions of people to question official rationalizations for the war by engaging directly with primary documents and rarely heard critical voices (1, 2). See also Gettleman's later reflections on these works and their impact (3).

The work of the Committee of Concerned Asia Scholars during US intervention in Indochina was seminal. For one account of their work, see Douglas

Allen (4). Major collective CCAS efforts included an overall work on the United States and Indochina (5), and works on Laos (6) and Cambodia (7). Their journal, the *Bulletin of Concerned Asian Scholars*, has been renamed *Critical Asian Studies* (8).

Early books by Noam Chomsky on Indochina (9–11) have been reprinted by the New Press (http://www.thenewpress.com) and by AK Press (http://www.akpress.org).

Important works by Marcus Raskin and colleagues at the Institute for Policy Studies (12) were influential in the advancement of critical thinking about the war (13, 14).

Works by George T. Kahin of Cornell University, a pivotal figure in the development of the academic study of Southeast Asia in the United States, remain essential (15, 16).

Jeffrey Race provided a major empirical study of the National Liberation Front in one village in South Vietnam (17).

The crucial Senator Gravel edition of the *Pentagon Papers*, containing material not present in the US government edition, was published by Beacon Press in 1971. Volume V of this edition, "Critical Essays," was edited by Howard Zinn and Noam Chomsky. This latter volume contains perspectives of exceptional importance by Gabriel Kolko, John Dower, and a host of other historians and analysts. Volume V also contains detailed subject and name indices of the *Pentagon Papers* (18).

On the aftermath of the US wars in Indochina, see the important work of Douglas Allen and Ngô Vĩnh Long (19). A noteworthy recent work on war crimes in Vietnam is by Deborah Nelson (20).

On the US domestic antiwar movement see the inspiring work of Paul Joseph (21). See also, generally, the work of Marilyn Young (22).

The collections of photographs of Vietnam by the late British photographer Philip Jones Griffiths remain indispensable for understanding the reality of US intervention in Vietnam (23, 24).

1. Gettleman, Marvin. *Conflict in Indo-China; a Reader on the Widening War in Laos and Cambodia*. New York: Random House, 1970.

2. Gettleman, Marvin. *Vietnam; History, Documents, and Opinions on a Major World Crisis*. Greenwich, CT: Fawcett Publications, 1965.

3. Gettleman, Marvin. "Against Cartesianism: Three Generations of Vietnam Scholarship." In *Coming to Terms: Indochina, the United States, and the War*,

edited by Douglas Allen, 209–302. Boulder, CO: Westview Press, 1991.

4. Allen, Douglas, "Scholars of Asia and the War." In *Coming to Terms: Indochina, the United States, and the War*, edited by Douglas Allen, 211–49. Boulder: Westview Press, 1991.

5. Committee of Concerned Asian Scholars. *The Indochina Story; a Fully Document-ed Account*. New York: Pantheon Books, 1970.

6. Adams, Nina S., Alfred W. McCoy, and Committee of Concerned Asian Schol-ars. *Laos: War and Revolution*. New York: Harper and Row, 1970.

7. Grant, Jonathan S. *Cambodia; the Widening War in Indochina*. New York: Wash-ington Square Press, 1971.

8. *Critical Asian Studies*, available online at http://bcasnet.org.

9. Chomsky, Noam. *American Power and the New Mandarins*. New York: Pantheon Books, 1969.

10. ——— *At War with Asia*. Edinburgh; Oakland, CA: AK Press, 2005.

11. ——— *For Reasons of State*. New York: New Press, 2003.

12. *Institute for Policy Studies*, available online at http://www.ips-dc.org.

15. Raskin, Marcus G. and Bernard B. Fall. *The Viet-Nam Reader: Articles and Doc-uments on American Foreign Policy and the Viet-Nam Crisis*. New York: Random House, 1965.

16. Stavins, Ralph, Richard J. Barnet, and Marcus G. Raskin. *Washington Plans an Aggressive War*. New York: Random House, 1971.

17. Kahin, George M. and John W. Lewis. *The United States in Vietnam*. New York: Dial Press, 1967.

18. Kahin, George M. *Intervention: How America Became Involved in Vietnam*. New York: Knopf, 1986.

19. Race, Jeffrey. *War Comes to Long An; Revolutionary Conflict in a Vietnamese Province*. Berkeley: University of California Press, 1972.

20. US Department of Defense and Gravel, Senator Mike, ed. *The Pentagon Papers: The Defense Department History of United States Decisionmaking on Vietnam*. 5 vols. Boston: Beacon Press, 1971.

21. Allen, Douglas and Ngô Vĩnh Long. *Coming to Terms: Indochina, the United States, and the War*. Boulder, CO: Westview Press, 1991.

22. Nelson, Deborah. *The War Behind Me: Vietnam Veterans Confront the Truth about U.S. War Crimes*. New York: Basic Books, 2008.

23. Joseph, Paul. *Cracks in the Empire: State Politics in the Vietnam War*. New York: Columbia University Press, 1987.

24. Young, Marilyn. *The Vietnam Wars, 1945–1990*. New York: HarperCollins, 1991.

25. Griffiths, P. J. *Vietnam Inc*. London: Phaidon, 2006.

26. Griffiths, P. J. *Agent Orange: "Collateral Damage" in Vietnam*. London: Trolley, 2004.

Further Readings Suggested by Tuan V. Nguyen:

Allen, Robert. *The Dioxin War—Truth and Lies About a Perfect Poison*. London: Pluto Press, 2004.

Bao Ninh. *The Sorrow of War*. New York: Riverhead Books, 1996.

Berman, Larry. *Perfect Spy*. New York: Collins, 2007.

Bilton, Michael and Kevin Sim. *Four Hours in My Lai*. New York: Penguin Books, 1992.

Capdeville, Yvonne, Francis Gendreau, Jean Meynard, eds. *L'agent orange au Viet-nam: Crime d'hier, tragédie d'aujourd'hui*. Paris: Tiresias Editions, 2005.

Ellsberg, Daniel. *Secrets*. New York: Penguin, 2003.

Gibson, James W. *The Perfect War: Technowar in Vietnam*. New York: Atlantic Monthly Press, 2000.

Gilbert, Marc. *Why the North Won the Vietnam War*. New York: Palgrave, 2002.

Gough, Michael. *Dioxin, Agent Orange*. New York: Plenum, 1986.

Griffiths, P. J. *Agent Orange: "Collateral Damage" in Vietnam*. London: Trolley, 2004.

Herring, George. *America's Longest War: The United States and Vietnam 1950–1975*. New York: McGraw-Hill, 1995.

Committee to Review the Health Effects in Vietnam Veterans of Herbicides, Institute of Medicine. *Veterans and Agent Orange: Update 2006*. Washington, DC: National Academies Press, 2007.

Karnow, Stanley. *Vietnam: A History*. New York: Penguin Books, 1997.

Le Xuan Khoa. *Viet Nam, 1945–1995* (in Vietnamese). Maryland: Tien Rong Publishing House, 2004.

Le Cao Dai. *Agent Orange in the Vietnam War: History and Consequences* [in Vietnamese]. Hanoi: Vietnam Red Cross Society, 2000.

Nguyen Van Tuan. *Agent Orange, Dioxin: Their Residual Effects on Health* [in Vietnamese]. Ho Chi Minh City: Tre Publishing House, 2004.

Schecter, Arnold and Thomas Gasiewicz, eds. *Dioxins and Health*. Hoboken, NJ: Wiley Interscience, 2003.

Schuck, Peter. *Agent Orange on Trial*. New York: Belknap Press, 2006.

Spector, Ronald H. *After Tet: The Bloodiest Year in Vietnam*. New York: Vintage, 1993.

Trung tâm Nghiên cuu Gioi, Gia dình và Môi truong trong Phát trien [Center for Study of Gender, Family and Environmental Development]. *Nhung câu chuyen cua nan nhân Chat doc Da cam/Dioxin—Viet Nam* [Stories of Victims of Agent Orange]. Hanoi: World Publishing House, 2004.

Truong Nhu Tang. *A Vietcong Memoir: An Inside Account of the Vietnam War and Its Aftermath*. New York: Vintage, 1986.

Wilcox, Fred A. *Waiting for an Army to Die: The Tragedy of Agent Orange*. Santa Ana, CA: Seven Locks Press, 1989.

Acknowledgments

This book was inspired by the work of the Indochina Resource Center, the Indochina Mobile Education Project, and the US antiwar movement generally.

It has been a great privilege to work with all the contributors to this book, all of whom donated their work, insight, and expertise.

Thanks in particular to Noam Chomsky for his extensive help and advice throughout this book's development.

Thank you to Channapha Khamvongsa and Elaine Russell for the list of NGOs currently working in Indochina.

Kristina Bobe and Tim Cash at Georgetown University Library were both immensely helpful.

—Mark Pavlick, Editor

Permissions

Chapter 3 in this volume, "Legacies of War: Cluster Bombs in Laos," was published previously in *Critical Asian Studies* 41, no. 2 (2009), 281–306. It has been updated to reflect important changes and developments since 2008.

Chapter 8 in this volume, "So Many People Died: The US System of Suffering, 1965–2014," is excerpted from Nick Turse's book *Kill Anything That Moves: The Real American War in Vietnam* (American Enterprise Project, 2013).

Grateful acknowledgment is made to South End Press (http://www.southendpress.org) for permission to reprint "Bloodbaths in Indochina: Constructive, Nefarious, and Mythical," Chapter 5 of *The Political Economy of Human Rights* (Boston: South End Press, 1979).

Grateful acknowledgment is made to Trolley Books (http://www.trolleynet.com) and to the late Philip Jones Griffiths for permission to reprint his photos of Agent Orange victims in Vietnam. These first appeared in Jones's book *Agent Orange: "Collateral Damage" in Vietnam* (London: Trolley, Ltd., 2004). The Philip Jones Griffiths Foundation is at 195 Goldhawk Road, side entrance, London, W12 8EP, UK.

Notes

Epigraph
Justice Robert H. Jackson's opening address is available at http://www.roberthjackson.
org/Man/theman2-7-8-1; see also http://avalon.law.yale.edu/imt/11-21-45.asp.

Introduction
1. George Evans, "Revelations in the Mother Lode," *Sudden Dreams* (Minneapolis, MN: Coffee House Press, 1991).
2. William Shawcross, *Sideshow: Kissinger, Nixon, and the Destruction of Cambodia* (New York: Cooper Square Press, rev. ed., 2002).
3. Richard A. Falk, Gabriel Kolko, and Robert J. Lifton, eds., *Crimes of War; a Legal, Political-Documentary, and Psychological Inquiry into the Responsibility of Leaders, Citizens, and Soldiers for Criminal Acts in Wars* (New York: Random House, 1971).
4. U.S. Department of the Army and U.S. Marine Corps, *The U.S. Army/Marine Corps Counterinsurgency Field Manual*, U.S. Army Field Manual No. 3-24, Marine Corps Warfighting Publications No. 3-33.5 (Chicago: University of Chicago Press, 2007).
5. Quoted in Stanley W. Cloud, "Exorcising an Old Demon," *Time*, March 11, 1991, 52.
6. Michael McClintock, *Instruments of Statecraft: U.S. Guerrilla Warfare, Counterinsurgency, and Counterterrorism, 1940–1990* (New York: Pantheon, 1992).

Chapter 1: War Crimes in Indochina and Our Troubled National Soul
1. Available at http://www.comp.nus.edu.sg/~nguyenvu/Artists/TC_Son/Songs/TCSon_songs---Bai_ca_danh_cho_xac_nguoi.htm.
2. James McMillan, *Five Men at Nuremberg* (London: Harrap, 1985), 25–26.
3. History News Network, "Vietnam Thirty Years Later: What John Kerry Said on *Meet the Press*," interview with Tim Russert May 6, 2001, with audiotape from April 18, 1971; available at http://hnn.us/articles/3552.html.
4. Richard A. Falk, Gabriel Kolko, and Robert J. Lifton, eds., *Crimes of War; a Legal, Political-Documentary, and Psychological Inquiry into the Responsibility of Leaders, Citizens, and Soldiers for Criminal Acts in Wars* (New York: Random House, 1971).
5. *Congressional Record* 121 (May 11, 1975), 14622–14626.
6. Robert S. McNamara et al., *Argument Without End: In Search of Answers to the*

Vietnam Tragedy (New York: Public Affairs, 1999).

7. Arnold C. Brackman, *The Other Nuremberg: The Untold Story of the Tokyo War Crimes Trials* (New York: William Morrow, 1987).

8. Raphaelle Branche, "Torture and Other Violations of the Law by the French Army during the Algerian War," in Adam Jones, ed., *Genocide, War Crimes and the West: History and Complicity* (London: Zed Books, 2005), 134–45.

9. Rick Perlstein, *Nixonland: The Rise of a President and the Fracturing of America* (New York: Scribner, 2008).

10. Tom Brokaw, *Boom! Voices of the Sixties: Personal Reflections on the '60s and Today* (New York: Random House, 2007), 566ff.

11. Richard A. Falk, Irene Gendzier, and Robert J. Lifton, eds., *Crimes of War: Iraq* (New York: Nation Books, 2006).

12. Michael Sallah and Mitch Weiss, "Buried Secrets, Brutal Truths," *Toledo Blade*, October 19–23, 2003.

13. Joe Conason, "Smear Boat Veterans for Bush," Salon.com, May 4, 2004, available at http://dir.salon.com/story/opinion/conason/2004/05/04/swift/.

14. Available at http://avalon.law.yale.edu/20th_century/hague04.asp.

15. Jonathan Schell, *The Village of Ben Suc* (New York: Knopf, 1967).

16. Sidney Schanberg, "A Cambodian Landscape: Bomb Pits, Rubble, Ashes," *New York Times*, May 24, 1973, 2.

17. Figure cited to the author by a US attaché in a press briefing in Phnom Penh in spring 1973.

18. Vietnam Veterans Against the War, *The Winter Soldier Investigation: An Inquiry into American War Crimes* (Boston: Beacon Press, 1972).

19. Michael Sallah and Mitch Weiss, *Tiger Force: A True Story of Men and War* (New York: Little, Brown, 2006).

20. Alfred W. McCoy, *A Question of Torture: CIA Interrogation, from the Cold War to the War on Terror* (New York: Henry Holt and Company, 2006), 60–69.

21. Brokaw, *Boom! Voices of the Sixties*, 450.

Chapter 2: Excerpts from *Voices from the Plain of Jars*

All stories and drawings are from Fred Branfman's *Voices from the Plain of Jars: Life Under an Air War*, 2nd ed. (Madison, WI: University of Wisconsin Press, 2013).

Chapter 3: Legacies of War: Cluster Bombs in Laos

1. *Congressional Record*, May 14, 1975, S14, 266.

2. The civilian population is protected under the Geneva Conventions and these protections are not affected by the presence of combatants in the population (Protocol I, Article 50, Section 3). These protections include the right to be free from attacks, reprisals, acts meant to instill terror, and indiscriminate attacks. Civilian populations must not be used as civilian shields (Protocol I, Article 51); see 1949 Geneva Convention II, in W. Michael Reisman and Chris T. Antonioni, *The Laws of War: A Comprehensive Collection of Primary Documents on*

International Laws Governing Armed Conflict (New York: Vintage Books, 1994).

3. "Documentation of American Bombing of Civilian Targets in Laos, Appendix II," prepared by Fred Branfman, from Hearings before Senate Subcommittee to Investigate Problems Connected with Refugees and Escapees (Subcommittee of the Committee on War-Related Civilian Problems in Indochina, Part II: Laos and Cambodia), April 21–22, 1971, 89–113.

4. Richard G. Kidd IV, "U.S. Intervention on Humanitarian Impacts of Cluster Munitions," Office of Weapons Removal and Abatement, June 20, 2007, available at http://www.mineaction.org/downloads/1/Statement%20of%20the%20 United%20States%20Richard%20Kidd%2020%20June%202007.pdf.

5. US White House, Office of the Press Secretary, "Joint Declaration between the United States of America and the Lao People's Democratic Republic," press release, September 6, 2016, https://obamawhitehouse.archives.gov/the -press-office/2016/09/06/joint-declaration-between-united-states-america -and-lao-peoples.

6. International Campaign to Ban Land Mines, *Landmine and Cluster Munition Monitors*, years 1996– 2017 (New York: Human Rights Watch), http://www .the-monitor.org/en-gb/home.aspx.

7. See http://www.bullfrogfilms.com/catalog/bombie.html.

8. See http://www.bombharvest.com/filmmakers.html.

9. See http://www.eastsilver.net/taxonomy/term/518.

10. Legacies of War, website, http://legaciesofwar.org/laobama/press-coverage -related-resources.

11. Convention on Cluster Munitions, website, http://www.clusterconvention.org.

12. Martin Stuart-Fox, *A History of Laos* (Cambridge: Cambridge University Press, 1997), 6.

13. Ibid., 9–10.

14. Ibid., 24–29.

15. Grant Evans, *A Short History of Laos, The Land in Between* (Crows Nest, Australia: Allen & Unwin, 2002), 59.

16. Ibid., 82–83.

17. Ibid., 95–96.

18. Walt Haney, "The Pentagon Papers and the United States Involvement in Laos," in Noam Chomsky and Howard Zinn, eds., *The Pentagon Papers, Gravel Edition: Critical Essays*, vol. V (Boston: Beacon Press, 1972), 53–54.

19. Ibid., 253.

20. This refers to the fantasy land in the movie *The Wizard of Oz*.

21. Haney, 265. See also Charles Stevenson, *The End of Nowhere: American Policy toward Laos Since 1954* (Boston: Beacon Press, 1972), 180.

22. Story from Fred Branfman's *Voices from the Plain of Jars: Life Under an Air War* (New York: Harper & Row, 1972).

23. Haney, 275.

24. Haney, 275.

25. *Congressional Record*, May 14, 1975, S14,266.

26. Handicap International, *Circle of Impact, The Fatal Footprint of Cluster Munitions on People and Communities* (Brussels: Handicap International Belgium, May 2007), 30. Available at http://www.handicapinternational.be.

27. United Nations Department of Economic and Social Affairs, *United Nations Demographic Yearbook 1979* (New York, 1980).

28. International Campaign to Ban Landmines, *Landmine Monitor Report 2005, Laos* (New York: Human Rights Watch, 2006).

29. Walt Haney, "A Survey of Civilian Casualties Among Refugees from the Plain of Jars, Laos," testimony before the Subcommittee to Investigate Problems Connected with Refugees and Escapees of the Committee on the Judiciary, United State Senate, July 22, 1971.

30. Ibid.

31. Haney, "The Pentagon Papers and the United States Involvement in Laos," 277.

32. Evans, *A Short History of Laos*, 178.

33. Legacies of War, "Four-Decade-Old Bomb Mistaken for Toy, Kills and Injures 13 in Laos," press release, March 23, 2017, http://legaciesofwar.org/four-decade-old-bomb-mistaken-for-toy-kills-and-injures-13-in-laos.

34. National Regulatory Authority, *National Survey of UXO Victims and Accidents, Phase I* (Vientiane, Lao PDR: National Regulatory Authority, 2009), http://www.nra.gov.la/resources/Reports%20and%20Studies/NRA%20Phase%201%20VA%20Report%20FINAL.pdf.

35. Handicap International Belgium, *Living with UXO—Final Report on the National Survey on the Socio-Economic Impact of UXO in Lao PDR* (Brussels: HIB, 1997), https://www.gichd.org/resources/publications/detail/publication/living-with-uxo-final-report/#.WgZJWLaZOb8.

36. Laos report at the gathering of UXO clearance agencies from Laos, Vietnam, and Cambodia hosted by the US State Department in Washington, DC, June, 2017.

37. US Department of State, *To Walk the Earth in Safety*, http://www.state.gov/t/pm/rls/rpt/walkearth/.

38. UNDP and Lao PDR Ministry of Planning and Investment, *8th 5-Year Socio-Economic Development Plan 2016–2020* (Vientiane, Lao PDR: UNDP, June 2016), http://www.la.one.un.org/images/publications/8th_NSEDP_2016-2020.pdf.

39. World Bank Group, *Lao Economic Monitor: Safeguarding Stability: an Ongoing Agenda* (June 2018), http://documents.worldbank.org/curated/en/418261529002464394/Lao-PDR-economic-monitor-safeguarding-stability-an-ongoing-agenda-thematic-section-how-can-farmers-get-more-for-their-rice-and-consumers-pay-less.

40. World Bank, *World Development Indicators 2016*, https://data.worldbank.org/products/wdi.

41. Tim Horner, "Intervention on Behalf of the United Nations Development Programme," speech before the Convention on Certain Conventional Weapons, June 20, 2007, available at: http://www.undp.org/cpr/documents/we_do/lao_TimHorner.pdf.

42. Central Intelligence Agency, "The World Factbook: Laos," 2007, at http://www

.cia.gov/library/publications/the-world-factbook/geos/la.html.

43. World Bank, *Lao PDR Environment Monitor* (Washington, DC: World Bank, 2007).

44. World Food Programme, *Lao People's Democatric Republic Country Strategic Plan (2017–2021),*February23,2017,http://documents.wfp.org/stellent/groups/internal /documents/projects/wfp291733.pdf?_ga=2.31950398.1464003336.1510097173 -290005273.1510097173.

45. Lao Statistics Bureau, Results of *Population and Housing Census 2015* (Vientiane, Lao PDR: Lao Statistics Bureau, 2015), http://lao.unfpa.org/sites/default /files/pub-pdf/PHC-ENG-FNAL-WEB_0.pdf.

46. Communication from Joe Pereira of COPE, September 18, 2008.

47. Funds for NGOs, "USAID/Thailand: Seeking Applications for Disability Support Sector Activity in Lao PDR," website listing, https://www2.fundsforngos .org/disability/usaidthailand-seeking-applications-disability-sector-support -activity-lao-pdr.

48. "Majority of Mental Health Issues Remain Untreated,"*Laotian Times,*July 7,2017, https://laotiantimes.com/2017/07/07/majority-mental-health-issues-remain -untreated-laos.

49. World Bank, *Lao PDR Environment Monitor*, 18.

50. Ibid., 23–24.

51. Legacies of War website, available at: http://www.legaciesofwar.org.

Chapter 4: Agent Orange in Vietnam

1. "Vietnam: 'The Biggest Chemical War' in History," *Le Nouvel Observateur*, March 14, 2004.

2. Ayres S, et al. Is 2,3,7,8-TCDD (dioxin) a carcinogen for humans? *Environ Health Perspect* 1985;62:329; see also Crosby DG, et al. Environmental generation and degradation of dibenzodioxins and dibenzofurans. *Environ Health Perspect* 1973;5:259.

3. Committee to Review the Health Effects in Vietnam Veterans of Exposure to Herbicides, *Veterans and Agent Orange: Update 2004* (Washington, DC: National Academies Press: 2005) 184, 186.

4. O. P. Gupta, *Modern Weed Management* (Jodhpur: Agrobios, 2000).

5. Pokorny R. Some chlorophenoxyacetic acids. *J Amer Chem Soc.* 1941;63:1768; see also Zimmerman PW and Hitchcock AE. Substituted phenoxy and benzoic acid growth substances in the relation of structure to physiological activity. *Contr. Boyce Thompson Inst* 1942; 12:321–344.

6. Barton J. Bernstein, "Origins of the U.S. Biological Warfare Program," in Susan Wright, ed., *Preventing a Biological Arms Race* (Boston: MIT Press, 1991), 9–25.

7. *Royal Air Force, the Malayan Emergency, 1948–1960* (London: Ministry of Defence, 1970), 113–114, 152, quoted in William A. Buckingham, Jr., *Operation Ranch Hand: Herbicides in Southeast Asia 1961–1971* (Washington, DC: Government Printing Office for Office of Air Force History, 1982).

8. NSAM 115, Subject: Defoliant Operations in Vietnam, November 30, 1961;

Message, Department of State to American Embassy in Saigon, Joint State–Defense Message Number 561, November 30, 1962.

9.   Record, 4th SECDEF Conference, HQ CINCPAC, March 21, 1962.

10. "Scientists Protest Viet Crop Destruction," *Science*, January 21, 1966, 309.

11. "5,000 Scientists Ask Ban on Gas in Vietnam," *Washington Post*, February 15, 1967, A-1.

12. Report, "Assessment of Ecological Effects of Extensive or Repeated Use of Herbicides," Midwest Research Institute, ARPA Order no. 1086, AD824314, January 12, 1967, 290–292.

13. Project CHECO, Southeast Asia Report, Ranch Hand Herbicide Operations in SEA, July 13, 1971, 32, 104.

14. Stellman JM, Stellman SD, Christian R, Weber T, Tomasallo C. The extent and patterns of usage of Agent Orange and other herbicides in Vietnam. *Nature* 2003; 422:681–687.

15. Ibid.

16. Ibid.

17. John Dux and P. J. Young, *Agent Orange: The Bitter Harvest* (Sydney: Hodder and Stoughton, 1980). See Chapter 3.

18. Peter H. Schuck, *Agent Orange on Trial* (Cambridge: Harvard University Press, 1986), 17.

19. Schuck, *Agent Orange on Trial*, 18.

20. Stellman JM, et al. The extent and patterns of usage of Agent Orange and other herbicides on Vietnam. *Nature* 2003;422:681–687.

21. Schechter A, et al. Agent Orange and the Vietnamese: the persistence of elevated dioxin levels in human tissues. *Am J Publ Health* 1995;85:516–22.

22. Schecter A, Quynh HT, Pavuk M, Papke O, Malish R, Constable JD. Food as a source of dioxin exposure in the residents of Bien Hoa City, Vietnam. *J Occup Environ Med* 2003;45:781–788.

23. Pirkle JL, et al. Estimates of the half-life of 2,3,7,8-tetrachlorodibenzo-p-dioxin in Vietnam veterans of Operation Ranch Hand. *Environ Health Perspect* 1998;106 Suppl 2:671–8.

24. Mocarelli P, et al. Paternal concentration of dioxin and sex ratio of offspring. *Lancet* 2000;355:1858–1863. Also see Rawls A, O'Sullivan DA. *Chem & Eng News* 54, August 23, 1976; Hay A. *Nature* 1976; 262:770.

25. Committee to Review the Health Effects in Vietnam Veterans of Exposure to Herbicides, *Veterans and Agent Orange: Update 2006* (Washington, DC: National Academies Press, 2007).

26. Agence France-Presse, "Study Finds Sharply Increased Risk of Cancer in Dioxin-Exposed Vietnam Veterans," January 22, 2004.

27. Michalek JE, et al. Serum dioxin, insulin, fasting glucose, and sex hormone-binding globulin in veterans of Operation Ranch Hand. *J Clin Endocrinol Metab* 1999;84:1540–3.

28. Bertazzi PA, Consonni D, Bachetti S, Rubagotti M, Baccarelli A, Zocchetti C, Pesatori AC. Health effects of dioxin exposure: a 20-year mortality study. *Am J*

Epidemiol 2001 Jun 1;153(11):1031–44.

29. John Lewallen, *Ecology of Devastation: Indochina* (Baltimore, MD: Penguin Books, 1971), 116.

30. Admiral Elmo R. Zumwalt, Report to the Secretary of the Department of Veterans' Affairs on the Association Between Adverse Health Effects and Exposure to Agent Orange, DVA Report, 1990.

31. Nessel CS, Gallo MA. Dioxins and related compounds; see Morton Lippmann, ed., *Environmental Toxicants* (New York: Van Nostrand Reinhold, 1992); DeVito MJ, Birnbaum LS. Dioxins: model chemicals for assessing receptor-mediated toxicity. *Toxicology* 1995;102:115–23.

32. Bryant PL, Reid LM, Schmid JE, Buckalew AR, Abbott BD. Effects of 2,3,7,8-tetrachlorodibenzo-p-dioxin (TCDD) on fetal mouse urinary tract epithelium in vitro. *Toxicology* 2001;162:23–34.

33. Cited in Lewallen, *Ecology of Devastation: Indochina*, 116.

34. *New York Times*, December 30, 1970, quoted in Lewallen, *Ecology of Devastation: Indochina*, 116.

35. Thomas Whiteside, *Defoliation* (New York: Ballantine, 1970), 31.

36. Bellett AJ. Agent Orange controversy. *Nature* 1990;343:586.

37. Ewing T. Agent Orange "Not guilty" verdict challenged. *Nature* 1989;342:217.

38. Nessel CS, Gallo MA. Dioxins and related compounds; see Morton Lippmann, ed., *Environmental Toxicants* (New York: Van Nostrand Reinhold, 1992); DeVito MJ, Birnbaum LS. Dioxins: model chemicals for assessing receptor-mediated toxicity. *Toxicology* 1995;102:115–23.

39. List of studies of association between Agent Orange exposure and birth defects are as follows: (1) Erickson JD, et al. Vietnam veterans' risks for fathering babies with birth defects. *JAMA* 1984;252: 903–12; (2) Lathrop GD et al. An epidemiological investigation of health effects in Air Force personnel following exposure to herbicides. Baseline morbidity study results. Brooks Air Force Base, TX: U.S. Air Force School of Aerospace Medicine, Aerospace Medical Division, 1984; (3) Donovan J, et al. Vietnam service and the risk of congenital anomalies. A case-control study. *Med J Aust* 1984;140:394–397; (4) CDC (Center for Disease Control). Health Status of Vietnam Veterans. III. Reproductive Health. *JAMA* 1988;259:2715–2719; (5) Field B and Kerr C. Reproductive behavior and consistent patterns of abnormalities in offspring of Vietnam veterans. *J Med Genet* 1988;25:819–826; (6) Aschengrau A and Monson RR. Paternal military service in Vietnam and the risk of late adverse pregnancy outcomes. *Am J Publ Health* 1990;80:1218–1224; (7) Wolfe WH, Michalek JE, et al. Air Force Health Study. An epidemiologic investigation of health effects in Air Force personnel following exposure to herbicides. Reproductive Outcomes, Brooks Air Force Base, TX: Epidemiology Research Division, Armstrong Laboratory, Human System Division (AFSC), 1992; (8) Wolfe WH, Michalek JE, et al. Paternal serum dioxin and reproductive outcomes among veterans of Operation Ranch Hand. *Epidemiology* 1995;6:17–22; (9) Kang HK, Mahan CM, et al. Pregnancy outcomes among US women Vietnam veterans. *Am J Ind Med* 2000;38:447–454; (10) Khoa ND.

Some biological parameters collected on the groups of people in an area affected by chemicals. First International Conference of Agent Orange/Dioxin, Hanoi, 1983; (11) Phuong NTN and Huong LTD. Consequence of chemical warfare on reproductive outcomes—an epidemiological survey in two localities in the South of Vietnam. First International Conference of Agent Orange/Dioxin, Ho Chi Minh City, 1983; (12) Can N, Xiem NT, et al. A case-control survey of congenital defects in Myvan district, Haihung province. First International Conference of Agent Orange/Dioxin, Hanoi, 1983; (13) Can N, Xiem NT, et al. An epidemiological survey of pregnancies in the North of Vietnam. First International Conference of Agent Orange/Dioxin, Hanoi, 1983; (14) Lang TD, Tung TT, et al. Mutagenic effects on the first generation after exposure to Agent Orange. First International Conference of Agent Orange/Dioxin, Hanoi, 1983; (15) Tanh V, Chi HTK, et al. Cohort study on reproductive anomalies in two villages in Song Be province, Vietnam. Second International Conference of Agent Orange/Dioxin, Hanoi, 1987; (16) Phuong NTN, Thuy TT, et al. An estimate of reproductive abnormalities in women inhabiting herbicide sprayed and non-herbicide sprayed areas in the South of Vietnam, 1952–1981. *Chemosphere* 1989;18:843–846; (17) Phuong NTN, Thang TM, et al. Survey on long-term effects of defoliations and herbicides on human reproduction at Uminh district Minh hai province. Second International Conference of Agent Orange/Dioxin, Hanoi, 1993; (18) Phuong NTN, Thuy TT, et al. An estimate of differences among women giving birth to deformed babies and among those with hydatid-iform mole seen at the Ob-Gyn hospital of Ho Chi Minh City in the South of Vietnam. *Chemosphere* 1989;18(1-6): 801–3; (19) Dai B, Gia Q, et al. Survey on diseases and reproductive abnormalities among soldiers deployed in chemicals sprayed areas in comparison with unexposed control. Second International Conference of Agent Orange/Dioxin, Hanoi, 1994; (20) Dai C, Quynh HT, et al. An investigation on the reproductive abnormalities in family of North Vietnam veterans exposed to herbicides during wartime. Second International Proceedings of Agent Orange/Dioxin. Hanoi, 1994; (21) 10-80 Committee and Hatfield Consultants Ltd., eds., *Retrospective Epidemiological Survey in Four Communes—Aso, Huong Lam, Hong Thuong and Hong Van*; 10-80 Committee and Hatfield Consultants Ltd., eds., *Study of Impact and Development of Mitigation Strategies Related to the Use of Agent Orange Herbicides in the A Luoi Valley Thua Thien Hue Province* (Hanoi: 10-80 Committee, 2000), 2:161–210; (22) Hung TM, Cuc PTK, et al. *Spina Bifida Investigated by Spinal X-Ray Among Children of Veterans Exposed to Defoliant in the War: Consequences of Chemicals Used in Vietnam War 1961-1971* (Hanoi: 10-80 Committee, 2000) 2:50–59.

40. Section 2, Chapter 1, Article 23 of Convention (IV) Respecting the Laws and Customs of War on Land, with Annex of Regulations, October 18, 1907, 1910 U.K.T.S. 9, 187 CTS 227; 1 Bevans 631, available at http://avalon.law.yale.edu/20th_century/hague04.asp.

41. Protocol for the Prohibition of the Use of Asphyxiating, Poisonous or Other Gases, and of Bacteriological Methods of Warfare: Geneva, June 17, 1925.

42. L. Craig Johnstone, "Ecocide and the Geneva Protocol," *Foreign Affairs* 49 (July 1971): 715, 8n.

43. Cathy Scott-Clark and Adrian Levy, "Spectre Orange," *Guardian*, March 29, 2003.

44. Article 5 of the European Convention for the Protection of Human Rights and Fundamental Freedoms, September 3, 1953; Article 10 of the American Convention on Human Rights, July 18, 1978, cited in Karen Parker and Jennifer Chew, "Compensation for Japan's World War II War-Rape Victims," *Hastings International and Comparative Law Review* 49 (1994):527, 177n.

45. Letter from Dr. James R. Clary to Senator Tom Daschle, September 9, 1988. Dr. Clary is a former government scientist with the Chemical Weapons Branch, BW/CW Division, Air Force Armament Development Laboratory, Eglin APE, Florida. Dr. Clary was instrumental in designing the specifications for the A/A 45y-1 spray tank (ADO 42) and was also the scientist who prepared the final report on Operation Ranch Hand: Herbicide Operations in Southeast Asia, July 1979.

46. Environmental Agents Service, Department of Veteran Affairs, United States of America, "Agent Orange: Information for Veterans who Served in Vietnam; General Information," September 1999.

47. Commenting on the outcome of the trial, a spokesman for Dow Chemical Co. said, "We believe that defoliant saved lives by protecting allied forces from enemy ambush and did not create adverse health effects," quoted in S. Berger, "Agent Orange Victims Furious As Court Denies Them Compensation," *Daily Telegraph* (UK), April 28, 2005.

48. "Central Payments Approved for Victims of Agent Orange," *Vietnam Investment Review*, March 6, 2000, quoted in Palmer MG. The legacy of Agent Orange: empirical evidence from central Vietnam. *Soc Sci Med* 2005;60(5):1061–70.

Chapter 5: Iraq, Another Vietnam? Consider Cambodia

1. *New York Times*, October 14, 2002; emphasis added.

2. See Ben Kiernan, *How Pol Pot Came to Power: Colonialism, Nationalism and Communism in Cambodia, 1930–1975* (New Haven, Connecticut: Yale University Press, Second Edition, 2004), 284, 345, 349–57, 390.

3. Seymour Hersh, "Where Is the Iraq War Headed Next?," *The New Yorker*, December 12, 2005.

4. "U.S. Military Steps Up War-Zone Airstrikes," *USA Today*, October 21, 2007.

5. Ibid.

6. Ibid.

7. *BBC News*, September 10, 2007, available at http://news.bbc.co.uk/2/hi/middle_east/6983841.stm.

8. To be precise, 35,914 US B-52 sorties had bombed Cambodia in 1969 and 1970.

9. See Kiernan, *How Pol Pot Came to Power*, 350.

10. Seymour Hersh, *The Price of Power: Kissinger in the Nixon White House* (New York: Summit Books, 1984), 69.

11. The GIS database comprised data originally recovered by the National Combat Command Information Processing System (NIPS) on missions conducted

between 1965 and 1975. The data was classified top secret and maintained by the joint chiefs of staff until declassified and delivered to the National Archives in 1976. It was originally compiled in four separate databases. These files are Combat Activities File (CACTA—October 1965–December 1970); Southeast Asia Database (SEADAB—January 1970–June 1975); the Strategic Air Command's Combat Activities report (SACCOACT—June 1965–August 1973); and herbicide data files (HERBS—July 1965–February 1971). E. Miguel and G. Roland, "The Long Run Impact of Bombing Vietnam" (manuscript, 2005), 45, and Tom Smith, "Southeast Asia Air Combat Data," *The DISAM Journal* (Winter Issue), 2001.

12. See Taylor Owen and Ben Kiernan, "Bombs over Cambodia," *The Walrus* (Toronto), October 2006, 62–69; Ben Kiernan and Taylor Owen, "Roots of U.S. Troubles in Afghanistan: Civilian Bombing Casualties and the Cambodian Precedent," *Asia-Pacific Journal*, June 28, 2010, http://japanfocus.org/-Ben -Kiernan/3380; and Ben Kiernan and Taylor Owen, "Making More Enemies than We Kill? Calculating U.S. Bomb Tonnages Dropped on Laos and Cambodia, and Weighing Their Implications," *Asia-Pacific Journal*, April 27, 2015, http://japanfocus.org/-Taylor-Owen/4313/article.html.

13. For Henry Kissinger's views, see his *Ending the Vietnam War: A History of America's Involvement in and Extrication from the Vietnam War* (New York: Simon & Schuster, 2003), and *Diplomacy* (New York: Touchstone, 1994); Henry Kissinger and Clare Boothe Luce, *The White House Years* (Boston: Little, Brown, 1979).

14. Grolier, 1996, cited but not fully referenced in Miguel and Roland, "Long Run Impact."

15. Miguel and Roland, "Long Run Impact," 2.

16. Over four years, this group conducted 1,835 missions and captured 24 prisoners, but did not find the Vietcong command center. William Shawcross, *Sideshow: Kissinger, Nixon and the Destruction of Cambodia* (New York: Simon & Schuster, 1979), 64.

17. *The Australian*, January 15, 1966, quoted in Kiernan, *How Pol Pot Came to Power*, 285.

18. Shawcross, *Sideshow*, 311.

19. Ibid., 191.

20. Kissinger made the case for escalation, stating "our analysis was that the Khmer Rouge would agree to a negotiated settlement only if denied of hope of military victory." Kissinger, *Ending the Vietnam War*, 476.

21. Ben Kiernan, "The American Bombardment of Kampuchea, 1969–1973," *Vietnam Generation* 1, no. 1 (Winter 1989): 4–41; see also https://gsp.yale.edu /case-studies/cambodian-genocide-program/us-involvement/united-states -bombing-cambodia-1965-1973.

22. "Efforts of Khmer Insurgents to Exploit for Propaganda Purposes Damage Done by Airstrikes in Kandal Province," CIA Intelligence Information Cable, May 2, 1973; for more details see Ben Kiernan, *The Pol Pot Regime: Race, Power and Genocide in Cambodia under the Khmer Rouge, 1975–1979*, 3rd ed. (New Ha-

ven, Connecticut: Yale University Press, 2008), 22.

23. Ben Kiernan, "'Collateral Damage' Means Real People," *Bangkok Post*, October 20, 2002.

Chapter 6: My Lai and the American Way of War Crimes

1. "The My Lai Massacre," *Vietnam Online*, PBS, available at http://www.pbs.org /wgbh/amex/vietnam/trenches/my_lai.html.
2. Ken Burns and Geoffrey C. Ward, *The Vietnam War: An Intimate History* (New York: Penguin Random House, 2017).
3. *United States v. Calley*, 46, C.M.R 131 (ACMR 1973), in Joseph Goldstein, William R. Peers, Jack Schwartz, and Burke Marshall, *The My Lai Massacre and Its Cover-Up: Beyond the Reach of Law?* (New York: Free Press, 1976), 505.
4. "The Massacre at Mylai," *Life*, December 5, 1969, 67.
5. Max D. Hutson, Testimony to US Army CID, 1969, in James S. Olson and Randy Roberts, *My Lai: A Brief History with Documents* (New York: Bedford/St. Martin's, 1998), 63.
6. Harry Stanley, Testimony to US Army CID, 1969, in Olson and Roberts, *My Lai: A Brief History with Documents*, 65.
7. Seymour Hersh, *Cover-Up: The Army's Secret Investigation of the Massacre at My Lai 4* (New York: Random House, 1972), 10–11.
8. The Peers Commission Report, in Goldstein, Peers, Schwartz, and Marshall, *The My Lai Massacre and Its Cover-Up*, 193.
9. Ibid.
10. Ibid., 319.
11. Ibid., 227.
12. Ibid., 211.
13. Ibid., 212.
14. The author obtained an electronic facsimile of MACV Directive 525-3, dated October 14, 1966, from the files of the US Army Heritage & Education Center, US Army Military History Institute, Carlisle, Pennsylvania, March 14, 2008.
15. The Peers Commission Report, in Goldstein, Peers, Schwartz, and Marshall, *The My Lai Massacre and Its Cover-Up*, 213.
16. MACV Directive 525-3, October 14, 1966.
17. The Peers Commission Report, in Goldstein, Peers, Schwartz, and Marshall, *The My Lai Massacre and Its Cover-Up*, 213.
18. MACV Directive 525-3, October 14, 1966.
19. Memorandum for the president by Robert S. McNamara, March 16, 1964, in *The Pentagon Papers*, Senator Gravel edition, vol. III (Boston: Beacon Press, 1972), 501.
20. *Pentagon Papers*, Gravel ed., vol. III, 462.
21. David Hunt, "Organizing for Revolution in Vietnam," *Radical America* 8 (January–April 1974): 42–54. Hunt's estimate of the depopulation of the Vietcong zone was based on the published interviews of prisoners and defectors undertaken by the RAND Corporation. See note 34.

22. The Peers Commission Report, in Goldstein, Peers, Schwartz, and Marshall, *The My Lai Massacre and Its Cover-Up*, 212.

23. William C. Westmoreland, *A Soldier Reports* (New York: Doubleday, 1976), 152.

24. Hersh, *Cover-Up*, 183.

25. The Peers Commission Report, in Goldstein, Peers, Schwartz, and Marshall, *The My Lai Massacre and Its Cover-Up*, 284–85.

26. Michael Sallah and Mitch Weiss, *Tiger Force: A True Story of Men and War* (New York: Back Bay Books, 2006), 29–30.

27. Michael D. Sallah and Mitch Weiss, " 'Free-fire' Situation Set Stage for Abuses," *Toledo Blade*, October 22, 2003.

28. Gareth Porter, "My Lai Probe Hid Policy that Led to Massacre," InterPress Service, March 15, 2008, available at http://ipsnews.net/news.asp?idnews=41608.

29. Lewy, *America in Vietnam*, 106, 475n104.

30. Hersh, *Cover-Up*, 4–5.

31. *St. Louis Post-Dispatch*, July 7, 1966, excerpted in Seymour Melman and Richard Falk, *In the Name of America* (Boston: E.P. Dutton & Co., 1968), 225.

32. Jonathan Schell, *The Military Half: An Account of Destruction in Quang Ngai and Quang Tin* (New York: Vintage Books, 1968), 16–19, 24.

33. Ibid.

34. On the RAND "Viet Cong Motivation and Morale" project, see W. Phillips Davison, *User's Guide to the Rand Interviews in Vietnam* (Santa Monica, CA: RAND Corporation, 1972), David Landau, "The Viet Cong Motivation and Morale Project," *Ramparts* (November 1972), and Anthony Russo, "Looking Backward: Rand and Vietnam in Retrospect," *Ramparts* (November 1972).

35. David Hunt, "Villagers at War: The National Liberation Front in My Tho Province, 1965–1967," *Radical America* 8 (January–April 1974): 1–2.

36. Ibid.

37. L. Goure, A. J. Russo, and D. Scott, *Some Findings of the Viet Cong Motivation and Morale Study: June–December 1965*, RM-4911-2-ISA/ARPA (Santa Monica, CA: RAND Corporation, February 1966), 9, 26, 31, 33, 41.

38. Testimony of Robert S. McNamara, January 21, 1966, *Hearings on Supplemental Defense Appropriations for Fiscal Year 1966*, Committee on Armed Services, US Senate, Eighty-Ninth Congress, Second Session (US Government Printing Office, Washington DC: 1966), 26.

39. Ibid.

Chapter 7: The Indonesian Domino

1. This chapter is dedicated to the late Dr. Andrew McNaughtan, an outstanding Australian activist.

2. National Archives of Australia (NAA): A5799, 94/1958, report by Defence Committee, "Importance of Indonesia to Australia and Regional Defence, 1958."

3. Greg Pemberton, *All the Way: Australia's Road to Vietnam* (Sydney: Allen and Unwin, 1987), 71.

4. John Burton, personal letter to F. K. Officer, August 27, 1948, "Documents on

Australian Foreign Policy 1937–49," vol. XIII, Indonesia, 270.

5. Merle Ricklefs, *A History of Modern Indonesia since c. 1300*, 2nd edition (London: Macmillan, 1993), 238.

6. Herb Feith, "Indonesia," in George Kahin, ed., *Governments and Politics of Southeast Asia*, 2nd ed. (Ithaca: Cornell University Press, 1964), 203.

7. Donald W. Fryer, *Emerging Southeast Asia: A Study in Growth and Stagnation* (London: George Philip and Son, 1970), 334–35.

8. Fryer, *Emerging Southeast Asia*, 324.

9. Ricklefs, *A History of Modern Indonesia since c. 1300*, 238–42.

10. NAA: A5799, 94/1958.

11. Benedict Anderson and Ruth McVey, "What Happened in Indonesia?," *New York Review of Books* (June 1, 1978), 25, no. 9.

12. Don Hindley, *The Communist Party of Indonesia* (Berkeley: University of California Press, 1964).

13. Harold Crouch, *The Army and Politics in Indonesia* (Ithaca: Cornell University Press, 1978), 351.

14. Foreign Relations of the United States (FRUS), *Indonesia 1958–1960, Vol. XVII*, (Washington, DC: US Government Printing Office, 1994).

15. Larissa Efimova, "New Evidence on the Establishment of Soviet-Indonesian Diplomatic Relations (1949–53)," *Indonesia and the Malay World* 29, no. 85 (2001): 231.

16. Larissa Efimova, "Who Gave Instructions to the Indonesian Communist Leader Musso in 1948?," *Indonesia and the Malay World* 31, no. 90 (2003):187.

17. NAA: A5799, 94/1958.

18. Foreign Relations of the United States (FRUS), *Indonesia 1964–1968, Vol. XXVI*, (Washington, DC: US Government Printing Office, 1994), 292.

19. Matthew Jones, "US Relations with Indonesia, the Kennedy-Johnson Transition, and the Vietnam Connection, 1963–1965," *Diplomatic History* 26, no. 2 (2002): 253n14.

20. George Kahin and Audrey Kahin, *Subversion as Foreign Policy* (New York: New Press, 1995), 93.

21. Brian Toohey and William Pinwill, *Oyster: The Story of the Australian Secret Intelligence Service* (Melbourne: Heinemann, 1989), 70–71.

22. Kahin and Kahin, *Subversion as Foreign Policy*, 132.

23. Ibid., 46–47.

24. Kenneth Conboy and James Morrison, *Feet to the Fire* (Naval Institute Press: Annapolis, 1999), 57–67.

25. Toohey and Pinwill, *Oyster*, 68–73.

26. Kahin and Kahin, *Subversion as Foreign Policy*, 151–57.

27. H. Brands, "The Limits of Manipulation," *Journal of American History* 76 (1989) 792.

28. FRUS, *Indonesia 1958–1960*, 257.

29. Ibid., 256–58.

30. D. Easter, "Keep the Indonesian Pot Boiling: Western Covert Intervention in

Indonesia, October 1965–March 1965" Cold War History 5, no. 1 (2005): 58–60.

31. Benedict Anderson, "How Did the Generals Die?," *Indonesia* (1987), 110.

32. FRUS, *Indonesia 1958–1960*, 387.

33. Ibid., 346.

34. Helen-Louise Hunter, *Sukarno and the Indonesian Coup: The Untold Story* (West-port: Praeger Security International, 2007), xi.

35. Brands, "The Limits of Manipulation," 803.

36. Karim Najjarine and Drew Cottle, "The Department of External Affairs, the ABC, and Reporting of the Indonesian Crisis 1965–1969," *Australian Journal of Politics and History* 49, no. 1 (2003): 48–60.

37. Easter, "Keep the Indonesian Pot Boiling," 64.

38. Mark Curtis, *Web of Deceit: Britain's Real Role in the World* (London: Vintage, 2003), 389.

39. John Roosa, *Pretext for Mass Murder* (Madison: University of Wisconsin Press, 2006), 225.

40. Scott Burchill, "Absolving the Dictator," *Australian Quarterly: Journal of Contemporary Analysis* 73, no. 3 (May–June 2001).

41. David Bourchier, "Lineages of Organicist Political Thought in Indonesia," unpublished PhD. thesis, Monash University, 1996.

42. A. Murtopo, "Twenty-five Years of Accelerated Modernisation," in D. Bourchier and V. Hadiz, eds., *Indonesian Politics and Society: A Reader* (London: Routledge, 2003), 45–46.

43. David Fromkin and James Chace, "What Are the Lessons of Vietnam?," *Foreign Affairs* 63, no. 4 (1985): 722–46; Harrison Salisbury, ed., *Vietnam Reconsidered: Lessons from a War* (New York: Harper and Row, 1984), 52.

44. Fromkin and Chace, "What Are the Lessons of Vietnam?"

45. Frank C. Darling, *Thailand and the United States* (Washington, DC: Public Affairs Press, 1965).

46. Ibid.

47. *Strategic Basis of Australian Defence Policy* (January 1959).

48. Australian Delegation memo, Colombo, January 11, 1950.

49. Daniel Oakman, *Facing Asia: A History of the Colombo Plan* (Canberra: ANU Press, 2010), 141.

50. ANZAM paper, cited by Greg Lockhart, *The Minefield: An Australian Tragedy in Vietnam* (Crows Nest, Sydney: Allen & Unwin, 2007), 7.

51. Appreciation by the Australian Chiefs of Staff (September 1950); Greg Lockhart, "We're So Alone: Two Versions of the Void in Australian Military History," *Australian Historical Studies* 33, no. 120 (2002).

52. Nuchlas J. White, *British Business in Post-Colonial Malaysia, 1957–70* (London: RoutledgeCurzon, 2004), 2.

53. *The Pentagon Papers*, Gravel edition, vol. IV, chapter 1, "The Air War in North Vietnam, 1965–1968," (Boston: Beacon Press, 1971).

Chapter 8: "So Many People Died": The American System of Suffering, 1965–2014

1. Dave Moniz, "Some Veterans of Vietnam See Iraq Parallel," *USA Today*, November 7, 2003. http://usatoday30.usatoday.com/news/world/iraq/2003-11-06 -vets-usat_x.htm; Frank Newport and Joseph Carroll, "Iraq Versus Vietnam: A Comparison of Public Opinion," Gallup poll, August 24, 2005, www.gallup .com/poll/18097/iraq-versus-vietnam-comparison-public-opinion.aspx; Jeffrey Record and W. Andrew Terrill, *Iraq and Vietnam: Differences, Similarities, and Insights* (Carlisle, PA: Strategic Studies Institute, 2004), http://ssi.armywarcollege .edu/pdffiles/00367.pdf.

2. John Barry, "Could Afghanistan Be Obama's Vietnam?" *Newsweek*, January 30, 2009, www.newsweek.com/could-afghanistan-be-obamas-vietnam-77749.

3. "Will Afghanistan Turn Into Another Vietnam?" CNN poll, October 19, 2009, http://politicalticker.blogs.cnn.com/2009/10/19/cnn-poll-will-afghanistan -turn-into-another-vietnam/.

4. Lewis Sorley, "The Real Afghan Lessons from Vietnam," *Wall Street Journal*, October 11, 2009, https://www.wsj.com/articles/SB10001424052748703746604574463024150622310; Peter Speigel and Jonathan Weisman, "Behind Afghan War Debate, a Battle of Two Books Rages," *Wall Street Journal*, October 7, 2009, https://www.wsj.com/articles/SB125487333320069331; Nick Turse, "The Pentagon Book Club," *Nation*, April 29, 2010, https://www.thenation.com/article /pentagon-book-club/.

5. Max Fisher, "How Afghanistan Is and Isn't Another Vietnam," *Atlantic*, December 2, 2009, https://www.theatlantic.com/international/archive/2009/12/how -afghanistan-is-and-isn-t-another-vietnam/347395/; Nick Turse, "Tet '68, Kabul '12: We Still Don't Get It," op-ed, *Los Angeles Times*, April 24, 2012, http://articles.latimes.com/2012/apr/24/opinion/la-oe-turse-afghanistan-and -vietnam-20120424; Turse, "The Pentagon Book Club."

6. Evan MacAskill, "Iraq Rejects US Request to Maintain Bases after Troop Withdrawal," *Guardian*, October 21, 2011, https://www.theguardian.com /world/2011/oct/21/iraq-rejects-us-plea-bases; Denis D. Gray, "Police: Afghan Policewoman Kills US Adviser," *USA Today*, December 24, 2012, https:// www.usatoday.com/story/news/world/2012/12/24/police-afghanistan-us -kabul/1788779/; David Zucchino, "Drone Strikes in Pakistan Have Killed Many Civilians, Study Says," *Los Angeles Times*, September 24, 2012, http:// articles.latimes.com/2012/sep/24/world/la-fg-drone-study-20120925; Adam Baron, "US Drone Strikes in Yemen Increase," *Miami Herald*, December 27, 2012, www.miamiherald.com/latest-news/article1945847.html; Tom Engelhardt, "The Fall of the American Empire: History, Farce, and David Petraeus," *TomDispatch*, November 20, 2012, www.tomdispatch.com/post/175619.

7. Richard D. Hooker Jr. and Joseph J. Collins, eds., *Lessons Encountered: Learning from the Long War* (Washington, DC: National Defense University Press, 2012), http://ndupress.ndu.edu/Portals/68/Documents/Books/lessons-encountered /lessons-encountered.pdf.

8. UNICEF, "Patterns in Conflict: Civilians Are Now the Target," https://www

.unicef.org/graca/patterns.htm; John Tirman, "Why Do We Ignore the Civilians Killed in American Wars?" op-ed, *Washington Post*, January 6, 2012, https://www.washingtonpost.com/opinions/why-do-we-ignore-the-civilians-killed-in-american-wars/2011/12/05/gIQALCO4eP_story.html.

9. Senate Subcommittee to Investigate Problems Connected with Refugees and Escapees, Committee on the Judiciary, *Humanitarian Problems in South Vietnam and Cambodia: Two Years after the Cease-Fire*, 94th US Congress (Washington, DC: US Printing Office, 1975); Jeanne Mager Stellman, et al., "The Extent and Patterns of Usage of Agent Orange and other Herbicides in Vietnam," *Nature* 422 (2003): 681–87.

10. National Archives, Foreign Commonwealth Office, "Middle East and North Africa: Iraq," reviewed; David Brown, "Study Claims Iraq's 'Excess Death' Toll Has Reached 655,000," *Washington Post*, October 11, 2006, www.washingtonpost.com/wp-dyn/content/article/2006/10/10/AR2006101001442.html.

11. Tina Susman, "Poll: Civilian Toll in Iraq May Top 1M," *Los Angeles Times*, September 14, 2007, www.latimes.com/world/la-fg-iraq14sep14-story.html.

12. Kim Gamel, "Official Report, Other Data Show More Than 110,600 Iraqi Deaths," Boston.com, April 24, 2009, http://archive.boston.com/news/world/middleeast/articles/2009/04/24/official_report_other_data_show_more_than_110600_iraqi_deaths/.

13. World Health Organization, "New Study Estimates 151,000 Violent Iraqi Deaths Since 2003 Invasion," news release, January 9, 2008, www.who.int/mediacentre/news/releases/2008/pr02/en/.

14. Iraq Body Count, https://www.iraqbodycount.org/, as of this writing.

15. Brown University, Watson Institute for International and Public Affairs, "Costs of War: Refugees & Health," updated December 2016, http://watson.brown.edu/costsofwar/costs/human/refugees.

16. Andrew E. Kramer, "After Nearly 9 Years of War, Too Many Widows," *New York Times*, November 24, 2011, www.nytimes.com/2011/11/25/world/middleeast/iraqi-widows-numbers-have-grown-but-aid-lags.html?_r=0.

17. Caroline Hawley, "Iraq Conflict: Crisis of an Orphaned Generation," *BBC News*, November 28, 2012, www.bbc.com/news/world-middle-east-20461110.

18. Michael Schwartz, "Iraq's Tidal Wave of Misery: The First History of the Planet's Worst Refugee Crisis," *TomDispatch*, February 10, 2008, www.tomdispatch.com/post/174892/michael_schwartz_the_iraqi_brain_drain.

19. *PBS NewsHour*, "VA Adds 1,600 Workers to Fix Backlog, but 'Always More We Can Do,'" April 19, 2012, www.pbs.org/newshour/bb/health-jan-june12-vamentalhealth_04-19/.

20. Chalmers Johnson, "Abolish the CIA!" *TomDispatch*, November 5, 2004, www.tomdispatch.com/post/1984/chalmers_johnson_abolish_the_cia.

21. Brown University, Watson Institute for International and Public Affairs, "Costs of War: Refugees & Health: Afghan Refugees," updated December 2016, http://watson.brown.edu/costsofwar/costs/human/refugees/afghan; Voice of America, "Roadside Bomb Kills 10 Afghan Civilians," November 29, 2012, http://blogs

.voanews.com/breaking-news/2012/11/29/roadside-bomb-kills-10-afghan
-civilians/; Carlotta Gall and Tajmoor Shah, "Afghan Villagers Describe Chaos
of U.S. Strikes," *New York Times*, May 14, 2009, www.nytimes.com/2009/05/15
/world/asia/15farah.html?pagewanted=all&_r=0; Rob Nordland, "Insurgent
Attacks Taking Toll on Afghan Civilians," *New York Times*, August 18, 2011,
www.nytimes.com/2011/08/19/world/asia/19afghanistan.html; Hashim Shu-
koor, McClatchy-Tribune News Service, "Helicopter Gunners Kill 9 Afghan
Boys Gathering Firewood; Petraeus Apologizes," Cleveland.com, March 2,
2011, www.cleveland.com/world/index.ssf/2011/03/helicopter_gunners_kill_9
_afgh.html; Emma Graham-Harrison, "NATO'S Afghan Night Raids Come
with High Civilian Cost," Reuters, February 24, 2011, www.reuters.com/article
/us-afghanistan-raids-idUSTRE71N15U20110224; Kim Murphy, "Afghanistan Massacre: Bales Was Denied Promotion Before Incident," *Los Angeles
Times*, November 7, 2012, http://articles.latimes.com/2012/nov/07/nation/la
-na-nn-robert-bales-afghanistan-massacre-20121107.

22. World Health Organization, Global Health Workforce Alliance, "Afghanistan,"
www.who.int/workforcealliance/countries/afg/en/; Emma Graham-Harrison,
"Afghan Refugees Abandoned by Their Own Government, Report Finds,"
Guardian, February 23, 2012, https://www.theguardian.com/world/2012/feb
/23/afghan-refugees-amnesty-report; Andrew North, "Anger as Afghan Children Freeze," BBC News, February 22, 2012, www.bbc.com/news/world
-asia-17116592; Rod Nordland, "Winter's Deadly Bite Returns to Refugee Camps of Kabul," *New York Times*, December 29, 2012, www.nytimes
.com/2012/12/30/world/asia/deadly-bite-of-winter-returns-to-ill-prepared
-refugee-camps-of-kabul.html.

23. Brown University, "Costs of War: Afghan Refugees"; Alex Rodriguez, "Pakistan Extends Refugee Status for Afghans by Six Months," *Los Angeles Times*,
December 13, 2012, http://articles.latimes.com/2012/dec/13/news/la-pakistan
-afghan-refugees-20121213.

24. Laura Lynch, "Afghanistan's Widows Face a Bleak Fight for Survival," PRI,
September 27, 2011, https://www.pri.org/stories/2011-09-27/afghanistans
-widows-face-bleak-fight-survival.

25. Asieh Namdar, "Afghan Orphans Embark on US Road Trip," CNN, February
10, 2012, www.cnn.com/2012/02/03/world/americas/afghanistan-orphanage
-tour/index.html.

26. Jay Loschky, "Afghans' Outlook on Lives Remains Bleak," Gallup poll, August 6,
2012, www.gallup.com/poll/156443/Afghans-Outlook-Lives-Remains-Bleak.aspx.

27. Associated Press, "Census: US Poverty Rates Spike, 50 Million Americans Affected," November 15, 2012, CBS DC, http://washington.cbslocal.
com/2012/11/15/census-u-s-poverty-rate-spikes-nearly-50-million-americans
-affected/.

28. *Rolling Stone*, "The Kill Team Photos," March 27, 2011, www.rollingstone.com
/politics/pictures/the-kill-team-photos-20110327/0742506; BBC News,
"US Marine Joseph Chamblin Sentenced for Afghan Urination Video," De-

cember 21, 2012, www.bbc.com/news/world-us-canada-20807182; M. J. Lee, "Magazine: Troops Mutilated Corpses," March 28, 2011, www.politico.com /politico44/perm/0311/kill_team_d664b005-6479-4a0b-ab2b-9be235920a0c. html; David Zucchino, "US Troops Posed with Body Parts of Afghan Bombers," *Los Angeles Times*, April 18, 2012, http://articles.latimes.com/2012/apr/18 /nation/la-na-afghan-photos-20120418; Reuters, "Soldier Weeps Describing Role in Rape and Killings in Iraq,"*New York Times*, February 22, 2007, www.nytimes .com/2007/02/22/world/middleeast/22confess.html; Kirk Johnson, "Army Seeks Death Penalty in Afghan Massacre," *New York Times*, November 13, 2012, www.nytimes.com/2012/11/14/us/army-seeks-death-penalty-for-robert-bales -in-massacre.html; Gene Johnson, "US Soldier Gets Life Sentence in Afghan Killings," Yahoo! News, November 11, 2011, https://www.yahoo.com/news/us -soldier-gets-life-sentence-afghan-killings-024116265.html.

29. *Los Angeles Times*, "Mexico under Siege," March 9, 2016, www.latimes.com /world/drug-war/la-fg-mexico-under-siege-20160309-storygallery.html#/its -a-war; Gabriel Stargardtner, "Mexico's New President Faces Long Grind on Poverty," Reuters, July 25, 2012, www.reuters.com/article/us-mexico-poverty -idUSBRE86O1PY20120725; Rodriguez, "Pakistan Extends Refugee Status for Afghans by Six Months."

30. Stephen Silverman, "Stars Turn out for Katrina Telethons," *People*, September 12, 2005, http://people.com/celebrity/stars-turn-out-for-katrina-telethons/; Kara Warner, "12-12-12 Concert Raises $30 Million for Sandy Relief," MTV. com, www.mtv.com/news/1698922/12-12-12-concert-raised-30-million-sandy -relief/; Empire State Relief Fund, www.empirestaterelief.com/.

31. Matthew Rosenberg, "US Fund to Rebuild Afghanistan is Criticized," *New York Times*, July 30, 2012, www.nytimes.com/2012/07/30/world/asia/us-fund-to-rebuild -afghanistan-is-criticized.html; Timothy Williams, "US Fails to Complete, or Cuts Back, Iraqi Projects," *New York Times*, July 3, 2010, www.nytimes .com/2010/07/04/world/middleeast/04reconstruct.html; Ernesto Londoño, "Demise of Iraqi Water Park Illustrates Limitations, Abuse of US Funding Program," *Washington Post*, January 3, 2011, www.washingtonpost.com/wp-dyn/content /article/2011/01/02/AR2011010202491.html; Peter Van Buren, "How Not to Reconstruct Iraq, Afghanistan—or America," *TomDispatch*, August 16, 2012, www.tomdispatch.com/blog/175583/.

32. Nick Turse and Deborah Nelson, "A Tortured Past," *Los Angeles Times*, August 20, 2006, http://articles.latimes.com/2006/aug/20/nation/na-vietnam20; Nick Turse and Deborah Nelson, "Vietnam Horrors: Darker Yet," *Los Angeles Times*, August 6, 2006, http://articles.latimes.com/2006/aug/06/nation/na-vietnam6; Deborah Nelson and Nick Turse, "Lasting Pain, Minimal Punishment," *Los Angeles Times*, August 20, 2006, http://articles.latimes.com/2006/aug/20/nation /na-vietside20; Nick Turse, "A My Lai a Month," *Nation*, November 13, 2008, https://www.thenation.com/article/my-lai-month/.

33. Veterans Book Project, www.veteransbookproject.com/the-veterans-book -project/; Steve Vogel, "War Stories Echo an Earlier Winter," *Washington Post*,

March 15, 2008, www.washingtonpost.com/wp-dyn/content/story/2008/03/14/ST2008031403909.html.

Chapter 9: Bloodbaths in Indochina: Constructive, Nefarious, and Mythical

1. Examples will appear below.
2. In the apologetic model, of course, the civilians were terrorized by the NLF and were thus harboring the terrorists out of fear and coercion. Most of the less hysterical apologists knew that this coercion theory of support was highly suspect. See "French and Diemist Bloodbaths" and "Revolutionary Terror in Theory and Practice," this chapter.
3. Sidney Hook, "Lord Russell and the War Crimes 'Trial,'" *New Leader*, October 24, 1966; "The Knight of the Double Standard," *The Humanist*, January 1971.
4. The restriction is regrettable as the systematic character of US aggression in Indochina can only be appreciated by an account that shows how the war machine was unleashed against North Vietnam, Laos, and Cambodia in ever more savage efforts to maintain US control at least of South Vietnam.
5. For our own views and background for them, see Edward S. Herman and Richard B. Du Boff, *America's Vietnam Policy, The Strategy of Deception* (New York: Public Affairs Press, 1966); E. S. Herman, *Atrocities in Vietnam: Myths and Realities* (Philadelphia: Pilgrim Press, 1970); Noam Chomsky, *American Power and the New Mandarins* (New York: Pantheon, 1969); *At War with Asia* (New York: Pantheon, 1970); *For Reasons of State* (New York: Pantheon, 1973); and many other publications.
6. Philippe Devillers, *Histoire du Vietnam* (Paris: Editions du Seuil, 1952), 337.
7. See section 5.2.2 of Noam Chomsky and Edward S. Herman, *The Political Economy of Human Rights* (Boston: South End Press, 1979).
8. "The Problem of Democracy in Vietnam," *The World Today*, February 1960, 73. Later he was to write that by 1956 "it was already clear that . . . [Diem] . . . was establishing an authoritarian regime which would tolerate no political dissent" (P. J. Honey, "Viet Nam Argument," *Encounter*, November 1965), though if it was already clear in 1956, one did not learn this from his pen. The *Encounter* article was devoted to showing how much things were improving since the "popular revolt headed by the army" that overthrew Diem, that is, the US-backed military coup.
9. See "Phoenix: A Case Study of Indiscriminate 'Selective' Terror" and "The Last Years of the Thieu Regime," this chapter.
10. Jean Lacouture, *Vietnam: Between Two Truces* (New York: Vintage Books, 1969), 29.
11. David Hotham, in Richard Lindholm, ed., *Vietnam: The First Five Years* (East Lansing, MI: Michigan State University Press, 1959), 359
12. J. J. Zasloff, *Origins of the Insurgency in South Vietnam, 1954–1960: The Role of the Southern Vietminh Cadres* (Santa Monica, CA: RAND Corporation, 1967), 11.
13. Ibid., 12–13.
14. See Joseph Buttinger, *Vietnam: The Unforgettable Tragedy* (New York: Horizon Books, 1977), for some documentation on his advisory role and also for an ac-

count of his radical change in view, which led him to believe that "future historians may very likely regard the claims that in South Vietnam the United States was defending a free country against foreign aggression among the great political lies of this century" (p. 34)—a lie that, however, like others of its genre, is generally believed (or at least propounded) by the intelligentsia of the state that produced it. See, for example, Arthur M. Schlesinger, Jr., *A Thousand Days: John F. Kennedy in the White House*, (New York: Fawcett Books, 1967 edition), 695: "1962 had not been a bad year: . . . aggression checked in Vietnam." In fact, 1962 was the first year in which US military forces were directly engaged in combat and combat support, bombing of villages, gunning down of peasants from helicopters, defoliation, etc. Only three years later, in April 1965, did US intelligence report the presence of the first North Vietnamese battalion in the South. The "aggression" was of the sort that liberal intellectuals like to call "internal aggression"; see above, p. 99. For many more examples, see the above references of note 5. On the internal US government analysis of "North Vietnamese aggression," see Chomsky, "The Pentagon Papers as Propaganda and as History," in Noam Chomsky and Howard Zinn, eds., *The Pentagon Papers: Critical Essays*, published with an index to volumes I–IV as volume V of the Senator Gravel edition of the *Pentagon Papers* (Boston: Beacon Press, 1971–72).

15. "Lösung für Vietnam," *Neues Forum* (August/September 1969), 459. Later, Buttinger was to write that "Communist control of the whole country [North and South] was achieved without the use of force, not of course because the Vietnamese Communists reject force as a means to gain power, but for the simple reason that in the absence of any effective political resistance, the Communists needed no force to establish control over the whole of Vietnam." (Buttinger, *Vietnam: The Unforgettable Tragedy*, 17.) For exactly the same reason, substantial use of force was required by the United States and its clients to suppress the Vietminh movement that had successfully withstood the French invasion. As Buttinger remarks, "It required a tidal wave of falsehood to persuade Americans into accepting the myth that not French, but Communist, aggression was responsible for the first Indochina war," (ibid., 22), as was constantly trumpeted by Dean Acheson and a host of sycophants.

16. Jeffrey Race, *War Comes to Long An*, (Berkeley: University of California Press, 1971), 197; to date, the best account of the origins of the insurgency under the US-Diem regime. There is also important material on this subject in the massive "Viet Cong Motivation and Morale Study" undertaken by the RAND Corporation. For an interesting study based on this generally ignored material, see David Hunt, "Organizing for Revolution in Vietnam," *Radical America* 8, nos. 1–2 (1974). See also Georges Chaffard, *Les deux guerres du Vietnam* (Paris: La Table Ronde, 1969). US government sources, in addition to the *Pentagon Papers*, also contain much useful information: see Robert L. Sansom, *The Economics of Insurgency In the Mekong Delta* (Boston: MIT Press, 1970); Douglas Pike, *Viet Cong*, (Boston: MIT Press, 1966) (here, one must be careful to distinguish the documentary evidence presented from the conclusions asserted); William A. Nighswonger,

Rural Pacification in Vietnam (New York: Praeger, 1967).

17. Pentagon Papers, Gravel ed., vol. I, 259. See also the government edition of the Pentagon Papers, US Department of Defense, United States Vietnam Relations, 1945–67, 12 vols., Government Printing Office, Washington, 1971; henceforth: DOD. See note 35, this chapter.

18. Pentagon Papers, Gravel ed., vol. I, 259.

19. Ibid., 254.

20. Ibid.

21. Ibid., 255.

22. Ibid., 243.

23. Diem had publicly repudiated the Accords in January 1955 and the US gave him complete support until he became a liability and was removed (indeed, eliminated) in 1963 in a US-backed generals' coup. The same record was replayed eighteen years later when Washington signed a "peace agreement" in Paris in January 1973 with much fanfare (even collecting a Nobel Prize) but immediately announced with utter clarity that it had not the slightest intention of observing its terms, which it proceeded at once to subvert quite openly—all of this before the eyes of the media, which remained silent and obedient.

24. Race, War Comes to Long An, 104.

25. Bernard Fall, "Vietcong—The Unseen Enemy in Vietnam," New Society, April 22, 1965; reprinted in Bernard Fall and Marcus G. Raskin, eds., The Vietnam Reader (New York: Vintage, 1965). Fall, basically a military man, was no dove.

26. The problem was seen to be, in part, the "tremendous sense of dependence on the U.S." of countries like the Philippines and South Korea. National Security Council Working Group Project—Courses of Action, Southeast Asia (November 10, 1964), Pentagon Papers, Gravel ed., vol. I, 627.

27. In the State Department's view, "a fundamental source of danger we face in the Far East derives from Communist China's rate of economic growth which will probably continue to outstrip that of free Asian countries, with the possible exception of Japan." (DOD, bk. 10, 1198). The Department urged that we do what we can to retard the progress of Asian Communist states. The assault on North and South Vietnam certainly contributed to that end, as did the no less violent attacks on Laos and Cambodia.

28. The NSC Working Group Project says that "In South Korea, there is . . . some discouragement at the failure to make as much progress politically and economically as North Korea (from a much more favorable initial position) has made." See note 26, this chapter. Recall that North Korea had been almost totally demolished in the Korean War, including even the bombing of dams to destroy the food supply of the population when the US Air Force could find no more targets.

29. An intelligence estimate of 1959 concluded that "development will lag behind that in the North, and the GVN will continue to rely heavily upon US support. . . ." In the North, while life is "grim and regimented . . . the national effort is concentrated on building for the future." (DOD, bk. 10, 1191–1193). In essence, this forecast proved to be correct.

30. Revised Bundy/McNaughton Draft of November 21, 1964, *Pentagon Papers*, Gravel ed., vol. III, 661.

31. Ibid.

32. Dean Acheson, *Present at the Creation* (New York: Norton, 1969), 219.

33. Gabriel Kolko, "The American Goals in Vietnam," *Pentagon Papers*, Gravel ed., vol. V, *Critical Essays*, 2.

34. On this matter, see John Dower, *The Superdomino in Postwar Asia: Japan in and out of the Pentagon Papers*, in *Pentagon Papers*, Gravel ed., vol. V., *Critical Essays*.

35. As should be obvious, the *Pentagon Papers*, though a useful source, must be regarded with the same caution that one would use in the case of productions, even for internal use, by scholars and bureaucrats working for other states. In fact, there is substantial misrepresentation, particularly with regard to such ideologically crucial matters as the origins of insurgency. For discussion, see Chomsky, "The Pentagon Papers as Propaganda and as History," in *Pentagon Papers*, Gravel ed., vol. V, *Critical Essays*. The same is true with regard to intelligence analyses. It is necessary to study the record to see how dominated the intelligence agencies were by the framework of propaganda that they themselves were helping to construct in their disinformation campaigns. To mention one striking example, the *Pentagon Papers* analysts were able to discover only one staff paper in a record of more than two decades "which treats communist reactions primarily in terms of the separate national interests of Hanoi, Moscow, and Peiping," rather than regarding Hanoi simply as an agent of international communism, directed from abroad. One expects this from Dean Acheson, Dean Rusk, and the more chauvinist elements of academic scholarship, but it is surprising to find such total subordination to state dogma in the intelligence agencies as well. For discussion, see Chomsky, *For Reasons of State*, 51.

36. See NSC Working Group on Vietnam, Sec. 1: "Intelligence Assessment: The Situation in Vietnam," November 24, 1964, Doc. 240, *Pentagon Papers*, Gravel ed., vol. III, 651–56.

37. In an unpublished and untitled memorandum on pacification problems circulated within the military in 1965, a copy of which was given by Vann to Professor Alex Carey, University of New South Wales, Australia.

38. See vol. I, chapter 3, note 5 in Chomsky and Herman, *The Political Economy of Human Rights*.

39. For the intellectual backup of a policy of terror and violence, see Charles Wolf, Jr., *United States Policy and the Third World* (Boston: Little, Brown, 1967). Wolf was Senior Economist for the RAND Corporation.

40. For references, and a general review of Komer's theories and policies, see Chomsky, *For Reasons of State*, 84–85.

41. Cited by Richard Critchfield, *The Long Charade* (New York: Harcourt Brace and World, 1968), 173.

42. For references, see vol. II, chapter 3 of Chomsky and Herman, *The Political Economy of Human Rights*.

43. Douglas Kinnard, *The War Managers* (Hanover, NH: University Press of New

England, 1977), 75, 47.

44. Katsuichi Honda, *Vietnam—A Voice from the Villages* (Tokyo: Committee for the English Publication, 1969), published in English translation in Tokyo, though it never reached the status of a bestseller in the United States. (See note 52, this chapter.)

45. Letter from a US soldier in Vietnam to Senator Fulbright, reprinted in the *Congressional Record*, June 16, 1967.

46. See Rafael Littauer and Norman Uphoff, eds., *The Air War in Indochina*, revised edition (Boston: Beacon, 1971), 62.

47. Ibid., 55.

48. Michael J. Uhl, Hearings Before Subcommittee of House Committee on Government Operations, *U.S. Assistance Programs in Vietnam* (July/August 1971), 315; henceforth, *U.S. Assistance Programs*. For a more extensive quote, see text at note 101, this chapter.

49. Quoted in Arthur M. Schlesinger, Jr., *The Bitter Heritage* (Boston: Houghton Mifflin, 1967), 47.

50. Indochina Resource Center, "A Statistical Fact Sheet on the Indochina War," September 27, 1972.

51. Littauer and Uphoff, *The Air War in Indochina*, 63.

52. See, for example, Herman, *Atrocities in Vietnam*, chapter 3; Seymour Hersh, *My Lai 4* (New York: Random House, 1971); Katsuichi Honda, *Vietnam War: A Report Through Asian Eyes* (Tokyo: Mirai-sha, 1972); Jonathan Schell, *The Military Half: An Account of Destruction in Quang Ngai and Quang Tin* (New York: Vintage, 1968); James Kunen, *Standard Operating Procedure* (New York: Avon, 1971).

53. Shimkin, who was killed in Vietnam, was an International Voluntary Services (IVS) worker who had aroused the ire of the US-Saigon authorities when he "told a *New York Times* reporter about the forced use of farm labor to clear a mine field in Ba Chuc village in the Mekong Delta when American officials there refused to act even after some of the farm people were killed and several wounded" (Don Luce, "Tell Your Friends That We're People," in *Pentagon Papers*, Gravel ed., volume V, *Critical Essays*). IVS was later expelled for being "too political." Its director had protested before the Kennedy Refugee Subcommittee of the Senate on "the forced movement of the Montagnards from their mountain homes into the city slums" (Luce). Kevin Buckley was the head of the *Newsweek* Bureau in Saigon. We are indebted to Buckley for allowing us to use his original notes for the *Newsweek* article in which his account of Speedy Express was partially reported ("Pacification's Deadly Price," *Newsweek*, June 19, 1972). Quotes are from Buckley's notes unless identified as *Newsweek*, in which case they are from the published article.

54. See Peter Braestrup, *Big Story*, vol. II, *Documents* (Boulder, CO: Westview Press, 1977), 20.

55. On the behavior of the Ninth Division and its commander, see Daniel Ellsberg, "Bombing and Other Crimes," in his *Papers on the War* (New York: Simon & Schuster, 1972). Ellsberg writes in part on the basis of direct observation as a

DOD analyst in Vietnam.

56. See the references cited in Chomsky, *For Reasons of State*, xx, xxxiii.

57. Earl S. Martin, *Reaching the Other Side* (New York: Crown, 1978), 133–34.

58. Gordon S. Livingston, "Letter from a Vietnam Veteran," *Saturday Review*, September 20, 1969.

59. Ithiel de Sola Pool, letter, *New York Review of Books*, February 13, 1969. For news reports on the exploits of the Ninth Division at the time, see Chomsky, *At War with Asia*, 99–100.

60. See also Henry Kamm, *New York Times*, November 29, 1969. This forcible evacuation complicated the task of the investigators of the My Lai massacre, he reported.

61. For references and further details, see Chomsky, *At War with Asia*, 104; *For Reasons of State*, 225; see Martin, *Reaching the Other Side*, 133, for an eyewitness account; also the testimony by Martin Teitel of the American Friends Service Committee, *Hearing before the Subcommittee to Investigate Problems Connected with Refugees and Escapees*, Committee on the Judiciary (Kennedy Subcommittee), US Senate, 92nd Congress, Second Session, May 8, 1972. Teitel also describes US-GVN atrocities of April 1972 in the same area subsequent to the virtually bloodless liberation by the NLF-NVA—the victims, once again, included remnants of the My Lai massacre, whose torment was endless. (See note 206, this chapter.)

62. Guenter Lewy, *America in Vietnam* (Oxford: Oxford University Press, 1978), 143. Lewy could have referred not only to *Newsweek* but also to the material cited here from Buckley's original notes, which had already been published. See Chomsky, "U.S. Involvement in Vietnam," *Bridge: An Asian American Perspective*, November 1975; "From Mad Jack to Mad Henry," *Vietnam Quarterly*, Winter 1976. In the case of Operation Bold Mariner Lewy avoids reference either to press reports or to reports by the AFSC observers at congressional hearings and elsewhere, and thus has no need to comment on purposeful destruction of dikes to deny food and the numerous recorded atrocities, again revealing his scholarly technique in this effort to show that the United States cannot justly be accused of war crimes. See also Lewy, *America in Vietnam*, 139–40. We will see below (note 173, this chapter) how Lewy deals with alleged crimes of the official enemy.

63. Two thousand Koreans were dispatched on January 8, 1965. The Honolulu meeting of April 20, 1965, recommended that the numbers be increased to 7,250 (just at the time of the first notice by intelligence that there might be a North Vietnamese battalion in the South; as late as July 1965 the Pentagon was still concerned over the *possibility* that there might be such forces in or near South Vietnam). See Chomsky, *For Reasons of State*, 122, for references. Koreans are reported to have been involved in an attack on a Cambodian village in February 1967; see Chomsky, *At War With Asia*, 122.

64. Robert M. Smith, "Vietnam Killings Laid to Koreans," *New York Times*, January 10, 1970.

65. Craig Whitney of the *New York Times*, who was given extensive documentation

on South Korean murders by Diane and Michael Jones, summarized their findings briefly toward the end of an article focusing on the future role of the South
Koreans in Vietnam. Toward the beginning of his article, Whitney states that
"they [the South Koreans] have been providing a military shield [Whitney does
not say for whom] in a poorly defended section of the central coast...." ("Korean
Troops End Vietnam Combat Role," *New York Times*, November 9, 1972).

66. A large number of South Korean murders were "random" in the sense of not
being attributable to any ongoing military actions.

67. The RAND Corporation's "Viet Cong Motivation and Morale Study" of 1966,
which gave documentary evidence of indiscriminate South Korean murders of
civilians, was classified and suppressed. See *American Report*, July 28, 1972.

68. Letter in the *New York Times*, January 25, 1970.

69. "Security" is another Orwellism consistently applied to Vietnam by official
spokesmen for the United States, and applied in analogous fashion throughout
the empire. With reference to Vietnam it meant unthreatened control by the US
client regime in Saigon. If Saigon controlled by sheer force and violence—often
the case—the people and hamlet were "secure"; if the NLF controlled without
force, the hamlet and its people were "insecure." Similarly, a National Intelligence
Estimate of June 1953 gloomily discussed the inability of the French "to provide security for the Vietnamese population," who warned the guerrillas of the
presence of French Union forces, thus permitting them to take cover. In short,
popular support for the Vietminh made it difficult for France to provide security
for the population from the Vietminh. *Pentagon Papers*, Gravel ed., vol. I, 396.

70. See " 'Pacification' by Calculated Frightfulness: The Testimony of Diane and Michael Jones on the Massacres of South Vietnamese Civilians by South Korean
Mercenary Troops," *Pacification Monograph Number 2*; edited with an introduction
by Edward S. Herman (Philadelphia: University of Pennsylvania Press, 1973).

71. The same tendencies quickly manifested themselves in the Australian "pacification" effort. See the documentation in Alex Carey, *Australian Atrocities in Vietnam* (Sydney, N.S.W.: R. S. Gould, 1968).

72. On the interaction of US-Diem terror and NLF counterterror, see above. Nevertheless, we will adhere to the terminology of the propaganda system here and
refer to the US assassination programs as "counterterror."

73. *U.S. Assistance Programs*, 183.

74. We will not review the depressing record of apologetics. To cite one example,
when Senator Kennedy, in congressional hearings, brought to the attention of
William Sullivan (then deputy assistant secretary of state for the Bureau of East
Asian and Pacific Affairs) a Saigon government report stating that the Phoenix
program was launched in order to "eradicate Communist infrastructure" and that
it reported "40,994 killed by assassination," Sullivan corrected the record, noting
that it said just "killed," not "assassinated," and then added that "some could
have been killed in taking part in military action." As for the Phoenix program,
"the Phoenix, basically, is only a program for the interchange of information
and intelligence," he asserted. *Hearings before the Subcommittee on Refugees and*

Escapees of the Committee on the Judiciary, U.S. Senate, 92nd Congress, Second Session, September 28, 1972 (Washington, DC: US Government Printing Office), 21–22.

75. An earlier predecessor was the "counterterror," or "CT" program organized by the CIA in the mid-1960s to use assassination and other forms of terror against the NLF leadership and cadres. See Wayne Cooper, "Operation Phoenix: A Vietnam Fiasco Seen From Within," *Washington Post*, June 8, 1972. See also Nighswonger, *Rural Pacification in Vietnam*, 136–37, on earlier US efforts to develop "assassination teams" and "prosecutor-executioners."

76. *Pentagon Papers*, Gravel ed., vol. II, 429, 585.

77. Ibid., 503–4.

78. Ibid., vol. IV, 578.

79. Richard S. Winslow, a former AID employee, pointed out that Phoenix program language at one time spoke of the "elimination" of VCI. " 'Elimination,' however, gave the unfortunate impression to some Congressmen and to the interested public that someone was being 'eliminated.' Now the major goal is 'neutralization' of the VCI. Of course, the same proportion of VCI are being killed . . . .But Congress seems mollified now that suspected Vietcong are 'neutralized,' rather than 'eliminated.'" *U.S. Assistance Programs*, 244.

80. *U.S. Assistance Programs*, 207.

81. Saigon Ministry of Information, *Vietnam 1967–1971, Toward Peace and Prosperity* (Saigon: Saigon Ministry of Information, 1971), 52.

82. *U.S. Assistance Programs*, 207.

83. Ibid., 184, 225.

84. Ibid., 183.

85. Ibid., 212.

86. Ibid., 186.

87. For Robert Komer, writing in April 1967, the problem is that "we are just not getting enough payoff yet from the massive intelligence we are increasingly collecting. Police/military coordination is sadly lacking both in collection and in swift reaction." *Pentagon Papers*, Gravel ed., vol. IV, 441.

88. Ibid., vol. II, 407, referring to the officials of Bien Hoa province.

89. See Jon Cooper, "Operation Phoenix," Department of History, Dartmouth College, 1971, mimeographed. The IVS volunteer was Don Luce.

90. *U.S. Assistance Programs*, 314.

91. *New York Times*, August 13, 1972.

92. *Washington Post*, February 17, 1970.

93. *U.S. Assistance Programs*, 314.

94. Dispatch News Service International, No. 376, July 6, 1972.

95. *U.S. Assistance Programs*, 321.

96. Tad Szulc, *New York Times*, April 7, 1971. Saigon costs were also borne by the United States, overwhelmingly.

97. Frances Starner, "I'll Do It My Way," *Far East Economic Review*, November 6, 1971.

98. Richard West, "Vietnam: 'The Year of the Rat,'" *New Statesman*, February 25, 1972.

99. *U.S. Assistance Programs*, 252.

100. Ibid., 314.

101. Ibid., 314–15. US intelligence nets were infiltrated by right-wing Vietnamese who had their own reasons for inciting terror, according to former intelligence agents. See the report by Jeffrey Stein, an agent-handler in 1968–69, *Boston Phoenix*, May 10, 1972.

102. *U.S. Assistance Programs*, 321.

103. Ibid., 252.

104. UPI, *Le Monde*, November 5, 1971.

105. After the Phoenix program was officially phased out, as a result of the bad publicity it received, a new program under the code name "F-6" of a similar nature was instituted, according to a number of former US intelligence officers. Earl Martin came across some independent evidence in support of this not-very-surprising allegation. Shortly before the Saigon army fled from Quang Ngai (which, he reports, was liberated by NLF troops without a shot being fired), Martin was picked up by the Saigon army and kept briefly in the local Provincial Interrogation Center, where the main torturers had operated. He happened to notice an organizational chart on which every number began with "F-6." Martin, *Rural Pacification in Vietnam*, 82.

It is interesting to see how the indiscriminate character of Phoenix murders is used by some of the current apologists for US terrorism in Indochina. Guenter Lewy, for example, points out that very few of those killed under the Phoenix program were specifically targeted. He argues that "the fact that so few of those killed were on the Phoenix target list certainly undermines the charge that the Phoenix program was a program of planned assassinations" (*Rural Pacification in Vietnam*, 281). The logic is astounding. Actually, the facts Lewy cites merely show that this program of planned assassination degenerated into indiscriminate slaughter, as we have discussed, not a surprising fact given the background and context, which Lewy characteristically ignores in his apologetics. As in the cases noted earlier (see note 62, this chapter), Lewy selectively cites government documents, carefully omitting testimony from participants in Phoenix operations or reports by journalists and others on the scene that would permit a serious scholar to determine the character and significance of the programs he seeks to justify.

106. Nazi extermination camps, of course, occupy a place by themselves, but for systematic torture and brutalization of ordinary citizens, often using sophisticated technology, the "Free Vietnam" established by US force bears comparison to European fascism.

107. For extensive documentation on this point, see *After the Signing of the Paris Agreements, Documents on South Vietnam's Political Prisoners* (Narmic/VRC, 1973), 27; Communauté Vietnamienne, *Saigon: un régime en question: les prisonniers politiques* (Paris: Sudestasie, 1974); *A Cry of Alarm, New Revelations on Repression*

and Deportations in South Vietnam (Saigon, 1972); Jean-Pierre Debris and André Menras, *Rescapes des bagnes de Saigon, nous accusons* (Paris: Editeurs Francais Réunis, 1973); *The Forgotten Prisoners of Nguyen Van Thieu* (Paris, 1973); Holmes Brown and Don Luce, *Hostages of War, Saigon's Political Prisoners* (Washington, DC: Indochina Mobile Education Project, 1973); *Pham Tam, Imprisonment and Torture in South Vietnam* (Fellowship of Reconciliation, undated); *Prisonniers Politiques au Sud Vietnam, Listes de Prisonniers, Appel des 30 Mouvements* (Saigon, February 1973).

108. Quoted in Brown and Luce, *Hostages of War*, 14.
109. Ibid., 15.
110. Ibid., 32.
111. Quaker Team in Quang Ngai province, "To Report Truthfully on the Treatment of Prisoners in 1972."
112. *After the Signing*, 32.
113. *U.S. Assistance Programs*, 314.
114. *After the Signing*, 27.
115. Ibid., 26–27.
116. Ibid., 33.
117. Ibid., 33–34.
118. Michael Field, *The Prevailing Wind: Witness in Indo-China* (London: Methuen, 1965), 210.
119. "M. Thieu . . . Appliquons la Loi des Cowboys," *Le Monde*, January 27, 1973.
120. Nothing new in that. For example, the May 1969 meeting of the Council on Vietnamese Studies, which pretended to be a scholarly organization, was devoted to a discussion led by Harvard's Samuel Huntington on the apparently insuperable problems that would face the United States and its local client if compelled to enter into political competition with the NLF, admittedly "the most powerful purely political national organization." Huntington suggested various forms of deceit and chicanery that might overcome the advantages of the enemy, but apparently without convincing his more skeptical colleagues. For discussion, in the context of the plans being developed in the early 1970s by US scholars for incorporating South Vietnam permanently within the US system, see Chomsky, *For Reasons of State*, chapter 4.
121. *Boston Globe*, June 24, 1972.
122. *San Francisco Chronicle*, June 4, 1972.
123. Cited in *Saigon: un régime en question: les prisonniers politiques*, 69, from the *Washington Post*, November 10, 1972, in a discussion of the intensifying terror.
124. *Le Monde*, May 17, 1973.
125. Chris Jenkins, "Thieu's Campaign of Terror," *American Report*, January 29, 1973; letter of the Committee Campaigning for the Improvement of the Prison System of South Vietnam, December 9, 1972; *After the Signing*, 35ff.
126. Sylvan Fox, "Saigon Bypasses Accord by Freeing Many Prisoners," *New York Times*, February 6, 1973.
127. The press also failed to note the suspiciousness of the huge number (forty thou-

sand) allegedly being released, and the illogic in the contention that the political component, numbering ten thousand, had "renounced communism." (All at once? If not, why were they held to this point?)

128. *Prison News* of the Committee Campaigning for the Improvement of the Prison System of South Vietnam, December 14, 1972.

129. *Prison News*, December 9, 1972; Ngô Vĩnh Long, "Thieu Starving Refugees to Keep the Throne," *Boston Phoenix*, December 12, 1972, citing South Vietnamese newspaper reports; *After the Signing*, 35ff.

130. *Le Monde*, January 3, 1973.

131. Ibid.

132. *New York Times*, January 27, 1973.

133. *U.S. Assistance Programs*, 5.

134. *GAO Report* (July 1972), 42.

135. *U.S. Assistance Programs*, 197.

136. Ibid., 224.

137. Ibid., 96.

138. Ibid., 177, 179. (Our emphasis.)

139. AID, Fiscal 1971 Program and Project Data Presentation to Congress; cited by Michael T. Klare, "America's Global Police," *American Report*, September 15, 1972.

140. Ibid., 48–49.

141. *U.S. Assistance Programs*, 186ff, 197. One illustration of "improvement" cited by William Colby was that confessions obtained during "interrogations," which "used to be used exclusively . . . are not used exclusively any more."

142. Quoted in Brown and Luce, *Hostages of War*, 32.

143. Ibid., 36.

144. Ibid., 111.

145. See Chomsky and Herman, *The Political Economy of Human Rights*, vol. II, chapter 1.

146. For a discussion of the 1967 attack on Dak Son and this general issue, see Herman, *Atrocities in Vietnam*, 46–54.

147. The quote is from a captured communist document dated March 1960, cited at length in Race, *War Comes to Long An*, 116–19. The specific quote is on page 119.

148. Douglas Pike, *Vietcong*, 91–92.

149. Ibid., 101. This conclusion is generally accepted even by scholars who bend over backward to find evidence for Hanoi's aggression. See, e.g., King C. Chen, "Hanoi's Three Decisions and the Escalation of the Vietnam War," *Political Science Quarterly* 90, no. 2 (Summer 1975): 258: "It was the growing military campaign of the Diem regime against the Communists with America's support that compelled Hanoi to decide to revert to war."

150. Race, *War Comes to Long An*, 184. Law 10/59 initiated a system of military courts that, within three days of a charge, were to sentence to death "whoever commits or attempts to commit . . . crimes with the aim of sabotage, or of infringing upon the security of the State" (Article 1), as well as "whoever belongs to an organiza-

tion designed to help to prepare or to perpetrate [these] crimes" (Article 3). This law made all dissent and opposition subversive and punishable by death.

151. However absurd it may be, this picture was widely disseminated throughout the Indochina wars, and still is, in essence: For example, it is seriously argued today that a tiny group of Paris-educated fanatics ("nine men at the top") held the entire country of Cambodia in their grip as they proceeded systematically to massacre and starve the population—the reason for this policy, according to the widely praised account that has reached by far the largest international audience, may be that their leader suffers from "chronic impotence." The same authorities (John Barron and Anthony Paul of the *Reader's Digest*) hold that a tiny group of completely inconsequential leaders succeeded through the use of terror to organize a force capable of defeating the world's greatest military power and the government it supported. This is put forth with utter seriousness in a work lauded for its insights throughout the Western world. Meanwhile another authority regarded with much awe among the intelligentsia (François Ponchaud) assures us that the group of fanatics who held the terrorized country in their iron grasp were proceeding to eliminate some five million–seven million people out of a total of eight million, including all but the young.

152. Race, *War Comes to Long An*, 196–97. Emphasis added.

153. Ibid., 188–89, 25n.

154. Ibid., 104.

155. Ibid., 110–11.

156. Ibid., 94–95, 116, 184ff.

157. Ibid., 140.

158. Ibid., 211.

159. Ibid., 200. After talking with the Saigon leadership in 1965, James Reston wrote: "Even Premier Ky told this reporter today that the communists were closer to the people's yearnings for social justice and an independent life than his own government," *New York Times*, September 1, 1965. It was a constant refrain apart from propaganda exercises.

160. Race, *War Comes to Long An*, 200.

161. These reports reached flood proportions during the DRV offensive of 1972, with the *New York Times* contributing its share in the writings of Joseph Treaster and Fox Butterfield. Their reports, heavily dependent on official handouts of Saigon and US information officers, do not withstand close scrutiny. See, for example, Tom Fox, "The Binh Dinh 'Massacre,'" *American Report*, September 15, 1972; *Le Monde*, May 28–29, 1972 (report of interviews with refugees by an AFP special correspondent). See also notes 179, 205, 206, this chapter.

162. When we speak of "mythical bloodbaths" we do not mean to imply that no killings took place. In fact they did, on a considerable scale. But the evidence seems to us decisive that the core of truth was distorted, misrepresented, inflated, and embellished with sheer fabrication for propaganda purposes. As to the events themselves, we are not attempting to offer any definitive account, but rather to compare the evidence available with its interpretation by the government and

the media.

163. This system of responsiveness extended into the military sphere, helping to explain the "astonishing" fighting capacity and "almost incredibly resilient morale" of DRV soldiers, who benefit from a system of "morale restitution . . . designed to lend great emotional and physical support to its members," a system that "anticipates and alleviates possible future morale troubles." Konrad Kellen, *1971 and Beyond: The View from Hanoi*, (Santa Monica, CA: RAND Corporation, 1971), 9.

164. In Pfeffer, ed., *No More Vietnams?*, 227.

165. Race, *War Comes to Long An*, 182–83, 22n.

166. Diane Johnstone, "'Communist Bloodbath' in North Vietnam Is Propaganda Myth, Says Former Saigon Psychological Warfare Chief," *St. Louis Post-Dispatch*, September 24, 1972.

167. The analysis that follows is based on D. Gareth Porter, *The Myth of the Bloodbath: North Vietnam's Land Reform Reconsidered*, Interim Report No. 2, (Ithaca, NY: Cornell University International Relations of East Asia, 1972). See also the abbreviated version in the *Bulletin of the Concerned Asian Scholars*, September 1973.

168. Porter, *Myth of the Bloodbath*, 26–28.

169. Ibid., 44–45.

170. "Figure on N. Vietnam's Killing 'Just a Guess,' Author Says," *Washington Post*, September 13, 1972.

171. Late 1954 was also a period of famine in much of North Vietnam, affecting the very area in which Chi had lived, which further compromises his inferences drawn from a count of village deaths by starvation.

172. Frances FitzGerald, *Fire in the Lake* (Boston: Little, Brown, 1972), 223. FitzGerald gives no footnote reference for this estimate, but she relies heavily on Fall and her language is similar to his.

173. Author (not Congressman) Michael Harrington writes that he and other "socialist cadre . . . knew that Ho and his comrades had killed thousands of peasants during forced collectivization in North Vietnam during the '50s (a fact they themselves had confessed)," *Dissent*, Spring 1973. In fact, the only known "confessions" are the fabrications that had been exposed many months earlier, and neither Harrington nor other Western observers "know" what took place during the land reform. Note the claim that "Ho and his comrades had killed thousands of peasants," when in fact there is no evidence that the leadership ordered or organized mass executions of peasants. Guenter Lewy writes that "the Communists in the North had severe problems with their own 'counterrevolutionaries.' In 1955–56 perhaps as many as 50,000 were executed in connection with the land reform law of 1953. . . . A North Vietnamese exile puts the number of victims at one-half million," (Lewy, *America in Vietnam*, 16). His two footnote references for these estimates are Chi for the latter and Fall (who appears to have relied on Chi) for the former. Lewy then adds, "Attempts by the Hanoi sympathizer D. Gareth Porter to deny the scope of this terror remain unconvincing." This exhausts Lewy's discussion, and once again reveals clearly the scholarly standards of this apologist for US terror. The material just reviewed is nowhere

discussed. For Lewy, an extrapolation from one execution reported in one village by a highly unreliable source to an estimate of fifty thousand executions (or five hundred thousand victims) for all of North Vietnam is quite legitimate, and there is no need to concern oneself over Chi's demonstrated fabrications, Chau's report that the whole story was an intelligence fabrication, the results of Moise's careful study (see note 170, this chapter), or any of the abundant evidence that calls this parody into question. This reference to alleged crimes of the enemy is a natural counterpart to Lewy's efforts to deny US crimes, in the manner already illustrated (see notes 62 and 104, this chapter).

174. Porter, *Myth of the Bloodbath*, 55.

175. See his "Land Reform and Land Reform Errors in North Vietnam," *Pacific Affairs*, Spring 1976, and his University of Michigan PhD dissertation, 1978. We quote from the former.

176. The analysis below is based primarily on D. Gareth Porter, "U.S. Political Warfare in Vietnam—The 1968 'Hue Massacre,'" *Indochina Chronicle*, no. 33 (June 24, 1974) (reprinted in the *Congressional Record*, February 19, 1975); and Edward S. Herman and D. Gareth Porter, "The Myth of the Hue Massacre," *Ramparts*, May–June 1975. See also references cited below.

177. Stewart Harris, *London Times*, March 27, 1968.

178. Marc Riboud, *Le Monde*, April 13, 1968. Riboud reports four thousand civilians killed during the reconquest of the "assassinated city" of Hue by US forces.

179. Report by John Sullivan of the AFSC, May 9, 1968. He reports that none of the AFSC workers who were in Hue throughout the fighting had heard of abusive or atrocious behavior by the NLF-NVA.

180. Len Ackland, "Hue," unpublished; one of the sources used by Don Oberdorfer in *Tet* (New York: Doubleday and Co., 1971).

181. Richard West, *New Statesman*, January 28, 1972.

182. And despite Pike's government position and quite remarkable record as a propagandist. For some samples, see N. Chomsky, *American Power and the New Mandarins*, 365–66.

183. FitzGerald, *Fire in the Lake*, 174–75. In a subsequent edition of her book, FitzGerald qualified her earlier wholesale acceptance of the myth, but the impact was slight.

184. "Op-Ed," *New York Times*, June 15, 1972. In his book, *No Exit From Vietnam*, (New York: David McKay Company, Updated Edition, 1970), Thompson says, "Normally Communist behavior toward the mass of the population is irreproachable and the use of terror is highly selective" (p. 40); but that work, while biased, involved some effort at understanding and contained a residue of integrity, entirely absent in the *New York Times* piece.

185. *Congressional Record*, May 3, 1972.

186. Porter, "U.S. Political Warfare in Vietnam."

187. Ibid.

188. Ibid.

189. Ibid.

190. See Chomsky and Herman, *The Political Economy of Human Rights*, vol. II, chapters 1 and 4.

191. Quoted in Townsend Hoopes, *The Limits of Intervention* (New York: David McKay Company, 1969), 142.

192. Philip Jones Griffiths, *Vietnam Inc.* (London: Palgrave-Macmillan, 1971), 137

193. Cited in Herman and Porter, "The Myth of the Hue Massacre."

194. See Harris, *London Times*, March 27, 1968.

195. Hoopes, *The Limits of Intervention*, 141–42.

196. Riboud, *Le Monde*, April 13, 1968.

197. See Wilfred Burchett, *Guardian* (New York), December 6, 1969.

198. Riboud, *Le Monde*, April 13, 1968.

199. Interview with Mr. Tony Zangrilli, February 2, 1973.

200. Alje Vennema, *The Tragedy of Hue*, unpublished; quoted by Porter, *Myth of the Bloodbath*. Subsequently Vennema changed his views on Hue. He returned for a visit during which he collected secondary and tertiary source information, which he then used in a book in which his own personal firsthand observations were shunted aside. See Alje Vennema, *The Viet Cong Massacre at Hue* (New York: Vantage Press, 1976).

201. Oriana Fallaci, "Working Up to Killing," *Washington Monthly*, February 1972.

202. John Lengel, AP, A010—Hue Descriptive, February 10, 1968, cited by Peter Braestrup, *Big Story*, vol. I, 268–69. After the reference to a psychological warfare program pinning the blame on the communists, Braestrup adds a footnote that reads: "At this point, the 'Hue massacre' by the Vietcong was still unknown to newsmen." It naturally does not occur to him to ask whether this "massacre" may not relate to the psywar program so desperately needed. While Braestrup cites Porter's critique, he assumes without comment or discussion that the official line must be correct, as does his Freedom House sponsor, a typical manifestation of subservience to official dogmas. See note 173, this chapter.

203. D. Gareth Porter and Len E. Ackland, "Vietnam: The Bloodbath Argument," *Christian Century*, November 5, 1969.

204. Ibid.

205. Katsuichi Honda, *Vietnam War: A Report Through Asian Eyes*, (Tokyo: Mira Sha, 1972), 55–69.

206. Martin Teitel, *Hearing before the Subcommittee to Investigate Problems Connected with Refugees and Escapees, Committee on the Judiciary* (Kennedy Subcommittee), U.S. Senate, 92nd Congress, Second Session, May 8, 1972, p. 17; "Again, the Suffering of My Lai," *New York Times*, June 7, 1972. In the same Senate hearings Teitel reports other instances of terrorism attributed to the NLF but apparently carried out by ARVN.

Chapter 10: From Mad Jack to Mad Henry: The United States in Vietnam

1.   *Far Eastern Economic Review*, May 23, 1975.

2.   Truong Buu Lam, *Patterns of Vietnamese Response to Foreign Intervention: 1858–1900*, Monograph Series No. 11, Southeast Asia Studies (New Haven: Yale Uni-

versity, 1967).

3. Helen B. Lamb, *Vietnam's Will to Live* (New York: Monthly Review Press, 1972).

4. Cited by Ngô Vĩnh Long, *Before the Revolution* (Cambridge: MIT Press, 1973).

5. *Viet Nam: A Historical Sketch* (Hanoi: Foreign Languages Publishing House, 1974).

6. Paulin Vial, cited by Lam, *Patterns of Vietnamese Response to Foreign Intervention*.

7. Léopold Pallu, cited by Lamb, *Vietnam's Will to Live*.

8. French resident minister Muselier, 1897, cited in *Vietnam: Fundamental Problems*, Vietnamese Studies no. 12 (Hanoi: Foreign Languages Publishing House, 1966).

9. Lam, *Patterns of Vietnamese Response to Foreign Intervention*.

10. Cited in *Viet Nam: A Historical Sketch*.

11. Frank M. White, an officer (major) in the Secret Intelligence Section of OSS (essentially, the predecessor of the CIA), who was in Vietnam in 1945–46, testified before Congress that in the first French regiment that landed in September 1945, "I doubt if there were half a dozen Frenchmen in the entire group. They were mainly Germans from POW camps." *Causes, Origins, and Lessons of the Vietnam War*, *Hearings before the Committee on Foreign Relations*, U.S. Senate, 92nd Congress, second session, May 1972 (Washington, DC: U.S. Government Printing Office, 1973).

12. Philippe Devillers, " 'Supporting' the French in Indochina?" in Noam Chomsky and Howard Zinn, eds., *The Pentagon Papers: Critical Essays*, Gravel edition, vol. V (Boston: Beacon Press, 1972). His emphasis.

13. Telegram cited by Philippe Devillers and Jean Lacouture, *End of a War: Indochina 1954* (New York: Praeger, 1969).

14. *Pentagon Papers*, Gravel ed., vol. III, 3. This assessment, by the *Pentagon Papers* historian, is only accurate in its recognition that the US government dismissed the interests of the Vietnamese. But in fact, the context of US policy toward Vietnam was primarily East Asia. We return to the matter below.

15. Devillers, " 'Supporting' the French in Indochina?" Devillers notes that the context of Washington's backing of the Vietnamese Quisling governments was of course different from the analogues cited.

16. Major F. M. Small, memorandum of Strategic Services Unit, War Department, October 25, 1945, cited in *Causes, Origins, and Lessons of the Vietnam War* (see note 11). The intelligence reports cited below are from the same source.

17. Congressional testimony, May 11, 1972, in *Causes, Origins, and Lessons of the Vietnam War*.

18. Cited from the government edition of the *Pentagon Papers* in my *For Reasons of State* (New York: Pantheon, 1973), 128. Unless otherwise indicated, citations from the *Pentagon Papers* are given with precise sources here.

19. For a review of the intelligence record as presented in the *Pentagon Papers*, see *For Reasons of State*, 51f.

20. Arthur M. Schlesinger, Jr., *A Thousand Days* (New York: Fawcett Crest, 1965), 695.

21. See note 60, below.

22. For some discussion, see my article in *Ramparts*, July 1975.

23. Ithiel de Sola Pool, formerly chairman of the Council on Vietnamese Studies of SEADAG and chairman of the political science department at MIT, cited, with some discussion, in my *American Power and the New Mandarins* (New York: Pantheon, 1969), 36. For further discussion of his contributions and those of his colleague, Samuel Huntington, also past chairman of the Council on Vietnamese Studies and chairman of the department of government at Harvard, see my *At War with Asia* (New York: Pantheon, 1970), 54–63, and *For Reasons of State*. It was Huntington who first explained how "In an absent-minded way the United States in Vietnam may well have stumbled upon the answer to 'wars of national liberation,'" namely, "forced-draft urbanization and modernization" by application of military power "on such a massive scale as to produce a massive migration from countryside to city."

24. George K. Tanham and Dennis J. Duncanson, "Some Dilemmas of Counterinsurgency," *Foreign Affairs* 48, no. 1 (1969).

25. For evidence on this matter, see Jeffrey Race, *War Comes to Long An* (Berkeley: University of California Press, 1971); Robert L. Sansom, *The Economics of Insurgency in the Mekong Delta* (Cambridge: MIT Press, 1970); Georges Chaffard, *Les Deux Guerres du Vietnam* (Paris: La Table Ronde, 1969); David Hunt, "Organizing for Revolution in Vietnam," *Radical America* 8, nos. 1 and 2 (1974). Race and Sansom were associated with the US military; Hunt's study is based on material released from the RAND Corporation's "Viet Cong Motivation and Morale" project; Chaffard was a French journalist with many years' experience in Vietnam. There are many other sources. For the "Mansfield Reports," cited below, see *Two Reports on Vietnam and Southeast Asia*, December 18, 1962, and December 17, 1965 (Washington, DC: U.S. Government Printing Office, April 1973). For a despairing assessment of the success of the guerrillas and the popularity of the Hanoi government, see Konrad Kellen, "1971 and Beyond: the View from Hanoi," June 1971; paper delivered at SEADAG meeting, May 8, 1971. Kellen is a RAND analyst.

26. Alex Carey, "Clockwork Vietnam: Psychology of Pacification (i)," mimeographed, 1972. See *Meanjin Quarterly*, 1973 (Australia), for parts of this and subsequent sections of his "Clockwork Vietnam." Carey is lecturer in Psychology of International Relations at the University of New South Wales. His investigations are based in part on several months' research in South Vietnam in 1970.

27. See, for example, Charles Wolf, *United States Policy and the Third World* (Boston: Little, Brown & Co., 1967). For discussion of this and other similar contributions, see *American Power and the New Mandarins*, chapter 1; my *Problems of Knowledge and Freedom* (New York: Pantheon, 1972), chapter 2, and *For Reasons of State*, 98f.

28. *Hearings before the Subcommittee on Health of the Committee on Labor and Public Welfare*, U.S. Senate, Ninety-Third Congress, First Session, February 21 and 22, 1973, part 1 (Washington, DC: U.S. Government Printing Office, 1973), 268.

For the original study, see Dr. Lloyd Cotter, *American Journal of Psychiatry*, July 1967.

29. See the obituary in *Newsweek*, June 19, 1972.

30. Carey, "Clockwork Vietnam: the Social Engineers Take Over (2)," *Meanjin Quarterly*.

31. Quotes in Carey, "Clockwork Vietnam: Psychology of Pacification (i)," from Colonel Reuben Nathan, "Psychological Warfare: Key of Success in Vietnam," *Orbis*, Spring 1967. Nathan was director of US psychological warfare in Vietnam.

32. On the collapse of the military forces, see David Cortwright, *Soldiers in Revolt* (New York: Doubleday, 1975).

33. Ithiel de Sola Pool, Introduction, *Reprints of Publications on Vietnam: 1966–1970*, privately printed, May 1971.

34. David G. Marr, "The Rise and Fall of 'Counterinsurgency,'" in Chomsky and Zinn, *The Pentagon Papers: Critical Essays*, Gravel ed., vol V., 208. Marr was a US Marine Corps intelligence officer, the only Vietnamese-speaking American in the first marine helicopter squadron sent to Vietnam by President Kennedy.

35. For a review of such programs, see *For Reasons of State*, chapter 4.

36. "Max Austerlitz," pseudonym of a journalist who remained in Danang after its "fall," "After the Fall of Danang," *New Republic*, May 17, 1973.

37. Samuel Huntington, "Getting Ready for Political Competition in South Vietnam," paper delivered at the May 1969 meeting of the Council on Vietnamese Studies, explaining how, by various forms of chicanery, we might be able to overcome the fact that the NLF is "the most powerful purely political national organization."

38. NSC Memorandum 5612/1, September 5, 1956, in *United States—Vietnam Relations 1945–67*, vol. 10 (Washington, DC: U.S. Government Printing Office, 1971), the government edition of the *Pentagon Papers*.

39. On this period in Cambodia, see D. R. SarDesai, *Indian Foreign Policy in Cambodia, Laos, and Vietnam, 1947–1964* (Berkeley: University of California Press, 1968). Also Malcolm Caldwell and Lek Tan, *Cambodia in the Southeast Asian War* (New York: Monthly Review Press, 1973). See also references cited in *For Reasons of State*, chapter 2.

40. Philip Jones Griffiths, *Vietnam Inc.* (New York: Macmillan, 1971), 137. Griffiths was a British journalist-photographer who was in Hue at the time. For more on the massacres at Hue, both the actual and the fabricated ones, see *For Reasons of State*, 230f; Noam Chomsky and Edward S. Herman, *Counterrevolutionary Violence* (New York: Warner Modular Inc., 1973); and references cited in these sources. For a recent summary, see E. S. Herman and D. G. Porter, "The Myth of the Hue Massacre," *Ramparts*, May–June 1975.

41. Interview with Vann in Carey, "Clockwork Vietnam: Psychology of Pacification (i)." On the great progress allegedly being made on all fronts by the Saigon government, as revealed by "applied social science," see Pool, *Reprints of Publications in Vietnam*. His final conclusion: "Not that South Vietnam will fall after American combat troops are withdrawn; it seems too strong for that."

42. See *For Reasons of State*, chapter 2, and references cited there; *Counterrevolution-*

ary Violence; and many other sources. For further information on the bombing of Cambodia, see "Bombing in Cambodia," *Hearings before the Committee on Armed Services*, US Senate, 93rd Congress, First Session, July–August 1973, (Washington, DC.: US Government Printing Office, 1973); Statement of Information, "Bombing of Cambodia," *Hearings before the Committee on the Judiciary, House of Representatives*, 93rd Congress, Second Session, Book XI, May–June 1974 (Washington, DC: US Government Printing Office, 1974).

43. Quarterly Review Staff Study, "The Attack on the Irrigation Dams in North Korea," *Air University Quarterly Review* 6, no.4 (Winter 1953–54). See also Robert Frank Futrell, *The United States Air Force in Korea 1950–1953* (New York: Duell, Sloan and Pearce, 1961), 623f.

44. See note 25.

45. On the relative US-DRV troop levels, as revealed by the *Pentagon Papers*, see my article "The *Pentagon Papers* as Propaganda and as History," in Chomsky and Zinn, eds., *The Pentagon Papers: Critical Essays*, Gravel ed., vol. V; also *For Reasons of State*, 82 (and note 147), 239f.

46. General Maxwell D. Taylor, *Swords and Plowshares* (New York: Norton, 1972).

47. Speaking in Paris, January 26, 1965, Khanh released correspondence with Huynh Tan Phat, then vice president of the Central Committee of the NLF, from late January 1965, indicating that agreement was close. See my article in *Ramparts*, July 1975, for further details. There is, incidentally, also evidence that the Diem regime may have been approaching a negotiated settlement just prior to the US-backed coup in which Diem was murdered. See Chaffard, *Les Deux Guerres du Vietnam*, chapter 8, and Mieczyslaw Maneli, *War of the Vanquished* (New York: Harper and Row, 1971). John P. Roche, an unreconstructed hawk, claims that he had furnished evidence to the *Pentagon Papers* historians, which they ignored, that the Kennedy administration had decided not to permit a deal between Diem and Ho Chi Minh. See his "Pentagon Papers," *Political Science Quarterly* 87, no. 2 (1972).

48. For details on this important document, misrepresented beyond recognition in the *Pentagon Papers* history, see *For Reasons of State*, 100f.

49. For details on these matters see my "Endgame: the Tactics of Peace in Vietnam," *Ramparts*, April 1973; and "Reporting Indochina: the News Media and the Legitimation of Lies," *Social Policy*, September–October 1973.

50. On US intervention in Laos, see the articles by Haney and Chomsky in Chomsky and Zinn, eds., *The Pentagon Papers: Critical Essays*, Gravel ed., vol. V; also *At War with Asia*, chapter 4, and *For Reasons of State*, chapter 2, and the references cited there.

51. Henry A. Kissinger, "The Vietnam Negotiations," in his *American Foreign Policy* (New York: Norton, 1969), 131; reprinted from *Foreign Affairs*, January 1969.

52. See the comment by the editors in *Dissent*, Spring 1975, in response to a letter of mine correcting a wholly fabricated version of my criticisms of their earlier editorial position. As indicated in their response, they prefer to restrict attention to the fabrication rather than attending to the entirely different original, which

suggests that they perhaps do have some reservations about their long-held position. For further details, see the interchange in the *New Republic* referred to in this exchange.

53. Kissinger, "The Vietnam Negotiations," 104–6.

54. Koji Nakamura, "Japan: a New Face for Asia," *Far Eastern Economic Review*, May 23, 1975.

55. Correspondent, "Putting Washington Before ASEAN," *Far Eastern Economic Review*, May 23, 1975. The text gives the date as 1968 instead of 1972, presumably an error.

56. See *At War with Asia*, chapter 1; *For Reasons of State*, chapter 1, section V; the articles by John W. Dower, Richard B. Du Boff, and Gabriel Kolko in Chomsky and Zinn, eds., *The Pentagon Papers: Critical Essays*, Gravel ed., vol. V.

57. For discussion of some misunderstandings of this critique by Richard Tucker, Charles Kindleberger, and others, see *For Reasons of State*, 42–46, 56–58.

58. John K. Fairbank, "Our Vietnam Tragedy," *Newsletter*, Harvard Graduate Society for Advanced Study and Research, June 1975. Fairbank also remarks that our "greatly accelerating the urbanization of Vietnam" after 1965 was "not necessarily to our credit or to the benefit of South Vietnam." Scholarly caution was perhaps appropriate in an issue of the *Newsletter* that announced a new professorship of Vietnamese Studies named for Kenneth T. Young, formerly chairman of SEADAG and director of Southeast Asian Affairs in the State Department in 1954–58, when the United States took over direct responsibility for repression and massacre in South Vietnam. Young was one of those to urge publicly that the United States and its local subordinates "should deliberately increase urbanized markets and the town groupings coupled with fewer remote villages and fewer dispersed hamlets outside the modernizing environment" to "outmatch and outclass the Viet Cong where they are weak" (see note 23), thus making "a virtue out of necessity." *Asian Survey*, August 1967. At that time, no rational person could be deceived as to how "urban realignment," as Young called it, was being and must be effected by the American Expeditionary Force. Perhaps someday the University of Berlin will institute an Eichmann Chair of Jewish Studies.

59. NSC Working Group Project, November 21, 1964, in *Pentagon Papers*, Gravel ed., vol. III, 661.

60. William Y. Elliott, ed., *The Political Economy of American Foreign Policy* (New York: Holt, 1955), 42.

61. Quoted in Iriye Akira, *Across the Pacific* (New York: Harcourt, Brace, and World, 1967), 77.

62. Cited by Frank Freidel in *Dissent in Three American Wars* (Cambridge: Harvard University Press, 1970).

63. Evelyn Keene, *Boston Globe*, May 18, 1975; commencement address at Bentley College.

64. Anthony Lewis, "The Morning After," *New York Times*, May 19, 1975.

65. John Osborne, *New Republic*, June 7, 1975.

66. James McCartney, *Boston Globe*, May 29, 1975.

Chapter 11: After "Mad Henry": US Policy Toward Indochina Since 1975

1. Henry Kissinger, *Years of Renewal* (New York: Simon and Schuster, 1999), 566–75. On these pages Kissinger gives details as to why May 14, 1975, was the busiest and most stressful day in his entire life and yet he would not delay the order for the sanctions on Cambodia and Vietnam for another day.

2. "A Silly War," *Los Angeles Times*, November 13, 1975; *Vietnam Southeast Asia International*, October–November 1975. For details on the official reasons for and justifications of the trade embargo, see "United States Embargo of Trade with South Vietnam and Cambodia," *Hearings Before the Subcommittee on International Trade and Commerce*, House of Representatives, 94th Congress, First Session, June 1975 (Washington, DC: U.S. Government Printing Office, 1975), 1–6. At this hearing members of the Ford administration explained that the authority to impose the sanctions had been "delegated" to the secretary of state and that President Ford himself had not been involved in the decision because it was not "required of by the President."

3. Edwin A. Martini, *Invisible Enemies: The American War on Vietnam*, 1975–2000 (Amherst, MA: University of Massachusetts Press, 2007), 15.

4. "United States Embargo of Trade with South Vietnam and Cambodia," 6.

5. The US embassy in Stockholm cabled this message to Kissinger on May 7, 1975. See National Security Advisor: Kissinger-Scowcroft West Wing Office Files: 1969–1977, Box 34, Ford Presidential Library.

6. *Washington Star*, May 14, 1975, 3.

7. Daniel Patrick Moynihan, *A Dangerous Place* (Boston: The Atlantic Monthly Press, 1978), 142–43, 145. Emphasis in original.

8. Telegram from Daniel Moynihan to Kissinger: "Admission of Vietnam to the United Nations," in National Security Council Institutional Files: Selected Documents 1974–1977, boxes 24–57, Ford Presidential Library. On Moynihan's statement, see *Department of State Bulletin*, September 15, 1975 (Washington, DC: U.S. Department of State, 1975), 421.

9. *Department of State Bulletin*, August 16, 1976 (Washington, DC: U.S. Department of State, 1976), 250.

10. *Fifty Years of Activities of the Communist Party of Vietnam* (Hanoi: Foreign Language Publishing House, 1980), 255–57. Also see Dao Van Tap, ed., *35 nam kinh te Viet Nam, 1945–1980* [Thirty-Five Years of the Vietnamese Economy, 1945–180] (Hanoi: Vien Kinh Te Hoc, 1980), 130–33.

11. Listed in *Lich Su Giao Thong Van Tai Viet Nam* [History of Communication and Transportation in Vietnam] (Hanoi: Nha Xuat Ban Giao Thong Van Tai, 1999), 541.

12. Stanley I. Kutler, *Encyclopedia of the Vietnam War* (New York: Charles Scribner's Sons, 1966), 103–104.

13. J. M. Stellman et al., "The extent and patterns of usage of Agent Orange and other herbicides in Vietnam," *Nature*, no. 422 (April 2003): 681–87.

14. Ibid.

15. Seymour M. Hersh, "Our Chemical War," *New York Review of Books*, April 25,

1968.

16. "Agriculture in the Vietnam Economy: A System for Economic Analysis," *FDD Field Report 32* (Washington, DC: U.S. Department of Agriculture and U.S. Agency for International Development, June 1973), 148–51. According to other sources, by 1971 at least 43 percent of South Vietnam's population was living in urban areas. Saigon's population had doubled to 4.5 million while other provincial cities had grown by as much as 500 percent. See Nigel Thrift and Dean Forbes, *The Price of War: Urbanisation in Vietnam, 1954–1985* (London: Allen and Unwin, 1986), 125, 154; Khong Dien, *Dan So va Dan So Toc Nguoi o Vietnam* [Population and Ethnic Population in Vietnam] (Hanoi: Nha Xuat Ban Khoa Hoc Xa Hoi, 1995), 204–5.

17. "Relief and Rehabilitation of War Victims in Indo-China, Part IV: South Vietnam and Regional Problems," *Hearings Before the Subcommittee to Investigate Problems Connected with Refugees and Escapees of the Committee on the Judiciary*, United States Senate, 93rd Congress (Washington, DC: U.S. Government Printing Office, 1973), 8.

18. Official statistics cited in the October 28, 1973 issue of *Dai Dan Toc* (The Great Populace) indicated that by mid-1971, 3,874,000 peasants had left for the urban areas and the refugee camps around the cities. After that, another 600,000 refugees were added to this number. According to this article, several million persons were unemployed. Official AID statistics revealed that 213,000 refugees were created during the period from January 28 to February 16, 1973, alone (i.e., right after the signing of the Paris Peace Agreement when the Thieu regime started its land-grabbing campaign). This statistic was itself scaled down by at least 70,000 persons (*New York Times*, Senate Subcommittee on Refugees Report, February 28, 1973)

.19. *Dai Dan Toc* ["The Greater National Community," a Saigon daily run by a group of deputies in the Lower House], November 1, 1974.

20. *FFD Field Report 32*, 154–57, 311–12.

21. As Major General Peter Olenchuck testified before the Senate Armed Services Committee on May 8, 1973, "We shortchanged ourselves within our overall inventories. We also shortchanged the reserve units in terms of prime assets. In certain instances, we also diverted equipment that would have gone to Europe." See "Fiscal Year 1974 Authorization for Military Procurement, Research and Development, Construction Authorization for Safeguard ABM, and Active Duty and Selected Reserve Strengths," *Hearings Before the Committee on Armed Services*, United States Senate, 93rd Congress, part 3, Authorizations (Washington, DC: U.S. Government Printing Office, 1973), 1383. In fiscal year 1974, Congress gave Saigon $1 billion more in military aid. Saigon expended as much ammunition as it could—$700 million worth. This left a stockpile of at least $300 million, a violation of the Paris Agreement, which stipulated that equipment could only be replaced on a one-to-one basis. For fiscal year 1975, Congress again authorized $1 billion in military aid, but appropriated $700 million—about what was actually spent in 1974.

22. Economic aid to the Thieu regime during the same period was also increased and channeled through various programs such as the Foreign Assistance Act and "Food for Peace." For example, on December 17 and 18, 1974, Congress passed the Foreign Assistance Act, authorizing $450 million in economic aid to Saigon. This was $100 million more than the amount authorized by Congress in fiscal year 1974. According to the January 16, 1975 issue of *Dien Tin*, 90 percent of US economic aid to the Thieu regime had been used to maintain the war. For detailed reports on the economic blockade and its impact, see the *Congressional Record*, May 20, 1974, and June 4, 1974.

23. *Dai Dan Toc*, August 8, 1974.

24. *Dai Dan Toc*, August 30, 1974.

25. *Chinh Luan* ["Official Discussion," a very conservative Saigon daily newspaper, which was accused by others as having a CIA connection at the time], November 5, 1974.

26. *Dien Tin*, September 6, 20, 22, and 24, 1974; *Dai Dan Toc*, September 30, 1974.

27. See, for example, *Tap Chi Cong San* ["Communist Review"], December 1975, 17, and March 1977, 59.

28. Chu Van Lam et al., *Hop Tac Hoa Nong Nghiep Viet Nam: Lich Su, Van De, Trien Vong* [Agricultural Collectivization in Vietnam: History, Problems, and Prospects] (Hanoi: Nha Xuat Ban Su That, 1992), 44–45. Some of the resolutions and directives include: Resolution 254-BCT of the Politburo in June 1976; Directive 236-CT/TW of the Central Committee in September 1976, entitled "On Implementing the Resolution of the Politburo Regarding the Land Situation in the South"; Decision 188-CP of the Government Council in September 1976, entitled "On the Policy of Total Eradication of the Vestiges of Colonial and Feudal Usurpation of Land and other Forms of Colonial and Feudal Exploitation in South Vietnam"; and Directive 28-CT/TW of the Central Committee in December 1977, entitled "Complete the Total Eradication of the Vestiges of Feudalism with Regards to Land, Develop Forms of Organizing Cooperation in Labor and Production, and Construct Pilot Cooperative Programs in the South."

29. *Vietnam Courir*, November 1975, 10.

30. For details see Ngô Vĩnh Long, "Agrarian Differentiation in the Southern Region of Vietnam," *Journal of Contemporary Asia* 14, no. 3 (1984): 283–305.

31. For details also see: Nguyen Xuan Lai, "Questions of Agrarian Structures and Agricultural Development in Southern Vietnam," *Vietnamese Studies* 5 [New Series] (Hanoi, 1984), 30–49.

32. Ngô Vĩnh Hai, "Postwar Vietnam: Political Economy," in Douglas Allen and Ngô Vĩnh Long eds., *Coming to Terms: The United States, Indochina and the War* (Boulder, Colorado: Westview Press, 1991), 68–70. For the official reports, see: *Bao Cao Tong Ket Danh Tu San Mai Ban o Cac Tinh Phia Nam Sau Ngay Giai Phong* [Report of the Overall Results of the Attack on Comprador Capitalists in the Southern Provinces after Liberation] (Hanoi: Ban Cai Tao Cong Thuong Nghiep Tu Doanh Trung Uong, Dang Cong San Viet Nam) and *Giai Cap Tu San Mai Ban o Nam Viet Nam* [The Comprador Capitalist Class in South Viet-

nam] (Ban Cai Tao Cong Thuong Nghiep Tu Doanh Trung Uong, Dang Cong San Viet Nam, 1977).

33. Lam et al., *Hop Tac Hoa Nong Nghiep Viet Nam*, 47–48.

34. Lam Quang Huyen, *Cach Mang Ruong Dat o Mien Nam Viet Nam* [Land Revolution in Southern Vietnam] (Hanoi: Nha Xuat Ban Khoa Hoc Xa Hoi, 1997), 171–73.

35. Nguyen Huy, "35 Nam Thuc Hien Duong Loi Phat Trien Nong Nghiep cua Dang," [Thirty-Five Years of Implementing the Policies for Agricultural Development of the Party] in Dao Van Tap, *35 Nam Kinh Te Viet Nam*, 132–35.

36. Le Minh Ngoc, "Ve Tang Lop Trung Nong o Dong Bang Song Cuu Long" [On the Middle-Peasant Class in the Mekong Delta], in *Mot So Van De Khoa Hoc Xa Hoi ve Dong Bang Song Cuu Long* [A Number of Social Science Questions on the Mekong Delta] (Hanoi: Nha Xuat Ban Khoa Hoc Xa Hoi, 1982), 215–25.

37. Grant Evans and Kelvin Rowley, *Red Brotherhood at War* (London: Verso, 1984), 115–126; On June 30, 1988, Agence France-Presse published an interview with Lieutenant General Le Khai Phieu, the deputy commander of the Vietnamese forces in Cambodia, in which he was reported to have disclosed that thirty thousand Vietnamese soldiers had been killed in 1977 and 1978 defending the border provinces against Pol Pot forces, as compared to the twenty-five thousand killed on the battlefields in Cambodia from December 1978, when Vietnam counterattacked in the attempt to get rid of Pol Pot, to June 1988. It seems that either the general or Agence France-Presse was in error and that the thirty thousand killed during 1977–1978 should be described as civilians instead of soldiers.

38. D. R. SarDesai, *Vietnam: The Struggle for National Identity* (Boulder, Colorado: Westview Press, 1992), 123–24.

39. Ibid., 126–127.

40. Nguyen Khac Vien, *Vietnam Ten Years After* (Hanoi: Foreign Publishing House, 1985), 17.

41. Ngo Vinh Hai, "Postwar Vietnam," in Allen and Long, *Coming to Terms*, 76.

42. Vietnamese title of the directive is "Ve viec nam vung va day manh cong tac cai tao nong nghiep mien Nam" [On holding firmly to and pushing strongly the activities of transforming agriculture in Southern Vietnam]. See Lam et al., *Hop Tac Hoa Nong Nghiep Viet Nam*, 45.

43. *45 năm kinh te Viet Nam (1945–1990)* [Forty-Five Years of the Vietnamese Economy, 1945–1990] (Hanoi: Nhà Xuat Ban Khoa Hoc Xã Hoi, 1990), 102. According to this volume, during this decade the government supplied the peasants with millions of tons of staples.

44. From November 1979 to mid-June 1980 this writer was in Vietnam at the invitation of Mr. Nguyen Khac Vien, the director of the Foreign Publishing House, and Mr. Hoang Tung, at that time head of the Party Committee for Propaganda and Indoctrination (*Ban Tuyen Huan*) as well as secretary of the Party Central Committee and editor-in-chief of *Nhan Dan* ("The People"), to conduct an independent survey of the rural situation in Vietnam. These population estimates as well as reasons for collectivization were provided to this writer by these two

men as well as Vietnamese researchers that this writer worked with during this period. Mr. Nguyen Khac Vien and Mr. Hoang Tung told this writer that about half the national budget of Vietnam went to the armed forces. Since the beginning of 1978 Mr. Hoang Tung had become the party's point man for pushing cooperativization in the South. Unknown to this writer at the time, by the end of 1979 Mr. Hoang Tung and many party leaders already had serious doubts about this effort. Hence they made arrangements for this writer to conduct studies of the rural situation in several provinces in both the northern and southern halves of the country (perhaps with the aim of using this writer's assessment to convince others for a change of direction?) of. Ngo Vinh Hai writes that Vietnam's armed forces now numbered around 1.2 million, or many times larger than the combined NLF and North Vietnam armed forces during the war years, in Allen and Long, *Coming to Terms*, 77.

45. For details see Ngo Vinh Long, "Some Aspects of Cooperativization in the Mekong Delta" in David G. Marr and Christine Pelzer White, eds., *Postwar Vietnam: Dilemmas in Socialist Development* (Ithaca, NY: Southeast Asia Program, Cornell University, 1988), 168–70.

46. Lam et al., *Hop Tac Hoa Nong Nghiep Viet Nam*, 47–48.

47. Ngô Vĩnh Long, "Some Aspects of Cooperativization in the Mekong Delta," in Allen and Long, *Coming to Terms*, 170–71.

48. See *Hearings Before the Subcommittee on Asian and Pacific Affairs,* Committee on International Affairs of the House of Representatives, 95th Congress, First Session, July 19, 1978, Appendix 13 (Washington, DC: U.S. Government Printing Office), 56. See also Kyodo News Service, July 10, 1978, and Agence France-Presse, July 14, 1978.

49. *Far Eastern Economic Review*, August 18, 1978, 11.

50. *Congressional Record,* August 22, 1978, S14007-9.

51. Zbigniew Brzezinski, *Power and Principle: Memoirs of the National Security Advisor 1977–1981* (London: Weidenfeld and Nicolson, 1983), 228.

52. Marilyn B. Young, *The Vietnam Wars 1945–1990* (New York: Harper Perennial, 1991), 310.

53. Brzezinski, *Power and Principle*, 409.

54. Young, *The Vietnam Wars*, 311–12.

55. See *1990 Yearbook* of Tong Cuc Thong Ke [General Statistical Office], 38, and the article entitled "Sau 30 Nam Hop Tac Hoa Nong Nghiep: Doi Song Nong Dan va Van De Quan Ly San Xuat Nong Nghiep Hien Nay" [After Thirty Years of Agricultural Cooperativization: The Living Conditions of the Peasants and the Question of Managing Agricultural Production at the Present Time] in Nguyen Luc, ed., *Thuc Trang Kinh Te Xa Hoi Viet Nam Giai Doan 1986–1990* [The Real Economic and Social Conditions of Vietnam in the 1986–1990 Period] (Hanoi: Statistical Journal Publishing House, 1990), 27–60.

56. This lengthy document was published in full in *Nhan Dan*, April 12, 1988, 1–3.

57. Lam et al., *Hop Tac Hoa Nong Nghiep Viet Nam*, 63.

58. Nayan Chanda, "A Troubled Friendship: Moscow Loses Patience with Hanoi

Over Economy and Cambodia," *Far Eastern Economic Review,* June 9, 1988, 16.

59. Raymond Burghardt, "US-Vietnam: Discreet Friendship Under China's Shadow," Yale Global Online, November 22, 2005, available at http://yaleglobal. yale.edu/display.article?id=6546.

Chapter 12: My Experiences with Laos and the Indochina Wars, Interview with Fred Branfman

1. Students for a Democratic Society (SDS) was a student activist movement founded in 1960 and solidified in 1962 with its manifesto, the Port Huron Statement. As the United States escalated involvement in Vietnam, SDS emerged as a major antiwar force, organizing protests, teach-ins, and sit-ins at campuses and elsewhere around the country. SDS was dissolved in 1969.

2. Erich Maria Remarque, *All Quiet on the Western Front,* trans. A. W. Wheen (London: G. P. Putnam's Sons, 1929).

3. Morton Kaplan, *Dissent and the State in Peace and War* (New York: Dunellen Co., 1970).

4. The Arusha Declaration, made by president Julius Nyerere on February 5, 1967, called for an overhaul of Tanzania's economic system in the interest of promoting rural development through *ujamaa,* or "villagization."

5. Alfred W. McCoy, Cathleen P. Read, and Leonard P. Adams, *The Politics of Heroin in Southeast Asia* (New York: Harper & Row, 1972).

6. Fred Branfman, James A. Hafner, and Joel M. Halpern, *The Village of the Deep Pond, Ban Xa Phang Meuk, Laos* (Amherst, MA: International Area Studies Program, University of Massachusetts at Amherst, 1978).

7. Fred Branfman, Joel M. Halpern, and James A. Hafner, *The Old Man: a Biographical Account of a Lao Villager* (Amherst, MA: International Area Studies Program, University of Massachusetts at Amherst, 1979).

8. J. R. R. Tolkien, *Lord of the Rings,* 3 vol. (Boston: Houghton Mifflin, 1954).

9. Jacques Decornoy, "Life in the Pathet Lao Liberated Zone," in N.S. Adams and Alfred W. McCoy, eds., *Laos: War and Revolution* (New York: Harper & Row, 1970) 411–23.

10. T. D. "Ted" Allman is a prolific investigative journalist who has written extensively on the "secret war" in Laos, among innumerable other topics, including the massacres in Cambodia. He has been a staff writer for the *New Yorker* and a foreign correspondent for *Vanity Fair,* and has written for *Harper's,* the *New York Times,* the *Washington Post, Rolling Stone, National Geographic,* the *New York Review of Books,* and many others. His books range from *Unmanifest Destiny: Mayhem and Illusion in American Foreign Policy—from the Monroe Doctrine to Reagan's War in El Salvador* (Dial Press, 1984) to *Rogue State: America at War with the World* (Nation Books, 2004).

11. Noam Chomsky, *At War With Asia: Essays on Indochina* (New York: Pantheon, 1969) 188–258.

12. Seymour M. Hersh, "How We Ran the Secret Air War in Laos," *New York Times Magazine,* October 29, 1972, 18–28.

13. Fred Branfman, *Voices from the Plain of Jars: Life Under an Air War* (New York:

Harper & Row, 1972).

14. Dispatch News Service, a left-of-center, Washington-based news agency founded in 1968 by David Obst and Michael Morrow, was the original outlet Seymour Hersh found for his November 1968 exposé of the My Lai massacre.

15. Fred Branfman, "Laos: One Day the Airplanes Came," *New York Times*, July 16, 1971.

16. Gloria Emerson, *Winners and Losers: Battles, Retreats, Gains, Losses, and Ruins from the Vietnam War* (New York: Penguin Books, 1985).

17. Strobe Talbott, "The Sounds of Silence," *Time*, July 17, 1972.

18. *CBS Evening News with Walter Cronkite*, Tuesday, July 13, 1973, available at http://openweb.tvnews.vanderbilt.edu/1971-7/1971-07-13-CBS-9.html.

19. Sidney Schanberg, "A Cambodian Landscape: Bomb Pits, Rubble, Ashes," *New York Times*, May 24, 1973.

20. Sidney Schanberg, "Embassy Still Controls Cambodia Raids," *New York Times*, May 11, 1973.

21. Tom Hayden, "Cutting Off Funding for War: The 1973 Indochina Case," The *Huffington Post*, May 20, 2007, available at http://www.huffingtonpost.com/tom-hayden/cutting-off-funding-for-w_b_43917.html.

22. Committee on International Relations, *The Vietnam Cambodia Emergency 1975. Part III—Vietnam Evacuation: Testimony of Graham A. Martin* (U.S. Government Printing Office: Washington, DC, 1975).

Chapter 13: Interview with Noam Chomsky

1. The Avalon Project at Yale Law School, "The Common Plan or Conspiracy and Aggressive War," in Nuremberg documents; available at http://www.yale.edu/lawweb/avalon/imt/proc/judnazi.htm#common.

2. The Avalon Project at Yale Law School, "The Webster-Ashburton Treaty—The *Caroline* Case"; available at http://www.yale.edu/lawweb/avalon/diplomacy/britain/br-1842d.htm.

3. United Nations, *A More Secure World: Our Shared Responsibility—A Report of the U.N. Panel on Threats, Challenges, and Change* (New York: United Nations, 2004).

4. United Nations, *2005 World Summit Outcome* (New York: United Nations, 2005).

5. The Avalon Project at Yale Law School, 1996; available at http://www.yale.edu/lawweb/avalon/avalon.htm.

6. Noam Chomsky, *Rethinking Camelot: JFK, the Vietnam War, and U.S. Political Culture* (Boston: South End Press, 1993).

7. Noam Chomsky and Edward Herman, *The Political Economy of Human Rights* (Boston: South End Press, 1979).

8. See note 6.

9. Hatfield Consultants—Contaminant Monitoring/Agent Orange; available at http://www.hatfieldgroup.com/services/contaminantagentorange.aspx.

10. P. J. Griffiths, *Agent Orange: "Collateral Damage" in Viet Nam* (London: Trolley, 2004).

11. The American Presidency Project, The President's News Conference of March

24, 1977; available at http://www.presidency.ucsb.edu/ws/index.php?pid=7229.

12. Barbara Crossette, "Hanoi Said to Vow to Give M.I.A. Data," *New York Times*, October 24, 1992.

13. Elizabeth Becker, "Kissinger Tapes Describe Crises, War, and Stark Photos of Abuse," *New York Times*, May 27, 2004.

14. Francis Jennings, *Empire of Fortune: Crowns, Colonies, and Tribes in the Seven Years War in America* (New York: Norton, 1988).

15. Arthur M. Schlesinger, *Journals, 1952–2000* (New York: Penguin Press, 2007).

16. "Last Chance in Vietnam," Editorial, *Dissent* 11 (Summer 1964): 275–78.

17. Irving Howe, "Vietnam: Sorrow and Pity," *Dissent* 22 (Summer 1975): 213–14.

18. Robert S. McNamara and Brian Van De Mark, *In Retrospect: The Tragedy and Lessons of Vietnam* (New York: Vintage Books, 1996).

19. Noam Chomsky, "Memories," *Z Magazine*, Summer 1995.

20. Noam Chomsky, "Hamlet Without the Prince of Denmark," *Diplomatic History* 20, no. 3 (Summer 1996): 450–55.

21. Noam Chomsky and Edward Herman, *After the Cataclysm: Postwar Indochina and the Reconstruction of Imperial Ideology* (Boston: South End Press, 1979).

22. Noam Chomsky and Edward Herman, *The Political Economy of Human Rights* (Boston: South End Press, 1979).

23. Joseph Nevins, *A Not-So-Distant Horror: Mass Violence in East Timor* (Ithaca: Cornell University Press, 2005).

24. American Association for the Advancement of Science, "Guatemala, Memory of Silence," Report for the Guatemalan Commission for Historical Clarification (Washington, DC: 1999).

25. UN Security Council, Annex, *From Madness to Hope: The 12-Year War in El Salvador*, Report of the Commission on the Truth for El Salvador (San Salvador and New York: United Nations Press, 1993).

26. Tommie Sue Montgomery, *Revolution in El Salvador: From Civil Strife to Civil Peace* (Boulder, CO: Westview Press, 1995).

27. Steven M. Streeter, *Managing the Counterrevolution: The United States and Guatemala, 1954–1961* (Athens, OH: Ohio University Center for International Studies, 2000).

28. Suzanne Jonas, *The Battle for Guatemala: Rebels, Death Squads, and U.S. Power* (Boulder, CO: Westview Press, 1991).

29. Archbishopric of Guatemala, Office of Human Rights, *Guatemala: Nunca Más!* (Guatemala City: REHMI, 1998; Maryknoll, New York: Orbis Books, 1999).

30. Thomas W. Walker, *Nicaragua: Living in the Shadow of the Eagle* (Boulder, Colorado: Westview Press, 2003).

31. John A. Booth, Christine J. Wade, and Thomas W. Walker, *Understanding Central America: Global Forces, Rebellion, and Change* (Boulder, Colorado: Westview Press, 2006).

32. Noam Chomsky, *Turning the Tide: U.S. Intervention in Central America and the Struggle for Peace* (Boston: South End Press, 1985).

33. ZNet, available at http://www.zcommunications.org/znet.

34. Noam Chomsky, *A New Generation Draws the Line: Kosovo, East Timor and the Standards of the West* (London, New York: Verso, 2000).

35. James Fallows, "Double Moral Standards," *Atlantic Monthly*, February 1982, 82–87.

36. Edward Herman and Noam Chomsky, *Manufacturing Consent: The Political Economy of the Mass Media* (New York: Pantheon Books, 2002).

37. Arthur M. Schlesinger, *The Bitter Heritage: Vietnam and American Democracy, 1941–1966* (Boston: Houghton Mifflin, 1967).

38. Noam Chomsky, "*The Bitter Heritage*: A Review," in *American Power and the New Mandarins* (Pantheon: New York, 1967) 295–307.

39. Anthony Lewis, "Ghosts," Op-Ed, *New York Times*, May 6, 2000.

40. Bernard B. Fall, *Last Reflections on a War* (Garden City, NY: Doubleday, 1967).

41. John E. Rielly, ed., *American Public Opinion and U.S. Foreign Policy 1975* (Chicago: Chicago Council on Foreign Relations, 1979); also available at http://www.ccfr.org/index.php.

42. "Out Now," Editorial, *Boston Globe*, 1969, 22.

INDEX

Contributors

Fred Branfman is the author of *Voices from the Plain of Jars*, originally printed in 1970 and reissued by University of Wisconsin Press in 2013. Fred founded and served as co-director of the crucial antiwar organizations, Project Air War and the Indochina Resource Center, in Washington, DC. Following the end of the US wars in Indochina, Fred worked in Democratic national politics for several years before turning his attention to the issue of climate change. In the 1990s Fred embarked on studies of spirituality and existential humanism, which informed his impassioned activism on environmental issues. He was interviewed in the 2008 documentary about the Laos bombing campaign, *The Most Secret Place on Earth*. In the last several years of Fred's life, he lived with his wife, Zsuzsanna Berkovits Branfman, in Budapest. Fred died in September 2014.

Noam Chomsky is widely regarded as one of the foremost critics of US foreign policy. He has published numerous groundbreaking books, articles, and essays on global politics, history, and linguistics. His recent books include *Hegemony or Survival*, *Failed States*, *Who Rules the World?*, *Requiem for the American Dream*, *Hopes and Prospects*, and *Masters of Mankind*.

Richard A. Falk is the Albert G. Milbank Professor of International Law and Practice, Emeritus, and Professor of Politics and International Affairs, Emeritus, at Princeton. He is the author of *Law, War, and Morality in the Contemporary World*; *The Role of Domestic Courts in the International Legal Order*; *Legal Order in a Violent World*; *The Status of Law in International Society*; *This Endangered Planet*; *A Study of Future Worlds*; *Human Rights and State Sovereignty*; *The End of World Order*; *Reviving the World Court*; *The Promise of World Order*; *Revolutionaries and Functionaries*; *Revitalizing International Law*; *Explorations at the Edge of Time*; *On Humane Governance: Toward a New Global Politics*; and *Law in an Emerging Global Village: A Post-Westphalian Perspective*, and editor or co-editor of more than twenty books. He has been a fellow at the Center for Advanced Study in the Behavioral Sciences, a Guggenheim Fellow, the Olaf Palme Visiting Professor in Stockholm, and Visiting Distinguished Professor at the Mediterranean Academy of Diplomatic Studies, University of Malta. JSD, Harvard University.

Clinton Fernandes is in the International and Political Studies program at the University of New South Wales in Canberra, Australia. He has lectured on Southeast Asian politics and Australia's foreign and defense policy. He is the author of *Reluctant Saviour: Australia, Indonesia and the Independence of East Timor*. He is a former Australian Army officer.

Edward Herman is professor emeritus of finance at the Wharton School, University of Pennsylvania, and has written extensively on economics, political economy, and the media. Among his books are *Corporate Control, Corporate Power* (Cambridge University Press, 1981), *The Real Terror Network* (South End Press, 1982), and, with Noam Chomsky, *The Political Economy of Human Rights* (South End Press, 1979) and *Manufacturing Consent* (Pantheon, 2002).

Channapha Khamvongsa is founder and executive director of Legacies of War, an organization that seeks to address the problem of unexploded ordnance in Laos, to provide space for healing the wounds of war, and to create greater hope for a future of peace. The organization uses art, culture, education, and community organizing, especially among the Lao diaspora, to create healing and transformation out of the wreckage of war. Legacies of War has successfully advocated for an increase in US funding for bomb clearance in Laos, from an annual average of $2 million in 2008 to $30 million in 2016. In September 2016, president Barack Obama acknowledged Channapha's advocacy efforts in Laos, when he became the first US president to visit the country. Channapha has written and spoken widely about the secret war in Laos and its aftermath and has appeared in the *New York Times*, *Democracy Now!*, CNN, ABC, PBS, and CBS News. She was most recently featured in an interview with the team of *Anthony Bourdain: Parts Unknown*. She previously worked at the Ford Foundation and NEO Philanthropy on immigrant rights, civil society, civic engagement, capacity building, and transformational leadership. She has served on the Seattle Women's Commission as well as on the boards of the Refugee Women's Alliance and the Conference on Asian Pacific American Leadership (CAPAL). She was born in Vientiane, Laos, and came to the United States as a refugee at the age of seven. Channapha received her bachelor's of science degree in public administration from George Mason University and a master's in public policy from Georgetown University.

Ben Kiernan is the A. Whitney Griswold Professor of History and Professor of International and Area Studies at Yale University. From 1994 to 2015 he was founding director of the Genocide Studies Program (gsp.yale.edu) and, from 2010 to 2015, chair of the Council on Southeast Asia Studies at Yale. His books include *Việt Nam: A History from Earliest Times to the Present* (2017); *How Pol Pot Came to Power* (1985); *The Pol Pot Regime* (1996); *Genocide and Resistance in Southeast Asia* (2007); and *Blood and Soil: A World History of Genocide and Extermination from Sparta to Darfur* (2007). For thirty years he documented the crimes of Pol Pot's Khmer Rouge regime in Cambodia. He founded the Cambodian Genocide Program, which uncovered the archives of the Khmer Rouge secret police, detailed the case for an international tribunal, and won many awards.

Ngô Vĩnh Long received a PhD in East Asian history and Far Eastern languages from Harvard University in 1978. He currently teaches at the University of Maine. He is at work on a history of modern Vietnam. Among his works are *Before the Revolution: The Vietnamese Peasants under the French* (MIT Press, 1973; Columbia University Press, October 1991), *Vietnamese Women in Society and Revolution: The French Colonial Period* (Cambridge: Vietnam Resource Center, 1974), and, co-editor with Douglas Allen, *Coming to Terms: Indochina, the United States and the War* (Westview Press, 1991). See also http://www.umaine.edu/history/faculty/long.htm.

Caroline Luft is an editor and writer based in New York City.

Dr. Tuan V. Nguyen is an associate professor of medicine and an epidemiologist with a keen interest in Agent Orange. He has written numerous commentary articles and published a book (in Vietnamese) on the residual effects of Agent Orange in Vietnam. He can be reached at tuan.nguyen@unsw.edu.au.

Taylor Owen is a doctoral candidate and Trudeau Scholar at the University of Oxford. He was a postgraduate fellow in the Genocide Studies Program at Yale University and received an MA from the University of British Columbia, based at the Liu Institute for Global Issues. He has worked at the International Peace Research Institute (PRIO) and the International Development Research Centre and has written widely on the concept and operationalization of human security, the causes and consequences of conflict, and EU, Canadian, and US foreign policy. He writes online at taylorowen.com and oxblog.com.

Mark Pavlick is an editor. This is his first book.

Gareth Porter is an independent investigative journalist and historian specializing in US wars and interventions abroad. He wrote regularly for Inter Press Service from 2004 through 2014, and has contributed in recent years to the *Nation, Truthdig, Truthout*, Consortium News, and *Foreign Policy*, among other publications. He is the author of four books on Vietnam and the US war in Indochina, the most recent of which is *Perils of Dominance: Imbalance of Power and the Road to War in Vietnam*, published in 2005. His most recent book is *Manufactured Crisis: The Untold Story of the Iran Nuclear Scare*, published in 2014.

Elaine Russell is a volunteer with and former board member of Legacies of War, who has written about the Vietnam-era war in Laos and its aftermath. She is the author of nonfiction and fiction, including "Laos—Living with Unexploded Ordnance: Past Memories and Present Realities" in *Interaction with a Violent Past: Reading Post-Conflict Landscapes in Cambodia, Laos and Vietnam*, edited by Vatthana Pholsena and Oliver Tappe; and the award-winning novel *Across the Mekong River*. Her children's books include the young adult novel *Montana in A Minor*, the *Martin McMillan* mystery series (ages 9 to 13), and the picture book *All About Thailand*. Elaine has a history degree from the University of California at Davis and a master›s in economics from California State University, Sacramento.

Nick Turse is an investigative reporter, a fellow at the Nation Institute, the managing editor of TomDispatch.com, a contributing writer at the *Intercept*, and the cofounder of Dispatch Books. He is the author, most recently, of *Next Time They'll Come to Count the Dead: War and Survival in South Sudan* as well as the *New York Times* bestseller *Kill Anything That Moves: The Real American War in Vietnam*, which received a 2014 American Book Award. His previous books include *Tomorrow's Battlefield*, *The Changing Face of Empire*, *The Complex*, and *The Case for Withdrawal from Afghanistan*. He has reported from the Middle East, Southeast Asia, and Africa and written for the *New York Times*, the *Los Angeles Times*, *Harper's*, *Vice*, the *San Francisco Chronicle*, the *Nation*, BBC.com, the *Daily Beast*, *GOOD*, *In These Times*, *Mother Jones*, and the *Village Voice*, among other print and online publications. His website is NickTurse.com.

About Haymarket Books

Haymarket Books is a radical, independent, nonprofit book publisher based in Chicago.

Our mission is to publish books that contribute to struggles for social and economic justice. We strive to make our books a vibrant and organic part of social movements and the education and development of a critical, engaged, international left.

We take inspiration and courage from our namesakes, the Haymarket martyrs, who gave their lives fighting for a better world. Their 1886 struggle for the eight-hour day—which gave us May Day, the international workers' holiday—reminds workers around the world that ordinary people can organize and struggle for their own liberation. These struggles continue today across the globe—struggles against oppression, exploitation, poverty, and war.

Since our founding in 2001, Haymarket Books has published more than five hundred titles. Radically independent, we seek to drive a wedge into the risk-averse world of corporate book publishing. Our authors include Noam Chomsky, Arundhati Roy, Rebecca Solnit, Angela Y. Davis, Howard Zinn, Amy Goodman, Wallace Shawn, Mike Davis, Winona LaDuke, Ilan Pappé, Richard Wolff, Dave Zirin, Keeanga-Yamahtta Taylor, Nick Turse, Dahr Jamail, David Barsamian, Elizabeth Laird, Amira Hass, Mark Steel, Avi Lewis, Naomi Klein, and Neil Davidson. We are also the trade publishers of the acclaimed Historical Materialism Book Series and of Dispatch Books.

Also Available from Haymarket Books

After the Cataclysm: The Political Economy of Human Rights: Volume II
Noam Chomsky and Edward S. Herman

American Insurgents: A Brief History of American Anti-Imperialism
Richard Seymour

Exile: Conversations With Pramoedya Ananta Toer
Edited by Nagesh Rao

In the Shadows of the American Century: The Rise and Decline of US Global Power
Alfred W. McCoy

Rethinking Camelot: JFK, the Vietnam War, and U.S. Political Culture
Noam Chomsky

Soldiers in Revolt: GI Resistance During the Vietnam War
David Cortright, Introduction by Howard Zinn

Urban Revolt: State Power and the Rise of People's Movements in the Global South
Edited by Immanuel Ness, Trevor Ngwane, and Luke Sinwell

Vietnam: The (Last) War the U.S. Lost
Joe Allen, Foreword by John Pilger

Vietnam: The Logic of Withdrawal
Howard Zinn

Winter Soldiers: An Oral History of the Vietnam Veterans Against the War
Richard Stacewicz